The Cambridge Companion to Christopher Marlowe

The Cambridge Companion to Christopher Marlowe provides a full introduction to one of the great pioneers of both the Elizabethan stage and modern English poetry. It recalls that Marlowe was an inventor of the English history play (*Edward II*) and of Ovidian narrative verse (*Hero and Leander*), as well as being author of such masterpieces of tragedy and lyric as *Doctor Faustus* and 'The Passionate Shepherd to His Love'. Seventeen leading scholars provide accessible and authoritative chapters on Marlowe's life, texts, style, politics, religion, and classicism. The volume also considers his literary and patronage relationships and his representations of sexuality and gender and of geography and identity; his presence in modern film and theatre; and finally his influence on subsequent writers. The *Companion* includes a chronology of Marlowe's life, a note on reference works, and a reading list for each chapter.

Portrait (putative) of Christopher Marlowe. Courtesy of the Master and Fellows of Corpus Christi College, Cambridge. The College cannot vouch for the identity of the portrait.

THE CAMBRIDGE
COMPANION TO
CHRISTOPHER
MARLOWE

EDITED BY
PATRICK CHENEY
Pennsylvania State University

CAMBRIDGE
UNIVERSITY PRESS

PUBLISHED BY THE PRESS SYNDICATE OF THE UNIVERSITY OF CAMBRIDGE
The Pitt Building, Trumpington Street, Cambridge, United Kingdom

CAMBRIDGE UNIVERSITY PRESS
The Edinburgh Building, Cambridge CB2 2RU, UK
40 West 20th Street, New York NY 10011-4211, USA
477 Williamstown Road, Port Melbourne, VIC 3207, Australia
Ruiz de Alarcón 13, 28014 Madrid, Spain
Dock House, The Waterfront, Cape Town 8001, South Africa

http://www.cambridge.org

First published 2004
Reprinted 2005

Printed in the United Kingdom at the University Press, Cambridge

Typeface Sabon 10/13 pt   *System* LATEX 2$_\varepsilon$ [TB]

A catalogue record for this book is available from the British Library

Library of Congress Cataloguing in Publication data

The Cambridge companion to Christopher Marlowe / edited by Patrick Cheney.
p.   cm. – (Cambridge Companions to Literature)
Includes bibliographical references and index.
ISBN 0 521 82034 0 – ISBN 0 521 52734 1 (pbk.)
1. Marlowe, Christopher, 1564–1593 – Criticism and interpretation – Handbooks,
manuals, etc.   I. Cheney, Patrick Gerard, 1949 –   II. Series.
PR2673.C36   2004
822′.3–dc22   2003069690

ISBN 0 521 82034 0 hardback
ISBN 0 521 52734 1 paperback

In memory of Clifford Leech

CONTENTS

ILLUSTRATIONS

CONTRIBUTORS

JAMES P. BEDNARZ, Long Island University
GEORGIA E. BROWN, University of Cambridge
MARK THORNTON BURNETT, Queen's University of Belfast
THOMAS CARTELLI, Muhlenberg College
KATE CHEDGZOY, University of Newcastle
PATRICK CHENEY, Pennsylvania State University
SARA MUNSON DEATS, University of South Florida
THOMAS HEALY, University of London
LISA HOPKINS, Sheffield Hallam University
JULIA REINHARD LUPTON, University of California – Irvine
LAURIE E. MAGUIRE, University of Oxford
RUSS MCDONALD, University of North Carolina – Greensboro
LOIS POTTER, University of Delaware
DAVID RIGGS, Stanford University
GARRETT A. SULLIVAN, JR, Pennsylvania State University
PAUL WHITFIELD WHITE, Purdue University
RICHARD WILSON, University of Lancaster

ACKNOWLEDGEMENTS

The origin of this *Companion* traces to the reception held by Cambridge University Press for Andrew Hadfield's *Cambridge Companion to Edmund Spenser* on 7 July 2001. Thanks to David Galbraith of Victoria College, University of Toronto, for generously introducing me to Sarah Stanton, the editor also of the present *Companion*, who has been both its originator and its guide. Without her thought, care, and support, this volume would not exist, and I remain grateful to her for inviting me to be its editor.

At the Press, I am also grateful to Jackie Warren, for courteously overseeing the production phase of the project; and to Margaret Berrill, for expertly copy-editing the manuscript.

I would also like to thank three friends and colleagues, Mark Thornton Burnett, Robert R. Edwards, and Garrett Sullivan, who served as judicious advisers and readers throughout the project. Others who supplied hearty comments on my introduction and other material include James P. Bednarz, Park Honan, and David Riggs. Richard McCabe hosted my Visiting Research Fellowship at Merton College, Oxford, in 2001, when much of the work on the volume began, while Andrew Hadfield supplied guidance, only in part through his model *Companion to Spenser*. Correspondence and conversation with this learned band of scholars and friends has been one of the joys of editing the volume.

Another has been communication with the sixteen other contributors, who have done a superb job of helping keep the volume on track. I count the volume and the field to be lucky in benefiting from such a deep reservoir of expertise on the life and works of Christopher Marlowe.

Also important has been the Marlowe Society of America, for its great and warming work on behalf of Marlowe studies (and for support of my own work during the past decade), especially Constance Brown Kuriyama, Robert A. Logan, Sara Munson Deats, Bruce E. Brandt, and Roslyn Knutson.

Finally, I would like to thank David Goldfarb, who helped with the initial stages of research for the introduction and the note on Marlowe reference works; and Letitia Montgomery, who served as a loyal and conscientious Research Intern, helping with the copy-editing of the chapters, as well as with checking quotations and citations for the introduction.

I first studied Marlowe in 1969 at the University of Montana under the inspiring teaching of the late Walter N. King. Then in 1974–5 I enrolled in the year-long graduate seminar on Marlowe at the University of Toronto taught by a distinguished editor of Marlowe, the late Millar MacLure. I shall never forget those early days.

The volume is dedicated to the memory of Clifford Leech, whose contributions to Marlowe studies were also historically important, as the volume introduction attempts to record. During the academic year 1973–4, I took Professor Leech's 'Shakespeare the Text' seminar at the University of Toronto, receiving my introduction to textual scholarship but also to the energy, care, and humour of a great teacher, scholar, and man of the theatre.

ABBREVIATIONS

BJRL	*Bibliography of the John Rylands Library*
CahiersE	*Cahiers Elisabéthains*
CritI	*Critical Inquiry*
DF	*Doctor Faustus*
Dido	*Dido, Queen of Carthage*
EII	*Edward II*
ELR	*English Literary Renaissance*
English	*English: The Journal of the English Association*
ESC	*English Studies in Canada*
HL	*Hero and Leander*
JM	*The Jew of Malta*
JMEMS	*Journal of Medieval and Early Modern Studies*
JMRS	*Journal of Medieval and Renaissance Studies*
JWCI	*Journal of the Warburg and Courtauld Institutes*
LFB	*Lucan's First Book*
Library	*Library: The Transactions of the Bibliographical Society*
LnL	*Language and Literature*
MacLure	Millar MacLure (ed.), *Marlowe: The Critical Heritage 1588–1896* (London: Routledge, 1979)
Manwood	Epitaph on Sir Roger Manwood
MLN	*Modern Language Notes*
MLQ	*Modern Language Quarterly*
MLR	*Modern Language Review*
MP	*The Massacre at Paris*
MRDE	*Medieval and Renaissance Drama in England*
MSAN	*Marlowe Society of America Newsletter*
N&Q	*Notes & Queries*
OE	*Ovid's Elegies*
OED	*Oxford English Dictionary*

PBA	*Proceedings of the British Academy*
Pembroke Dedication	The Dedicatory Epistle to the Countess of Pembroke
'PS'	"The Passionate Shepherd to His Love"
RenD	*Renaissance Drama*
RES	*Review of English Studies*
RenP	*Renaissance Papers*
RORD	*Research Opportunities in Renaissance Drama*
RQ	*Renaissance Quarterly*
SAQ	*South Atlantic Quarterly*
SB	*Studies in Bibliography*
SEL	*Studies in English Literature 1500–1900*
ShakS	*Shakespeare Studies*
ShS	*Shakespeare Survey*
SoH	*Southern History*
SN	*Studia Neophilologica*
SP	*Studies in Philology*
SQ	*Shakespeare Quarterly*
SR	*Sewanee Review*
SWR	*Southwest Review*
StHR	*Stanford Humanities Review*
1 Tamb.	*Tamburlaine, Part One*
2 Tamb.	*Tamburlaine, Part Two*
Thomas and Tydeman	Vivien Thomas and William Tydeman (eds.), *Christopher Marlowe: The Plays and Their Sources* (London: Routledge, 1994)
TDR	*Tulane Drama Review*
TJ	*Theatre Journal*
TLS	*Times Literary Supplement*

1564   Marlowe born in Canterbury. Son of John Marlowe and Katherine Arthur Marlowe.
26 Feb. Christened at St George the Martyr.
26 Apr. William Shakespeare baptized at Holy Trinity Church, Stratford-upon-Avon.

1572   *24 Aug.* St Bartholomew Day's Massacre, France.

1576   Opening of the Theatre, Shoreditch, first regular commercial playhouse in London, built by James Burbage.

1579–80   Holds scholarship at the King's School, Canterbury.

1580   Begins residence at Corpus Christi College, Cambridge. Sir Francis Drake circumnavigates the globe.

1581   Matriculates as a 'pensioner' at Corpus Christi. Thomas Watson's *Antigone* published.
7–11 May. Elected to a Matthew Parker scholarship at Corpus Christi.

1584   Completes the BA degree at Cambridge University.

1585   Probably composes *Ovid's Elegies*. *Dido, Queen of Carthage* probably first written while Marlowe is at Cambridge. Watson's *Aminta* published.
31 Mar. Admitted to candidacy for the MA degree at Cambridge.
Nov. Witnesses the will of Katherine Benchkin of Canterbury.

1586   Death of Sir Philip Sidney. Babington Plot to assassinate Queen Elizabeth exposed.

1587–8   *Tamburlaine, Parts One* and *Two* performed in London; Marlowe works for the Admiral's Men, Edward Alleyn its leading actor. Possibly composes 'The Passionate Shepherd to His Love'.

1587   *29 Jun.* The Privy Council writes a letter to the Cambridge authorities exonerating Marlowe for his absences and supporting his candidacy for the MA degree. Marlowe probably doing secret service work for the Queen's Privy Council. The Rose theatre built on Bankside (Southwark) by Philip Henslowe. Execution of Mary, Queen of Scots, mother of James VI of Scotland, future king of England (James I). *Historia von D. Iohañ Fausten* published at Frankfurt, Germany.

1588   England defeats the Spanish Armada. Robert Greene charges Marlowe with atheism in his *Epistle to Perimedes the Blacksmith*. Thomas Herriot's *A Brief and True Report of the New Found land of Virginia* published.

1588–92 Writes *Doctor Faustus, The Jew of Malta, The Massacre at Paris, Edward II*, although the order of composition and the precise dates remain uncertain.

1589   *Sept.–Dec.* Engages in swordfight on 18 Sept. in Hog Lane, London, with William Bradley, who is killed by Thomas Watson, Marlowe's friend and fellow poet–playwright. Watson and Marlowe are jailed on suspicion of murder in Newgate Prison but eventually released.

1590   *Tamburlaine, Parts One* and *Two* published, without Marlowe's name on the title page. Edmund Spenser's epic poem, *The Faerie Queene* (Books 1–3), also published. Death of Sir Francis Walsingham.

1591   Shares room with Thomas Kyd, author of *The Spanish Tragedy*. Seeks patronage from Ferdinando Stanley, Lord Strange, whose acting company, Lord Strange's Men, performs his plays.

1592–3 Plague breaks out in London, closing the theatres.

1592   *The Historie of the damnable life, and deserved death of Doctor Iohn Faustus* published (the earliest extant English translation of the 1577 *Historia*). The Gabriel Harvey–Thomas Nashe dispute begins.

26 Jan. Accused of counterfeiting by Richard Baines in Flushing, the Netherlands, and sent back to London by Sir Robert Sidney, Governor of Flushing, to be examined by the Treasurer, William Cecil, Lord Burleigh, but is evidently released. According to Sidney, Marlowe admitted to counterfeiting, but claimed he was prompted by curiosity.

9 May. Bound to keep the peace by the constable and subconstable of Holywell Street, Shoreditch.

3 Sept. Robert Greene dies. The posthumously published *Greene's Groatsworth of Wit*, perhaps co-authored by Henry Chettle, again accuses Marlowe of atheism.

15 Sept. Fights with William Corkine in Canterbury. Corkine's suit against Marlowe is settled out of court.

26 Sept. Watson buried at St Bartholomew the Less, London, perhaps a victim of plague. Watson's *Amintae gaudia* published posthumously, with Marlowe contributing a Latin *Dedicatory Epistle* to Mary Sidney Herbert, Countess of Pembroke.

14 Dec. Death of Sir Roger Manwood, Canterbury jurist. Marlowe writes Manwood's epitaph sometime during the next few months.

1593 Perhaps under the patronage of Thomas Walsingham, of Scadbury, Kent, translates *Lucan's First Book* and writes *Hero and Leander*. Shakespeare's *Venus and Adonis* published.

5 May. Libel attacking Protestant immigrants is posted on the wall of the Dutch Church in London. It is signed 'per Tamberlaine' and contains several allusions to Marlowe's plays.

11 May. The Privy Council orders the Lord Mayor to arrest and examine persons suspected in connection with the Dutch Church Libel.

12 May. Thomas Kyd arrested on suspicion of libel, imprisoned, and tortured. Investigators discover a heretical document in Kyd's room, but he claims it is Marlowe's.

?12–27 May. An unnamed spy writes 'Remembrances of words & matter against Richard Cholmeley', which reports that Marlowe has been lecturing on behalf of atheism.

18 May. The Privy Council issues a warrant for Marlowe's arrest.

20 May. Appears before the Privy Council and is instructed to give his 'daily attendance'; released on his own cognizance.

27 May. Possible delivery of the Baines Note accusing Marlowe of atheism.

30 May. Killed by Ingram Frizer at the house of Eleanor Bull, Deptford. Witnesses in the room are Robert Poley and Nicholas Skeres. The official coroner's report says that Marlowe attacked Frizer over a dispute about who would pay the 'reckoning' or bill.

1 Jun. A jury determines that Frizer acted in self-defence for the killing of Christopher Marlowe. Buried in a nameless grave at St Nicholas's Church, Deptford. Soon afterwards, Kyd writes two documents to the Lord Keeper, Sir John Puckering, accusing Marlowe of atheism and of being an injurious person.

	29 Jun. Richard Cholmley admits he has been influenced by Marlowe's atheism.
	28 Sept. Lucan's First Book and *Hero and Leander* entered together in the Stationers' Register.
1594	Publication of *Dido, Queen of Carthage* and *Edward II*, the first works bearing Marlowe's name on the title page, although Thomas Nashe's name also appears on *Dido*. Possible publication of *The Massacre at Paris*. Publication of Shakespeare's *The Rape of Lucrece* and *Titus Andronicus*. Nashe's *The Unfortunate Traveller* also published.
1597	Thomas Beard's *The Theatre of God's Judgments* published.
1598	*Hero and Leander* published, first as an 818-line poem and later as a Homeric and Virgilian epic, divided into 'sestiads', and completed by George Chapman.
1599	The Bishop of London and Archbishop of Canterbury ban *Ovid's Elegies* (probably published in mid- to late-1590s), along with Sir John Davies's *Epigrams*, and have them burned in public. *The Passionate Pilgrim* published, with Shakespeare's name on the title page, and including versions of 'The Passionate Shepherd' and Ralegh's 'The Nymph's Reply'.
1600	*Lucan's First Book* published with Marlowe's name on the title page. *England's Helicon* published, including versions of 'The Passionate Shepherd' and Ralegh's 'The Nymph's Reply'.
1602	Philip Henslowe, manager of the Admiral's Men, pays William Birde and Samuel Rowley £4 for additions to *Doctor Faustus*.
1603	Death of Queen Elizabeth I. Succession of James VI of Scotland as James I.
1604	'A' text of *Doctor Faustus* published, with Marlowe's name on the title page.
1616	The 'B' text of *Doctor Faustus* published, with Marlowe's name on the title page.
1633	Thomas Heywood publishes *The Jew of Malta*, identifying Marlowe as the author.

I

PATRICK CHENEY

Introduction: Marlowe in the twenty-first century

...that pure elemental wit Chr. Marlowe, whose ghost or genius is to be seen walk the Churchyard in (at the least) three or four sheets.[1]

Christopher Marlowe (1564–93) enters the twenty-first century arguably the most enigmatic genius of the English literary Renaissance. While the enigma of Marlowe's genius remains difficult to circumscribe, it conjures up that special relation his literary works have long been held to have with his life. In 1588, fellow writer Robert Greene inaugurates printed commentary by accusing Marlowe of 'daring god out of heaven with that Atheist Tamburlan' (MacLure, p. 29), an imitation of Marlowe's description of his own protagonist, whose 'looks do menace heaven and dare the gods' (1 *Tamb.* 1.2.157), and indicating that the Marlovian 'ghost or genius' rather slyly haunts his own historical making. Perhaps the enigma continues to fascinate today because the brilliant creator of such masterpieces in lyric and tragedy as 'The Passionate Shepherd to His Love' and *Doctor Faustus* was ignominiously arrested no fewer than four times – three for street-fighting and a fourth for counterfeiting – and was under house arrest for (potentially) dissident behaviour when he received a fatal knife-wound to the right temple in what proved his darkest hour. If his life was dissident, his works were iconoclastic, and both are difficult to capture. Reflecting variously on the enigma of Marlovian genius, the present *Companion* includes sixteen subsequent chapters by distinguished women and men from the United Kingdom and the United States spread over as many topics as such a volume can contain.

The volume design follows a tripartite format. After the present Introduction, the first part divides into five chapters offering orientation to essential features of Marlowe and his works. The first three of these chapters concentrate on topics that underlie the others, and address the genuine difficulty we have in gauging and interpreting Marlowe: his life and career; his texts and authorship; and his style. The next two chapters explore Marlowe in his cultural contexts, probing the interrelation between religion and politics and examining the English literary scene in the late 1580s and early 1590s.

The second part of the *Companion*, which forms the bulk and centre, consists of six chapters on Marlowe's works, divided according to the two broad literary forms he produced. One chapter examines his poems by emphasizing what they have in common: a vigorous response to classicism. The following five chapters range over his extant plays, with one chapter each on those plays taught more frequently (*Tamburlaine, Parts One* and *Two*; *The Jew of Malta*; *Edward II*; and *Doctor Faustus*) and a single chapter combining those plays that are taught less often (*Dido, Queen of Carthage* and *The Massacre at Paris*).

Finally, the third part of the companion consists of five chapters. The first bridges the second and third parts by focusing on Marlowe's foundational dramatic genre, tragedy, filtered through important themes of representation, patronage, and power. The next two chapters also deal with themes of Marlovian representation that commentators have found especially important and original: geography and identity; and gender and sexuality. The final two chapters concern Marlowe's afterlife, from his day to ours: Marlowe in theatre and film; and his reception and influence. The present *Companion* also features an initial chronology of Marlowe's life and works, emphasizing dates and events important to the various chapters; a reading list at the close of each chapter, recommending selected works of commentary; and, at the end of the volume, a brief note on reference works available on Marlowe (biographies, editions, bibliographies, concordances, periodicals, other research tools, collections of essays, 'Marlowe on the Internet'). Underlying many of the chapters is an attempt to unravel the enigma of Marlowe's life and works; precisely because of this enigma, we can expect varying, even contradictory assessments and interpretations. In this introductory chapter, we will consider issues not covered in detail elsewhere in order to approach the haunting genius we inherit today.[2]

Marlowe's own contemporaries discover a deep furrow marking the genius of the young author's brow. For instance, the sublime author whom the poet Michael Drayton imagined 'bath[ing] . . . in the Thespian springs' and who 'Had in him those brave translunary things, / That the first Poets had', was evidently the same 'barking dog' whom the Puritan polemicist Thomas Beard damningly found 'the Lord' *hooking* by 'the nostrils': 'a playmaker, and a Poet of scurrilitie' whose 'manner of . . . death' was 'terrible (for hee even cursed and blasphemed to his last gaspe, and togither with his breath an oath flew out of his mouth)' (MacLure, pp. 47, 41–2). If Drayton could rhapsodically discover in Marlowe the 'fine madness' of high Platonic fury 'which rightly should possess a Poets braine', another Puritan, William Vaughan, referred more gruesomely to the fatal point of entry at the poet's unsacred temple: Marlowe died with 'his braines comming out at the daggers point' (MacLure, p. 47).

How could 'the best of Poets in that age', as the dramatist Thomas Heywood called Marlowe in 1633, be 'intemperate & of a cruel hart', as his former room-mate and the author of *The Spanish Tragedy*, Thomas Kyd, claimed back in 1593 (MacLure, pp. 49, 33)? How are we to reconcile fellow poet George Peele's fond testimony about 'Marley, the Muses darling for thy verse' with Kyd's accusation against a dangerous atheist with 'monstruous opinions' who would 'attempt...soden pryvie injuries to men' (MacLure, pp. 39, 35–6)? Evidently, the same sexually charged youth who deftly versified the loss of female virginity more powerfully than perhaps any English male poet before or since – 'Jewels being lost are found again, this never;/ 'Tis lost but once, and once lost, lost for ever' (*HL* 1.85–6) – relied on 'table talk' to 'report St John to be our saviour Christes Alexis...that is[,] that Christ did love him with an extraordinary love' (Kyd, in MacLure, p. 35). At one point, a deep religious sensibility bequeaths one of our most haunting testimonies to the loss of Christian faith: 'Think'st thou', Mephistopheles says to Faustus, 'that I, who saw the face of God / And tasted the eternal joys of heaven / Am not tormented with ten thousand hells / In being deprived of everlasting bliss? (*DF* 'A' text 1.3.77–80). Yet, at another point, that same sensibility opprobriously 'jest[s] at the devine scriptures[,] gybe[s]...at praires', as Kyd claimed, or, as fellow-spy Richard Baines put it in his infamous deposition, callously joke that 'the sacrament' 'instituted' by Christ 'would have bin much better being administred in a Tobacco pipe' (MacLure, pp. 35, 37). While Kyd and Baines both portray a Marlowe who considers Moses and Jesus to be dishonest mountebanks, they also show a young man with a deep religious imagination, complexly cut, as Paul Whitfield White shows in his chapter here, along sectarian lines. As Baines reports, Marlowe claimed that 'if there be any god or any good Religion, then it is in the papistes because the service of god is performed with more Cerimonies...That all protestantes are Hypocriticall asses' (MacLure, p. 37).

In the political sphere, we can further discover troubling contradiction. If Marlowe could nobly use his art in the grand republican manner to 'defend...freedom 'gainst a monarchy' (*1 Tamb.* 2.1.56), he could, Kyd writes, 'perswade with men of quallitie to goe unto the k[ing] of Scotts' (MacLure, p. 36) – a treasonous offence before the 1603 accession of James VI of Scotland to the English throne. Indeed, the archive leaves us with little but murky political ink, ranging from Kyd's accusation of 'mutinous sedition towrd the state' (MacLure, p. 35) to the Privy Council's exonerating letter to the authorities at Cambridge University, who tried to stop the young scholar from receiving his MA degree because he was rumoured to have gone to the Catholic seminary in Rheims, France: 'in all his actions he had behaved him selfe orderlie and discreetelie whereby he had done her Majestie good service, and deserved to be rewarded for his faithful dealinge'.[3] What are we to believe? Shall Marlowe be rewarded for his faithful dealing? Or should the barking dog be hooked by the nose for his cruel and intemperate heart?

While the biographical record makes it difficult to gain purchase on this baffling figure (as David Riggs ably shows in the volume's second chapter), we can seek surer footing by gauging Marlowe's standing in English literary history. Yet even here (as the subsequent chapter by Laurie Maguire makes clear) we enter difficult terrain, in part because the texts of Marlowe's works make assessments about his authorship precarious; in part because our understanding of those texts continues to evolve imperfectly. The Marlowe canon (perhaps like its inventor's personality) has never been stable. In his 1753 *Lives of the Poets*, for instance, Theophilus Cibber believed Marlowe the author of *Lust's Dominion* (MacLure, p. 56), a play no longer ascribed to him, while Thomas Warton in his 1781 *History of English Poetry* believed Marlowe had 'translated Coluthus' 'Rape of Helen' into English rhyme, in the year 1587, even though Warton confessed he had 'never seen it' (MacLure, p. 58); nor have we. In 1850, a short entry appeared in *Notes and Queries* signed by one 'm', who mentions a manuscript transcribing an eclogue and sixteen sonnets written by 'Ch.M.'. This manuscript remained lost, but by 1942 the biographer John Bakeless could speculate hopefully that 'Marlowe's lost sonnets may have been genuine.' Bakeless believed the probability increased because of the technical mastery that he and C. F. Tucker Brooke thought Marlowe displayed in the ottava rima stanza in some verses printed in *England's Helicon* (1600), titled 'Description of Seas, Waters, Rivers &c'.[4] In 1988, however, Sukanta Chaudhuri was able to print the 'lost' manuscript of eclogue and sonnets, but concluded that Marlowe had no hand in it – as, alas, seems likely.[5] Today, unlike at the beginning of the past century, neither those poems nor the priceless hydrologic verses in *England's Helicon* make their way into a Marlowe edition.

The works that do make their way constitute a startlingly brief yet brilliant canon created within a short span of six or perhaps eight years (1585–93) – brief indeed, for an author with such canonical status today. Marlowe is now generally believed to be the author of seven extant plays: *Dido*; *Tamburlaine, Parts One* and *Two*; *The Jew*; *Edward II*; *The Massacre*; and *Faustus*. Recent scholarship encourages us to view that last play as two, since we have two different texts, each with its own historical authority, yet both published well after Marlowe's death: the so-called 'A' text of 1604 and the 'B' text of 1616. As these dates alone indicate, the question of the chronology of Marlowe's plays is a thorny one, and it has long spawned contentious debate.

As Riggs and Maguire reveal, however, most textual scholars now believe that Marlowe wrote *Dido* first, the two *Tamburlaine* plays next, followed by *The Jew*; and that he wrote *Edward II* and *The Massacre* late in his career, although not necessarily in this order. During the last century, scholars were divided over whether Marlowe wrote *Doctor Faustus* 'early' (1588–9) or 'late' (1592–3), with some believing that he might have written two versions at different times, and today most seem willing to entertain an early date. In his chapter on this play, Thomas Healy emphasizes how the two texts, rather than being of interest only to textual scholars, can profitably direct interpretation itself. The larger chronology of Marlowe's plays has been important because it has been thought to hold the key to the locked secret absorbing scholars since the Victorian era: the obsession with 'Marlowe's development' as an autonomous author.

The fascination holds, but it has not impeded Marlowe's latest editor from choosing a quite different method for organizing the plays: a chronology not of composition but of publication, in keeping with recent textual scholarship privileging the 'materiality of the text'. Thus, Mark Thornton Burnett in his 1999 Everyman edition of *The Complete Plays* begins with the two *Tamburlaine* plays, which were the only works of Marlowe's published during his lifetime (1590). Burnett follows with two works published the year after Marlowe's death, *Edward II* and *Dido* (1594), continues with *The Massacre*, published after 1594 but of uncertain date during the Elizabethan era, and next he prints the two Jacobean versions of *Faustus* (1604 and 1616). Burnett concludes with *The Jew*, not published by Heywood until the Caroline period (1633). Thus, even though the canon of plays has not changed during the last century, the printing of it today has changed dramatically. If earlier editions arrange the plays according to the author's dates of composition (and performance), Burnett's edition prints them according to the reception the author received in print. Commentary derived from the one method may differ from commentary derived from the other, but one can imagine that Marlowe would have been cheered by the mystery of this difference. He is so mysterious that some prefer to replace 'Marlowe' with a 'Marlowe effect'.[6]

In addition to the plays, Marlowe wrote five extant poems, none of which was published during his lifetime. As with the plays, here we do not know the order in which Marlowe composed, but the situation is even less certain about when most of these works were published. *Ovid's Elegies*, a line-for-line translation of Ovid's *Amores*, is usually placed as Marlowe's first poetic composition (while he was a student at Cambridge University, around 1584–5); its date of publication is also uncertain, but it is generally believed to have been printed between the latter half of the 1590s and the early years of the seventeenth century. *Ovid's Elegies* appears in three different editions, the first two printing only ten poems and the third the complete sequence of three books or 48 poems. 'The Passionate Shepherd to His Love', Marlowe's famous pastoral lyric, is also of uncertain compositional date, but it is generally assigned to the mid to late 1580s, since it was widely imitated during the period, including by Marlowe himself in *Dido*, the *Tamburlaine* plays, *The Jew*, and *Edward II*; it appears in various printed forms, from four to seven stanzas, with a four-stanza version printed in *The Passionate Pilgrim* (1599) and a six-stanza version in *England's Helicon*. *Lucan's First Book*, a translation of Book 1 of Lucan's epic poem, *The Pharsalia*, is the only poem whose publication we can date with certainty, even though it was not published until 1600. Scholars are divided over whether to place its composition early or late in Marlowe's career, but its superior merit in versification suggests a late date, as does its presence in the Stationers' Register on 28 September 1593, back to back with *Hero and Leander*, which scholars tend to place in the last year of Marlowe's life. This famous epyllion or Ovidian narrative poem appeared in two different versions published in 1598, the first an 818-line poem that ends with an editor's insertion, *'desunt nonnulla'* (something missing). The second version divides the poem into two 'sestiads', which were continued by George Chapman, who contributed four more sestiads and turned Marlowe's work into the only epyllion in the period printed as a minor epic in the grand tradition of Homer and Virgil, each sestiad prefaced with a verse argument. Marlowe's fifth poem, a short Latin epitaph on Sir Roger Manwood, a Canterbury jurist, is preserved only in manuscript, but it must have been written between December 1592, the time of Manwood's death, and May 1593, when Marlowe died. Additionally, Marlowe is now credited as the author of a Latin prose *Dedicatory Epistle* addressed to Mary Sidney Herbert, Countess of Pembroke (sister to Sir Philip Sidney), which prefaces Thomas Watson's 1592 poem, *Amintae gaudia*, and which sheds intriguing light on Marlowe's career as a poet and thus is now conventionally printed alongside his poems.

In short, the Marlowe canon is not merely in motion; it is paradoxically truncated. The image recalls Henry Petowe, in his *Dedicatory Epistle* to *The Second Part of 'Hero and Leander', Containing their Future Fortunes* (1598): 'This history, of *Hero and Leander*, penned by that admired poet Marlowe, but not finished (being prevented by sudden death) and the same…resting like a head separated from the body'.[7] Unlike Ben Jonson or Samuel Daniel, Marlowe did not live to bring out an edition of his own poems and plays; nor did he benefit, as Edmund Spenser and William Shakespeare did, from a folio edition published by colleagues soon after his death, preserving his canon for posterity.

The truncated state of Marlowe's works confounds attempts at holistic commentary, rendering our efforts tenuous and controversial. Students of Marlowe might view this predicament as less a warning than a challenge. The question is: how can we view clearly what is inherently opaque? Perhaps the occasion affords a genuine opportunity, and we may wonder whether the spy who was suspected of going 'beyond the seas to Reames' knew it (qtd in Kuriyama, p. 202). In viewing his life and works, we might experience the excitement an archaeologist presumably feels when first discovering the bright shard of a broken vase – or perhaps more appropriate here, scabbard.

While the present *Companion* affords a frame for viewing such a shard, we need to register the singular feature of Marlowe's standing in English literary history: his absolute inaugural power. Nearly four hundred years ago, Drayton first located in Marlowe's brain the brave translunary things 'that the first Poets had' – what Drayton himself considered the mysterious rapture of air and fire that makes Marlowe's verses clear. The word 'first' is applied to Marlowe so often during the next centuries that we might wonder whether Spenser or Shakespeare could outstrip him in the race of literary originality (like the word *genius*, the word *first* occasionally slips into a second meaning: *best*). The achievement is all the more remarkable because the Muses' darling is dead at twenty-nine. No wonder the energy circulating around his corpus continues to be electrifying. As William Hazlitt expressed it in the nineteenth century, somewhat ambivalently, 'There is a lust of power in his writings, a hunger and thirst after unrighteousness, a glow of the imagination, unhallowed by any thing but its own energies' (MacLure, p. 78).

Like Hazlitt during the Romantic era, both Petowe and Heywood in the early modern era place Marlowe at the forefront of English literary history. Petowe says of 'th' admired Marlowe' that his 'honey-flowing vein / No English writer can as yet attain' (58–60), while Heywood calls him 'the best of Poets in that age' – a phrase quoted throughout the seventeenth and eighteenth centuries. In the first years of the nineteenth century (1808), Charles Lamb singled out 'the death-scene' of *Edward II* as moving 'pity and terror beyond any scene, ancient or modern, with which I am acquainted' (MacLure, p. 69). In an unsigned review from 1818, a commentator considered *The Jew of Malta* 'the first regular and consistent English drama; . . . Marlowe was the first poet before Shakespeare who possessed any thing like real *dramatic* genius' (MacLure, pp. 70–1; reviewer's emphasis). By 1820, Hazlitt is a bit more guarded, but not much: 'Marlowe is a name that stands high, and almost first in this list of dramatic worthies' (MacLure, p. 78). In 1830, James Broughton went further by specifying that Dr Faustus's 'last impassioned soliloquy of agony and despair' is 'surpassed by nothing in the whole circle of the English Drama', even though it is *Edward II*, 'by far the best of Marlowe's plays', that 'place[s] Marlowe in the first class of dramatic writers' (MacLure, p. 87). Perhaps echoing Drayton, Leigh Hunt marvelled in 1844, 'If ever there was a born poet, Marlowe was one... He... prepared the way for the versification, the dignity, and the pathos of his successors... and his imagination, like Spenser's, haunted those purely poetic regions of ancient fabling and modern rapture... Marlowe and Spenser are the first of our poets who perceived the beauty of words' (MacLure, pp. 89–91).

In 1879, when modern scholarship on Marlowe is first being consolidated,[8] Edward Dowden finds that Marlowe, 'of all the Elizabethan dramatists, stands next to Shakspere in poetical stature' (MacLure, p. 100). In 1875, A. W. Ward, writing *A History of English Dramatic Literature*, can summarize Marlowe's originality in a judgement that basically holds true today: 'His services to our dramatic literature are two-fold. As the author who first introduced blank verse to the popular stage he rendered to our drama a service which it would be difficult to overestimate... His second service to the progress of our dramatic literature' is that he 'first inspired with true poetic passion the form of literature to which his chief efforts were consecrated...; and it is this gift of passion which, together with his services to the outward form of the English drama, makes Marlowe worthy to be called not a predecessor, but the earliest in the immortal company, of our great dramatists' (MacLure, pp. 120–1). [9]

For these reasons, John Addington Symmonds in 1884 can style Marlowe 'the father and founder of English dramatic poetry' (MacLure, p. 133); and A. H. Bullen in 1885, 'the father of the English drama' (MacLure, p. 136). In 1887, James Russell Lowell can poignantly say, 'Yes, Drayton was right', for Marlowe 'was indeed... that most indefinable thing, an original man... He was the herald that dropped dead' (MacLure, pp. 159–62). In 1887 as well, George Saintsbury could state that the 'riot of passion and of delight in the beauty of colour and form which characterises his version of "Hero and Leander" has never been approached by any writer' (MacLure, p. 163). That same year, Havelock Ellis agreed: 'It is the brightest flower of the English Renaissance' (MacLure, p. 167). No one, however, rhapsodized more than Algernon Charles Swinburne, who termed Marlowe 'alone... the true Apollo of our dawn, the bright and morning star of the full midsummer day of English poetry at its highest... The first great English poet was the father of English tragedy and the creator of English blank verse... the first English poet whose powers can be called sublime... He is the greatest discoverer, the most daring and inspired pioneer, in all our poetic literature' (MacLure, pp. 175–84).

Pioneer, discoverer, morning star, herald, original man, first dramatic genius, first poet: this is an astonishing set of representational claims for the
enigma of Marlovian genius. While the twentieth century sharpened its view
of Marlowe's role in English literary history, it did not substantively change
these earlier assessments about his original contribution to English drama.
Opening a groundbreaking 1964 Twentieth Century Views *Marlowe*, for instance, Clifford Leech writes, 'There is wide enough agreement that Marlowe
is one of the major figures in English dramatic writing. That he was the most
important of Shakespeare's predecessors... is not disputed, nor is the poetic
excellence of... Marlowe's "mighty line".'[10]

Leech's essay conveniently serves as an intermediary between earlier and
later commentary, reminding us that the leaders of Renaissance studies
throughout the twentieth century felt drawn to the genius of the Marlowe
enigma: from A. C. Bradley, T. S. Eliot, G. Wilson Knight, Muriel C.
Bradbrook, Cleanth Brooks, C. S. Lewis, William Empson, Harry Levin,
and C. L. Barber, to Harold Bloom, Stephen Orgel, David Bevington,
A. Bartlett Giamatti, Stephen Greenblatt, Jonathan Dollimore, Catherine
Belsey, Jonathan Goldberg, and Marjorie Garber.[11] Yet Leech does alter
the earlier view of Marlowe as a madcap dreamer absorbed in the exul-
tant power of his imagination, demarcating 'three ways in which Marlowe
criticism has taken new directions' up to the early 1960s (p. 3), even as he
acknowledges that 'the nature of Marlowe's drama remains a thing that most
readers are still groping after' (p. 9). First, Marlowe now enjoys the 'intellectual stature' of 'learning', through which he 'conscious[ly]' moulds and
extends 'tradition' (p. 4), represented in the work of Paul Kocher.[12] Second,
Marlowe's writing thus acquires new 'complexity', including 'the comic element', wherein Marlowe recognizes 'the puniness of human ambition', which
leads to 'a wider range of interpretations... extending from Christian to ag-
nostic views' (pp. 5–6), represented in work by Roy Battenhouse and Una
Ellis-Fermor.[13] And third, Marlowe's plays, after long absence from the theatre, begin to demonstrate their stage-worthiness, the dramatist exhibiting
an 'eye' for specifically theatrical effect (p. 9), represented by Leech himself.[14]
For Leech, Marlowe had 'large-mindedness', a 'double view of the aspiring
mind', a 'notion of the irresponsibility with which the universe functions',
and 'a profound sense of the Christian scheme: no one has written better in
English of the beatific vision and the wrath of God' (pp. 9–10).

After Leech declared that 'the beginnings of Marlowe criticism are with us'
(p. 11), a virtual industry emerged, as Marlowe in the later 1960s, the 70s,
80s, and 90s became subject to large-scale investigation on diverse fronts. We
may conveniently identify five broad, interwoven categories: (1) *subjectivity*
(matters of the mind: inwardness, interiority, psychology); (2) *sexuality*

(matters of the body: desire, gender, homoeroticism/heterosexuality); (3) *politics* (matters of the state: culture, ideology, sociology, family); (4) *religion* (matters of the Church: theology, belief, the Reformation); and (5) *poetics* (matters of art, or literariness: authorship, language/rhetoric, genre, influence/intertextuality, theatricality/film/performance).[15]

Among works produced in the second half of the twentieth century, Levin's groundbreaking 1954 study of Marlowe as 'the overreacher' continues to resound today, while Greenblatt's 'new historicist' Marlowe remains the most influential formulation in the last quarter century: 'a fathomless and eerily playful self-estrangement' that Greenblatt calls the 'will to play' – 'play on the brink of an abyss, *absolute* play'.[16] As Mark Burnett writes in his 1999 'Marlowe and the Critic', 'With one or two exceptions, the construction of Marlowe as a political subversive has gained a wide currency over the last twenty years' (ed., p. 617) – though we could extend Marlovian subversion to the categories of subjectivity, sexuality, religion, and poetics.[17]

The investment that Greenblatt shares with Leech in a theatrical Marlowe has a characteristic twentieth-century liability: a neglect of Marlowe's poems. While commentators from the late-seventeenth century to the nineteenth praise Marlowe exuberantly for his achievements in drama, they have surprisingly little to say about his poems as a body of work in its own right, and even less praise.[18] Commentators in this period do recognize *Hero and Leander*, as we have seen, but it takes until 1781 for Warton to recognize fully Marlowe's 'PURE POETRY': *Ovid's Elegies, Lucan's First Book*, and even 'The Passionate Shepherd' (MacLure, pp. 59–60; see MacLure's comment, p. 24). Between Warton and Swinburne, commentators refer to various of the poems only intermittently, as if, under the pressure of the Shakespeare factor, no one is quite sure what to do with a playwright who, like Shakespeare, wrote some of the most gifted poems in the language.[19] The General Catalogue to the British Library sets the official classification that prevails today: 'Marlowe (Christopher) the Dramatist'.

In the latter half of the twentieth century, however, counter forces were assembling.[20] Levin himself led the rearguard action, in a series of brilliant observations spliced into his dramatic view of the overreacher. He was followed more emphatically by J. B. Steane in his 1964 *Marlowe: A Critical Study*, which devotes chapters to *Lucan, Ovid*, and *Hero* (curiously ignoring 'The Passionate Shepherd').[21] Even Leech's posthumously published *Poet for the Stage* (1986) includes two chapters on the poems (pp. 26–42, 175–98). While most studies throughout the century focused exclusively on 'Marlovian drama', some included chapters on *Hero and Leander*, while simultaneously this Ovidian poem was attracting an impressive string of fine analyses, from C. S. Lewis to David Lee Miller and beyond.[22]

The problem of Marlovian classification appears enshrined in the 1987 article on Marlowe in *The Dictionary of Literary Biography*, printed in the volume on *Elizabethan Dramatists*, rather than in *The Sixteenth-Century Non-Dramatic Poets*. Written by the late Roma Gill, the opening paragraph confirms what we have learned about Marlowe's standing in English literary history but tacitly resists the narrowness of the volume's generic frame, as if Marlowe's 'ghost or genius' were too infinite to be encircled by such artificial boundaries:

> The achievement of Christopher Marlowe, poet and dramatist, was enormous – surpassed by that of his exact contemporary, Shakespeare. A few months the elder, Marlowe was usually the leader, although Shakespeare was able to bring his art to a higher perfection. Most dramatic poets of the sixteenth century followed where Marlowe had led, especially in their use of language and the blank-verse line ... English drama was never to be the same again.[23]

Nor, we may add, was English poetry ever to be the same. For Gill, Marlowe is a 'poet and dramatist'; we may take her cue, recalling that we have had access to this version of Marlovian authorship for a long time. In 1891, for instance, producer–actor Henry Irving unveiled the Marlowe Commemoration at Canterbury, Marlowe's city of birth, with a memorable formulation: 'of all those illustrious dead, the greatest is CHRISTOPHER MARLOWE. He was the first, the only, herald of SHAKESPEARE. He was the father of the great family of English dramatic poets, and a lyrical poet of the first order among Elizabethans' (MacLure, p. 185).

Following Irving and Gill, we may usher in our own century by identifying another first for Marlowe: he is the first major English author to combine poems and plays substantively within a single literary career. A few previous English authors – John Skelton, for instance, or George Gascoigne, or even Marlowe's fellow street-fighter Watson – had combined at least one play in their otherwise non-dramatic careers – but Marlowe moves beyond this haphazard-looking professional profile by taking both forms to heart.[24] Today, Marlowe may be best remembered as the father of English drama, but his achievements in poetry are no less astonishing, once we pause to consider them, as Georgia Brown does in her chapter here. It is not simply that two of his poems are recognized as the first of their kind – *Ovid's Elegies*, the first translation of the *Amores* into any European vernacular; *Lucan's First Book*, the first in English – but also that no fewer than three of the five have been singled out as 'masterpieces'. *Hero and Leander* has long been known to be the most superior Ovidian narrative poem in the language, greater even than Shakespeare's *Venus and Adonis*, asserted C. S. Lewis: 'I do not know that any other poet has rivalled its peculiar excellence.'[25] In the history of praise, however, few poems can rival 'The Passionate Shepherd' – 'one of the most faultless lyrics . . . in the whole range of descriptive and fanciful poetry', rhapsodized Swinburne (MacLure, p. 183); 'the most popular of all Elizabethan lyrics', rationalized Millar MacLure (ed., *Poems*, p. xxxvii). As for *Lucan's First Book*, Lewis judged it 'of very great merit', so much so that he was tempted to deny Marlowe's authorship of it (*English Literature*, p. 486), while the classicist Charles Martindale calls it 'arguably one of the underrated masterpieces of Elizabethan literature'.[26] Given that scholars are only now looking into the 1590s as the original groundplot of seventeenth-century English republicanism, we may expect this original translation to come closer to centre stage.

All told, when we match such utterances as Martindale's with those made about the plays, we discover an unprecedented literary achievement: the first sustained combination in English of poems and plays at an artistically superior level. We may thus come to view Marlowe as the founding father of a distinctly sixteenth-century form of authorship: the English poet–playwright.[27] *Ovid's Elegies* suggests that Marlowe looked back to Ovid as the progenitor of his own twin production, since the *Amores* tells a clear authorial narrative, interleaved with an erotic one: Ovid struggles to write both epic and tragedy, the high Aristotelian genres from the *Poetics*; he becomes impeded in this professional ambition by his erotic obsession with love elegy (1.1, 2.1, 2.18, 3.1); but finally he succeeds in announcing his turn from elegy to tragedy (3.15; in *Ovid's Elegies*, 3.14), setting up the expectation that he will eventually turn to epic. Ovid fulfils the expectations of both generic turns. As he reports in the *Tristia* towards the end of his life, he has 'given to the kings of tragedy their royal scepter and speech suited to the buskin's dignity' (2.551–3) – referring to his *Medea*, a tragedy extant in two lines and praised in antiquity as the true measure of Ovid's genius (Cheney, *Marlowe's Counterfeit Profession*, pp. 31–48, 89–98). And as Ovid writes to open the *Metamorphoses* (1.1–4), he is metamorphosing from 'elegist into epicist'.[28]

While Marlowe may have self-consciously imitated Ovid, we need to situate his imitation within a broader sixteenth-century European movement, represented diversely in the careers of Marguerite de Navarre in France, Lope de Vega in Spain, and Torquato Tasso in Italy, all of whom combined poems with plays in their careers. Even if today we do not recognize Marlowe's status as an English poet–playwright, his own contemporaries most emphatically did – from Beard's grim classification of 'a playmaker, and a Poet of scurrilitie' to Heywood's citation of both *Hero and Leander* and the *Tamburlaine* plays in his commemoration of 'the best of Poets in that age'.

Presumably because of Marlowe's pioneering combination, his two most important English heirs, Shakespeare and Ben Jonson, went on to combine poems and plays in even more influential ways. Together, Marlowe, Shakespeare, and Jonson gave birth to a new standard of English authorship, evident in the seventeenth and eighteenth centuries through the careers of Milton and John Dryden; in the nineteenth century through the Romantics, especially Lord Byron; and in the twentieth century through William Butler Yeats and John Millington Synge, T. S. Eliot and W. H. Auden, and even in our own time, such authors as Derek Walcott and Sam Shepard.

Marlowe's pioneering role as England's first great poet–playwright speaks to another paradox: despite his painfully brief career and sadly truncated canon, this author appears to have possessed an ambition we may call Dantean. In the *Inferno*, the great medieval poet of Italian Christian epic pauses to place himself in the company of a select band of pagan authors. As the guide Virgil tells the pilgrim Dante:

> That other shade is Homer, the consummate poet;
> The other one is Horace, satirist;
> The third is Ovid, and the last is Lucan.[29]

In *The Cambridge Companion to Virgil*, Charles Martindale enables us to see a signature peculiarity of Marlowe's career when he recalls this moment: 'Authors elect their own precursors, by allusion, quotation, imitation, translation, homage, at once creating a canon and making a claim for their own inclusion in it.'[30] For reasons to which we will never be privy, by the time Marlowe was in his late twenties he had translated two of Dante's five classical authors, Ovid and Lucan; he had put a third, Virgil, on the stage; and he had dramatized a fourth, Homer, in one of the most famous appropriations on record; in a play now celebrated as a world masterpiece, Faustus conjures up Helen of Troy, 'the face that launched a thousand ships' ('A' text 5.1.89). As Faustus earlier exclaims to Mephistopheles, 'Have not I made blind Homer sing to me / Of Alexander's love and Oenon's death?' ('A' text 2.3.26–7). (Perhaps not surprisingly, the poet who felt compelled to complete *Hero and Leander*, George Chapman, became the great early modern translator of Homer, as Keats fondly remembered.) From Dante's company of poets, only the 'satirist' Horace appears to escape the Marlovian imagination, although we might wonder whether Marlowe's well-known satirical pose towards the world does not have at least some Horatian origin.[31] Yet even without Horace, the company Marlowe keeps is notable for its canonicity. Quickly, we discern something askew. On the surface, Marlowe appears to engage in the self-conscious canon-formation that Martindale attributes to Virgil and Dante, and that we could extend to Spenser and Milton. Yet who with confidence would make such an attribution to Marlowe? Whatever canon the Muses' darling might create, the barking dog breaks asunder.

Marlowe boldly raises the spectres of Homer, Virgil, Ovid, and Lucan, only to draw a magical circle around them; more to the point, he turns the author of the *Iliad* into a love poet of demonic energy – his great epic into an erotic epyllion – and he sets Ovid and Lucan against Virgil. Marlowe is arguably England's first canonical dissident writer.

Martindale recalls the broad European political quest for empire, *translatio imperii*, and its accompanying literary vehicle, *translatio studii*, 'with Virgil at its core' ('Introduction', p. 3), allowing us to see further the vast cultural enterprise that Marlowe dares to break up. Furthermore, in his chapter on geography and identity in the present companion, Garrett Sullivan permits us to see that in four of seven plays Marlowe migrates his plot along the east–west route of empire and learning: *Dido*, with its obvious trajectory from Troy to Carthage to Rome; the two *Tamburlaine* plays, wherein the 'monarch of the East' (*1 Tamb.* 1.1.43) 'write[s] him] . . . self great lord of Africa: / . . . from the East unto the furthest West' (3.3.245–6); and *The Jew of Malta*, set on 'an island', Levin reminds us, where, 'if anywhere, East met West' (p. 65). We could add three of Marlowe's five poems: *Ovid's Elegies*, set in Rome in opposition to Virgil's epic imperialism; *Lucan's First Book*, rehearsing Rome's civil war also in opposition to Virgilian empire; and even *Hero and Leander*, as Chapman reminds us in his translation of Marlowe's source text, the poem by the same name written by the fifth-century grammarian Musaeus, whom Marlowe and the Renaissance thought one of the legendary founders of poetry, along with Orpheus: 'Abydus and Sestus were two ancient Towns; one in Europe, another in Asia; East and West, opposites.'[32] Marlowe habitually rehearses his plots along the expansive imperial track precisely to blockade it, from early in his career to the very end, both on stage and on page.

Despite this consistent representation, the truncated quality of Marlowe's works and our imperfect knowledge of his life prevent us from attributing to him the kind of political organization that Richard Helgerson and others attribute to other early modern individuals who wrote the English nation, such as Spenser and Shakespeare, who managed to survive their twenties.[33] Nonetheless, as Marlowe's counter-imperial track hints, enough representational evidence exists to discern the outlines of a concerted project.

In *Marlowe's Counterfeit Profession*, I argued that Marlowe's Ovidian poems and plays inscribe a 'counter-nationhood', a non-patriotic form of nationalism that subverts Elizabethan royal power with what Ovid calls *libertas* (*Amores* 3.15.9) – and Marlowe translates as 'liberty' (*OE* 3.14.9) – in order to present 'the poet' as 'the true nation':[34] 'Verse is immortal, and shall ne'er decay. / To verse let kings give place, and kingly shows' (*OE* 1.15.32–3). Marlowe's Lucanian poetry, however, needs to be re-routed as a second

classical road into the Elizabethan political sphere – specifically, as a republican form of nationalism in opposition to monarchical power. Marlowe's
twin translations of Rome's two greatest counter-imperial epicists,[35] at the
beginning and the end of his career, construct for his work a bifold representational framework that includes, rather complexly, both Ovidian counter-
nationalism and Lucanian republicanism. Any full study of Marlowe's representational politics needs to distinguish between the two and then to discern
their concurrent, interwoven texture.

Marlowe deserves to be placed at the forefront of any conversation about
the rise of English republicanism, simply because he is the first Englishman
to translate Lucan's counter-imperial epic, also known as Lucan's *Civil War*
(*De Bello Civili*).[36] According to David Norbrook, Lucan is 'the central poet
of the republican imagination' (p. 24). As the original Lucanian voice in
England, Marlowe qualifies as the first Elizabethan poet of the republican
imagination. We do not know what Marlowe's plans were for his partial
translation, but Norbrook helps us understand what Marlovians neglect:
'The first book of the *Pharsalia* was in fact much cited by two of the leading seventeenth-century theorists of republicanism, James Harrington and
Algernon Sidney' (pp. 36–7). Whatever Marlowe's intentions might have
been, we can guardedly classify his translation of Lucan's first book as
a republican document – perhaps the first great literary representation of
republicanism in the English 'Renaissance'.

Because *Lucan's First Book* shows up in the Stationers' Register with
Hero and Leander, we may see how these two proto-epic documents at
the end of Marlowe's career cohere with documents traditionally placed
at the beginning, in elegy and tragedy (*Ovid's Elegies* and *Dido*), thereby
completing a Marlovian *cursus* that imitates the generic pattern of Ovid's
career. Marlowe's counter-Virgilian Ovidian art joins his counter-Virgilian,
Lucanian art as solid evidence for looking further into the representational
politics informing Marlowe's career.[37]

Marlowe's experiments in tragedy (discussed in the chapter here by
Richard Wilson) can also be identified as in some sense republican documents. Stephen Greenblatt and his heirs – notably Emily C. Bartels –
emphasize Marlowe's theatrical originality in putting at centre stage a series
of aliens, outsiders, and exiles – an African queen, a Scythian shepherd, a
German scholar, a Maltese Jew, even an English homoerotic king who lacks
political organization – without recognizing such figuration as forming a
strong republican ethos.[38] Marlowe describes Tamburlaine as one who 'with
shepherds and a little spoil / Durst, in disdain of wrong and tyranny, / Defend his freedom 'gainst a monarchy' (*1 Tamb.* 2.1.54–6). Thus, Marlowe's
much-debated interest in Machiavelli needs to be reconsidered, since it is well

known that in *The Jew of Malta* he is the first to put the arch-republican author of *The Prince* and *The Discourses* on to the English stage.[39] To this *dramatis personae*, we can add, from Marlowe's poems, an Ovidian lover, a passionate shepherd, a pair of star-crossed lovers, and of course those egregious Gemini of anti-republicanism at the core of Lucan's Roman civil war, Caesar and Pompey.

Accordingly, the famed Marlovian narrative, in both poems and plays, tells how a freedom-seeking individual is oppressed, always to annihilation, by authorities in power, whether represented by a corrupt government or by the angry gods – often by both: 'My God, my God, look not so fierce on me! / Adders, and serpents, let me breathe a while!' (*DF* 'A' text 5.2.119–20). The precise goal of Faustus's turn to magic helps us recognize what the authorities would be so swift to annihilate: a longing to 'make man to live eternally' ('A' text 1.1.24; see Cheney, *Marlowe's Counterfeit Profession*, p. 82). Intriguingly, this line has an earlier instantiation in the *Inferno*, where the pilgrim Dante recalls how Ser Brunetto, damned for sodomy, 'taught [him] . . . how man makes himself eternal' (15.85). Ser Brunetto is Dante's most powerful icon of earthly fame; not simply does he tell Dante that his 'company has clerics / and men of letters and of great fame' (106–7), but the great teacher makes a request that marks his signature character: 'Let my *Tesero*, in which I still live, / be precious to you; and I ask no more' (119–20). For Dante, Ser Brunetto is the author of a book that makes himself famous and teaches others how to be famous 'upon the earth' (108). He is the supreme exemplar in the entire *Commedia* of an author who writes a book violating Dante's own authorship in service of Christian glory. For his part, Marlowe overgoes Dante, for Faustus uses the book of magic not simply to become famous on earth but to create eternal life within time – an art that forms the ultimate blasphemy against the Christian God and yet hauntingly anticipates the goal of modern medicine and science. As in so much else, Marlowe's daring search for freedom attracted the strong hand of government.

Patrick Collinson has made famous the notion that Elizabeth's government was really a 'monarchical republic', and much recent scholarship, in English studies as in history, has been intrigued to map out such a complex public sphere.[40] Presumably, such a government allows for the birth of Marlovian freedom and puts it under surveillance. Yet here we might distinguish between republicanism as a form of government – conveniently defined by Norbrook as '"a state which was not headed by a king and in which the hereditary principle did not prevail in whole or in part in determining the headship"' (p. 17; quoting Zera S. Fink) – and the representation of republicanism in literary documents. Was Marlowe a republican? To quote Marlowe himself in *Hero and Leander*, 'O who can tell' (2.23)? What we can tell very plainly is what we might call the literary form of Marlowe's representational republicanism. His poems and plays constitute a significant register and clear herald of republican representation, both in the late Elizabethan era and finally in the early seventeenth century, as the English nation moves ever closer to the nightmare of a Lucanian Civil War.

Lucan's First Book ends with an inset hymn to the god Apollo by a Bacchic Roman matron, who futilely uses her prophetic power to head off Roman civil war. Philip Hardie finds the counter-Virgilian Lucan himself lurking in the original Latin representation (pp. 107–8), suggesting that Lucan uses characters to voice his republican programme. Surely, Marlowe saw this and delighted in cross-dressing his own English voice in his translation.[41] As is well known today, and as Kate Chedgzoy shows in her chapter here, Marlowe achieves another first worth emphasizing: he is the first English author to foreground his own homoerotic experience, in both poems and plays. This Marlovian originality appears most notably in the relationship between Edward and Gaveston in *Edward II*, but also in the inset tale of Leander with Neptune and the opening episode of *Dido* with Jupiter and Ganymede (see the chapter here by Sara Munson Deats).

For all Marlowe's inventiveness, however, no one could have predicted, until the last few years or so, Marlowe's most uncanny originality: not simply his staging of Jews, taken up famously by Shakespeare in *The Merchant of Venice*, but also his invention of a sub-genre of plays about Islam, taken up by such competing heirs as Robert Greene in *Alphonsus King of Aragon* (1587) and Peele in *The Battle of Alcazar* (1589).[42] In his chapter on *Edward II* here, Thomas Cartelli notes how Marlowe has recently emerged as 'early modern England's most modern playwright'; nowhere is this more striking than in Marlowe's centralized staging of two cultural topics now absorbing the world, the fate of Jews and the role of Islam. Furthermore, as the chapters by Julia Lupton and Mark Burnett emphasize, Marlowe's world of Barabas and Tamburlaine, recording a cultural environment in which Christians, Jews, and Muslims occupy the same political space, is a striking prediction of the world we inhabit today.

By way of conclusion, we might recall that Marlowe himself seems to have been fascinated by the idea of firstness. The word *first* appears over 130 times in his truncated corpus, and he manages to record a capacious series of first happenings: from the 'first mover of that sphere' (*1 Tamb.* 4.2.8) to 'he that first invented war' (*1 Tamb.* 2.4.1); from 'the first day of [Adam's]...creation' (*DF* 'A' text 2.2.109) to the 'first verse' of his own poetic creation (*OE* 1.1.21); and from the 'first letter' of Lechery's 'name' (*DF* 'A' text 2.2.169–70) to Leander's 'first sight' of Hero (*HL* 1.176). As this last example reminds us, the idea of firstness imprints one of Marlowe's most famous lines, quoted by Shakespeare in *As You Like It* (3.5.83): 'Who ever loved, that loved not at first sight.' In a manner not perhaps uncharacteristic of him, Marlowe indeed appears to have been (secretly) involved in the invention of his own standing as England's first major poet–playwright.

What is finally so striking about Marlowe is his signature yoking of literature with violence – not simply in his works but in his life. Contemporaries such as Spenser had used terms of violence to represent the art of writing, but surely England's New Poet did not make such a marriage the heart of his work.[43] In contrast to Spenser, Marlowe (one suspects) did: this young man made out of his author's life and works one of the most haunting fusions of the literary and the violent on record, and he was the first in England to do so in a nationally visible theatre. Yet even so, perhaps we can discern in the strange Marlovian fusion something more than a tormented psyche and its sadly truncated product: perhaps it is the historical birth passage of authorial freedom itself. Back in 1600, Thomas Thorpe, the publisher of Marlowe's *Lucan*, initially captured the historical constraint of Marlovian freedom when imagining a ghost or genius walking the churchyard in three or four sheets.

The notion of Marlovian firstness might help us further appreciate today the enigma of Marlowe's original genius. Clarke Hulse, observing that Marlowe wrote a poem paraphrasing 'divine Musaeus' (*HL* 1.52), calls Marlowe 'the Primeval Poet' and *Hero and Leander* the inaugural poem of an Elizabethan 'genre of primeval poetry'.[44] Marlowe might have been drawn especially to the primeval poets as a republican community because, as some Renaissance scholars thought, poets preceded monarchs in the evolution of civilization.[45] By recalling the remarkable line of commemoration identifying Marlowe's original achievement in English poetry and drama, from his day to ours, we may wonder whether it was the Muses' darling bathing in the Thespian springs, or perhaps the barking dog hooked by the nose, who cultivated for posterity the absolute fame of originality. Christopher Marlowe enters the twenty-first century the enigmatic genius of canonical dissidence.

NOTES

For helpful readings of this introduction, I am grateful to James P. Bednarz, Mark Thornton Burnett, Robert R. Edwards, Park Honan, David Riggs, and Garrett A. Sullivan.

1. Thomas Thorpe, *Dedicatory Epistle* to *Lucan's First Book* (1600), in Millar MacLure (ed.), *The Poems: Christopher Marlowe*, the Revels Plays (London: Methuen, 1968), p. 221. In this chapter all quotations from Marlowe's poems are taken from this edition. Quotations from the plays are from Mark Thornton

Burnett (ed.), *Christopher Marlowe: The Complete Plays*, Everyman Library (London: Dent; Rutland, VT: Tuttle, 1999). The i–j and u–v have been modernized in all quotations (Marlowe and otherwise), as have other obsolete typographical conventions, such as the italicizing of places and names.

2. The chapters by Lois Potter (pp. 262–81) and Lisa Hopkins (pp. 282–96) touch on interrelated matters. For recent recuperations of 'genius', a word that originally meant *attendant spirit* but that quite naturally came to mean *creative brilliance*, see Jonathan Bate, *The Genius of Shakespeare* (London: Picador, 1997); and Harold Bloom, *Genius: A Mosaic of One Hundred Exemplary Creative Minds* (New York: Warner, 2002). Marlowe's 'genius' has long been debated, but supporters from the sixteenth century onwards include (in MacLure, *Critical Heritage*) George Peele, Michael Drayton, Thomas Heywood, Ben Jonson, Thomas Warton, William Hazlitt, Leigh Hunt, Edward Dowden, A. C. Bradley, John Addington Symonds, James Russell Lowell, George Saintsbury, and Algernon Charles Swinburne. T. S. Eliot ushers in modern criticism by judging that Marlowe wrote 'indubitably great poetry' ('Christopher Marlowe', in *Elizabethan Dramatists* (London: Faber, 1963), pp. 65–6).

3. Rpt in Constance Brown Kuriyama, *Christopher Marlowe: A Renaissance Life* (Ithaca: Cornell University Press, 2002), pp. 202–3.

4. John Bakeless, *The Tragical History of Christopher Marlowe*, 2 vols. (1942; Hamden, CT: Archon, 1964), 2: 161 (see 2: 290).

5. Sukanta Chaudhuri, 'Marlowe, Madrigals, and a New Elizabethan Poet', *RES* 39 (1988), 199–216.

6. Leah S. Marcus, 'Textual Indeterminacy and Ideological Difference: the Case of *Dr Faustus*', *RenD* 20 (1989), 1–29; Thomas Healy, *Christopher Marlowe* (Plymouth: Northcote House in Association with the British Council, 1994), pp. 1–9.

7. Rpt in Stephen Orgel (ed.), *Christopher Marlowe: The Complete Poems and Translations* (Harmondsworth: Penguin, 1971), p. 91.

8. See Thomas Dabbs, *Reforming Marlowe: The Nineteenth-Century Canonization of a Renaissance Dramatist* (London: Associated University Presses, 1991).

9. Marlowe was not the first to bring blank verse to the stage (it emerged in such pre-Marlovian plays as *Gorboduc*), but he was famed in his own time for having made blank verse the standard line for the stage, as Jonson recognized by singling out 'Marlowes mighty line' in his memorial poem on Shakespeare (rpt in *The Riverside Shakespeare*, G. Blakemore Evans, et al. (eds.) (Boston: Houghton, 1997), p. 97). On this topic, see McDonald in the present volume, pp. 55–69.

10. Clifford Leech (ed.), 'Introduction', *Marlowe: A Collection of Critical Essays*, Twentieth Century Views (Englewood Cliffs, NJ: Prentice-Hall, 1964), p. 1.

11. These and other critics can be found in Leech and other important collections: Brian Morris (ed.), *Christopher Marlowe* (New York: Hill, 1968); Judith O'Neill (ed.), *Critics on Marlowe* (Coral Gables: University of Miami Press, 1970); Alvin B. Kernan (ed.), *Two Renaissance Mythmakers: Christopher Marlowe and Ben Jonson* (Baltimore: Johns Hopkins University Press, 1977); Harold Bloom (ed.), *Christopher Marlowe* (New York: Chelsea, 1986); Emily C. Bartels (ed.), *Critical Essays on Christopher Marlowe* (New York: G. K. Hall; and London: Prentice, 1996); and Richard Wilson (ed.), *Christopher Marlowe* (London: Longman, 1999).

12. Paul H. Kocher, *Christopher Marlowe: A Study of His Thought, Learning, and Character* (1946; New York: Russell, 1962).

13. Roy W. Battenhouse, *Marlowe's 'Tamburlaine': A Study in Renaissance Moral Philosophy* (Nashville: Vanderbilt University Press, 1941); and Una Ellis-Fermor, *Christopher Marlowe* (1927: Hamden, CT: Archon, 1967).

14. Clifford Leech, *Christopher Marlowe: Poet for the Stage*, Anne Lancashire (ed.) (New York: AMS Press, 1986), esp. 'The Acting of Marlowe and Shakespeare' (pp. 199–218).

15. See Patrick Cheney, 'Recent Studies in Marlowe (1987–1998)', *ELR* 31 (2001), 288–328. See earlier instalments in Jonathan Post, 'Recent Studies in Marlowe: 1968–1976', *ELR* 6 (1977), 382–99; and Ronald Levao, 'Recent Studies in Marlowe (1977–1987)', *ELR* 18 (1988), 329–41.

16. Stephen Greenblatt, 'Marlowe and the Will to Absolute Play', in *Renaissance Self-Fashioning: More to Shakespeare* (University of Chicago Press, 1980), pp. 193–221 (quotations from p. 220; his emphasis); and Harry Levin, *The Overreacher: A Study of Christopher Marlowe* (Cambridge, MA: Harvard University Press, 1954).

17. Cf. Irving Ribner, 'Marlowe and the Critics', *TDR* 8 (1964), 211–24.

18. For a recent overview, see Mark Thornton Burnett (ed.), 'Introduction', *Christopher Marlowe: The Complete Poems*, Everyman Poetry (London: Dent; Rutland, VT: Tuttle, 2000), pp. xiv–xx. Cf. MacLure (ed.), *Poems*, pp. xix–xliv; and Harry Morris, 'Marlowe's Poetry', *TDR* 8 (1963), 134–54.

19. Patrick Cheney, *Marlowe's Counterfeit Profession: Ovid, Spenser, Counter-Nationhood* (University of Toronto Press, 1997), pp. 259–64, esp. p. 343n6.

20. For a fuller inventory, see Patrick Cheney, 'Materials', in Cheney and Anne Lake Prescott (eds.), *Approaches to Teaching Shorter Elizabethan Poetry* (New York: MLA, 2000), pp. 46–50.

21. J. B. Steane, *Marlowe: A Critical Study* (Cambridge University Press, 1964).

22. C. S. Lewis, 'Hero and Leander', *PBA* 28 (1952), 23–37, rpt in Paul J. Alpers (ed.), *Elizabethan Poetry: Modern Essays in Criticism* (London: Oxford University Press, 1967), pp. 235–50; David Lee Miller, 'The Death of the Modern: Gender and Desire in Marlowe's *Hero and Leander*', *SAQ* 88 (1989), 757–87. Books on Marlowe's plays with a chapter on *Hero and Leander* include Malcolm Kelsall, *Christopher Marlowe* (Leiden: Brill, 1981); and William Zunder, *Elizabethan Marlowe: Writing and Culture in the English Renaissance* (Cottingham: Unity, 1994). Fred B. Tromly's *Playing with Desire: Christopher Marlowe and the Art of Tantalization* (University of Toronto Press, 1998) signals a new trend that combines poems with plays, although he neglects *Lucan's First Book*.

23. Roma Gill, 'Christopher Marlowe', in vol. 62 of Fredson Bowers (ed.), *The Dictionary of Literary Biography: Elizabethan Dramatists* (Detroit: Gale Research Group, 1987), pp. 212–31 (quotation from p. 213).

24. In his chapter on the English literary scene, pp. 90–105, James P. Bednarz examines Marlowe in relation specifically to Watson, Greene, and Shakespeare.

25. C. S. Lewis, *English Literature of the Sixteenth Century, Excluding Drama* (1954; London: Oxford University Press, 1973), p. 488 (see p. 487).

26. Charles Martindale, *Redeeming the Text: Latin Poetry and the Hermeneutics of Reception* (Cambridge University Press, 1993), p. 97.

27. Patrick Cheney, '"O, Let My Books be...Dumb Presagers": Poetry and Theater in Shakespeare's Sonnets', *SQ* 52 (2001), 222–54; and *Shakespeare, National Poet–Playwright* (Cambridge University Press, 2004).

28. E. J. Kenney, 'Ovid', in Kenney (ed.), *Latin Literature* (Cambridge University Press, 1982), vol. 2 of Kenney (ed.), *The Cambridge History of Classical Literature* (Cambridge University Press, 1982–5), 2: 433.

29. Dante, *Inferno* 4.88–90, in *The Divine Comedy of Dante: Inferno, Purgatorio, Paradiso*, Allen Mandelbaum (trans.) (New York: Bantam Doubleday, 1982).

30. Charles Martindale, 'Introduction: "The Classic of all Europe"', in Martindale (ed.), *The Cambridge Companion to Virgil* (Cambridge University Press, 1997), p. 2.

31. The Horatian connection is neglected, but for Marlowe as an Erasmian ironist, see Judith Weil, *Christopher Marlowe: Merlin's Prophet* (Cambridge University Press, 1977).

32. George Chapman (trans.), *Hero and Leander*, in Richard Herne Shepherd (ed.), *The Works of George Chapman*, 3 vols. (London: Chatto, 1911–24), 2: 94.

33. Richard Helgerson, *Forms of Nationhood: The Elizabethan Writing of England* (University of Chicago Press, 1992). See also Andrew D. Hadfield, *Literature, Politics, and National Identity: Reformation to Renaissance* (Cambridge University Press, 1994); and Claire McEachern, *The Poetics of English Nationalism, 1590–1612* (Cambridge University Press, 1996).

34. Leo Braudy, *The Frenzy of Renown: Fame and Its History* (New York: Oxford University Press, 1986), p. 135.

35. See Philip Hardie, *The Epic Successors of Virgil* (Cambridge University Press, 1993).

36. Critics neglect Marlowe's inaugural role in the rise of English republicanism: e.g., David Norbrook, *Writing the English Republic: Poetry, Rhetoric, and Politics, 1627–1660* (Cambridge University Press, 1999), p. 41; and Andrew Hadfield, 'Was Spenser a Republican?', *English* 47 (1998), 169–82 and *Shakespeare and Renaissance Political Culture* (forthcoming).

37. Marlowe critics tend to overlook Lucan, but see James Shapiro, '"Metre Meete to Furnish Lucans Style": Reconsidering Marlowe's *Lucan*', in Kenneth Friedenreich, Roma Gill, and Constance B. Kuriyama (eds.), *'A Poet and a Filthy Playmaker': New Essays on Christopher Marlowe* (New York: AMS Press, 1988), pp. 315–25.

38. Emily C. Bartels, *Spectacles of Strangeness: Imperialism, Alienation, and Marlowe* (Philadelphia: University of Pennsylvania Press, 1993).

39. Graham Hammill is researching this topic.

40. Patrick Collinson, 'The Monarchical Republic of Queen Elizabeth I', *BJRL* 69 (1987), 394–424.

41. On this Elizabethan strategy elsewhere in Renaissance literature, see Wendy Wall, *The Imprint of Gender: Authorship and Publication in the English Renaissance* (Ithaca: Cornell University Press, 1993), pp. 227–78.

42. On the Islam plays, see Peter Berek, '*Tamburlaine*'s Weak Sons: Imitation as Interpretation before 1593', *RenD* 13 (1982), 55–82. For a convenient listing, see Leech's 'Proposed Chronology of Marlowe's Works: in Relation to Certain Types of Writing During and Shortly After His Time' (*Poet for the Stage*, pp. 219–22).

This topic is now being increasingly studied by such critics as Emily C. Bartels and Daniel J. Vitkus. See Daniel Vitkus (ed.), *Three Turk Plays from Early Modern England: 'Selimus,' 'A Christian Turned Turk,' and 'The Renegado'* (New York: Columbia University Press, 2000). On the Jews in early modern England, see James Shapiro, *Shakespeare and the Jews* (New York: Columbia University Press, 1996).

43. On 'the violence of writing' in Spenser, see Theresa M. Krier, *Birth Passages: Maternity, Nostalgia, Antiquity to Shakespeare* (Ithaca: Cornell University Press), p. 221, indebted to Jonathan Goldberg, *Writing Matter: From the Hands of the English Renaissance* (Stanford University Press, 1990), pp. 57–107; and Gordon Teskey, *Allegory and Violence* (Ithaca: Cornell University Press, 1996), pp. 168–88. For Senecan origins, see Gorden Braden, *Renaissance Tragedy and the Senecan Tradition: Anger's Privilege* (New Haven: Yale University Press, 1985).

44. Clarke Hulse, 'Marlowe, the Primeval Poet', in *Metamorphic Verse: The Elizabethan Minor Epic* (Princeton University Press, 1981), pp. 93–140.

45. See, e.g., George Puttenham, *The Arte of English Poesie*, in G. Gregory Smith (ed.), *Elizabethan Critical Essays*, 2 vols. (London: Oxford University Press, 1904), 2: 7–8. Thanks to David Riggs.

READING LIST

Bartels, Emily C. *Spectacles of Strangeness: Imperialism, Alienation, and Marlowe.* Philadelphia: University of Pennsylvania Press, 1993.

Cartelli, Thomas. *Marlowe, Shakespeare, and the Economy of Theatrical Experience.* Philadelphia: University of Pennsylvania Press, 1991.

Cheney, Patrick. *Marlowe's Counterfeit Profession: Ovid, Spenser, Counter-Nationhood.* University of Toronto Press, 1997.

Eliot, T. S. 'Christopher Marlowe'. *Elizabethan Dramatists.* London: Faber and Faber, 1963, pp. 58–66.

Ellis-Fermor, Una. *Christopher Marlowe.* 1927; Hamden, CT: Archon, 1967.

Gill, Roma. 'Christopher Marlowe'. In Fredson Bowers (ed.), *The Dictionary of Literary Biography: Elizabethan Dramatists.* Detroit: Gale Research Group, 1987, 62: 212–31.

Greenblatt, Stephen. 'Marlowe and the Will to Absolute Play'. *Renaissance Self-Fashioning: More to Shakespeare.* University of Chicago Press, 1980, pp. 193–221.

Healy, Thomas. *Christopher Marlowe.* Plymouth, Northcote House in Association with the British Council, 1994.

Kocher, Paul. *Christopher Marlowe: A Study of His Thought, Learning, and Character.* 1946; New York: Russell, 1962.

Leech, Clifford. *Christopher Marlowe: Poet for the Stage.* Anne Lancashire (ed.). New York: AMS Press, 1986.

Levin, Harry. *The Overreacher: A Study of Christopher Marlowe.* Cambridge, MA: Harvard University Press, 1954.

Kuriyama, Constance Brown. *Christopher Marlowe: A Renaissance Life.* Ithaca: Cornell University Press, 2002.

MacLure, Millar (ed.). *Marlowe: The Critical Heritage 1588–1896*. London: Routledge and Kegan Paul, 1979.

Nicholl, Charles. *The Reckoning: The Murder of Christopher Marlowe*. New York: Harcourt, 1992.

Riggs, David. 'The Killing of Christopher Marlowe'. *StHR* 8 (2000), 239–51.

Steane, J. B. *Marlowe: A Critical Study*. Cambridge University Press, 1964.

2

DAVID RIGGS

Marlowe's life

Christopher Marlowe's contemporaries recalled a conflicted figure. 'Pity it is that wit so ill should dwell', wrote a student playwright at Cambridge, 'Wit lent from heaven, but vices sent from hell.' Other living witnesses lined up on either side of this divide. The poet George Peele called the dead playwright 'the Muses' darling'. William Shakespeare hailed the author of the magical verse, 'Who ever loved, that loved not at first sight?' Ben Jonson praised the inventor of 'Marlowe's mighty line'. Michael Drayton, another poet, proclaimed that Marlowe 'Had in him those brave translunary things, / That the first Poets have'. Marlowe's enemies were just as adamant about his vices. During the months leading up to Marlowe's death, the pamphleteer Robert Greene publicly predicted that if the 'famous gracer of tragedians' did not repent his blasphemies God would soon strike him down. Just a few days before Marlowe was murdered, the spy Richard Baines informed Queen Elizabeth's Privy Council that the playwright was a proselytizing atheist, a counterfeiter, and a consumer of 'boys and tobacco'. Protestant ministers viewed Marlowe's violent end in his twenty-ninth year as an act of divine vengeance. Marlowe had 'denied God and his son Christ', declared Thomas Beard, 'But see what a hook the Lord put in the nostrils of this barking dog.'[1]

Four hundred years later, we can agree about Marlowe's artistic genius, but the story of his wayward life remains elusive. He left no first-person utterances behind for us to interpret (the sole exception is a cryptic Latin dedication to the Countess of Pembroke). The facts of his adult life are few, scattered, and of doubtful accuracy. Only one of his works was published during his lifetime, and his name appears nowhere on the text. Despite his many encounters with the law, Marlowe seldom went to trial and was never convicted of anything.[2] The evidence about his transgressive temperament sits at one remove from his own voice. It consists of reported speech, observations by unfriendly witnesses, and passages drawn from his plays. Sceptics rightly insist that the atheist and troublemaker exists only in these documents. He is an irretrievably textual being.

Where does a biographer go from there? Seven of Marlowe's contemporaries allude in writing to his blasphemies; the number increases to eleven if we include writers who refer to him by pseudonyms.[3] This dossier is unprecedented in its intricacy and scope, its points of contact with literature and politics, and its murderous outcome. The fear of God was the bedrock of moral order in Marlowe's England. His contemporaries assumed that people who did not believe in the hand of divine correction would sin with reckless abandon. Within the history of modern unbelief, Marlowe bestrides the moment when atheism comes out of the closet and acquires a public face. In *The Theatre of God's Judgments*, Beard correctly identified him as the first Englishman to challenge comparison with the great blasphemers of antiquity: 'not inferior to any of the former in Atheism and impiety, and equal to all in manner of punishment'. During the last six years of his life, Marlowe was cited for defecting to the Roman Catholic seminary at Rheims, suspicion of murder, counterfeiting, disturbing the peace, felonious assault, and public atheism. The constables in his neighbourhood sought protection from the local magistrate because they were afraid of him. One informant accused him of planning to join 'the enemy', Catholic Spain, just four years after the coming of the Spanish Armada in 1588. Another linked him with a London gang-leader who was involved in a plot to assassinate Queen Elizabeth I.

In the jargon of today's intelligence agencies, there was a lot of 'chatter' around Christopher Marlowe, an array of signals that implicated him in covert operations and high-level conspiracies. Prosaic explanations for Marlowe's misadventures are readily available: the rumour about his going to Rheims could have been a simple mistake; maybe he took up counterfeiting because he needed money, and got away with it because the authorities did not bother to prosecute him; perhaps he was murdered in a drunken quarrel over a bar bill. But the chatter is still there.

The first question to ask about this evidence is not 'Did he or didn't he?' but rather 'Why Marlowe?' Why was he selected by history to fill this role? The answers to this question cannot lie in his conscious choices, about which there is little to know; they lie in the parts he was chosen to play.

His father, the migrant worker John Marlowe, moved to the cathedral city of Canterbury in the mid-1550s. He was twenty years old and came from Ospringe, beside the north Kent port of Faversham. Single men between the ages of twelve and twenty, the time when apprentices were indentured, took to the roads in search of work. Canterbury was not only a church capital, but also a regional centre located amid fertile farmlands. Families bearing the name of Marlowe, or Marley, had settled there during the fifteenth and earlier sixteenth centuries. John Marlowe could expect to find 'cousins' in a position to help him. Furthermore, the influenza epidemic of the late 1550s decreased the local population by a quarter. This demographic catastrophe encouraged looser policies of apprenticeship and admission to the trade guilds; it was far easier for outsiders to enter the workforce when local replacements were lacking.[4] By the autumn of 1560, John Marlowe had apprenticed himself to an ageing and impoverished shoemaker.

The following spring, Marlowe married Katherine Arthur, another outsider, who came to Canterbury from the coastal city of Dover. Like her husband, she was probably the child of peasants. A year later the newly-weds had a daughter named Mary. Their first son Christopher was baptized on 26 February 1564, just two months before Shakespeare was christened at Stratford-upon-Avon. All told, Katherine Marlowe bore nine children and saw five or six of them survive into adulthood. John Marlowe's master died intestate in 1564, during a severe outbreak of bubonic plague. His passing doubtless explains why Marlowe could join the Shoemakers' Guild a few weeks later, just four years after entering into his apprenticeship, instead of the statutory seven. The Marlowes remained a poor family: they were not on the subsidy rolls and received welfare assistance from local charities during Marlowe's boyhood. Yet the father did possess one unusual asset for a man in his position: he could sign his name and perform clerical tasks.

Christopher Marlowe's formal education began around the age of seven, when he memorized his *ABC and Catechism*. This ubiquitous little book was meant to induct impressionable children into the Church of England; but Canterbury remained a city of divided loyalties. The English state religion changed three times between 1547 and 1558, and Canterbury felt the full shock of these seismic alterations. Each time a new king came to the throne, everyone in the ecclesiastical establishment had to adapt or be deprived. These vacillations left parish life badly demoralized. When the Crown lawyer and antiquarian William Lambarde visited Canterbury during the 1560s, the city was a shadow of its former self: 'And therefore no marvel', he reckoned, 'if wealth withdrawn, and opinion of holiness removed, the places tumble headlong to ruin and decay.'[5]

Tradesmen's sons usually left school at the age of eight. Marlowe, however, proceeded to grammar school and began to study Latin. In the winter of 1579, just six weeks shy of his fifteenth birthday, he won a scholarship at the prestigious King's School in Canterbury. The School instituted these awards for 'fifty poor boys, both destitute of the help of friends and endowed with minds apt for learning'. When Marlowe became a scholar, perhaps half of the fifty really were poor, that is, the sons of small tradesmen or yeoman farmers. The head master reserved places for them because, as Archbishop Cranmer remarked when the school was founded, 'the poor man's son by painstaking for the most part will be learned, when the gentleman's son will not take the pain to get it'. Poor boys won many of the university scholarships for the same reason.

The 'chiefest labor' of grammar school, wrote a prominent schoolmaster, 'is to make those purest Authors our own, as Tully [Cicero] for prose, so Ovid and Virgil for verse, so to speak and write in Latin for the phrase, as they did'. The most gruelling ordeal was the extemporaneous oral composition of Ovidian and Virgilian hexameters. William Harrison, a Tudor social historian, reports that university scholarships were awarded to 'poor scholars' after they had mastered 'the rules of versifying, the trial whereof is made by certain apposers yearly appointed to examine them'. Archbishop Parker's son John, who oversaw the Parker scholarship that sent Marlowe to Corpus Christi College, Cambridge, wrote this career path into the terms of his father's bequest. Parker wanted this award to go to 'such as can make a verse'.[6] By the time Marlowe left grammar school, he had internalized the basic principles of Latin prosody (figures of speech, metrical resolution rules, relative stress) that underlaid his great contributions to the art of English poetry: the heroic couplet and the blank verse line.

Marlowe arrived at Corpus Christi during the second week of December, 1580. The student body included a mix of fee-paying gentlemen and base-born scholars. The division between these two groups laid the groundwork for many scenes of social conflict that arise in Marlowe's works. Parker endowed Marlowe's three-year scholarship for boys 'who were likely to proceed in Arts and afterwards make Divinity their study'. Students who intended to enter Holy Orders could hold them for an additional three years after the BA, and proceed to the MA. The Cambridge arts course, however, emphasized classical studies at the expense of Divinity. The 1570 statutes virtually eliminated scholastic philosophy, the cornerstone of Roman Catholic learning, from the list of set texts for university lecturers. The most important book in Master Robert Norgate's lesson plan for students at Corpus Christi is John Seton's *Dialectic*, the indispensable textbook on logic.[7] The dialecticians rejected formal validity, the guiding principle of scholastic logic, in favour of persuasiveness, the looser standard of proof that applies to rhetoric. The truest arguments, which could be borrowed from rhetoric and poetry, were the ones that 'compelled belief' on an *ad hoc* basis.

Marlowe learned this lesson well. His poetry and plays – from his signature lyric 'Come live with me and be my love' (1584?) to *Tamburlaine the Great* (1587–8), to his erotic narrative *Hero and Leander* (1592–3) – emphasize the power of persuasive speech to move the will.

Although there is no hard evidence to go on, most scholars put Marlowe's translation of Ovid's *Amores* at the beginning of his career. His line-by-line rendering of Ovid's unrhymed distiches into rhymed English couplets reproduces the snap and wit of Ovid's original; but *All Ovid's Elegies* (1584–5?) also contains the botched translations and metrical irregularities that are the telltale signs of apprentice work. The title page of *Dido, Queen of Carthage* (1584–5?) states that the play was prepared by Marlowe and his Cambridge contemporary Thomas Nashe, and performed by the Children of the Chapel Royal. Since the Chapel Children flourished in 1583–4, and then went into eclipse, we can infer that *Dido* was written *c.* 1584. The play dramatizes Books 1, 2, and 4 of Virgil's *Aeneid*; but Marlowe, following Ovid, emphasizes the plight of the abandoned queen, while reducing the status of Virgil's manly hero. Edmund Spenser had already positioned himself as the 'English Virgil'; Marlowe adopted the opposing role of the English Ovid. His masterly line-by-line translation of Lucan's *Civil War*, Book 1, is even harder to date, but Marlowe's commitment to Lucan, the other great anti-Virgilian poet of imperial Rome, complemented his Ovidian stance.

Marlowe received his BA in July 1584. Degree-holders had more mobility than undergraduates did and Marlowe took advantage of this. He was away from his college for about half of the academic year 1584–5, and the pattern of extended absences persisted until the end of his MA course. Marlowe's only recorded appearance outside of Cambridge during this period occurred in Canterbury. In August 1585, he signed the will of Widow Benchkin, a neighbour there; this is Marlowe's only extant autograph signature. With the benefit of hindsight, speculation about Marlowe's employment during his absences has focused on the secret service. The Jesuit mission to re-convert England, the mounting threat posed by Mary, Queen of Scots, and the outbreak of war with Spain in 1585 stimulated an acute demand for messengers, snoops, and undercover agents. Queen Elizabeth professional-ized her surveillance apparatus in 1581–2, when she authorized Sir Francis Walsingham to organize the first state-sponsored secret service in English history. By 1585, Walsingham's annual outlay for secret service work had leapt to about £7,000 a year; the figure for 1586 was upwards of £12,000, an enormous sum of money by Elizabethan standards.[8]

The intriguing puzzle of Marlowe's absences from Cambridge makes it easy to forget that he spent at least a year and a half in residence prepar-ing for his MA. Candidates for the MA were required to 'be constant at-tendants of lectures in philosophy, astronomy, optics [the science of sight], and the Greek language'. Cosmography, an interdisciplinary branch of op-tics that encompassed both geography and history, proved especially fruit-ful for Marlowe's intellectual development. Abraham Ortellius's pioneering atlas, *The Theatre of the World*, Andre Thevet's *Universal Cosmography*, and Francois Belleforest's *Universal Cosmography of the Whole World* sup-plied him with material for *Tamburlaine, Part Two*, and *The Jew of Malta*

(1589–91).[9] With the eclipse of scholastic learning, poetry became an important source for the study of philosophy. The author of *The Ethical, Scientific, and Historical Interpretation of Ovid's Fables*, published by the Cambridge University Press in 1584, explained that 'Poetry is nothing, if not philosophy joined together with metre and story.'[10] Ovid's naturalistic and libertine philosophy had a profound influence on Marlowe's atheistic worldview. The scientific metaphors of the four elements and the voyage into the heavens guided Marlowe's reading of Ovid's *Metamorphoses* and Lucretius' *On the Nature of Things*, and taught him to conceive of the universe as a self-perpetuating physical construction. These paradigms came to life in *Tamburlaine*, the play he completed in the year that he took his MA.

The mystery of Marlowe's absences grew more urgent in 1587. There was a 'rumour' that Marlowe 'was determined to have gone beyond the seas to Rheims there to remain'. The English seminary at Rheims was a prime destination for Catholic students-in-exile; it housed many of Queen Elizabeth's deadliest enemies. On 29 June, the queen's Privy Council informed university officials that Marlowe 'had done her Majesty good service . . . in matters touching the benefit of his country'. The Councillors denied that he had ever intended to 'remain' at Rheims, and finessed the intriguing question of whether or not he had actually gone there. In any case, their letter leaves the impression that Marlowe has carried out secret missions on the Council's behalf.

The major figures in Marlowe's postgraduate life, apart from the playwright Thomas Kyd, worked for the Elizabethan secret service. The spy Richard Baines, the poet Thomas Watson, and the Kentish squire Thomas Walsingham all belonged to the band of intelligence operatives that kept watch on the seminarians at Rheims and their English allies.[11] On the other hand, Marlowe's name nowhere appears in the Diary where the seminary kept its records. It is more likely, then, that he intended to visit Rheims, where he could have contacted one of Walsingham's agents such as the master spy Gilbert Gifford. Biographers assume that Marlowe was in Sir Francis Walsingham's employ; but the Council's letter to Cambridge was signed by Lord Treasurer Burleigh, the queen's closest adviser, and members of his faction, the 'peace party' who were negotiating with the Spanish army headquartered in Brussels. When Marlowe subsequently appears in government documents, he is dealing with Burleigh or his agents.

The Council frequently employed poets as messengers and go-betweens. Marlowe's case stands out because of the rumour about his switching sides. In its effort to scotch the rumour, the Privy Council identified the real Marlowe with the loyal subject ('he had no such intent'), implying that the seditious Marlowe was merely playing a part. Such distinctions often broke down in practice. The vast majority of secret agents toiled in a marginal and mercenary occupation. Their own employers held them in suspicion, believing that 'There be no trust to a knave that will deceive them that trust him' (Nicholl, p. 130). Field operatives rarely found posts in the civil service or the professions, and there is no reason to believe that Marlowe's prospects were any different.

The timing of the Council's letter to Cambridge dovetailed with Marlowe's decision to write for the newly erected London theatres; he was the first university graduate to forge a lasting professional bond with the adult players. Why was this collaboration so successful? Like his new employers, the secret agent was an actor, licensed by authority to perform the role of the outlaw, and shrewdly suspected of being the part he played. By commissioning Marlowe as a double agent, the authorities inserted him into opposing roles – loyal servant and subversive Other. As a government agent, he served the state by imitating the enemy whose presence justified the exercise of state power; the Crown authorized him to voice what it regarded as sedition and heresy (Goldberg).

Marlowe's *Tamburlaine the Great* was in the repertory of the Lord Admiral's Men by the autumn of 1587. A work of high literary accomplishment, and an unprecedented crowd-pleaser to boot, *Tamburlaine* marked an important advance in the quality of English professional theatre. Marlowe's major innovation was the sonorous, actor-friendly blank verse line that he bequeathed to Shakespeare and Milton. The author voices his scorn for 'rhyming mother wits', and promises to regale his audience with 'high astounding terms', in the opening lines of his Prologue. Marlowe writes this triumphalist version of literary history into the structure of his work. His base-born hero is an extemporaneous oral poet whose verses, the 'working words' that energize his followers, are his passport to wealth and dominion. This fable transforms the cycle of poverty, poetry, and social mobility that had cast Marlowe on the margins of Elizabethan society into an unexampled success story.

The Prologue to *Tamburlaine, Part Two* explains Marlowe's motive for writing the sequel. 'The general welcomes Tamburlaine received', he begins, 'When he arrived last upon our stage / Hath made our poet pen his second part / Where death cuts off the progress of his pomp' (1–4). *Part Two* offers a Lucretian meditation on the meaning of death. Characters who imagine themselves in a conscious afterlife, rewarded and punished by the gods, are ridiculed and tormented; characters who take the Epicurean view that the soul perishes with the body, dissolving into the elements, achieve tranquillity. Marlowe enforces this anti-Christian idea with satire and blasphemy. By the time Marlowe wrote *Part Two* (1587?), he had seen the First Book of Spenser's *Faerie Queene* in manuscript. He signalled his awareness of Spenser's masterpiece by inserting a travesty of one of his rival's most widely admired stanzas into his play: King Arthur, Spenser's Christian warrior, momentarily turns into Tamburlaine, the blaspheming tyrant.

Small wonder that Robert Greene complained the following March about 'daring God out of heaven with that atheist Tamburlaine'. Although Greene cloaks his remarks about Marlowe in cryptic allusions and figures, the thrust of his critique is clear enough. Two gentlemen have derided him 'for that I could not make my verses jet upon the stage' like that atheist Tamburlaine. But Greene refuses to 'wantonly set out such impious instances of intolerable poetry'. Instead he will adhere to his Horatian motto, and mix instruction with delight. Tamburlaine's verses delight but do not instruct. Greene would rather endure the gentlemen's insult than follow the lead of 'such mad and scoffing poets, that have prophetical spirits as bred of *Merlins* race'. Merlin was the legendary magician; but this was also the Elizabethan pronunciation of 'Marlin', the name Marlowe went by at Cambridge, while the mad and scoffing poets are his followers. Greene doubts that Marlowe has 'set the end of scholarism in an English blank verse', the term Greene invents to describe Marlowe's innovation. 'Scholarism' refers to the ill-fated attempt to write English poetry in classical metres. Although Greene will not concede that Merlin has rung the death knell of scholarism, that is precisely what Marlowe had done. Even Greene has to admit that *Tamburlaine* has set a trend. If Merlin made a bad example, he was also a prophet who inspired a race of imitators.

The earliest imitations of Marlowe include Greene's *Alphonsus King of Aragon*, George Peele's *The Battle of Alcazar*, Thomas Lodge's *Wounds of Civil War*, and the anonymous *Selimus*, all written within a few years of *Tamburlaine*. These works reduced Marlowe's conception to a marketable formula: poetry and spectacle transform regicide into effective theatre, a source of illicit pleasure. The protagonists speak in thumping blank verse thickly larded with hyperboles. The action reeks of egregious violence. The common practice of quoting or citing *Tamburlaine*, or of reproducing its most lurid scenes, gave Marlowe's work a bad eminence, as if 'Merlin' were responsible for the exorbitance of his imitators. Marlowe found his co-equal in his future chamber fellow Thomas Kyd. Kyd devised his own version of the blank verse line for *The Spanish Tragedy* (c. 1587). Like Marlowe, Kyd employs the scourge-of-God motif to obtain moral leverage on subaltern violence. Where Tamburlaine claims to be a flail sent from heaven, Kyd's protagonist Hieronimo is a high-minded magistrate driven mad, like Hamlet, by the contradictory roles of 'scourge and minister'. Kyd, too, attracted imitators, who penned blank verse revenge plays that revel in gratuitous cruelty and murder.

In a public letter 'To the Gentlemen Students of Both Universities' prefixed to Greene's novel *Menaphon* (1589), Thomas Nashe attacked the new fad of blank verse tragedy. Nashe complained about the capacity of blank verse to reproduce itself in the arena of popular culture; anyone could mimic its heavily accented rhythms. Other writers confirm Nashe's observation. Satirical vignettes by Shakespeare, Joseph Hall, and George Wither depict an urban sub-culture where plebeian poets gave extempore renditions of Tamburlaine in taverns. The art of making 'pure iambic verse', formerly the preserve of scholars, had become available to anyone who could afford standing room in the playhouse or the price of a drink. Nashe singles out Kyd, who never went to university, for censure. Greene, however, does allude to Marlowe, in the text of *Menaphon*. Making fun of what he calls a 'Canterbury tale', Greene remarks that it was told by a 'prophetical full mouth that as he were a Cobbler's eldest son, would by the last tell where another's shoe wrings'. Greene refers to the eldest son of the Canterbury cobbler John Marlowe. The would-be prophet's shoe wrings 'by the last' on which his father fashioned footwear. Like Kyd, Marlowe has left the trade into which he was born, transgressing the confines of his birth and status.

On 18 September 1589, between the hours of two and three in the afternoon, the flesh-and-blood Christopher Marlowe flashes into view. He was on Hog Lane, near the Theatre in Shoreditch, fighting with William Bradley, a 26-year-old innkeeper from nearby Bishopsgate. The poet and playwright Thomas Watson lurked nearby. Watson drew his sword, allegedly to 'separate' the two men and 'to keep the Queen's peace'. Bradley then turned on Watson, who killed his assailant with a thrust into the chest. Marlowe and Watson were arrested 'on suspicion of murder' and taken to Newgate Prison. Marlowe posted his bail on 1 October.

Marlowe's fellow prisoners at Newgate included John Poole, a Cheshire gentleman who had been arrested for counterfeiting in 1587. Richard Baines remembered Marlowe saying 'that he was acquainted with one poole, a prisoner in newgate who hath great Skill in mixture of metals'. Since Baines and Marlowe were later involved in a counterfeiting scheme, the informant was doubtless telling the truth in this case. Poole belonged to the Catholic underground and was related to the Earl of Derby's eldest son Ferdinando Stanley, Lord Strange. After the execution of Mary, Queen of Scots, Lord Strange became an important figurehead for papists who sought to replace Queen Elizabeth with a Catholic monarch. Poole took a lively interest in Strange's claim to the English crown. He also spoke warmly of another relative, the renegade English commander Sir William Stanley, who led a regiment of

'Spanish Elizabethans' headquartered in the Low Countries (Eccles, pp. 3–101; Nicholl, pp. 286–98).

Around the time of his imprisonment in Newgate, Marlowe began to write for Lord Strange's acting company, and in this way crossed the outer threshold of Ferdinando Stanley's retinue. Kyd, who seems to have been Strange's personal servant, later testified that 'my first acquaintance with this Marlowe, rose upon his bearing name to serve my Lord although his Lordship never knew his service but in writing for his players'. By 1591, Kyd and Marlowe were 'writing in one chamber'. Marlowe's *The Jew of Malta* contains verbal echoes of Kyd's *Spanish Tragedy*, and bears family resemblances to Kyd's intricate revenge plot. *The Jew* was already in the repertory of Strange's Men when they gave the first recorded performance on 26 February 1592.

Barabas, the Jew of Malta, personified the new breed of stateless intelligence operatives who made their living by playing both ends against the middle, shuttling back and forth between Protestants and Catholics while remaining loyal to no one but themselves: 'Thus loving neither will I live with both / Making a profit of my policy; / And he from whom my most advantage comes / Shall be my friend' (5.2.111–14). Marlowe's relationship to Lord Strange, who was both a potential patron and a primary object of surveillance, put the playwright in a similar position; he could work for Strange and the secret service at the same time. Marlowe's friend Watson had this kind of relationship with his patron, the prominent Catholic Sir William Cornwallis.

Most scholars now believe that the 1604 quarto of Marlowe's *Doctor Faustus* (1588–92) derives from an authorial manuscript by Marlowe, perhaps with the assistance of a collaborator who wrote the comic scenes. The second quarto (1616), on the other hand, contains many additions and revisions by Samuel Rowley and William Birde. The date of Marlowe's original manuscript remains an open question. The case for a later date is simple. Everyone agrees that Marlowe's primary source was P. F.'s translation of the German *Historia von D. Johann Fausten* (1587) into the English *History ... of Dr John Faustus*; and the earliest extant edition of P. F.'s *History* appeared in 1592. The case for an earlier date largely rests on evidence that a lost and unregistered edition of *The Damnable Life* was published *c.* 1588; and on the appearance of brief passages that closely resemble lines from *Doctor Faustus* in two plays printed before 1592. But we cannot assume that the authors of the two plays lifted these passages from an early text of *Doctor Faustus*. In the case of Shakespeare's *Henry VI* and Marlowe's *Edward II*, the one instance where the identity of the borrower can be decided on textual grounds, Marlowe was quoting Shakespeare.[12]

With no clear-cut answer from textual studies, the question of when Marlowe wrote *Doctor Faustus* (1588–92) becomes a matter of choice. From a biographical standpoint, the early date has much to recommend it. Marlowe altered his source to include a great deal of material drawn from university life, some of which pertains to Cambridge. The story of a recent graduate who must decide what to do with his life bore on Marlowe's personal circumstances in 1587–8. Putting *Doctor Faustus* in the late 1580s, next to *The Jew of Malta*, brings out the parallels between his two close imitations of the morality play. Barabas descends from the morality-play character called the Vice, and takes part in the traditional battle of the vices and virtues – though the Christians in *The Jew* turn out to be disconcertingly vicious. Dr Faustus recalls the allegorical figure of Mankind choosing between his Good Angel and his Evil Angel – though Marlowe insinuates that Faustus has already been chosen for sin and damnation. This chronology lends an attractive symmetry to Marlowe's career. He evolves from heroic drama written in the classical style (*Dido* and *Tamburlaine*) to the native form of the morality play (*Faustus* and *The Jew*), to the new vernacular genre of the history play (*Edward II* and *The Massacre at Paris*).

The winter of 1592 found Marlowe at Flushing, in the Low Countries, where he began to make counterfeit money with the spy Richard Baines and the goldsmith Gifford Gilbert. After the first coin was put in circulation, Baines, 'fearing the success', went to Sir Robert Sidney, the head of the English garrison there, and informed on his partners. In his letter of 26 January to Lord Treasurer Burleigh, Sidney further reported that Baines and Marlowe accused 'one another of intent to go to the enemy, or to Rome'. The 'enemy' resided at the Spanish headquarters in Brussels and at Sir William Stanley's encampment in Nijmegen. Marlowe told Sidney that he was 'very well known both to the Earl of Northumberland and my Lord Strange'. Northumberland and, especially, Strange were the leading heirs apparent in Catholic conspiracies to remove Elizabeth from the throne. Although both men denied any involvement with such plots, Sir William Stanley urged English Catholics to 'cast their eye upon Lord Strange'. Stanley's agents financed their ventures through theft and counterfeiting. Marlowe's own counterfeiting scheme coincided with the formation of the 'Stanley plot': the plotters intended to assassinate Queen Elizabeth while Stanley's regiment invaded from the North, where they would receive assistance from Lord Strange.[13]

There are, then, multiple explanations for Marlowe's criminal behaviour in Flushing. He just wanted, as he told Sidney, 'to see the goldsmith's cunning'. He wanted the money – the stereotypical figure of the poor scholar recurs throughout his later work. He wanted to penetrate the Stanley plot and gather intelligence for the Privy Council. He wanted to 'go to the enemy' in earnest. If these explanations are contradictory, they also represent options that remained open for an entrepreneurial double agent.

Sidney placed Marlowe and the goldsmith under arrest and sent all three men back to Lord Burleigh 'to take their trial as you shall think best'. There is no indication that Marlowe underwent any punishment. Why did Burleigh release him? Counterfeiting was high treason and carried the death penalty. Moreover, Baines's allegation that his chamber fellow intended to go to the enemy cast doubt on Marlowe's loyalty to the state. On the other hand, Marlowe's contacts with John Poole and Lord Strange, together with his initiative in Flushing, meant that he still could help lead Burleigh to the Stanley conspirators. The Lord Treasurer held Marlowe and Baines in reserve, 'banking his tools' like one of John Le Carré's spymasters, until the time came to use them. Marlowe was back on the streets by 9 May, when he was taken to court for his threats against two constables. The judge required Marlowe to 'keep the peace' towards the constables, and to appear at the General Sessions of the Peace for Middlesex County on 29 September.

That spring Marlowe encountered a new and potent rival. William Shakespeare's early trilogy about the reign of King Henry VI was strongly influenced by Marlowe's conqueror–hero, and contains many verbal echoes of *Tamburlaine*. Marlowe's *Edward II* (1592) in turn borrows passages from 2 and 3 *Henry VI* and adopts the basic plot formula of Shakespeare's trilogy, in which overmighty nobles and a strong-willed queen destroy a weak king. Marlowe's extraordinary variation on Shakespeare's plot-formula was to place the homosexual relationship between King Edward and his base-born favourites at the centre of the action. Although unvarnished history does not record any meetings between the two playwrights, 2 *Henry VI*, 3 *Henry VI*, and *Edward II* were all written for the up-and-coming Earl of Pembroke's Men.

Marlowe's groundbreaking representations of homoerotic attachments, together with Baines's remark about the playwright's preference for boys, raise the question of Marlowe's own sexual orientation. Unmarried persons in early modern England ordinarily had a same-sex bedfellow until they married, which usually occurred in their late twenties if they were men. Unless Marlowe was celibate, the readiest outlet for his sexual desire was other males. But the question 'Was Marlowe a homosexual?' is anachronistic. Elizabethans regarded homosexuality as an aspect of seditious behaviour, rather than a type of person. The crime of sodomy became visible in relation to other offences; otherwise, it went unrecognized. Thus the claim that

Marlowe said 'all they that love not boys and tobacco are fools' only arises in connection with Baines's allegation that Marlowe was an atheist and a counterfeiter.[14]

Marlowe began to acquire a bad reputation in addition to his criminal record. Late in the summer of 1592, Robert Greene levelled an extraordinary public accusation of atheism against the 'famous gracer of tragedians', a thinly disguised simulacrum of Marlowe. On 15 September, Marlowe was brawling on the streets again, this time in Canterbury, where he attacked the tailor William Corkine with a stick and dagger. Corkine vs. Marlowe was settled out of court during the first week of October. Marlowe's sycophantic Latin epitaph 'On the Death of Sir Roger Manwood' mourns the death of a powerful Kentish nobleman that December. The Manwood epitaph, his only known poem in praise of a contemporary figure, suggests that he was actively seeking patronage and protection at the end of 1592, and hoped to find it in Kent. By the following spring, he was residing at the Kentish manor house of Thomas Walsingham.

In the midst of his troubles, Marlowe grasped another opportunity to obtain a literary patron. When Thomas Watson died at the end of September, the task of seeing his Latin pastoral *Aminta gaudia* through the press fell to Marlowe. In keeping with Watson's wishes, Marlowe dedicated the work to Lady Mary Herbert, wife of the Earl of Pembroke and a generous patron of poets; Marlowe could well have known her through his affiliation with the Earl's acting company. He introduces himself to Lady Pembroke as an Ovidian poet in mid-career. He has translated the *Amores*; now the Countess is 'infusing the spirit of an exalted frenzy, whereby my poor self seems capable of exceeding what my own ripe talent is accustomed to bring forth'. What did Marlowe mean by this avowal? In the recently issued *Third Part* of Abraham Fraunce's *Ivychurch*, a book commissioned by Lady Pembroke and known to Marlowe, Fraunce notes that 'Leander *and* Hero's love is in every man's mouth' and cites standard versions of the story by Ovid and by the Spanish poet Juan Boscan. Marlowe took on the task of rendering Museaus' original, Greek version of the poem into English. Where the traditional story ends with Leander's drowning and Hero's suicide, Marlowe's *Hero and Leander* (1592–3) breaks off after the consummation of their love affair. It used to be thought that the poem was left unfinished because of the author's untimely death in May, 1593. Recent scholarship, however, sees it as a celebration of physical love that is complete and coherent as it stands.[15]

On 26 January 1593, Strange's Men performed Marlowe's *The Massacre at Paris* (1592). It was evidently a new work or at least one that the company had not performed before. The second half of the play, with its homosexual king and libertine minions, offers a reprise of *Edward II* (1592). The earliest edition of *The Massacre*, and the source-text for all subsequent printings, is a memorial reconstruction of the text that Marlowe had originally prepared for Strange's Men (see Maguire's chapter in this volume, pp. 41–54). Even in its truncated form, *The Massacre* reveals that Marlowe had an intricate, firsthand knowledge of the French civil wars. It includes details that were not available from printed sources, and thus bears out the hypothesis that he had performed diplomatic or secret-service work in France. In a more general way, *The Massacre* explores the role of intelligence in the history of Marlowe's own times. His plot works on the principle of discrepant awareness. First we see the forward-looking conspirators, then their unwitting victims. The only way to survive in this world is to know your enemies' plans in advance; without reliable intelligence; the play's victims are doomed.

On the night of 5 May, an anonymous rhymester who styled himself 'Tamberlaine' posted a provocative placard on the wall of the Dutch church-yard in London. Tamberlaine ventriloquized Marlowe's Tamburlaine in order to stir up mob violence against the immigrant community; he also alluded to *The Jew of Malta* and *The Massacre at Paris*. Tamberlaine caught the queen's attention. On 11 May the Council conveyed her vexation to the authorities, ordering them to examine 'such persons as may be in this case any way suspected', a broad-bottomed category that had to include Christopher Marlowe, despite the lack of any evidence that he had written the offending verses. Marlowe's former chamber-fellow Thomas Kyd was under arrest the following day. The authorities tortured Kyd, who said that he had inadvertently received a transcript of 'heretical conceits' from Marlowe. Kyd also could have told them that it was Marlowe's custom 'to jest at the divine scriptures [and] gibe at prayers'; or that 'He would report St John to be our saviour Christ's Alexis.' He subsequently wrote these and other allegations down in two letters to Thomas Puckering, Elizabeth's Lord Keeper of the Privy Seal; he had small incentive to withhold them under torture.

Puckering now commissioned a special agent, probably Thomas Drury, to procure more evidence relating to the case. Drury contacted the gang-leader Richard Cholmeley, who indicated that he had fallen under Marlowe's influence. Drury quoted Cholmeley as saying that that 'one Marlowe is able to show more sound reasons for Atheism than any divine in England is able to give to prove divinity'. An endorsement on the back of Drury's report refers to John and James Tipping and Henry Young, three Catholic insurrectionists who were involved in Sir William Stanley's plot to assassinate the queen. Now they had joined forces with Cholmeley and, by extension, Marlowe. On 18 May, or soon thereafter, the Council arrested Marlowe; he was released on bail two days later, but ordered to report to the Council on a daily basis. In the meantime, Drury procured Richard Baines's Note concerning Marlowe's 'Damnable Judgment of Religion and scorn of God's word' and delivered it to the Council around 27 May. The note contains a ribald, corrosive attack on Judeo-Christian religion; several sentences elaborate on irreligious jests that Kyd and Cholmeley had attributed to Marlowe. Was Marlowe a bona fide atheist and insurrectionist? Or was he a government spy attempting to entrap men suspected of these crimes? Within the fluid, opportunistic world of the double agent, it is hard to imagine what sort of evidence could categorically exclude either alternative. It has also been argued that all of this evidence was fabricated in order to destroy what Baines calls 'other great men', such as Sir Walter Ralegh, who allegedly heard Marlowe's atheist lecture. With respect to Marlowe, the most incriminating evidence in these documents concerns his peripheral involvement in the Stanley plot.

Drury subsequently recalled the moment when Baines's Note, 'the notablest and vilest articles of Atheism... were delivered to her highness and command given by herself to prosecute it to the full'. A few days later, on 30 May, Marlowe was murdered after a 'feast' at Eleanor Bull's house in nearby Deptford. Widow Bull was a notional cousin of Blanche Parry, formerly Elizabeth's head lady-in-waiting. Robert Poley, whose job was to foil assassination plots, was present at the scene of the crime along with the petty confidence man Nicholas Skerres and his partner, the swindler Ingram Frizer. Frizer, the killer, claimed that he had acted in self-defence, after a quarrel over 'the reckoning', a bill for food and drink. The queen's coroner William Danby accepted Frizer's plea, but Danby's contorted attempt to explain how Frizer, who was armed, killed Marlowe in self-defence, while Poley and Skerres passively stood by, does not inspire much confidence.

The archival records surrounding the death of Christopher Marlowe describe a conflict between the insurrectionist playwright and the court. This dispute came to a head when Baines's Note arrived at Greenwich and ended with the murder of Marlowe shortly thereafter. The fact that the coroner's inquest trivializes the killing should provoke scepticism, not easy acquiescence. Queen Elizabeth paid Marlowe the fatal compliment of taking him seriously, as a political agent to be reckoned with.[16]

For his epitaph, we may turn to Marlowe's friend Thomas Nashe: 'His life he contemned in comparison of the liberty of speech.'[17] Marlowe's project was to represent creeds that his society defined as alien and subversive. Tamburlaine the Great founds an idolatrous cult dedicated to violent appropriation. The Jew of Malta reduces all forms of organized religion to mockery. The Epicurean King Edward II elevates his lover Gaveston above the claims of the Church, the nobility, and his wife. The reprobate Dr Faustus proclaims hell a fable and sells his soul for twenty-four years of carnal pleasure. Arguments about the morally correct response to these villain–heroes miss the thrust of Marlowe's achievement, which was to make such figures conceivable within a public theatrical marketplace.

NOTES

I thank the John Simon Guggenheim Foundation and the National Endowment for the Humanities for supporting the research that underlies this essay.

1. Unless otherwise noted, references to Marlowe and his contemporaries can be identified through the indexes in John Bakeless, *The Tragicall History of Christopher Marlowe*, 2 vols. (1942; Hamden, CT: Archon, 1964); Patrick Cheney, *Marlowe's Counterfeit Profession: Ovid, Spenser, Counter-Nationhood* (University of Toronto Press, 1997); Mark Eccles, *Christopher Marlowe in London* (Cambridge, MA: Harvard University Press, 1934); Constance Brown Kuriyama, *Christopher Marlowe: A Renaissance Life* (Ithaca: Cornell University Press); MacLure; Charles Nicholl, *The Reckoning: The Murder of Christopher Marlowe*, 2nd edn (London: Vintage, 2000); William Urry, *Christopher Marlowe and Canterbury*, ed. Andrew Butcher (London: Faber and Faber, 1988). The first quotation is from 2 *The Return from Parnassus* qtd in MacLure, p. 46.

2. For a chronology of the events in Marlowe's life, see Kuriyama, *Christopher Marlowe*, pp. xiii–xix; for the relevant documents, see pp. 173–240. The most thorough, if occasionally speculative, account of Marlowe's encounters with the law is in Nicholl, *The Reckoning*.

3. David Riggs, 'Marlowe's Quarrel With God', in Emily Bartels (ed.), *Critical Essays on Christopher Marlowe* (New York: G. K. Hall, 1997), p. 56n8.

4. John S. Moore, 'Canterbury Visitations and the Demography of Mid-Tudor Kent', *SoH* 15 (1993), 36–85. Information about Marlowe's childhood and adolescence in this and the following three paragraphs is taken from Urry, *Christopher Marlowe and Canterbury*, pp. 1–61 unless otherwise noted.

5. William Lambarde, *A Perambulation of Kent* (London, 1576), p. 236.

6. Facts about Marlowe's grammar school education are taken from T. W. Baldwin, *Shakspere's Small Latine and Lesse Greeke*, 2 vols. (Urbana: University of Illinois Press, 1944). For the terms of Marlowe's Parker scholarship, see Bakeless, *Tragicall History*, 1: 47–50, 64.

7. Richard F. Hardin, 'Marlowe and the Fruits of Scholarism', *PQ* 63 (1984), 387–400.

8. Scott McMillin and Sally-Beth MacLean, *The Queen's Men and their Plays* (Cambridge University Press, 1998), p. 203.

9. The sources of Marlowe's plays are in Thomas and Tydeman.

10. G. Sabinus (ed.), *Fabularum Ovidii interpretatio ethica physica et historica* (Cambridge, 1584), sig. Q8^v: 'Poetica nihil aliud est nisi Philosophia numeris et fabulis concinna.'

11. Roy Kendall, 'Richard Baines and Christopher Marlowe's Milieu', *ELR* 24 (1994), 507–52.

12. R. Fehrenbach, 'A Pre-1592 English Faust Book and the Date of Marlowe's *Dr Faustus*', *Library* 2 (2001), 327–35. Christopher Marlowe, *Edward II*, ed. Charles Forker (Manchester University Press, 1994), p. 18.

13. Nicholl, *The Reckoning*, pp. 225–39; Ethel Seaton, 'Marlowe, Poley, and the Tippings', *RES* 5 (1929), 273–87.

14. Alan Bray, *Homosexuality in Renaissance England* (London: Gay Men's Press, 1982); and Goldberg, 'Sodomy and Society'.

15. Marion Campbell, '"Desunt Nonnulla": the Construction of Marlowe's *Hero and Leander* as an Unfinished Poem', *ELH* 51 (1984), 241–68.

16. The paragraphs on the death of Marlowe are based on Nicholl, *The Reckoning*, Kendall, *Christopher Marlowe and Richard Baines*, and Riggs, 'The Killing of Christopher Marlowe'. Anyone seriously interested in the death of Marlowe should also consult Kuriyama, *Christopher Marlowe*, pp. 120–41.

17. Lynette and Evelyn Feasy, "Nashe's *The Unfortunate Traveller*: Some Marlovian Echoes', *English* 7 (1948), 125–9.

READING LIST

Bakeless, John. *The Tragicall History of Christopher Marlowe*. 2 vols. 1942; Hamden, CT: Archon, 1964.

Cheney, Patrick. *Marlowe's Counterfeit Profession: Ovid, Spenser, Counter-Nationhood*. University of Toronto Press, 1997.

Eccles, Mark. *Christopher Marlowe in London*. Cambridge, MA: Harvard University Press, 1934.

Goldberg, Jonathan. 'Sodomy and Society: the Case of Christopher Marlowe', *SWR* 69 (1984), 371–8.

Grantley, Darryll and Peter Roberts (eds.). *Christopher Marlowe and English Renaissance Culture*. Aldershot: Scolar Press, 1996.

Hopkins, Lisa. *Christopher Marlowe – A Literary Life*. Basingstoke: Palgrave, 2000.

Kendall, Roy. *Christopher Marlowe and Richard Baines: Journeys through the Elizabethan Underworld*. London: Associated University Presses, 2003.

Kuriyama, Constance Brown. *Christopher Marlowe: A Renaissance Life*. Ithaca: Cornell University Press, 2002.

MacLure, Millar (ed.). *Marlowe: The Critical Heritage 1588–1896*. London: Routledge, 1979.

Nicholl, Charles. *The Reckoning: The Murder of Christopher Marlowe*. 2nd edn London: Vintage, 2002.

Riggs, David. 'The Killing of Christopher Marlowe'. *StHR* 8 (2000), 239–51.

Urry, William. *Christopher Marlowe and Canterbury*. Andrew Butcher (ed.). London: Faber and Faber, 1988.

3

LAURIE E. MAGUIRE

Marlovian texts and authorship

None of Marlowe's plays or poems exist in manuscript (for one partial exception, see the discussion of *The Massacre at Paris*, below). Our earliest witnesses are printed. Printed texts reveal a great deal about the circumstances of printing; but they can also be encouraged to speak about the circumstances of composition and consumption. A chapter about Marlovian texts and authorship is thus also a chapter about critics and readers, about tastes and preferences: not just about what Marlowe wrote but about how it was received.

The first of Marlowe's texts to reach print was *Tamburlaine*, possibly his first play. On 14 August 1590 the publisher Richard Jones made an entry in the Stationers' Register (the register in which publishers entered their right to a work) for the two parts of *Tamburlaine*. In the same year he published both parts as a single volume, in a small octavo format.

The title page is an endearing example of early modern advertising. It provides a racy plot summary, boasts of recent stage success, and promotes the quarto as hot off the press:

> *Tamburlaine the Great. Who, from a Scythian shepherd, by his rare and wonderful conquests, became a most puissant and mighty monarch, and (for his tyranny and terror in war) was termed 'The Scourge of God'. Divided into two tragical discourses, as they were sundry times showed upon stages in the city of London by the right honourable Lord Admiral his servants. Now first and newly published.*[1]

The tautology of this last claim ('first and newly published') is as excessive as the eye-catching graphics: there are no fewer than three typefaces (roman, italic, black letter) and at least seven point sizes. Printing was in its early days, and printers, like novice users of word-processing packages or PowerPoint, availed themselves of all the technical flourishes. Since title pages were displayed independently as posters, the typographical enthusiasm makes sense.

Tamburlaine was apparently on the boards by November 1587 when a letter describes an accident during a performance of an unnamed Admiral's Men's play: a loaded pistol used for a stage murder accidentally killed two audience members and wounded a third. The description of the stage action in which the misdirected gun was used corresponds approximately to the end of *Tamburlaine, Part Two*. The approximation is explained by the derivative nature of the testimony: 'though myself no witness thereof, yet I may be bold to verify it for an assured truth'.[2] If this 1587 account refers to *Tamburlaine, Part Two*, *Tamburlaine, Part One* must have been performed shortly before.

In 1587 Marlowe was still at Cambridge (he graduated in July); *Tamburlaine, Part One* is thus the work of an undergraduate student, not a practising playwright. The text has visible academic credentials: the scene divisions and the ends of acts are noted in Latin ('Actus II, Scaena II'; 'Finis Actus tertii'). Act 5 concludes with 'Finis Actus quinti & ultimi *huius primae parti*' (my italics). The Prologue to *Part Two* tells us that the sequel was prompted by the theatrical success of *Part One*. If this statement is correct, then the italicized material ('of this first part') must be a post-performance insertion by Marlowe. If, on the other hand, the Act 5 Latin notice is supplied by the publisher (who, as we saw, published the two parts together), it may suggest that the Latin act and scene divisions do not originate with Marlowe. The evidence is inconclusive.

Less ambiguous is the marked difference in the format of the stage directions between *Tamburlaine, Parts One* and *Two*. *Part One* is notable for its lack of 'Enter' instructions; scenes begin simply with a list of characters: 'Cosroe, Menaphon, Ortygius, Ceneus, with other Souldiers' (B4ᵛ). Although this habit continues in *Part Two*, it is matched by directions with 'Enter' (sixteen occurrences of each type). *Part One*'s lists suggest a classical author lining up his speakers; *Part Two*'s 'Enter' formulation suggests someone now familiarized to theatre, or a text marked up for professional performance.

Richard Jones's Stationers' Register entry registers the play as 'Two comical discourses of Tamburlaine'. The printed title page, however, advertises 'two Tragical discourses'. The metamorphosis of comedy into tragedy is explained by Jones in his epistle to the reader which prefaces the printed edition: 'I have (purposely) omitted and left out some fond and frivolous gestures, digressing (and in my poor opinion) far unmeet for the matter.' Jones claims to have turned aesthetic judgement into editorial action – that is, if his statement is a true witness to events. It is a perplexing claim. In the sixteenth century 'gesture' referred solely to bodily gesture. The *OED* cites the following examples from 1532 to 1592: 'with outward gesture of my body'; 'outward gesture and deed'; 'gesture of his body'. Jones may therefore be censoring stage action, presumably clowning, in which case his epistle offers an aesthetic excuse to disguise a practical problem: he did not possess the material which he claims to have omitted. However, if his claim of comic excision is true, the original *Tamburlaine* was clearly generically different from the extant text, although episodes like Mycetes's hiding of his crown (*1 Tamb.* 2.4) and the transfer of Zabina's crown to Zenocrate (*1 Tamb.* 3.3) indicate the plays' comic potential. The misnumbered scenes and omitted scene divisions in the printed text of *Tamburlaine* may support Jones's claim to have excised material. In *Tamburlaine, Part One*, 4.5 follows 4.3. In *Tamburlaine, Part Two* the nine scenes which comprise the first two acts run in a normal numerical sequence; thereafter they are numbered 3.1, 3.5, 2.1, 4.1, 4.3, 4.4, 5.1, 5.4, and 5.6. Richard Jones was something of a literary critic, judging by the contents of the prefatory epistles to other works he published, and could conceivably have expanded his literary role from commentator to editor (although we might note that his aversion to the otiose does not extend to his own prose. The tautology noticeable on the title page continues in the prefatory epistle: 'omitted and left out', 'fond and frivolous').

There are no further publications or Stationers' Register entries until 1593, the year of Marlowe's death. 1593 saw two Stationers' Register entries: *Edward II* (registered just weeks after Marlowe's murder although not published until 1594) and the narrative poem *Hero and Leander* (published in 1598). If the timing of the entries testifies to the publishers' opportunism, the delay in publication seems odd, but speculation about a lost first edition of either text seems groundless. The copy of *Edward II* in the Victoria and Albert Museum lacks the first two leaves, which have been supplied in manuscript; the manuscript title page bears the date 1593, suggesting that it was copied from a printed edition of that date. However, Richard Rowland notes that the compositors' errors in mislineation in the 1594 quarto are too discrepant if they were copying from a printed quarto, and the preliminaries, which would usually be printed first in a reprint, were printed last, as one would expect in a first edition.[3] The date on the manuscript remains intriguing but is not a reliable witness to a lost edition.

Marlowe was not an 'attached' dramatist (the term for someone exclusively contracted to a theatre company). *Tamburlaine* was performed by the Admiral's Men; *Edward II* was performed by Pembroke's Men; *Dido, Queen of Carthage* was performed by the Children of the Queen's Chapel. This company of boy actors with unbroken voices was associated with satires/burlesques and plays on mythological themes; *Dido* combines the two, being a tragicomic version of Books 1, 2, and 4 of Virgil's *Aeneid*. The play was published in 1594 with a title page advertising it as 'Written by Christopher Marlowe, and Thomas Nash. Gent'. Collaboration was the norm rather than the exception in the dramatic milieu of the 1590s (cf. the team writing of today's screenplays, and soap operas). Nonetheless, the post-Romantic conception of the writer as a solitary genius influences contemporary attitudes, and critics have long sought to identify (and separate) Nashe's share in *Dido*. Much has been made of the different and smaller typeface in which Nashe's name is printed on the title page; literary judgements give his share as anything from a few per cent to nothing.

The twentieth century developed statistical rather than literary methods for identifying authors' hands, the most reliable of which concentrates on function words and letters – areas over which authors have no conscious control. Whereas authors deliberately select their literary vocabulary (what Jonathan Bate calls their 'poetic plumage')[4] for elegance, sound, association, or meaning, they do not – cannot – exercise conscious control over function words – prepositions, pronouns, articles, conjunctions – or over letter frequencies. Nonetheless, the literary fingerprint, the verbal tic ('style') will reveal itself in these areas: one author will have a predilection for 'to' over 'with', another's phrasing will mean that certain letter combinations dominate. Computers can identify these networks.

The most exciting application of these approaches to Marlowe comes in the work of Thomas Merriam. He has recently identified the first half of *Dido* as being by Marlowe, the second half by Nashe.[5] Marlowe and Nashe were contemporaries at Cambridge, and Robert Greene associated them in 1592: 'With thee [Marlowe, whom Greene is addressing] I join young Juvenal, that biting Satirist' – a phrase usually taken to refer to Nashe.[6] Their collaboration is plausible; or, depending on the date of composition, perhaps Nashe completed a play left unfinished at the time of Marlowe's death. In either case, Merriam's analysis encourages us to accept the witness of the title page.

1594 is the date tentatively assigned to the publication of Marlowe's *The Massacre at Paris*, a play performed by the Admiral's Men, although the undated octavo may have been published as late as 1602. Performances of a tragedy of the Guise are recorded in the London repertory of Lord Strange's Men in January 1592–3, and in the Admiral's repertory in 1594. The published text, however, is unlikely to correspond to that performed on those occasions. A curious cartoon-strip history which covers the seventeen years of religious wars from the St Bartholomew's Day Massacre of 1572, the play compresses the deaths of thirteen main characters into a mere twelve hundred lines – little over an hour's playing time. The printer realized the play's brevity and compensated typographically: for instance, he printed single lines of dialogue as two lines. Thus the actual dialogue is only 1147 lines – half the length of a typical play of the 1590s.

The play is stylistically uneven, not at all what one expects from the author of *Tamburlaine* and *Edward II*; long and fluid speeches (notably those of the Guise) co-exist with short staccato speeches (e.g. 190–235).[7] Characters are blunt and over-explicit about their motives. Characterization tends to be two-dimensional, notably in the roles of Navarre and the Queen Mother, who are extremes of good and bad respectively. Verse structure is often lost, although the underlying iambic pentameter is discernible. The verbal quality deteriorates towards the end (compare Guise's soliloquy at 1031–43 with his earlier soliloquy at 108ff.), contributing further to the unevenness.

The major anomaly, however, appears in the form of repetitions. The dialogue both repeats itself verbatim and paraphrases itself loosely; it combines repeated short phrases into textual mosaics and repeats chunks from other plays. The Queen Mother paraphrases and repeats her own speech of 625–33 at lines 782–90; the Friar repeats her line 625 at 1420; Henry III repeats her line 627 at 1090. Thus it is not simply a case of an author penning a speech for one character, then deciding to use it elsewhere. The Guise's wife shares lines with Arden's wife in the contemporary *Arden of Faversham*:

> Sweet Mugeroune, tis he that hath my heart,
> And Guise vsurpes it, cause I am his wife.
>
> > (*MP* 795–6)

> Sweet Mosbie is the man that hath my hart:
> And he usurpes it, hauing nought but this,
> That I am tyed to him by marriage.
>
> > (*Arden* 99–101)[8]

These features – repetition, unevenness, wrecked verse – are not typical of Elizabethan drama; they are, however, shared by a handful of plays of the period. How are we to account for them?

We can begin to answer that question by calling another witness: a manuscript of scene 15 of *The Massacre at Paris*, the scene in which a soldier hired by the Guise murders Mugeroun, the man with whom the Guise's wife is having an affair. The soldier's speech, with which the scene opens, conveys the same information in both manuscript and printed texts. However, the printed version has instances of loose expansion and repetition; it contains the gist, with the vocabulary, of the manuscript but in a disordered manner; it keeps the punch-line but mangles the development of a piece of humour; and there are a host of indifferent variants (slight and apparently purposeless alterations). Although the soldier's speech is slightly longer in the manuscript version than in the printed octavo, the difference in length is so negligible as to obviate the possibility of deliberate abridgement. The concentration of trivial variants likewise reduces the likelihood of revision (although it is true that revising authors often tinker needlessly). The soldier's speech in the octavo seems to be an inaccurate attempt to reproduce the version in the manuscript.

Guise's subsequent speech is sixteen lines in the manuscript but only four lines in the octavo. The omitted material includes three lines of inessential embroidery, and nine lines of Machiavellian character development. The remaining four lines make perfectly adequate if abrupt sense, and the octavo reproduces them almost perfectly, with only one substantive variant (*as* for *yf*). The Guise's four-line octavo speech is clearly an abridgement of the manuscript's sixteen-line speech.

Thus in comparison with the manuscript, the octavo text gives evidence of two processes: abridgement and memorial reconstruction. Memory explains the lengthy repetitions, the mosaics of repeated phrases, and the purposeless variants. In the external echo from *Arden* we see a mind trying to remember one sequence of lines and inadvertently recalling another from a different play. But whose memory? The memory or memories of Admiral's Men actors, some of whom may not have performed the roles they were attempting to reproduce (hence the stylistic unevenness).

Memorial reconstruction is one of the most powerful textual theories of the twentieth century. It is not a perfect theory – it has a great many 'ifs' – and there is no external evidence to support it: no contemporary witness describes or explains memorial reconstruction. All we have are a number of suspect texts whose pervasive symptoms of faulty memory attest to disruption of a kind that cannot be explained by the normal routes, such as printing-house error. In the case of *The Massacre*, the theory is bolstered by the existence of a manuscript for comparison, but the auspices of the manuscript are unclear. Is it a theatre document? A copy for private use? If either, why is it a single self-contained scene? (The scene is a deliberate extract, not an accidental fragment: there is ample blank space for scene 16.) It is not in Marlowe's hand. It was once thought to be a forgery by the Victorian scholar John Payne Collier, but current Collier scholarship has convincingly disposed of that canard. Although enigmatic, the manuscript is helpful in suggesting the kind of text that must have lain behind the Admiral's Men's performances in 1592.

Although memorial reconstruction is often characterized as an underhand practice, there is nothing illicit about a company attempting to recreate the text of a play which it owned. Why they should wish to do so is a moot point. Edward Alleyn, the Admiral's Men's lead actor, owned the playbook of *The Massacre at Paris*. If the company was performing out of town, and if it divided in two for the purposes of touring (as we know happened), one branch might need to manufacture a text from which to perform. This suggestion is not without its problems: a reconstructed manuscript would lack the vital licence and signature of the Lord Chamberlain, without which theatre companies were not supposed to perform. Nor is the purpose of the abridgement clear: reduction in length, personnel, or simplification of staging? There are still loose ends to tie up.

By 1598 *Tamburlaine* had been reprinted twice (in 1592–3 and 1597) and *Edward II* once (in 1598). Fifteen ninety-eight also saw the publication of the epyllion *Hero and Leander* (entered in the Stationers' Register in 1593). This poem was the greatest success in the history of Marlowe in print: it had a second edition in 1598 and was again reprinted in 1600, 1606, 1609, 1613, 1617, 1622, 1629 and 1637. All the reprints from 1600 also included Marlowe's translation of *Lucan's First Book*. The epyllion may have been a poetic fashion of the 1590s but it was never out of date as a reading experience; it is as an Ovidian poet that Marlowe was most known in print.

Hero and Leander, an account of the inexperienced experiences of two young lovers, is by turns comic, bathetic, satirical, and cynical. The leisurely narrative ends abruptly and darkly after consummation. The first edition of 1598 concludes with the words 'Desunt nonnulla' ('some sections are missing'). The second edition, also in 1598, supplied the alleged lacunae: George Chapman continued and completed Marlowe's poem, providing twice as much again, albeit in a more moral vein. In the same year Henry Petowe's completion of the poem also reached print. Although several contemporary critics have argued that Marlowe's 818-line poem is complete as it stands, the Chapman and Petowe versions are witness to the fact that at least two sixteenth-century readers saw the poem as incomplete.

By 1599, Marlowe's translation of ten of Ovid's elegies (the *Amores*) had been published, in an edition with Sir John Davies's *Epigrams*. The book was burned, by episcopal order, in the same year. It was probably Davies's epigrams which prompted the order, for Marlowe's Ovid is not particularly licentious. Nonetheless, the number of early editions, some of them surreptitious, bears witness to the popularity of the volume. Fifteen-ninety-nine saw the publication of *The Passionate Pilgrim*, a poetic miscellany falsely attributed to Shakespeare, which included Marlowe's lyric poem 'The Passionate Shepherd to his Love'. This poem was reprinted the following year in a volume entitled *England's Helicon* which also included 'The Nymph's Reply' (by Ralegh) and an anonymous imitation. Phoebe's pastoral invitation to Endymion in lines 207–24 of Drayton's *Endimion and Phoebe: Ideas Latmus* (1595) also imitates Marlowe. We do not know when Marlowe's poem was written: Ithamore's variant of it in *The Jew of Malta* (which was performed in February 1592 and may have been written as early as 1588) may be a draft or a pastiche. If the latter, it is a witness to the poem's immediate popularity. As mentioned above, Marlowe's translation of *Lucan's First Book* was published in 1600. Thus the end of the sixteenth century saw all the Marlowe poems known to us in print.

The plays by which Marlowe is most regularly represented on stage today – *Doctor Faustus* and *The Jew of Malta* – had not yet been published, although theatre records attest to performances of both in 1594. The seventeenth century ushered them into print (*Doctor Faustus* in 1604, *The Jew of Malta* in 1633) in texts that raise a number of bibliographical questions. In the case of *Doctor Faustus* we have three dates with which to conjure: 1602, when the theatrical manager Philip Henslowe paid the dramatists William Birde and Samuel Rowley £4 for 'additions in Dr Faustus' (since £4 was a substantial sum, the additions must have been considerable); 1604, when *Doctor Faustus* was published in a text of 1,517 lines (known to critics as the 'A' text); 1616, when the play was published in a longer text of 2,119 lines (the 'B' text). The relationship between the two texts, between the two texts and Henslowe's payment, and between the two texts and the play as performed in 1594 (or earlier) must be resolved. The early twentieth century viewed the 'A' text as authentic, the mid-century the 'B' text, and the 1990s favoured the 'A' text once more; thus the text you read depends on the date of your edition. The most recent Revels edition prints both versions.[9]

The 'B' text is close to that of the 'A' text in Acts 1 and 5, but diverges in the middle, expanding the action at the Imperial Court and the material with Benvolio. (In chapter 4 of *A Textual Companion*, Eric Rasmussen provides an excellent thematic analysis of the differences.)[10] It is now clear to us that the 'B' text incorporates the additions by Birde and Rowley. The need for these revisions is explored by Leah Marcus, who argues that they were designed to update what she calls the 'Marlowe effect' – to keep the play at the cutting edge of theatrical daring.[11] Thus the 'B' text is a witness to Marlowe as performed and revised on the seventeenth-century stage; it is not a reliable witness to what Marlowe wrote.

Nor is the 'A' text – or so it seemed to textual critics for much of the twentieth century. The comic scene 10 (D3^v–D4^r; 3.2 in Bevington and Rasmussen's edition), in which the clowns conjure Faustus from Constantinople, has duplicate endings. In one, Mephistopheles changes the clowns and the vintner into animals and makes them vanish; in another the vintner flees and the business is extended with Mephistopheles's complaints and his conversation with the clowns. One comic scene (9) and one chorus (D2^v–D3^r) are misplaced. The reference to Dr Lopez, a Jewish Portuguese physician who attained notoriety in February 1594 for allegedly attempting to poison Queen Elizabeth, is clearly a topical reference which must postdate the original composition of the play. Thus the text as printed is distanced from Marlowe.

The evidence of the misplaced Chorus and the topical Lopez insertion is bibliographically clear. But twentieth-century bibliographers identified other lines and episodes as corruptions and insertions using a non-bibliographical criterion: taste. Viewing Faustus's papal pranks with horror, bibliographers found it easier to ascribe the tricks to textual corruption than to the conscious choice of a university graduate. W. W. Greg went further: he took theology as a yardstick in assessing the origins of the 'A' and 'B' texts, viewing the 'B' text as more authentic because more theologically orthodox. Michael Keefer wryly points out the folly of assuming that 'theological orthodoxy can be used – in this of all plays – as a textual criterion'.[12] The 'A' text cannot be deemed corrupt just because one does not approve of it.

For as long as critics believed that the longer 'B' text did not include the 1602 additions, it was easy to view the shorter 'A' text as a corrupt derivative of 'B'. The combination of clowning and brevity led to the conclusion that *Doctor Faustus*'s corruption, like that of *The Massacre at Paris*, was evidence of memorial reconstruction, even though 'A' *Doctor Faustus*'s textual quality is strikingly different from that of *The Massacre at Paris*: it has none of the verbal symptoms of memorial reconstruction. However, once the status of the 'B' text was reclassified as a revision, the 'A' text had to be reinvestigated.

The 'A' text gives witness to a text which has been prepared from an authorial manuscript. It is closer than is the 'B' text to the play's source, *The Damnable Life of Doctor Faustus* (a fact which tends to overrule the theory of memorial reconstruction by actors). The duplicate scene endings may thus indicate alternative actions or authorial revision (in the latter case the printer must accidentally have ignored a deletion mark).

Bevington and Rasmussen observe an interesting phenomenon which points not just to authorial papers but to dual authorship. The compositors of the 'A' text change stints mid-page, often at the beginning of a new scene or the entrance of a new character (Bevington and Rasmussen, pp. 68–9). This is unusual. Because of the process of folding the printed paper to form a quarto text, pages were not printed in numerical sequence. Pages 1, 8, 4, and 5 were printed on four quadrants of one large sheet of paper; pages 2, 7, 3, and 6 were printed on the reverse side. In the interests of efficiency, one compositor set the type for pages 1, 8, 4, and 5 while another set pages 2, 7, 3, and 6. The compositors therefore had to calculate how to distribute ('cast off') the manuscript copy from which they were working to correspond accurately with the printed pages. In the case of 'A' *Doctor Faustus* it seems that the normal process of casting off was frustrated by new scenes beginning on a new page. The logical explanation for this is collaborative authorial papers:

different handwriting made consistency of calculation difficult for the compositors. Thus current theory believes the 'A' text of *Doctor Faustus* to be based not on a memorial reconstruction but on the working manuscript of two authors. Marlowe's collaborator has not yet been identified with any confidence.

Nor has the date of original composition. Critics frequently favour a late date *c.* 1593 for no other reason than a desire to see this tragedy as the jewel in Marlowe's crown. What evidence there is, however, suggests a slightly earlier date. For example, mock-sweetheart tricks like that in *Doctor Faustus* 2.1 feature in *Orlando Furioso*, *John of Bordeaux*, and *A Knack to Know a Knave* (all plays on stage before June 1592 when *A Knack to Know a Knave* is first mentioned). In *John of Bordeaux* (*c.* 1590) the virtuous Rossalin refuses to yield to the sexual advances of Prince Ferdinand; the magician Vandermast placates the prince by summoning a devil, disguised as Rossalin, to appear to Ferdinand at night. In *Orlando Furioso* (played 21 February 1591–2) the clown appears to Orlando in disguise as his sweetheart Angelica. An analogous episode in *A Knack to Know a Knave* is rendered ambiguous by an incomplete stage direction, but it is clear that the episode involves a comic trick with a devil, a sweetheart, and a disguise. In *Doctor Faustus*, Faustus requests a wife, Mephistopheles agrees, and the stage direction in 'A' reads 'Enter with a diuell drest like a woman, / with fier workes' (C2^r). Clearly mock-sweethearts and comic anticlimax enjoyed something of a vogue in plays of the early 1590s. Whether Marlowe inaugurated the fashion or capitalized on it is not clear; or rather it cannot be established on textual grounds, although critical judgement – bias? – might incline us to view Marlowe, in this as in so much else, as the innovator.

It is clear that the mixed genres of Marlovian drama regularly cause critical anxiety, from Richard Jones's alleged unease in 1590 about the co-existence of comedy with tragedy in *Tamburlaine* to twentieth-century bibliographers' disapproval of the irreverent activities of Faustus. Bibliographers' anxiety about the text of *Doctor Faustus* was paralleled in their suspicions about the text of *The Jew of Malta*. The descent from tragedy into farce, relished by audiences familiar with the comedy of cruelty, caused problems for E. K. Chambers, who concluded that the play 'has only come down to us in a form rehandled to suit an audience of inferior mentality to that aimed at by the original author'.[13] Chambers's conclusion, as J. C. Maxwell pointed out, is 'disconcerting for those of us who have never detected anything more than a certain unevenness of quality, and now realize that we must have just the inferior mentality the adapter was aiming at'.[14]

The forty-year gap between Marlowe's death and the play's publication in 1633 encouraged bibliographers to attribute their unease with the play's generic instability to textual corruption. *The Jew of Malta* was revived in 1633 for performances at the Cockpit and the Court, for which Thomas Heywood wrote new Prologues and Epilogues. The fear is that Heywood may have written more. Tucker Brooke felt that the 1633 quarto was 'sadly corrupted and altered from that in which it left the hands of Marlowe'.[15] Note the emotive vocabulary: 'sadly' – because anything non-Marlovian is grievous even though it might tell us about Heywood and Caroline tastes – and 'corrupted' – because anything which time or theatre (or both) has altered is, ipso facto, diminution. Tucker Brooke is not interested in a textual witness to the conditions of 1633; he seeks a witness for the early 1590s.

In fact the text is probably a witness to both. The question we need to ask of *The Jew of Malta* is not why it was not published earlier (it was entered in the Stationers' Register in 1594) but why it was published when it was. A survey of dramatic publications in 1633 and adjacent years answers the question.

Philip Massinger's city comedy *A New Way to Pay Old Debts*, written in 1625, was published in 1633. The central comic character is a characteristically Marlovian overreacher, as his name indicates: Sir Giles Overreach. An extortioner who seeks title, land, and influence, he deprives his nephew of his estate, tries to marry his daughter to a lord, takes over his neighbour's lands by breaking his fences, trampling his corn, setting fire to his barns, and breaking his cattle's legs. His manifesto could have been uttered by Barabas:

> We worldly men, when we see friends, and kinsmen,
> Past hope sunk in their fortunes, lend no hand
> To lift 'em up, but rather set our feet
> Upon their heads, to press 'em to the bottom.
> (*A New Way* 3.3.50–6)[16]

Marlowe's *The Jew of Malta*, ahead of its time in the 1590s, was obviously valued in the 1630s for the superb city comedy it is. City comedies were popular in performance and print in Caroline London: Jonson's *The New Inn* (written 1629, published 1631), Massinger's *The City Madam* (written 1632), Brome's *The Weeding of the Covent Garden* (written 1632), Shirley's *A Bird in a Cage* (written and published 1633), and Jonson's *A Tale of a Tub* (revised 1633). Heywood's court Prologue to *The Jew of Malta* apologizes for presenting an old play 'mongst other playes that now in fashion are', an apology repeated in the Epilogue. Nigel Bawcutt takes Heywood at face value: 'the actors were prepared in advance for the play to be a failure' (p. 41). But in the theatre one apologizes only for one's most reliable offerings. It is inconceivable that the Caroline company resurrected an anticipated failure.

They resurrected *The Jew of Malta* because its genre meshed so perfectly with the prevailing vogue for city comedy.

In his play *The School of Night* (1992) Peter Whelan stages a conversation between Marlowe and Shakespeare about comedy. For Marlowe, humans are vulnerable when they laugh; laughter is 'the fish opening its mouth' and comedy is 'the bait that hides the hook'. (With such a philosophy Marlowe is inevitably disturbed by Shakespeare's question: 'But what if you only want to feed the fish . . . not catch them?').[17] Whelan's Marlowe aptly defines city comedy and inadvertently encapsulates *The Jew of Malta*.

The influence of Marlowe on Shakespeare and vice versa has long aroused interest. This interest incorporates the fictional (Whelan, Burgess,[18] *Shakespeare in Love*), the literary (Shapiro),[19] and the bibliographical (nineteenth-century Shakespeare disintegrators, twentieth-century stylometricists), although the bibliographical and the biographical often overlap, as in the work of those who insist Marlowe was Shakespeare. Recent stylometric work has resurrected the view that Marlowe's hand appears in several Shakespeare texts – in some of the *Henry VI* plays and *Titus Andronicus* – as well as introducing two new claims: that Marlowe contributed to *Edward III* (a play recently claimed for Shakespeare) and that Shakespeare's *Henry V* is a revision of a lost Marlowe original.[20] Limitations of space prevent me presenting the stylometric evidence in detail, but these tantalizing claims can be summarized.

Using function-word tests and relative letter frequencies, Thomas Merriam claims six scenes of *Titus Andronicus* for Marlowe (1.1, 2.1, 4.4, 5.1, 5.2, 5.3). The Marlowe scenes focus on revenge; the Shakespeare scenes focus on pathos and suffering. In *Henry V* the two contrasting visions of Henry – as admirable hero or as tactical politician – correlate to a linguistic division. *Henry V* contains words and phrases unique in the Shakespeare canon, which occur elsewhere only in the Marlowe canon: in *Tamburlaine*, in *Edward II*, *Dido*, and *Lucan*. Presumably Shakespeare revised a Marlovian original. In *Edward III* two scenes, anomalous in terms of twelve stylometric variables, emulate *Tamburlaine, Parts One* and *Two*, and suggest Marlowe's hand. Parallel passages in *1 Henry VI* and in the Marlowe canon, supported by logometric tests, indicate that Marlowe wrote Joan of Arc's penultimate scene.

Merriam's articles offer impressively restrained conclusions. He presents his logometric analyses graphically, with a clear spatial demarcation between results characteristic of the Shakespeare canon (or reliable portions thereof) and results characteristic of the Marlowe canon (or reliable portions thereof). All that Merriam claims – or that stylometry can claim – is that certain letter frequencies or function-word patterns have more in common with Marlowe's canon than with Shakespeare's. If we wish to interpret that statistical witness as bibliographical/biographical conclusion, that is up to us.

I save for the end stylometry's most startling claim: that the generically anomalous *Jew of Malta* has more in common with the work of Thomas Kyd than with that of Marlowe. Critics have long recognized the resemblances between *The Jew* and *The Spanish Tragedy*. Merriam supports this impression with evidence: 'principal component analysis, based on the letter frequencies of the whole alphabet in modern spelling editions, has shown a consistent alienation of *The Jew of Malta* from the other six Marlowe plays, combined with a consistent association with *The Spanish Tragedy* and *Soliman and Perseda*'.[21] Criticism is accustomed to claims which expand Marlowe's small canon; claims which reduce it are unusual. That *The Jew of Malta* should be by Kyd is perhaps more of a surprise than that it should not be by Marlowe. Nevertheless, given the resemblance between *The Jew of Malta* and the anonymous *Arden of Faversham* (a play stylometry also claims for Kyd), Merriam's reattribution is tempting.

We do not know as much about the history of Marlowe's texts as we'd like, and what we know is tantalizing and incomplete. It is based upon witnesses, ranging from stationers' transactions and publishers' statements to early modern performance records, Marlowe's texts themselves, and sixteenth-century critical reactions to them. These witnesses must be cross-examined so that we can decide which to trust. The fluctuation in critical trust in the last two centuries reveals as much about the generic challenges of the Marlovian canon as it does about the problems (real or perceived) in the published texts. An account of Marlowe's texts is thus an account of how we treat evidence: not a neutral description of bibliographical fact (fact is only what we agree it is) but an account of our assumptions, desires, and prejudices – in short, of ourselves as readers.

NOTES

1. STC 17425. I have modernized the spelling and punctuation.
2. E. K. Chambers, *The Elizabethan Stage*, 2 vols. (Oxford: Clarendon Press, 1923), 2: 135. I have modernized the spelling.
3. R. Rowland (ed.), *Edward II* (Oxford: Clarendon Press, 1994), p. xxxv.
4. Jonathan Bate (ed.), *Titus Andronicus* (London: Routledge, 1995), p. 83.
5. Thomas Merriam, 'Marlowe and Nashe in *Dido, Queen of Carthage*', *N&Q* 245 (2000), 425–8.
6. Robert Greene, *A Groatsworth of Wit* (London, 1592), F1[r].
7. Christopher Marlowe, *The Massacre at Paris*, ed. W. W. Greg (Oxford: Malone Society Reprint, 1929 for 1928).
8. Anon, *Arden of Faversham*, ed. Hugh Macdonald with D. Nichol Smith (Oxford: Malone Society Reprint, 1947 for 1940).

9. David Bevington and Eric Rasmussen (eds.), *Doctor Faustus, A and B Texts* (Manchester University Press, 1993).
10. Eric Rasmussen, *A Textual Companion to 'Doctor Faustus'* (Manchester University Press, 1993).
11. Leah Marcus, 'Textual Indeterminacy and Ideological Difference: the Case of *Doctor Faustus*', *RenD* n.s. 20 (1989): 1–29.
12. Michael H. Keefer (ed.), *Christopher Marlowe's Doctor Faustus* (Peterborough, Ontario: Broadview Press, 1991), p. xvi.
13. E. K. Chambers, review of J. S. Bennett (ed.), *The Jew of Malta*, MLR 27 (1932), 78.
14. J. C. Maxwell, "How Bad is the Text of *The Jew of Malta?*" MLR 48 (1953), 435.
15. Cited by Nigel Bawcutt (ed.), *The Jew of Malta* (Manchester University Press, 1978), p. 38.
16. Philip Massinger, *A New Way to Pay Old Debts*, ed. T. W. Craik (London: Ernest Benn, 1964).
17. Peter Whelan, *The School of Night* (London: Warner Chappell Plays, 1992), pp. 57, 58.
18. Anthony Burgess, *A Dead Man in Deptford* (London: Hutchinson, 1993).
19. James Shapiro, *Rival Playwrights* (New York: Columbia University Press, 1991).
20. See Thomas Merriam, 'Marlowe's Hand in *Edward III*', *Literary and Linguistic Computing* 8 (1993): 59–72; 'Possible Light on a Kyd Canon', *N&Q* 240 (1995): 340–1; 'Marlowe's Hand in *Edward III* Revisited', *Literary and Linguistic Computing* 11 (1996): 19–22; 'Tamburlaine Stalks in *Henry VI*', *Computers and the Humanities* 30 (1996): 267–80; 'The Tenor of Marlowe in *Henry V*', *N&Q* 243 (1998): 318–24; 'Influence Alone? More on the Authorship of *Titus Andronicus*', *N&Q* 243 (1998): 304–8; 'Marlowe and Nashe in *Dido, Queen of Carthage*', *N&Q* 245 (2000): 425–8; 'Faustian Joan', *N&Q* 245 (2000).
21. Merriam, 'Possible Light on a Kyd Canon', 340.

READING LIST

Bevington, David and Eric Rasmussen (eds.). *Doctor Faustus, A and B Texts*. Manchester University Press, 1993.
Keefer, Michael H. (ed.). *Christopher Marlowe's Doctor Faustus – A 1604-Version*. Peterborough, Ontario: Broadview Press, 1991.
Maguire, Laurie E. *Shakespearean Suspect Texts*. Cambridge University Press, 1996.
Marcus, Leah. 'Textual Indeterminacy and Ideological Difference: the Case of *Doctor Faustus*'. *RenD* n.s. 20 (1989), 1–29.
Proudfoot, Richard. 'Marlowe and the Editors'. In J. A. Downie and J. T. Parnell (eds.), *Constructing Christopher Marlowe*. Cambridge University Press, 2000, pp. 41–54.
Rasmussen, Eric. *A Textual Companion to 'Doctor Faustus'*. Manchester University Press, 1993.

4

RUSS McDONALD

Marlowe and style

Atheist, sodomite, smoker – the image of Christopher Marlowe persisting to the present day is attributable in part to the poet himself, who apparently cultivated an anti-establishment persona for professional ends. The Prologue to the first part of *Tamburlaine* declares that the audience should expect something different from the second-rate 'conceits' to which lesser writers have accustomed them, and whatever the mix of artistry and commerce that governed his work, Marlowe's iconoclastic themes and eloquent speakers certainly had the effect of selling theatre tickets and, later, books. However, the scurrilous personal reputation that attracts many in our day has not always appealed, certainly not (for example) to most arbiters of Georgian and Victorian culture: we find no evidence that any play by Marlowe was performed between 1663 and 1818, when Edmund Kean revived *The Jew of Malta*. The twentieth century, however, rediscovered his plays and poems, re-evaluated his persona, forgave him his putative sins, and took the poet and his works to its heart. One major benefit of this resuscitation has been an increased appreciation for Marlowe's foundational role in the development of English poetry and drama.

It is worth reminding ourselves that there was more to Marlowe than his bad-boy image connotes, and such a corrective is especially salutary when it comes to comprehending the mechanics and the significance of Marlowe's poetry. As a student in Canterbury he was sufficiently diligent to win a Parker scholarship to Cambridge; whatever the truth about his record at Corpus Christi, he educated himself well enough to prepare translations of important Latin poems and to attempt an audacious stage version of the *Aeneid*; he composed one of the most winning of all English lyrics; he wrote plays that filled the public theatres; and he served in some capacity in Elizabeth's government, perhaps in intelligence, perhaps not. We might say that his willingness to flout cultural and artistic standards depended upon a savvy sense of how to thrive within those conventions, and how to turn them to his advantage. Throughout literary history Marlowe's verse, like his persona, has been exaggerated and then admired or reviled, according to the taste of the reader and the times. Patrick Cheney, in the Introduction to this volume, collects some of the most memorable of those responses, such as William Hazlitt's 'a lust of power in his writings, a hunger and thirst after unrighteousness, a glow of the imagination'. Hazlitt's reading is itself hyperbolic, of course, but it is representative of the terms regularly invoked to describe Marlowe's creative achievement, and such instances of overstatement need to be tempered, or at least complemented with other views. Just as Marlowe the man is more complex than he is often portrayed, so is Marlowe the poet.

Marlowe's dramatic poetry proceeds from his unique combination of the transgressive and the conventional. The 'mighty line', to begin with Ben Jonson's famous phrase, is marked by irrepressible energy, thrilling sonorities, and dazzling verbal pictures, but it is still a *line*, an ordering system, an invariable and comforting rhythmic standard that organizes words and ideas. We acknowledge Marlowe as the greatest dramatic poet before Shakespeare, but we sometimes forget that he was the first English writer to create great poetry *and* great plays, and – the burden of my analysis – great poetry *in* great plays. He composed not only 'The Passionate Shepherd', *Hero and Leander*, and brilliant translations but also transformed the English popular play, thus ushering in the greatest age of English drama.[1] He gave the English theatre a voice, a voice the public applauded and other playwrights recognized, appropriated, and developed. Specifically, he taught his contemporaries that English verse could be made to sound magnificent, and that the way to achieve that effect was to do without rhyme.

In the introductory survey undertaken here I can do little more than glance at some of the traits that make Marlowe's verse what it is, always with an eye (or ear) to comprehending how these properties confer affective power on the verse, how they cohere to move the listener. The common thread of this analysis is Marlowe's ability to synthesize conflicting skills and ideas. Janus-faced as poet and dramatist, he looks backwards and forwards, his intimate acquaintance with the classics accompanied by a thirst for knowledge about the modern world. His expansive imagination stretches beyond accepted boundaries of geography, philosophy, and drama, but he transcends them by popular artistic means. This intellectual curiosity, exceptional even in a famously curious era, produced a great variety of themes – power, alienation, masculinity, ambition, transcendence, limitation – and such topics help to account for the distinctive texture of Marlowe's language, especially its acoustic properties. Critics as different as Jonson and Swinburne have recognized that the sound of the verse is one of its defining characteristics: commanding without being bombastic, it partakes of the affective power of artifice without seeming stiff or excessively rhetorical. Among several important contributions to English letters, Marlowe's most meaningful is his transformation of blank verse: his renovation and development of a hitherto undistinguished poetic form into the primary medium for the Elizabethan and Jacobean stage. Marlowe's poetic significance can hardly be overestimated: George Peele, his contemporary, supplied an apt label in referring to him as 'the Muses' darling'.[2]

The Renaissance poet and the world of words

Marlowe's status as a major early modern poet is not in doubt, but it must be said also that Marlowe is a major Renaissance poet. In other words, his art owes much of its vitality and distinction to his unmediated acquaintance with rediscovered classical texts. The characters, geography, and concerns of classical Rome permeate, as we would expect, the translations of Ovid's *Elegies* and *Lucan's First Book*, as well as *Dido, Queen of Carthage*. But Marlowe's immersion in classical literature also greatly influenced his original poems and his plays, imparting to them the flavour of tradition and learning characteristic of much early modern English literature. His speakers often place themselves and their actions in a classical context: Faustus praises Helen as 'Brighter ... than flaming Jupiter / When he appeared to hapless Semele' (5.1.105–6, 'A' text); Gaveston, returning to England to join Edward II, anticipates masques presenting 'a lovely boy in Dian's shape' and 'One like Actaeon peeping through the grove' (1.1.60, 66). C. S. Lewis grumbled that 'We forget Tamburlaine and Mortimer and even (at times) Faustus and think only of Rhodope and Persepolis and celestial spheres and spirits ...', and even though Lewis preferred lyric poetry to drama and had had the opportunity to see few of the plays on the stage, still he has a point, for Marlowe's learning at times threatens to swamp the ideas and episodes it is summoned to clarify.[3] And yet the classical allusions usually supply an acute comment on characters and their actions, as in the case of 'hapless Semele', who destroyed herself with a desire for knowledge that parallels Faustus's own intellectual aspirations.

The humanism that accounts for Marlowe's command of the classics also manifests itself in his fascination with the multiplicity of the early modern world. Having absorbed the major texts of classical literature and ancient history, he also sought to understand the conditions of his own culture and of the world at large. The charges of atheism may have been exaggerated, but clearly he thought deeply and unconventionally about politics, religion, commerce, sexuality, science, and other topics that were causing controversy throughout sixteenth-century Europe. The breadth and intensity of his imagination produce the energy, the hyperbole, and the persuasiveness of his expressive style. Further, the works attest to an unfailing interest in the possibilities of the English language during one of the most exciting periods of its development.

Marlowe's devotion to words and his skill at manipulating them were acknowledged immediately, most pointedly in the frequency with which other dramatists parodied his style. Tamburlaine was the principal target: Jonson, Marston, and Shakespeare all mocked the hero's majestic speech, usually by inflating it even further.[4] Marlowe, of course, was aware of the originality of his talent. The novice playwright's advertisement for himself in the Prologue to his first effort for the public stage—

> you shall hear the Scythian Tamburlaine
> Threat'ning the world with high astounding terms
> And scourging kingdoms with his conquering sword—[5]
> (*1 Tamb.* Prologue, 4–6)

constitutes a helpful précis of his dramatic style. It emphasizes the sound of the verse ('you shall hear'), establishes precisely the register of the play's language ('high astounding terms'), and formally identifies words and deeds. The audience will see the anti-hero 'Threat'ning . . . with . . . terms / And scourging . . . with his . . . sword'. This yoking of language and action is a recurrent *topos*: seventy lines into the play proper, the weak King Mycetes responds to his general's rousing speech by proclaiming that 'words are swords'. The emotional power of controlled language is never far from the consciousness of Marlowe's principal speakers.

Visual rather than aural audacity informs *Hero and Leander*, the erotic narrative that became one of Marlowe's most popular works. Circulated in manuscript but not published until 1598, the epyllion is Ovidian in spirit, deriving much of its brilliance from the young poet's insouciant self-awareness. Assurance and wit steer the reader through a poem that seems both traditional in subject – love among glamorous ancient mortals – and self-consciously up-to-date in the style of storytelling. Its ethos is established early by the hyperbole of the visual descriptions, a winning example being the heroine's ornate buskins: they are 'of shells all silver'd . . . / And branch'd with blushing coral'; at the knees 'sparrows perch'd, of hollow pearl and gold'; filled with water by her servant, the birds as she moved 'would chirrup through the bills' (1. 31–6). Such visual extravagance is matched by Marlowe's witty treatment of the pentameter couplets. Although nothing perhaps is as jocular as the initial description of Leander – 'I could tell ye / How smooth his breast was, and how white his belly' (66–7) – nevertheless the constant chiming of the end-rhymes adds another voice to the rhythmic and assonantal music of the poem. Such descriptive verve and witty commentary also animate the translation of Ovid's *Amores*. At the end of 'Corinnae concubitis', having described the mistress's body in detail, the speaker skips discreetly over the sexual act with a clever use of *occupatio* and finishes with an invocation: 'Judge you the rest: being tir'd she bade me kiss; / Jove send me more such afternoons as this' (1.5.25–66).

Restraint, on the other hand, is the dominant note in his translation of *Lucan's First Book*, in which the poet eschews rhyme in favour of blank verse.[6] Whatever the date of the translation, the impudence and eros of *Hero and Leander* are absent; instead, Marlowe renders a polished, sophisticated, and even moving version of Lucan's portrait of Caesar's campaign against Rome. The gravity of the subject involves no diminution of poetic verve. Lacking the music of end-rhyme, the poet devises alternative kinds of poetic replication:

> As soon as Caesar got unto the bank
> And bounds of Italy, 'Here, here', saith he,
> 'An end of peace; here end polluted laws;
> Hence, leagues and convenants; Fortune, thee I follow,
> War and the Destinies shall try my cause'.
> This said, the restless general through the dark
> (Swifter than bullets thrown from Spanish slings,
> Or darts which Parthians backward shoot) march'd on,
> And then (when Lucifer did shine alone,
> And some dim stars) he Ariminum enter'd.
> (*LFB* 225–34)

The language is largely determined by the Latin original, of course, and the poetic properties are not flashy, but the strategic doubling of words and the intricate interlacing of vowels and consonants produce a melody that overlays and accompanies the fundamental decasyllabic rhythm: 'Here, here . . . here'; 'end . . . end'; 'bank / And bounds', 'Swifter . . . Spanish slings', 'darts . . . Parthians . . . march'd', 'then (when', 'some dim . . . Ariminum enter'd'). The unrhymed line is a crucial factor in the potency of such duplication, magnifying as it does the reverberation of the internal rhymes and repeated consonants.

The effect of echo

The extract from Lucan conveniently establishes one source of Marlowe's poetic distinction, his taste for various types of reiteration. Aural duplication is accompanied by skeins of visual images and the ideational echoing of themes and ideas. Of course all poetry depends heavily on repetition – of words, of rhythmic units such as iambs, of consonants and vowels – and his predecessors and contemporaries employed and valued this technique. T. S. Eliot proposed that Marlowe learned such melodic techniques from Spenser,[7] and one need only scan two or three random sentences from *Euphues* or think back over various sonnet sequences to recognize the enthusiasm with which the Elizabethan ear responded to repeated patterns. Marlowe willingly catered to this taste for echo. In the 1604 text of *Doctor Faustus*, a play of 1,485 lines, the name 'Faustus' sounds 150 times. (Compare this figure to *Hamlet*, a play of some 3,900 lines, in which the prince's name is used 72 times.) Harry Levin has calculated that 15 per cent of all the lines in the two parts of *Tamburlaine* begin with the conjunction 'and', pointing out that many of these same lines also end with a polysyllabic proper noun.[8] The momentum and regularity thereby created lend a sense of inexorability appropriate to the Scythian's irresistible conquests. But the poet also achieves other musical and thematic effects by doubling his acoustic elements: sounds, words, and ideas form patterns that beguile the listener and establish a sympathetic relation between stage and audience.

One of the great arias from any of the plays might be cited to illustrate the potential power of such reiteration, but its impact is audible even in expository or conversational passages, as in Faustus's initial interrogation of Mephistopheles:

> FAUSTUS   And what are you that live with Lucifer?
> MEPHISTOPHELES   Unhappy spirits that fell with Lucifer,
>   Conspired against our God with Lucifer,
>   And are for ever damned with Lucifer.
> FAUSTUS   Where are you damned?
> MEPHISTOPHELES   In hell.
> FAUSTUS   How comes it then that thou art out of hell?
> MEPHISTOPHELES   Why, this is hell, nor am I out of it.
>   (*DF* 'A' text 1.3.70–7)

The poetic ingredients are not extraordinary in themselves, but Marlowe selects and employs them with an acute awareness of their capacity to combine into something greater than the sum of its parts. The most prominent tactic is ending four successive lines of dialogue on the phrase 'with Lucifer'. An example of the trope known as *antistrophe* or *epistrophe*, such artifice is liable, in the hands of a lesser poet, to sound stiff, perhaps even parodic. But Marlowe imbues the phrase with mystery by surrounding it with a neutral, relatively austere vocabulary: of the fifty-three words in the passage, forty-five are monosyllables, and of the eight polysyllables, four are 'Lucifer'. Thus the relatively simple backdrop magnifies the incantatory power of the few multisyllabic words, especially the liquid and sibilant name of the devil.

The monosyllables, however, are deceptive in their simplicity, augmenting the hushed tone with a musical effect based on phrasal, lexical, and syllabic repetition. *Damned* appears in two successive lines, *hell* in three (supported by a stray rhyme on *fell*), the phrase *out of* in the same location in the last two lines. We should note also the relatively insignificant *and, are, you, our, that*, words that gain power when repeated in proximity. Within lines the repetition of initial consonants or combinations of consonants and the resonance of repeated vowels intensify the effect of wonder: 'then that thou' (line 76), 'How...thou...out' (also 76), 'against our God' (72), 'are for ever' (73), 'this is' (77). The interweaving of sounds creates the impression of significance, even though precise meaning remains implicit or obscure. But the word music also functions particularly, in that a discussion of eternal mysteries sounds suitably reverential and solemn. Often the secret to Marlowe's poetic repetitions lies in their relative restraint, a quality that emerges when his lines are set against the insistent echoing of a play like *The Spanish Tragedy*.[9] Unlike Kyd's, Marlowe's patterns do not loudly proclaim their status as patterns.

The simple reiteration of 'Lucifer' in the passage cited also attests to an extraordinary care for diction. It is a commonplace that Marlowe takes particular delight in geographical nouns, apparently having studied atlases and other such texts for the express purpose of giving authority to his portrait of Tamburlaine, the world conqueror.[10] And a significant measure of that authority inheres in the music of the proper nouns and their adjectival derivatives: Scythia, Persepolis, Natolia, Trebizond, Tenedos, Persia (three syllables), Asia (three syllables), Pharsalia, Bythinia, Larissa plains, Mauritanian steeds, Cimmerian Styx, Tartarian hills. All these are taken from *Tamburlaine, Parts One* and *Two* and represent only a fraction of the total. Levin, again, calculates that 'in *Tamburlaine*, the amplest vehicle for Marlowe's fascination with proper names, we can count 1,410 of them. More than a third of these, 545, gain peculiar stress by coming at the end of a line' (61). Beyond adding tonal weight, such impressive polysyllables also afford acceleration and momentum: the music of the lengthy word sweeps the speaker through the pentameter line and on to the next. As might be expected, such geographical ostentation is especially prominent in these two plays, and while it is less insistent in others, it still serves the poet in *Dido, Queen of Carthage* and *The Jew of Malta*, with their Mediterranean settings, and in the universal arena of *Doctor Faustus*.

Marlowe appears to have taken unfailing delight in trisyllabic nouns, especially those accented (roughly speaking) on the first and last syllable.

This configuration, imported into English from Greek and Latin prosody, is known as the *amphimacer*, and the names of many of Marlowe's most vivid characters conform to its rhythmic shape: Tamburlaine, Bajazeth, Sigismond, Calyphas, Amyras, Barabas, Callepine (in two different plays), Calymath, Ithamore, Abigail, Gaveston, Mortimer, Helena. In addition, these sonorous proper nouns gain added power from what seems like totemic repetition. Especially in the associations many of them call to mind, they expose Marlowe's delight in hyperbole, his fascination with the breadth and multiplicity of the world, and the reach of his learning. Moreover, the rhythms of these terms, like most of the other poetic devices I have enumerated, fit handily into the fundamental iambic pattern.

Marlowe and blank verse

Marlowe's adoption of blank verse is one of the decisive moments in the history of English poetry. It is generally agreed that the Earl of Surrey devised the form of blank verse as a vehicle for translating Virgil into the vernacular: on the title page of the selections from the *Aeneid* (1557), the poetic kind is described as a 'straunge meter', meaning perhaps 'foreign', and Surrey may have adapted an Italian verse form. Blank verse was first spoken by actors shortly thereafter in *Gorboduc* (1559), Sackville and Norton's tragedy on the consequences of political division. In the first decades of Elizabeth's reign it attracted many talented poets, including Nicholas Grimald, George Turberville, George Gascoigne, George Peele, and (briefly) even Edmund Spenser. According to one influential view, early writers turned to blank verse as a means of 'simulating the exotic grace of Latin quantitative verse . . .'[11] But until Marlowe seized upon it the form had not yet become the default mode of dramatic speech. The formal properties of blank verse seem to have been especially hospitable to his poetic and theatrical aims. Jonson's reference to 'Marlowe's mighty line' is usually taken favourably, although some regard it as a critique of his predecessor's weakness for bombast. However we choose to read the adjective, Jonson got the noun right: Marlowe is the poet of the line.

For him and his immediate contemporaries and successors, the decasyllabic line is the determinant feature of blank verse, the frame that secures the stability of poetic expression. As George Saintsbury pointed out a century ago, the earliest practitioners seemed to think in ten-syllable blocks: in *Gorboduc* and *The Misfortunes of Arthur*, he complains, 'the stump of the verse is . . . painfully audible . . . [T]he want of ease, the terror of losing the mould, the ignorance of deliberate line-overlapping, and of substitution within the line, are still disastrously noticeable'.[12] The simplicity of the earliest examples, even including some of Marlowe's, affords unseemly mirth for Saintsbury and a few later readers. They condescend because they are familiar with the extraordinary rhythmic diversity that Shakespeare, after the first few apprentice plays, was able to wring from the line. A more productive response is to historicize Marlowe's distinctive form of blank verse, attempting insofar as we can to hear his lines as his early auditors would have heard them. Stephen Booth's complaint that critics are too often guilty of 'accusing the past of having been the past' is relevant not only to ideas but also to poetics.[13]

The rhythmic power of blank verse inheres chiefly in its uniformity: poetic segments of equivalent length follow one another incessantly and with little variation, creating a rhythmic pattern agreeable to the ear and gratifying to the mind. In most of Marlowe's dramatic verse the impression of regularity is enhanced by a correspondence between the semantic or syntactic unit and the rhythmic segment: in other words, the sentence usually conforms to the demands of the pentameter, ending as the poetic line ends or at least distributing its clauses and phrases so that they lie comfortably in the decasyllabic frame. Thus we find little evidence of enjambment and, as a concomitant, few instances of caesura. Such generalizations are subject to modification, of course, depending upon the work in question, but in all the plays the alignment of meaning and metrics furnishes vigour and the drive of inevitability. For all Marlowe's reputation as an overreacher, only rarely did he overreach the poetic line.

The uniformity or 'stump of the verse', the very feature Saintsbury deplores, can be appreciated as something of an achievement. The Marlovian line, especially its almost invariable regularity, offers a kind of simple symmetry, a framing pattern calling attention to 'like measure', or equivalent units of sound. In discarding end-rhyme, i.e. leaving a 'blank' in the verse where a terminal rhyme would have been expected, the poet abandons the more obvious organizing principle in favour of a subtler marker, the rhythmic unit, and so the preponderance of end-stopped lines actually helps the auditor to expect and enjoy the structured language.[14]

A famous speech of Tamburlaine's demonstrates the sensation of equivalence fostered by such linear arrangement:

> I hold the Fates bound fast in iron chains
> And with my hand turn Fortune's wheel about;
> And sooner shall the sun fall from his sphere
> Than Tamburlaine be slain or overcome.
> Draw forth thy sword, thou mighty man-at-arms,
> Intending but to raze my charmèd skin,

And Jove himself will stretch his hand from heaven
To ward the blow and shield me safe from harm.
(*1 Tamb.* 1.2.174–81)

In this relatively uncomplicated case of metric serialization or poetic parataxis, similar units of sound follow and replicate one another. As I have indicated, the continuous flow of equivalent lines conveys aurally the unimpeded succession of victories that make up Tamburlaine's career. But the propulsive energy of the line is also valuable generally for its effect upon the auditor. Even later, when the more experienced poet varies the musical effects and complicates the innards of the pentametric unit, lineal repetition ensures a rhythmic pulse that is dramatically irresistible. It is not too much to say that Marlowe's most vital contribution to English dramatic poetry is rhythmic, that by removing the obvious chime at the end of the line he discovered the expressive versatility of iambic pentameter.

The foundational regularity of the unrhymed line amplifies other forms of reiteration, including consonance and assonance, morphemic repetition, and other acoustic patterns. In *The Arte of English Poesie* (published 1589, but composed a few years earlier), George Puttenham promotes the poetic benefits of such a mixture of order and ornament:

> It is said by such as professe the Mathematicall sciences, that all things stand by proportion, and that without it nothing could stand to be good or beautiful... the Philosopher gathers a triple proportion, to wit, the Arithmeticall, the Geometricall, and the Musicall. And by one of these three is every other proportion guided of the things that have conveniencie by relation, as the visible by light colour and shadow: the audible by stirres, times and accents....[15]

Many kinds of pattern might be adduced to illustrate Puttenham's argument – parallel phrases, rhyme, consonance and assonance, strings of isomorphic clauses in prose – but his analysis is especially pertinent in elucidating the operation of blank verse. The key is counterpoint. Just as painting depends on the proper distribution of shadow and light in relation to each other, so poetic structures are grounded in aural relations, with sounds making an impact chiefly in relation to other sounds.

The regulatory function of the frame is modified by the complementary principle, variety or diversity. Potential diversity is the key to the sovereignty and survival of the pentameter line in English poetry, and it is in the invention and exploitation of variety that Marlowe exceeds all his contemporaries except Shakespeare. Many of them were able to produce a workable five-beat line, but Marlowe more than any was capable of filling the spaces of the ten-syllable unit with compelling, various, and pleasing details. His talent for elaboration appears in those characteristic poetic features already enumerated: the exotic nouns, particularly place names (Persepolis, Campania, Alexandria, Uz); the multi-syllabic proper names (Barabas, Gaveston, Usumcasane, Mephistopheles); the polysyllabic diction generally (*paramour, ceremonial, magnanimity*); the specific active verbs (*fortified, pronounce, defame, glut*). It is the combination of such elements, and especially their relation to one another, that provides the ornamentation, the complex music that enlivens each pentametric segment. Marlowe's poetic contemporaries – Spenser in his lyric poems and in *The Faerie Queene*, Sidney in *Astrophil and Stella*, Shakespeare in the earliest sonnets, *Venus and Adonis*, and *The Rape of Lucrece* – were inventively expanding the repertory of ornamental possibilities: puns, internal rhymes, rhythmic surprises, extravagant use of assonance and consonance. Obviously Marlowe was listening to and learning from them.

Colourful details thus enrich what is probably the most famous passage in all Marlowe, Faustus's apostrophe to the spirit of Helen of Troy:

> Was this the face that launched a thousand ships
> And burnt the topless towers of Ilium?
> Sweet Helen, make me immortal with a kiss.
> [*They kiss*]
> Her lips sucks forth my soul. See where it flies.
> Come, Helen, come, give me my soul again.
> [*They kiss*]
> Here will I dwell, for heaven be in these lips,
> And all is dross that is not Helena.
> (*DF* 'A' text 5.1.99–105)

The phonic and melodic particulars that ornament the speech work contrapuntally with the uniformity of the unrhymed lines. As in the earlier exchange with Mephistopheles, most of the words are monosyllabic, and thus the few polysyllables – *Ilium, immortal, Helena* – stand in relief. But the poet has also crafted an intricate system of lexical and literal relations, connections that create more matching patterns within the wider metrical structure. The abundantly repeated words, for instance, connect identical elements in different lines, and sometimes in the same line: *Helen, lips, my soul, come, is.* The ear is affected not only by the reiterated words but also by a complex reticulum of duplicated letters: 'th' in the first line, 't' and 'l' in the second, 'm' and 'l' in the third and fifth lines, 'h' and 'll' in the last two. Such co-operative tension among components within the line animates many typical speeches, such as Tamburlaine's famous remarks on aspiring minds, or Gaveston's fantasy about the life of pleasure at Edward's court.

It will now be helpful to return to the complementary impulses discussed initially, the transgressive and the conventional, and to suggest that this foundational Marlovian tension manifests itself in the productive opposition between poetic diversity and regularity. And while the keynote is uniformity, certain passages exhibit greater ornamentation within the individual line, as well as from line to line; this is the promise of poetic variety that Marlowe's successors would soon exploit. The lack of certain chronology makes it difficult to construct a developmental argument, but much of the verse in *Doctor Faustus* and *Edward II* sounds more diverse, more 'advanced', more various than that of the other plays.

> Fair blows the wind for France. Blow, gentle gale,
> Till Edmund be arrived for England's good.
> Nature, yield to my country's cause in this.
> A brother, no, a butcher of thy friends,
> Proud Edward, dost thou banish me thy presence?
>
> (*EII* 4.1.1–5)

Even this quiet, reflective soliloquy, spoken by the Earl of Kent on leaving England, exhibits a more sophisticated sense of rhythm than much Marlovian verse, particularly the rolling succession of equivalent lines heard in *Tamburlaine*, for example. Here the use of caesura is uncommonly abundant. Even if we distrust the punctuation supplied by editors (of whatever century, the sixteenth or the twenty-first), still it is clear that an actor must stop and start, and stop and start again and again, disrupting the rhythmic regularity and defeating the familiar Marlovian swagger.[16] It is significant that most of these stops come at the beginning of the line, as in the last three cited: the early stop creates aural variety but still permits the speaker to generate some velocity in moving to the end of the line. And many of the familiar poetic traits are still audible, notably the repeated words and phonetic duplications. In other words, the forms of internal ornament or poetic disorder which normally vary the lineal equilibrium are amplified even more by the additional rhythmic variations.

It is hardly surprising to find such poetic transgression at the climax of *Doctor Faustus*:

> The stars move still; time runs; the clock will strike;
> The devil will come, and Faustus must be damned.
> O, I'll leap up to my God! Who pulls me down?
> See, see where Christ's blood streams in the firmament!
> One drop would save my soul, half a drop. Ah, my Christ!
> Ah, rend not my heart for naming of my Christ!
> Yet I will call on him. O, spare me, Lucifer!

Where is it now? 'Tis gone; and see where God
Stretcheth out his arm and bends his ireful brows!
(DF 'A' text 5.2.67–75)

Taking for granted the familiar poetic properties, we perceive immediately that these lines resemble those from *Edward II* in their multiple internal stops. But what is unique here is the degree of hyper-metricality: of the nine lines quoted, six have more than ten syllables, syllables not easily elided, so that the normal comforts of the iambic pentameter are repeatedly threatened.[17] In this climactic moment Marlowe's verse reveals the brilliant future of dramatic poetry over the next four decades.

The inevitable comparison with you-know-who is, on this point at least, exact and instructive. We must keep in mind that Marlowe was one of Shakespeare's most influential teachers, that Shakespeare's plays would have been very different from what they are – and may not have been at all – were it not for the Marlovian example. At just this moment in theatre history, the first three years of the 1590s, Shakespeare introduces those rhythmic permutations that will make his blank verse the subtle, flexible instrument that it becomes in the years after Marlowe's death. Frequent syncopation, trochaic inversions, multiple caesurae, enjambed lines – these and other such modulations serve to distinguish the subtle expressivity of Brutus or Henry V or Hamlet from the relatively uncomplicated rhythms of the early histories. In the eloquence of such speakers we hear the nature of the promise that Marlowe himself might have fulfilled had the Muses spared their darling.

NOTES

1. Patrick Cheney seeks to remedy this separation of poet and playwright in his Introduction to the present collection.
2. The mention appears in the Prologue to Peele's 'The Honour of the Garter', in *The Life and Minor Poems of George Peele*, ed. David H. Horne (New Haven: Yale University Press, 1952), p. 246.
3. *English Literature in the Sixteenth Century Excluding Drama* (Oxford: Clarendon Press, 1954), p. 481.
4. See especially Shakespeare's Pistol (in *2 Henry IV* and *Henry V*), the Induction to Marston's *Antonio and Mellida*, and Jonson's disparagement in *Discoveries* of 'the Tamerlanes and Tamar-Chams of the late age' with their 'scenical strutting and furious vociferation' (*Ben Jonson*, ed. Ian Donaldson (Oxford University Press, 1985), lines 789–92).
5. In this chapter quotations from Marlowe's plays are taken from the edition by David Bevington and Eric Rasmussen, *Doctor Faustus and Other Plays* (Oxford University Press, 1995). Quotations from the poems are taken from *The Poems; Christopher Marlowe*, ed. Millar MacLure (London: Methuen, 1968).

6. The question of when Marlowe translated Lucan has been reopened. See James Shapiro, '"Metre Meete to Furnish Lucans Style": Reconsidering Marlowe's *Lucan*', in Kenneth Friedenreich, Roma Gill, and Constance B. Kuriyama (eds.), *'A Poet and a Filthy Play-maker': New Essays on Christopher Marlowe* (New York: AMS Press, 1988), pp. 315–25.

7. 'Christopher Marlowe', in *Essays on Elizabethan Drama* (New York: Harcourt, Brace, and World, 1960), pp. 58–61.

8. *The Overreacher: A Study of Christopher Marlowe* (London: Faber and Faber, 1954), p. 61.

9. For example, Lorenzo's description of his defeat at the hands of Horatio (2.1.119–33) resounds with the artificial, highly rhetorical patterns characteristic of the play. Such a counter-example should not be read as an effort to promote the 'sophisticated' Marlowe at the expense of the 'naïve' Kyd, but juxtaposition of the two styles reveals Marlowe's gift for exploiting poetic repetition while at the same time increasing the verisimilitude of the dialogue. It is this combination of tradition and originality that makes Marlowe's dramatic verse sound as it does.

10. Ethel Seaton, 'Marlowe's Map', *Essays and Studies by Members of the English Association*, 10 (1924), 13–35.

11. C. F. Tucker Brooke, 'Marlowe's Versification and Style', *SP* 19 (1922), 187–8.

12. *The History of English Prosody* (London: Macmillan, 1906), 1: 346.

13. 'The Function of Criticism at the Present Time and All Others', *SQ* 41 (1990), 265.

14. In apprehending this new verse, according to George T. Wright, 'the spectator's relatively frivolous delight in rhyme was replaced by the more austere pleasures of meter'. *Shakespeare's Metrical Art* (Berkeley: University of California Press, 1988), p. 97.

15. *The Arte of English Poesie*, Intro. Baxter Hathaway, A Facsimile Reproduction (Kent, OH: Kent State University Press, 1970), p. 78.

16. On the extremely corrupt textual state of Marlowe's plays, see Richard Proudfoot, 'Marlowe and the Editors', in J. A. Downie and J. T. Parnell (eds.), *Constructing Christopher Marlowe* (Cambridge University Press, 2000), pp. 41–54; and Laurie Maguire's chapter in this volume, pp. 41–54.

17. Some of this metrical irregularity is perhaps attributable to faulty transmission of the text; the version of this passage printed in 1616 (the 'B' text) is smoother, less ejaculatory.

READING LIST

Downie, J. A., and J. T. Parnell (eds.). *Constructing Christopher Marlowe*. Cambridge University Press, 2000.

Eliot, T. S. 'Christopher Marlowe'. In *Essays on Elizabethan Drama*. New York: Harcourt, Brace, and World, 1960, pp. 56–64.

Hardison, O. B., Jr. *Prosody and Purpose in the English Renaissance*. Baltimore: Johns Hopkins University Press, 1989.

Leech, Clifford. *Christopher Marlowe: Poet for the Stage*. Anne Lancashire (ed.). New York: AMS Press, 1986.

Levin, Harry. *The Overreacher: A Study of Christopher Marlowe*. London: Faber and Faber, 1954.

Morris, Harry. 'Marlowe's Poetry'. *TDR* 8 (1964), 134–54.

Shapiro, James. '"Metre Meete to Furnish Lucans Style": Reconsidering Marlowe's *Lucan*'. In Kenneth Friedenreich, Roma Gill, and Constance B. Kuriyama (eds.), *'A Poet and a Filthy Play-maker': New Essays on Christopher Marlowe*. New York: AMS Press, 1988, pp. 315–25.

Steane, J. B. *Marlowe: A Critical Study*. Cambridge University Press, 1964.

Tucker Brooke, C. F. 'Marlowe's Versification and Style'. *SP* 19 (1922), 186–205.

Wilson, F. P. *Marlowe and the Early Shakespeare*. Oxford: Clarendon Press, 1954.

5

PAUL WHITFIELD WHITE

Marlowe and the politics of religion

It is a critical commonplace that religion and politics were inseparably entwined in Marlowe's England. Queen Elizabeth was 'Supreme Governess' of the Church of England, and the Church of England's leading primate, Archbishop John Whitgift, wielded considerable authority as a member of her Privy Council. Since monarchical rule was divinely sanctioned with the queen herself as God's vice-regent, disobedience to her laws was not just a crime, but a sin against God; conversely, wilful dissent from the Church's official prescriptions of order and worship was not just a sin but a crime against the state. These ideas, of course, constituted the official ideology of the Elizabethan government, but English subjects (as well as foreigners) who disagreed politically with the Crown shared the notion that Church and state, religious and civil authority, sacred and secular values, are intimately and inextricably linked, whether they advocated the queen's overthrow (as Catholics loyal to Rome did after a Papal Bull excommunicated Elizabeth in 1570) or called for the routing of bishops and their hierarchical mode of ecclesiastical polity from the national church (as Puritan radicals did throughout the reign). Not surprisingly, Marlowe represents these complex intersections of religion and politics in his works, questioning many of the verities his audience took for granted about them. In the discussion of this topic which follows, my focus will be primarily on the plays with occasional reference to the poetry and translations.

Dissecting God's scourge

With no stage-heaven or -hell, no supernatural characters, and no explicit moralistic message expressed in jog-trot verse – all typical features of popular drama in 1580s London – *Tamburlaine, Part One* would appear to usher in the age of Elizabethan 'secular' theatre. And yet this play reverberates with religious language and iconography and provocatively interrogates the political implications of mainstream religious doctrine, particularly the notion of divine providence. Tamburlaine was most famously known in the historical narratives of Marlowe's own time as the 'scourge of God', and indeed this is how he is described on the title page to the 1590 edition. Moreover, both Tamburlaine himself and his enemies repeatedly make this identification throughout both plays. 'There is a God full of revenging wrath', Tamburlaine exclaims, 'Whose Scourge I am, and him will I obey.'[1] Tamburlaine illustrates the notion, popularized by Protestant writings in Elizabethan England, that while bloodthirsty tyrants are entirely responsible for their wicked deeds, they carry them out in accordance with God's will, and are thus used as 'scourges' or agents of divine justice to punish sinful individuals, communities, even entire nations.[2] The prototype of the biblical scourge is the Assyrian tyrant, described in the Books of Kings, Chronicles, and Isaiah, whom Marlowe may have seen staged in a revival of Nicholas Udall's Cambridge play *Ezechias*, in which the Assyrian conqueror is described as 'Huge in armament and of a huge body', a fitting physical profile of Tamburlaine himself.[3] Divine vengeance in the play is visited on the innocent as well as the wicked, most notably in the slaughter of the Virgins in *Tamburlaine, Part One* and the drowning of the citizens of Babylon in *Tamburlaine, Part Two*. As sensational and horrifying as these acts are, Elizabethan providential theory agreed that many good people suffer when entire nations are scourged (such as England during the Wars of the Roses, thematically treated in Shakespeare's *Richard III*). Nevertheless, the rival kings and rulers Tamburlaine defeats – Cosroe, Bajazeth, Orcanes, Calapine, and their allies – are all shown to be power-hungry infidels deserving of their fate. Treated in particularly contemptible terms is Bajazeth, the Turkish Emperor of *Tamburlaine, Part One*, who boasts about the Christian apostates who have joined his army. When this historical figure threatened Christendom itself by laying siege to Constantinople, the eastern centre of Christianity, European writers feared him as an agent of divine retribution on a decaying, divided Christendom. Tamburlaine becomes the scourge of the scourge when he defeats Bajazeth and lifts the siege of Constantinople, enlarging 'Those Christian captives, which you keep as slaves' (*1 Tamb.* 3.3.46–7). For this feat, the historical Tamburlaine was celebrated throughout Europe.

And yet Marlowe's *Tamburlaine* plays question whether providential explanations of events are human fictions which, in some instances, constitute self-deception, but in the hands of cunning politicians, are cynically appropriated and propagated to advance their power and subdue dissent. Marlowe's complex, if not ambivalent, treatment of Elizabethan providential theory is illustrated in the sub-plot featuring the Christian King Sigismund and the Turkish ruler Orcanes in the early scenes of *Tamburlaine, Part Two*. When the armies of the two leaders face off near the River Danube on the borders of

Christian Europe, Sigismund accepts the Turk's offer of a truce, made binding by a solemn oath to their respective deities, Sigismund vowing, 'By him that made the world and saved my soul, / . . . Sweet Jesus Christ, I solemnly protest, / And vow to keep this peace inviolable' (2 *Tamb.* 1.2.133–6). Sigismund's Christian allies, however, persuade him to break the league, arguing that oaths to infidels are not binding in the eyes of God and are not trustworthy with them anyway, and that the Turks' vulnerability is an opportunity given by divine providence to scourge their 'foul blasphemous paganism' (2 *Tamb.* 2.1.53). Yet despite heavy odds in their favour due to the depleted Turkish forces (much of their army moved south to challenge Tamburlaine), the Hungarian Christians are defeated, and Sigismund concludes that 'God hath thundered vengeance from on high, / For my accursed and hateful perjury' (2 *Tamb.* 2.3.2–3). Since Orcanes himself had called on Christ to punish the Christians for the sacrilegious oath-breaking (contrasting with Tamburlaine's later calling on Mahomet to avenge his sins, to no effect), the Turkish victory over the Europeans may be seen as an act of vengeance by the Christian God. Yet Marlowe undermines this providential explanation. When Orcanes asks Gazellus whether he agrees that the defeat is attributable to the justice and power of Christ, his fellow-Turk replies, ''Tis but the fortune of the wars my Lord, / Whose power is often proved a miracle' (2 *Tamb.* 2.3.31–2). This sounds very much like the statement fellow playwright Thomas Kyd attributed to Marlowe to illustrate his atheism: 'That things esteemed to be donn by devine power might have aswell been don by observation of men' (MacLure, p. 35).

The *Tamburlaine* plays raise other questions about the ways in which religious doctrine and military/political institutions are linked. Tamburlaine's career shows how it is possible through extraordinary will-power, personal charisma, brute strength, and military strategy, to rise from a lowly shepherd to become emperor of the Eastern world. This challenges the basis on which European royalty justified and maintained their rule – divinely ordained succession through primogeniture – and it legitimates radical mobility through the social ranks, which was discouraged, if not condemned, by orthodox religious and political notions of 'place' and social hierarchy. Even Tamburlaine's repeated claim to be a divinely ordained scourge suggests that he has simply adopted this identity to give a higher aura of authority to his rule and further his military and political aims. 'But since I exercise a greater name, / The scourge of God and terror of the world,' he asserts late in *Tamburlaine, Part Two*, '*I must apply my self to fit those terms*' (2 *Tamb.* 4.1.155–7; my italics).

The idea that Tamburlaine is simply exploiting religion is reinforced by the range of contradictory stances he takes towards it. He speaks, at least at one point, as a practising Muslim (2 *Tamb.* 1.3.109); at other times he is defiant of, or sees himself as superior to, all religious authority (e.g., *1 Tamb.* 1.2.174ff.); and certainly in the climactic scene of *Tamburlaine, Part Two,* where he burns the Koran and shakes his sword heavenward, taunting Mohammed to strike vengeance upon him, he appeared to his contemporaries as a blaspheming atheist.[4] Whatever playgoers are to think of Tamburlaine's own religious stance, the Koran-burning episode (which ends *without* Mahomet answering Tamburlaine with vengeance) is the culmination of a number of moments or scenes in the plays which question, if not confirm to the audience, the non-existence of the Muslim God and reveal Islam to be a religion of empty curses and providential threats. Time and again, Bajazeth and his allies predict a sensational, violent ending to Tamburlaine at the hands of Mahomet, but these never come true. When the fervent prayers of Bajazeth and Zabina to Mahomet go unheeded, the humiliated Turkish emperor calls out in frustrated rage, 'O *Mahomet*, Oh sleepy *Mahomet!*' (*1 Tamb.* 3.3.269), while his wife Zabina first curses Mahomet then loses her faith altogether before she and Bajazeth dash their brains out: 'Then is there left no *Mahomet*, no God?' (*1 Tamb.* 5.1.239). A godless religion or not, Marlowe's audience would have observed that Islam is a more tolerant religion than Christianity in *Tamburlaine, Part Two,* where Orcanes pays tribute to both Christ and Mahomet, a gesture not unheard of among sixteenth-century Muslims.[5]

While it is probably true that continental Catholicism, and specifically Catholic Spain, was the enemy Elizabethan England feared most in the 1580s, Marlowe's *Tamburlaine* gives us another important perspective on politico-religious relations of the time, suggesting that England shared with all European nations, Catholic as well as Protestant, the dread of a holy war waged by the Ottoman Empire against western Europe. When Bajazeth threatens Tamburlaine with the 'force of Turkish arms / Which lately made all Europe quake for fear' (*1 Tamb.* 3.3.134–5), he was not exaggerating but expressing a truth that was every bit as real for Europe in the late sixteenth century as in the play's early fifteenth-century setting. When facing this threat, many European Protestant and Catholic nations set aside their differences to see this as a threat against *Christendom.* This explains why nations of divided religious and political allegiances joined together to oppose the Muslim infidel, and why it was possible for English bishops to order prayers to be said on behalf of the mostly Catholic Christians in Malta to protect them against their Turkish invaders in 1565.[6] By the 1580s, the Elizabethan government was engaged in diplomatic relations with the Turks to increase their trade, and they were happy to exploit the enmity between the Ottoman Empire and their more immediate enemy the Spanish, who fiercely competed for control of commerce and territory in the Mediterranean. Within this context, then, Tamburlaine must have generated both admiration and fear for contemporary audiences: admiration for his military efficiency and his conquering the Ottoman Empire, a projected fantasy of Christian European nations; and at the same time, fear of a brutal tyrant, the 'Turkish Tamburlaine', as he was called, indistinguishable in most respects from the Turks themselves.[7]

Stranger Jews and Catholics

The other play Marlowe wrote in which the Turks figure prominently is *The Jew of Malta*. Religion, and particularly religious 'policy' (Plate 1), are more explicitly evident in this black farce set on the western Mediterranean island of Malta, which the Turks fiercely attacked and besieged but failed to capture in 1565. The island by this time was governed by the Catholic Knights of St John the Evangelist, an elite order commissioned by and answerable only to the Pope for the purpose of protecting pilgrims from the Turkish enemy on their travels to the holy land. After surrendering to the Turks on the island of Rhodes, the Knights were brought to Malta by Emperor Charles V of Spain. In Marlowe's play, they find themselves caught between their political commitment to the Muslim Turks, to whom they owe a ten-year tribute, and their religious allegiance to the Catholic Spaniards, represented by Admiral Del Bosco, who shames them for dealing with the infidel. To pay the tribute, Ferneze, the governor of the island, turns to the Jews in Malta, who are not citizens but 'strangers' because they will not convert to Christianity, and this is the action which leads to a series of vengeful acts by Barabas, the wealthiest of the Jews on the island, whose entire estate is seized and his home converted to a nunnery.[8]

What did Marlowe and his audience know about Jews and what was their attitude towards them? Jews had been expelled from England in 1290 and did not resettle legally in the country until 1655. Nevertheless, it has been estimated that about 200 lived in England in the late sixteenth century, with a community of about 80 Portuguese Morannos (Jews who converted to Christianity) settling in London, the most famous member of whom was Roderigo Lopez, physician to Queen Elizabeth. Accused of plotting to assassinate the queen and Don Antonio, pretender to the Portuguese throne, Lopez was hanged in 1594. His fervent claim at his execution 'that he loved the Queen as well as he loved Jesus Christ' was greeted with derisive laughter by the crowd witnessing it.[9] The public sensation surrounding the trial and execution of Lopez illustrates the explosive mix of racial prejudice, religion, and politics that lies at the centre of *The Jew of Malta*, which, not surprisingly, was revived for this event, staged fifteen times at the Rose playhouse

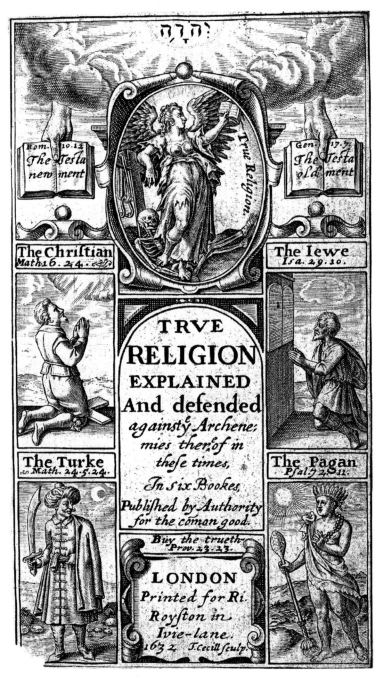

1 Frontispiece of Hugh Grotius's *True Religion Explained and Defended* (London, 1632).

in the summer of 1594, quite possibly motivating Shakespeare to write *The Merchant of Venice* around the same time.[10]

Marlowe's portrayal of Barabas combines historical facts about famous Jewish merchants of his day with a heavy dose of stage-stereotyping and centuries-old prejudice, which included the beliefs that Jews poisoned wells and crucified children (*JM* 2.3.181; 3.6.49). The name Barabas derives from the biblical thief whom the Jews asked Pontius Pilate to release in place of Christ before his crucifixion. According to the informer Richard Baines, Marlowe himself made the blasphemous claim 'That Crist deserved better to dy then Barrabas and that the Jewes made a good Choise, though Barrabas were both a theif and a murtherer' (MacLure, p. 37). This is certainly not the 'message' of Marlowe's play, and it is conceivable that Baines was inspired to invent the statement after viewing or hearing about *The Jew*, but it certainly captures the irreverent utterances of Barabas and the play's choric figure, Machiavel, who claims to be Barabas's mentor in the play's opening address. Machievel is a caricature of the Italian political theorist, Niccolo Machiavelli, who was notorious in England for advocating, among other things, the use of religion, when necessary, as an instrument of state power. Calling religion 'a childish toy' (Prologue 14), Machievel counts among his disciples the Guise, a French Catholic leader, and various popes for whom religion is a convenient mask behind which one murders one's way to high office. As he himself admits, Barabas is not after political power (*JM* 1.1.128), but rather the accumulation of wealth which brings its own kind of authority and influence. If Marlowe gives Barabas a well-developed Jewish identity, Judaism itself is represented as a bogus religion, one in which the 'Blessings promised' to Abraham are interpreted *not* as the spiritual rewards of faith in Christ (as the Protestantism of Marlowe's audience taught) but rather the worldly prosperity and economic superiority of God's chosen people.[11] In other words, Marlowe implies, Jewish religion justifies the acquisitive drive, restless pursuit of riches, and usurious money practices exemplified by Jewish merchants such as Barabas. Of course, as a disciple of Machiavel, Barabas himself does not take his own religion seriously; publicly, he professes it to his persecutors and to his fellow Jews, who take him to be their leader, but privately he admits to the audience, 'They say we are a scattered nation; I cannot tell', and deserts his co-religionists. His religious hypocrisy in the early scenes is matched by his pose as a Christian convert to trick the Friars later on.

It is important to note that Barabas's identity as a Jew, as perceived by both the play's Christians and by its Elizabethan audience, was not based only on theological belief. Jewishness was a racial and nationalistic category as well, increasingly recognized with the development of racial and nationalistic discourses in the sixteenth century (Shapiro, pp. 167–94). The widely accepted notion that the Jews themselves remained racially pure down through the ages may be traced back to the curse the Bible ascribed to them for their role in the crucifixion: 'Then answered all the people, and said, His blood be on us, and on our children' (Matt. 27: 25). This is brought up in the play, most notably in the counsel scene where one of the Maltese Knights says, 'If your first curse fall heavy on thy head, / And make thee poor and scorned of all the world, / 'Tis not our fault, but thy inherent sin' (*JM* 1.2.110–12). That Jews began to be considered more frequently in terms of nationhood as well as race is evident at a time when England and other European countries were defining their own sense of national identity and viewing the Jews both as a model of such nationhood (as illustrated in the Israelite people of the Old Testament) and a potential challenge. That threat was seen not only as social through intermarriage but economic as well. In the latter respect, the Jews were lumped together with other 'aliens' and 'strangers' in London, where riots and civil unrest arose over the perceived threat of foreign merchants and labourers to the livelihoods of London citizens, one series of incidents occurring in the spring of 1593, weeks after *The Jew* was staged at the Rose playhouse, and implicating Marlowe himself. As James Shapiro claims, 'Elizabethan theatergoers in 1593 would surely have been alert to how closely Barabas's activities in *The Jew of Malta* resembled those attributed to the dangerous aliens in their midst. Barabas is, after all, an alien merchant residing in the "Port-Town" of Malta who happily engrosses commodities into his own hands' (p. 184).

No less alienated in post-Reformation English society, of course, were Roman Catholics who, since the Excommunication of Queen Elizabeth by the Pope in 1570, were, along with Catholic priests and missionaries, subject to severe penalties and punishments for professing their faith. Whatever Marlowe's religious sympathies were (Baines's Marlowe favours Catholics and dismisses Protestants as 'Hypocriticall asses' (MacLure, p. 37)), in *The Jew of Malta* Catholicism is, like Judaism, represented as a false religion. Throughout the period Marlowe was writing plays in the 1580s and early 1590s, England was at war with Catholic nations abroad, most notably Spain (its Armada ignominiously defeated in 1588 when it attempted to invade England), and also Catholic principalities in France. Placed in opposition both to her villainous anti-Christian father and to the contemptible Catholic figures in the play is Barabas's daughter, Abigail. The sincerity and inward-centred nature of her faith contrast sharply with her father's dissembling and atheism and the Friars' avaricious, lecherous, and vow-breaking actions, which parody the Catholic formulae for spiritual regeneration: poverty, chastity, and obedience.[12] 'Witness that I dye a Christian', Abigail declares before her death, to which Friar Bernadine replies, 'I, and a Virgin too, that grieves me most' (*JM* 3.6.41). This is one of many instances of the play's anti-Catholic satire directed at the lechery, greed, and duplicity of the Friars and the wholly corrupted institutions to which they and the nuns belong.

Marlowe's anti-Catholicism clearly extends to include Ferneze and the other monastic Knights of St John who, historically, took their directive from the Papacy and are consistently addressed as 'the Christians' by Barabas. Their sanctimonious remarks and self-righteousness in the early council-house scene with Barabas and the other Jews shows faint echoes of the Pharisees at the trial of Christ (Hunter, pp. 212–13), and while Ferneze may not have appeared as a complete religious charlatan to Elizabethan audiences, his acts of 'policy', breaking oaths with the Turks and with Barabas and invoking religious authority to exploit the Jews for their wealth and to advance Maltese interests in his relations with both the Catholic Spaniard and the Muslim Turk, suggest his kinship with Machievel as well. Certainly his triumphant remarks at the play's conclusion ('let due praise be given / Neither to fate nor fortune, but to heaven' [*JM* 5.5.122–23]) are to be taken ironically.

Religion, politics, and sectarian violence

Without doubt the most ferociously anti-Catholic rhetoric to be found in Marlowe's plays occurs in *The Massacre at Paris*, the title of which refers to the mass killing of French Huguenots (i.e., Protestants) in Paris and other cities in August and September 1572. The Guise, the play's Machiavellian villain, combines Barabas's malevolent glee with Tamburlaine's penchant for violence. His religious cynicism is revealed directly to the audience early on in his notorious 'My policy hath framed religion' speech (*MP* 1.2.62–6). This comes close to summing up the play's view of institutionalized Catholicism, an oppressive political system hiding behind the mask of true religion. The audience is repeatedly reminded (chiefly by the Duke himself) that the Guise, his brother the Cardinal of Lorraine, along with the Queen Mother, the Italian-descended Catherine de Medici, are plotting the eradication of Protestantism in the service of the Pope and King Philip of Spain, Europe's most powerful Catholic monarch. *The Massacre*'s scenes of murder are shocking in their graphic realism, made all the more so by the coarse, sardonic humour of the Catholic assassins as they stab to death their enemies, whose pleas for mercy evoke sympathy and horror.

Recent criticism questions earlier opinion that *The Massacre* is simply a crude piece of Protestant propaganda, citing Marlowe's use of Catholic sources to depict the murders of the Duke of Guise and his Cardinal brother which parallel murder of Protestants earlier in the play.[13] Unfortunately, because of the corrupt and truncated condition of the text, it is very difficult to know how much is missing from the play's twenty-four scenes and, in turn, what the complete, original play in performance involved. Certainly, even as it stands, the surviving text shows religiously motivated violence on both sides and raises questions already posed in the *Tamburlaine* plays and *The Jew of Malta* about the cynical exploitation of religious authority and religiously induced fear in the pursuit of military force and political power. Relevant, moreover, is that the Crown's military support of the Protestant Henry IV against French Catholics from 1589 onwards was unpopular.[14] Having said that, there is no indication here that Marlowe was balancing his criticism of opposing religious parties. From beginning to end, the play is rabidly anti-Catholic, and its depiction of sectarian violence is designed to excite and cater to the militant Protestantism which English audiences shared in the immediate aftermath of the failed Spanish Armada.

The politics of Church and state

The tumultuous mixing of politics and religion is explored in a somewhat different way in *Edward II*. A nation's horrific descent into civil war is a theme Marlowe had addressed in his verse translation of *Lucan's First Book*, a work which betrays republican sympathies and a measure of scepticism about the role of providential intervention in human (and political) affairs.[15] Religion, nevertheless, was very much a part of the sixteenth-century debate over the right to resist constituted authority, particularly the authority of deeply corrupt or tyrannical monarchs. In England, the theory that under intolerable circumstances the governing class could lead a revolt against evil (read Catholic) kingship was developed by Protestant exiles during the Catholic reign of Elizabeth's elder sister Mary, and it found endorsement in one of the best-selling books of Marlowe's day, Calvin's *Institution of the Christian Religion*. This highly influential book was translated into English by Thomas Norton, the author of the Senecan tragedy *Gorboduc* (1561), itself a play which advocated a central role for Parliament and the aristocracy in monarchical government. In the heated political climate of the 1580s and early 1590s, any public sentiment justifying armed resistance to the monarch became associated with Jesuit plots to overthrow Elizabeth, but there is no question that these ideas were circulating on the Puritan left as well as on the Catholic right, and the fact that Edward II's deposition scene (unlike its counterpart in Shakespeare's *Richard II*) was not suppressed by censorship, not to mention the repeated treatment of the subject in history plays, indicates that some degree of discussion was at least tolerated.[16]

What is particularly intriguing in *Edward II*, however, is the Church's role in the challenge to kingly rule. Very early in the play, the Bishop of Coventry strenuously objects to the return of the exiled Gaveston, with the result that the king and his friend strip the bishop of his vestments, cast him into a ditch, and divest him of his title and possessions. It is this incident which precipitates the play's first major movement, the barons and the Church joining forces with the queen to banish Gaveston's presence and subsequent appointments of office at the royal court. To an Elizabethan audience fully conscious of Elizabeth's own excommunication by the Pope, the Archbishop of Canterbury's threat to Edward that unless the king banishes Gaveston he, in his role as papal legate, will absolve the barons of allegiance to the throne must have been particularly contemptible, and it precipitates Edward's subsequent tirade against the Church in Act 1, scene 4 (Heinemann, p. 183). Here, as in the Vatican scenes in *Doctor Faustus* where, in the 'B' text version, the conflict between Pope Adrian and the Emperor's election of an alternative pope is shown, the rivalry between Church and state for political power is dramatized, with the implicit condemnation of the intervention of ecclesiastical authorities in secular rule.

The great wealth, opulent lifestyle, lavish vestments, and elaborate ceremonials of the prelates in the Vatican scenes of 'A' and 'B' text versions of *Doctor Faustus* explicitly target the Pope's court at Rome, but it is not irrelevant that these were precisely the evils associated with *English* bishops in a series of unlicensed pamphlets known as *The Martin Marprelate Tracts* published around the time *Doctor Faustus* probably was first staged (1588–90). In England, the episcopal system of ecclesiastical polity was essentially intact from the pre-Reformation Church; its leader, Archbishop Whitgift, was widely despised for his secular role on the queen's Privy Council, which he used to persecute (and eventually to crush) militant Puritans who wished to replace episcopacy with a more democratically oriented church polity known as Presbyterianism. It is now widely accepted that the commercial theatre participated in the Marprelate controversy, so much so that the government intervened temporarily to suppress plays in London in November 1589, with a warning to the company associated with Marlowe himself, the Lord Admiral's Men. Other author/playwrights participated (John Lyly and Thomas Nashe certainly, Anthony Munday and Robert Greene probably), apparently on the side of the bishops, but we have no way of knowing whether Marlowe was involved. However, the anti-prelate scenes in *Doctor Faustus* and *Edward II* would have resonated with the large contingent of

Puritan sympathizers in attendance at amphitheatre performances in the late 1580s and early 1590s.[17]

Religion, politics, and censorship

Apart from the Vatican scenes, *Doctor Faustus* is perhaps the least overtly political, and the most explicitly religious, of Marlowe's plays, but in the tumultuous climate of the 1580s and 1590s when activism against the doctrinal and ecclesiastical teachings of the Church of England constituted a crime against the state, the play's provocative representation of religious dissidence, however inscribed within the tragedy's morality play framework with its edifying Prologue and Epilogue, may well have been perceived as politically subversive. Sceptical of religious orthodoxy, Faustus thinks hell's a fable and contemptuously dismisses the pains of the afterlife as 'trifles and mere old wives' tales' ('A' text 2.1.129, 137).[18] Moreover, he is inclined to side with the Evil Angel who regards contrition, prayer, and repentance as 'illusions, fruits of lunacy, / That make men foolish that do trust them most' ('A' text 2.1.18–19). Divinity, he says, is 'basest' of the learned professions, 'Unpleasant, harsh, contemptible and vile' ('A' text 1.1.110–11), and promptly dismisses it to pursue magic chiefly because of the notions of original sin and predestination ('A' text 1.1.37–50), cornerstone doctrines of the Elizabethan Church, the latter so important to Archbishop Whitgift's view of Protestant theology that he petitioned the queen (unsuccessfully it turned out) to have a more explicit, detailed statement about predestination included in the Church's official articles of religion.[19] And perhaps most shockingly, in a parody of Christ's final words on the cross, Faustus concludes his soul-selling pact with Lucifer with the utterance, '*Consummatum Est*' ('It is finished') ('A' text 1.4.74).

The Elizabethan government was too busy hunting down Jesuit missionaries and fanatical Puritans to concern itself with intellectual atheism, but it was sufficiently sensitive to public advocacy of its opinions to summon Marlowe himself for questioning. The Privy Council issued a warrant for his arrest on 18 May 1593, shortly after fellow playwright Thomas Kyd confessed to a document containing 'vile heretical conceits denying the deity of Jesus Christ our Saviour', which he claimed actually belonged to Marlowe with whom he lodged for a short time (MacLure, pp. 32–6). Both Kyd and the informer Richard Baines attributed to Marlowe a series of incriminating opinions. Among them were that the biblical account of Adam's creation six thousand years ago is historically untenable, that Moses was 'a juggler' who filled the Israelites' hearts with superstition, and that Christ was a bastard. 'The first beginning of Religion', Baines reports Marlowe as saying, 'was only to keep men in awe', and 'if he were to write a new Religion, he would vndertake both a more Excellent and Admirable methode and that all the new testament is filthily written' (MacLure, pp. 36–7). We will never know to what extent these statements represent Marlowe's own views, but they are sufficiently close to the anti-Christian sentiment expressed in *Doctor Faustus* to raise the question of whether the play was subject to state censorship.

Over the past century, many critics have argued that *Doctor Faustus* was indeed directly censored by the government, and they have offered this as an explanation for the broad discrepancies between the so-called 'A' text (published 1604) and the considerably longer 'B' text (published 1616). The most elaborate claim for state intervention is by William Empson, who argued that the Master of the Revels, Edmund Tilney (the court-appointed regulator of dramatic entertainments), initially licensed *Doctor Faustus* but then, in discovering its heretical implications in performance (which included the magician being saved from damnation) and feeling pressure from the newly formed Licensing Commission of 1589 involving the Archbishop of Canterbury and the London city council, extensively cut offending passages and scenes; this resulted in the 'A' text, a truncated version used for provincial touring. Subsequently, the impresario Philip Henslowe was able to get Tilney to restore much of Marlowe's original text, and hence the 'B' text, which, Empson surmises, was performed by the Admiral's Men through the 1590s.[20] Empson offers no convincing evidence to support this hypothesis, and it has now been largely discredited by Bevington and Rasmussen's more plausible reconstruction of the textual history, with the 'A' text close to Marlowe's 'foul papers' (original script), and the 'B' text a consequence of additions Henslowe commissioned in 1602.[21] Empson was following the commonly held assumption that state regulation of theatre, particularly in policing religious expression, was heavy-handed and repressive, an assumption that persists in criticism, much of it new historicist, which sees Marlowe engaging in self-censorship as a means of avoiding the supposed draconian measures imposed on dissident playwrights, even as he obliquely conveys the subversive, atheistic ideas given explicit expression in the Baines Note. Thus Catherine Minshull sees *Doctor Faustus* avoiding censorship measures by way of a 'rebellious subtext' in which 'the exercise of absolutist authority [is portrayed] as repressive, entrenched, unjust, and implacable'.[22]

There is perhaps some truth to the claim that Marlowe knew his limits in terms of what he could and could not stage before a popular audience (and before the watchful eye of the Master of the Revels), but as Richard Dutton has so convincingly shown in his review of censorship issues and *Doctor Faustus*, there simply was no elaborate machinery of state regulation which imposed repressive measures on the Elizabethan stage (Dutton, pp. 62–9). To be sure, proclamations dating back to the opening years of the queen's reign proposed severe restrictions on the expression of religious issues in plays, but it is quite clear from the numerous religious interludes and biblical plays on record for performance and publication throughout the period that these were not seriously enforced. Moreover, the frequently cited Licensing Commission of 1589, prompted by the Marprelate controversy, in which officers from the court, the City, and the Church were charged with perusing all plays for the purpose of striking out all matters relating to divinity and state, was never heard from after the controversy ended around 1590. What we can conclude, therefore, is that playwrights like Marlowe actually had considerable latitude in what they could represent in their plays, and it proved only to be in times of serious political crisis – notably the Marprelate controversy and the later Essex rebellion of 1601 – that severe measures were imposed. This helps to explain, moreover, how Lord Strange's Men in the early 1590s could include in its repertory Marlowe's anti-Catholic *The Massacre at Paris* alongside *The Book of Sir Thomas More*, a play about a Catholic heretic executed for opposing Henry VIII's act of royal supremacy.[23]

Religion, politics, and sexuality

If Archbishop Whitgift did not manage to censor Marlowe's writings as a member of the Licensing Commission of 1589, he succeeded a decade later, almost six years to the day after the playwright's death on 30 May 1593, by way of a proclamation known as the Bishops' Order. Co-ordered by Richard Bancroft, Bishop of London, the proclamation, issued on 1 June 1599, banned the publication of all satires and epigrams and ordered the burning of nine specifically selected books in the Stationers' Hall, one of which contained forty-eight of Sir John Davies's epigrams and ten of Marlowe's translations of Ovid's elegies from the *Amores*. Whitgift's purpose, expressed in an earlier 1596 order of High Commission, was to censor books of 'Ribaldry . . . superstition . . . and flat heresie' by which English subjects are allured 'to wantonness, corrupted in doctrine', and provoked into civil disobedience.[24] Marlowe's translation certainly fits these criteria. The frank eroticism of the *Amores* reflects Marlowe's refusal to follow precedent in 'Christianizing' Ovid. Indeed, several of the elegies are provocatively anti-religious, though some were omitted from the Marlowe–Davies book. 'God is a name, no substance, feared in vain, / And doth the world in fond belief detain', reads Elegy 3 from Book 3.[25] 'Or if there be a God', reads the next line, 'he loves fine wenches' (line 25). Elegy 8 from Book 3 states that 'When bad fates take good men, I am forbod / But secret thoughts to think there is a god' (35–6). Interestingly, Marlowe translates 'deos' (gods) as 'god' and emboldens the meaning of the original to accentuate its provocativeness (Leech, p. 32).

All of Marlowe's classically inspired love poetry and drama, i.e. the Ovidian *Amores* and *Hero and Leander*, and the Virgilian *Dido, Queen of Carthage*, comically defy Christian standards of sexual morality at the same time as they travesty the Christian, and specifically Protestant, notions of the sovereignty and complete transcendence of the godhead. However, if the poems revel in the sexual licence which pagan religion sanctions and the multitude of gods practise – one thinks of Jupiter doting over Ganymede as the boy sits on his lap; Neptune's equally homoerotic pursuit of Leander in the Hellespont – they also frequently remind us of the darker implications of erotic desire. As Claude Summers perceptively remarks with respect to Marlowe's treatment of homosexuality: 'What is most noteworthy about Marlowe's depiction of same-sex relations is that his posture is consistently oppositional *vis-à-vis* his society's official condemnation of homosexuality as sodomitical even as that condemnation inevitably and powerfully shapes his varied representations.'[26] This is very important as we turn our attention to *Edward II*, where Christian discourse defining same-sex physical relations as sodomy (the term derives from the Old Testament city of Sodom, a place of sexual vice), evoked in the horrific murder scene with its parody of physical sex between males, clashes with an Ovidian discourse of homoerotic play and desire characterizing the intimate exchanges between Edward and Gaveston. Until very recently, critics have tended to emphasize the former without sufficiently recognizing the importance of the latter in the play's representation of sexuality.

In considering *Edward II*'s complex mix of religion, politics, and sexuality, it is worth briefly comparing the play's climactic death scene with those in Marlowe's other tragedies. Certainly the tortuous deaths of the other villain–heroes, Faustus 'All torn asunder' by devils ('B' text), the multiple stabbing of the Guise, the boiling of Barabas in the cauldron of hot oil (a familiar medieval image of hell), cater to conventional notions of God's retribution for a life of sin. In this respect Marlowe is following Fulke Greville's dictate that tragedy's purpose is 'to point out God's revenging aspect upon every particular sin, to the despair or confusion of mortality'.[27] In *Edward II*, however, the king's murder by the insertion of a hot spit into his anus is the most shocking of all Marlowe's death scenes. We may ask, is this execution also to be perceived as divinely decreed, in this instance as the suitably prescribed punishment for sodomy? Or is it perhaps nothing more than the avenging act of Mortimer and Isabella?[28] As with the death of Tamburlaine after a sudden illness, Marlowe problematizes this conclusion as an example of divine justice in a play which many believe to be his most naturalistic depiction of human experience. *Edward II* contains no moralizing prologue or epilogue, and while the play stages state–Church conflicts, its characters are conspicuously free of the religious rhetoric exhibited in the other major tragedies. Edward's wretched final hours starkly contrast with Faustus's in that he does not dwell on his impending spiritual fate; there is little remorse for sin, and certainly no regrets about his relationship with Gaveston – however politically and personally disastrous its consequences, and it is only moments before his murder that he prays, 'Assist me, sweet God, and receive my soul!' (*EII* 5.5.108). Indeed, Edward's most passionate outcry amidst the stench, filth, and cold of the castle sewer is reserved for his beloved Gaveston, in whose cause he sees his impending death as a martyr's act of sacrifice: 'O Gaveston, it is for thee that I am wronged; / For me, both thou and both the Spencers died / And for their sakes a thousand wrongs I'll endure' (*EII* 5.3.41–3). On the one hand, Marlowe inherited a narrative from his historical sources in which Edward's passionate relationship with Gaveston leads providentially to 'a form of punishment that reenacts the sin it punishes'.[29] On the other hand, the absence of the transcendent in this tragedy, the very strong sense that the relentless pursuit of power and wilful self-destruction are what shape the characters' destiny, raises compelling questions about the use of a violent, sadistic killing as moralized example and a providentially ordained act.

Marlowe's political religion

All discussions of Marlowe's writings, at one point or another, lead back to the author himself. No poet–playwright of the Elizabethan age is more deeply implicated in his work than Marlowe; this is a historical constant of Marlovian scholarship despite theoretical assaults on the notion of autonomous authorship and the questions of collaboration surrounding the plays. Of course, we can never get back to the 'real' Marlowe and see inside his mind, but it is a useful exercise to speculate about what he believed and how he felt about religion, if only as a means of drawing some general conclusions about what his plays and poems collectively communicate to contemporary audiences and to us today on this complex topic. Although they are voices one step removed from Marlowe's own, the Marlovian persona of the Baines Note and the narrator of Ovid's Elegy 3.3 articulate a materialist, if not highly political, sense of religion and God: 'the first beginning of Religioun was only to keep men in awe', Baines's Marlowe asserts, and 'God is a name, no substance, feared in vain', Ovid's narrator claims (MacLure, p. 37; Elegy 3.3.23). However, the plays are more ambiguous than this. Is Sigismund's humiliating defeat an act of divine retribution for violating his oath with Christ, or is it a mere consequence of war?

What Marlowe does show is that religion is a potent and potentially destructive weapon in the hands of political leaders. Tamburlaine, Ferneze, and the Guise all illustrate how senseless acts of cruelty, greed, selfishness, and injustice can be carried out in the name of God and true religion; in the cases of Tamburlaine and the Guise, the exploitation seems self-conscious, while with Ferneze it is not so clear. Marlowe, at least in the poignant case of Barabas's genuinely pious daughter Abigail, effectively raises the question of why God allows bad things to happen to good people. Abigail, perhaps the only godly, sympathetic character in the play, is victimized by both her father and her supposed spiritual mentors before she dies of poison, reminding one once again of Marlowe's Ovid: 'Live godly, thou shalt die; though honour heaven, / Yet shall thy life be forcibly bereaven' (*JM* 3.8.35–6).

Critics have perceived this questioning of Protestant notions of divine justice elsewhere in Marlowe,[30] as we have noted its implications for transgressive sexuality in *Edward II*. In the cases of Friars Bernadine and Jacomo, Marlowe seems to suggest that the corrupt institutions they serve and the unrealistic vows they are required to follow inevitably result in hypocrisy and a disparity between religious ideals and practices. At the same time, as G. K. Hunter insightfully remarks, if Marlowe 'was an atheist in the modern sense at all, he was a God-haunted atheist', who especially in *Doctor Faustus* but also at moments in the other plays suggests a passionate identification with the experiences of remorse, fear of damnation, repentance, and worship. This was the religious culture of Marlowe's Cambridge, and given that intensely devout Catholics engaged in similar self-scrutiny and spiritual introspection, this was also part of the world he entered when visiting Catholic colleges abroad.

NOTES

1. *Tamburlaine the Great, Part One*, in *Christopher Marlowe: The Complete Plays*, Mark Thornton Burnett (ed.), Everyman (London: Dent, 1999), p. 135 (5.1.181 and 183). In this chapter all subsequent references to this and other plays by Marlowe are taken from Burnett's edition and appear parenthetically in the text.
2. See John Calvin, *The Institution of the Christian Religion*, Thomas Norton (trans.) (1561; rpt London, 1582), i: xvii; William Perkins, *The Workes* (London, 1608), i: 160 and 164. The notion is pervasive in Thomas Beard's Elizabethan pamphlet, *The Theatre of Gods Judgement* (London, 1648).
3. The only known performance was before the queen in King's College Chapel, Cambridge, in August 1564. See Paul Whitfield White, *Theatre and Reformation: Protestantism, Patronage and Playing in Tudor England* (Cambridge University Press, 1993), pp. 142–6.

4. Robert Greene, in reference to *Tamburlaine* in 1588, condemns Marlowe for 'daring God out of heauen with that Atheist Tamburlan' (MacLure, p. 29).

5. For the Muslim King of Morocco's affection for England because of its religion, see Rami Jaradat, 'Redefining the Role of the Turks in Elizabethan Literature', PhD Dissertation, Purdue University, 2002, chapter 1; and Simon Shepherd, *Marlowe and the Politics of Elizabethan Theatre* (New York: St Martin's Press, 1986), pp. 141–5.

6. For English prayers for the Maltese, see Andrew P. Vella, *An Elizabethan–Ottoman Conspiracy* (Valetta, Malta: Royal University of Malta Press, 1972), p. 14; cited in 'Introduction', *The Jew of Malta*, Roma Gill (ed.) (Oxford: Clarendon Press, 1995), p. xii.

7. 'Turkish *Tamberlaine*' is how Joseph Hall describes Marlowe's hero in his verse satire, 'Virgidemiarum' (1597–8); see MacLure, p. 40. For Tamburlaine and the Turks, see Shepherd, *Marlowe*, pp. 142–69; and Jaradat, 'Redefining the Role of the Turks'.

8. For a succinct introduction to the play, see 'Introduction to *The Jew of Malta*', in *English Renaissance Drama: A Norton Anthology*, David Bevington, et al. (eds.) (New York: Norton, 2002), pp. 287–92.

9. Cited in James Shapiro, *Shakespeare and the Jews* (New York: Columbia University Press, 1996), p. 38.

10. See E. K. Chambers, *The Elizabethan Stage*, 4 vols. (Oxford: Clarendon Press, 1923), 3: 424–5.

11. See G. K. Hunter, 'The Theology of Marlowe's *The Jew of Malta*', JWCI 28 (1964), 211–40.

12. The Elizabethan Homilies of 1563 condemned 'the three chief principal points, which they called the three essentials (or three chief foundations) of religion, that is to say, obedience, chastity and willful poverty'. See Michael Questier, *Conversion, Politics and Religion in England, 1580–1625* (Cambridge University Press, 1996), p. 61.

13. The most influential of these commentaries is Julia Briggs, 'Marlowe's *Massacre at Paris*: a Reconsideration', RES 34 (1983), 257–78.

14. See R. B. Wernham, *After the Armada: Elizabethan England and the Struggle for Western Europe 1588–1595* (Oxford University Press, 1984); Curtis Breight, *Surveillance, Militarism and Drama in the Elizabethan Era* (New York: St Martin's Press, 1996), p. 114.

15. For discussions of Marlowe's Lucan, see Patrick Cheney, *Marlowe's Counterfeit Profession: Ovid, Spenser, Counter-Nationhood* (University of Toronto Press, 1997), pp. 227–37; and Clifford Leech, *Christopher Marlowe: Poet for the Stage*, Anne Lancashire (ed.) (New York: AMS, 1980), pp. 33–5.

16. See Margot Heinemann, 'Political Drama', in A. R. Braunmuller and Michael Hattaway (eds.), *The Cambridge Companion to English Renaissance Drama* (Cambridge University Press, 1990): pp. 161–205; qtd from pp. 182–4.

17. For the players' involvement in the Marprelate controversy, see Scott McMillin and Sally-Beth MacLean, *The Queen's Men and Their Plays* (Cambridge University Press, 1998), pp. 52–4; Richard Dutton, *Licensing, Censorship, and Authorship in Early Modern England* (New York: Palgrave, 2000), pp. 74–6; and Charles Nicholl, *A Cup of News: The Life of Thomas Nashe* (London: Routledge, 1984), pp. 64–79.

18. For convenience, I quote mainly from the 'A' text of 1604. For further discussion of the 'A' and 'B' texts, see the chapters by Laurie Maguire and Thomas Healy in the present volume, pp. 41–54 and 174–92.

19. These came to be known as the Lambeth articles published in 1596. See *The Works of John Whitgift*, ed. John Ayre, 3 vols., Parker Society (Cambridge, 1851), 3: 612.

20. William Empson, *Faustus and the Censor: The English Faust-Book and Marlowe's 'Dr Faustus'* (Oxford: Blackwell, 1987).

21. David Bevington and Eric Rasmussen (eds.), 'Introduction,' *'Doctor Faustus' A- and B-texts (1604, 1616)* (Manchester University Press, 1993).

22. Catherine Minshull, 'The Dissident Sub-Text of Marlowe's *Dr Faustus*', *English* 39 (1990), 193–207; qtd from p. 205.

23. See Andrew Gurr, *Shakespearean Playing Companies* (Oxford: Clarendon Press, 1996), pp. 263–4.

24. See Ian Frederick Moulton, '"Printed Abroad and Uncastrated": Marlowe's *Elegies* with Davies' *Epigrams*', in Paul Whitfield White (ed.), *Marlowe, History, and Sexuality: New Critical Essays on Christopher Marlowe* (New York: AMS Press, 1998), pp. 77–90; qtd from p. 77.

25. *Christopher Marlowe: The Complete Poems and Translations*, Stephen Orgel (ed.) (New York: Penguin, 1971), p. 166 (lines 23–4).

26. Claude Summers, '*Hero and Leander*: the Arbitrariness of Desire', in J. A. Downie and J. T. Parnell (eds.), *Constructing Christopher Marlowe* (Cambridge University Press), pp. 133–47; qtd from p. 134.

27. Cited in Alan Sinfield, *Faultlines: Cultural Materialism and the Politics of Dissident Reading* (Berkeley: University of California Press, 1992), p. 217.

28. See Charles R. Forker's discussion of the criticism in his edition of *Edward the Second* (Manchester University Press, 1994), pp. 92–9.

29. I quote David Bevington in his 'Introduction to *Edward II*', in *English Renaissance Drama*. Bevington, et al. (eds.), p. 356.

30. See, for example, Bevington and Rassmussen (eds.), *Doctor Faustus*, pp. 30–1.

READING LIST

Bevington, David, and Eric Rasmussen (eds.). *'Doctor Faustus', A- and B-texts (1604, 1616)*. Revels Plays. Manchester University Press, 1993.

Dutton, Richard. *Licensing, Censorship, and Authorship in Early Modern England*. New York: Palgrave, 2000.

Heinemann, Margot. 'Political Drama'. In *The Cambridge Companion to English Renaissance Drama*. Cambridge University Press, 1990, pp. 161–205.

Hunter, G. K. 'The Theology of Marlowe's *The Jew of Malta*'. *JWCI* 28 (1964), 211–40.

Leech, Clifford. *Christopher Marlowe: Poet for the Stage*. Anne Lancashire (ed.). New York: AMS Press, 1980.

Questier, Michael. *Conversion, Politics and Religion in England, 1580–1625*. Cambridge University Press, 1996.

Riggs, David. 'Marlowe's Quarrel with God'. In Paul Whitfield White (ed.), *Marlowe, History and Sexuality: New Critical Essays on Christopher Marlowe*. New York: AMS Press, 1998, pp. 15–38.

Shapiro, James. *Shakespeare and the Jews*. New York: Columbia University Press, 1996.

Shepherd, Simon. *Marlowe and the Politics of Elizabethan Theatre*. New York: St Martin's Press, 1986.

Sinfield, Alan. *Faultlines: Cultural Materialism and the Politics of Dissident Reading*. Berkeley: University of California Press, 1992.

6

JAMES P. BEDNARZ

Marlowe and the English literary scene

Between 1587, when he left Cambridge, and his death in 1593, Marlowe's literary career developed in three social contexts: he found patronage and employment as a government spy; he associated with some of the most heterodox intellectuals of his age; and he became one of London's first professional writers. It is through these interconnected activities – reflected in Marlowe's relationships with Thomas Watson, Thomas Harriot, and William Shakespeare – that he transformed Elizabethan literature. Watson, a 'University Wit' like Marlowe, was a model of what a scholar could achieve in a career supported by patronage, publication, and playwrighting. Harriot, a brilliant scientist whose friendship resulted in accusations of their collusion in 'Sir Walter Ralegh's school of atheism', mirrored Marlowe's intellectual audacity. And Shakespeare, Marlowe's chief rival in the public theatre, engaged him in a theatrical dialogue on the meaning of history. The Marlovian moment lasted only six years, but its achievement was to prove that popular drama could be counted among those exclusive cultural activities which Thomas Nashe called 'the endeavors of art'.[1]

Thomas Watson was among a small group of writers now called the University Wits, who gained literary reputations in the 1580s after having studied at Cambridge or Oxford. As London's first set of university-trained professionals, the wits – whose best writers included Watson, Marlowe, Nashe, Robert Greene, George Peele, Thomas Lodge, and John Lyly – appeared at the moment when the cultural marketplace first made having a literary career viable. Watson, who killed William Bradley in 1589 while defending Marlowe, was a writer whose reputation seemed so assured that William Covell in *Polymanteia* (1595) called Shakespeare 'Watson's heir'.[2] Some seven years older than Marlowe, Watson, who had briefly studied at Oxford before finishing his education on the continent, was probably writing for the Queen's Men between 1583 and 1585, when his younger friend was still at Cambridge. Although he died in 1592, he had by that time become such an accomplished dramatist that Francis Meres would remember him six years later as being among 'our best for tragedy'.[3] He had proved that it was possible for a scholar to forge a career as a playwright and patronage poet, and Marlowe followed his precedent in dividing his original compositions between poetry, circulated in manuscript or print, and drama for the commercial stage. *Hecatompathia* (1582), Watson's collection of English sonnets (in eighteen lines), became so recognizable that the courtiers Lorenzo and Balthazar in *The Spanish Tragedy* flaunt their knowledge of contemporary love poetry by recalling eight lines from sonnet 48.[4] Praised by the scrupulous Cambridge don Gabriel Harvey as one of England's finest Latin poets, Watson produced a Latin translation of Sophocles' *Antigone* (1581) and responded to Tasso's Italian pastoral play *Aminta* in a Latin poem entitled *Amyntas* (1585). Marlowe shared Watson's enthusiasm for translation, which he also practised with varying degrees of fidelity, in paraphrasing Virgil's *Aeneid* in *Dido, Queen of Carthage*, producing English versions of *Ovid's Elegies* and the first book of Lucan's *Pharsalia*, and improvising on Musaeus' *Hero and Leander*. Furthermore, in his Latin epitaph 'On the Death of Sir Roger Manwood' (who had been lenient in the Bradley affair) and perhaps in the Latin dedication to the Countess of Pembroke (signed C. M.) of Watson's posthumously published *Amintae gaudia*, he served their combined interests. Marlowe's remarkable facility with English blank verse was, moreover, anchored in his knowledge of classical prosody.

In the early modern period, patronage signified a wide range of attachments and responsibilities, from the process of occasionally dedicating literary work to ongoing service as a secretary or tutor. Watson and Marlowe's association with Thomas Walsingham, a second cousin of Sir Francis Walsingham (Queen Elizabeth's secretary of state and the head of her secret service), suggests that they might have served as agents engaged in anti-Catholic intrigue. When Cambridge threatened to withhold Marlowe's degree, the Privy Council insisted that his apparent apostasy was a ploy and that 'he had done her majesty good service and deserved to be rewarded for his faithful dealing'.[5] He was not a Catholic, heading for the English College at Rheims, but had probably been gathering information about potentially dangerous nonconformists. Between 1576 and 1577, Watson had been admitted into the English College at Douai in Flanders, before it moved to Rheims. But when Sir Francis died in 1590, Watson expressed his grief in a pastoral dialogue called *Meliboeus* in which Corydon (Watson) and Tityrus (Thomas Walsingham) lament their benefactor's passing. Years later, Edward Blount, in dedicating *Hero and Leander*, reminded Thomas of the 'many kind favors' and 'liberal affection' he had shown its author. But with so little evidence, we can only wonder at the services Marlowe had rendered in what Charles Nicholl calls 'the secret theater' of Elizabethan espionage by the time he rode from Walsingham's estate to his death in Deptford on 30 May 1593.

That Marlowe had been employed to counterfeit his religious beliefs makes it impossible, at this late date, to determine his theological allegiances, which might have been in considerable turmoil. David Riggs cogently notes that although 'the Privy Council valued Marlowe because of his contacts in the recusant community, and because of his willingness to betray it', these were 'equally reasons not to trust him'. The modern reader faces the same interpretive problem in reading the plays. Tamburlaine, the scourge of God, who blasphemes as 'God's double agent', parallels Marlowe, whose own appearance of apostasy had been state sanctioned. Tamburlaine 'invokes the orthodox doctrine of obedience in a sophisticated right to disobey', Riggs explains, even as his status as scourge 'liberates him from the very God who enfranchises him'.[6] Tamburlaine rebels against the power that sanctions his transgression, and, in showing what C. L. Barber calls Marlowe's 'unstable appropriation of the divine for the human', makes blasphemy 'a heroic enterprise'.[7] This issue of Marlowe's poetic theology – his debate on the connection between the human and the divine – is particularly problematic when it is considered in the context of Ralegh's intellectual circle, which has been sensationalized by Muriel Bradbrook as a centre of occultism in *The School of Night*.

Ralegh's administrative, privateering, and colonial ventures were based at Durham House, his London residence, where Thomas Harriot was employed as his scientific adviser. Harriot, like Marlowe, was a bold innovator. One of the foremost mathematicians in Europe, Harriot familiarized Ralegh's navigators with the latest technology, while pursuing studies in astronomy, cosmology, astrology, alchemy, optics, ethnography, and linguistics. Through his friendship with Harriot, Marlowe stood at the epicentre of English colonialism. In 1584, Harriot wrote navigational instructions for Amadas and Barlowe's reconnaissance for the Roanoke colony, and, in the following year, he participated in the expedition, under John White, to plant it. Then, probably as part of Ralegh's plan for a new voyage, he published *A Brief and True Report of the New Found Land of Virginia* in 1588, just before it was discovered that the remaining settlers of England's first colony in the New World had mysteriously vanished. Although urged to publish more, he later wrote to Kepler that, 'Things with us are in such a condition that I still cannot philosophize freely.'[8] Richard Hakluyt included the *True Report* in his *Principal Navigations* in 1589, and in 1590 Theodor de Bry published a folio edition in Latin, English, French, and German, with engravings based on White's drawings, earning its author an international reputation. Marlowe not only shared Harriot's interests in the alien and exotic: magnates such as Ralegh and magi such as Harriot embodied the restless ambition of Tamburlaine, Faustus, Barabas, and the Guise.

Ralegh's enemies at court and on the continent demonized his enterprise. In 1592, a scandalous pamphlet based on the work of the Jesuit Robert Parsons mocked 'Sir Walter Ralegh's school of atheism' and Harriot as 'the conjurer that is master thereof'.[9] Throughout his career Harriot would be denounced as both a necromancer and rationalist who questioned Scripture. He is, for example, the target of Nashe's aspersion in *Pierce Penniless* that 'there be Mathematicians . . . harboured in high places' who believe that there were 'men before *Adam*' and 'that there are no devils' (1: 172). Domestic surveillance corroborated this view. Richard Baines quotes Marlowe as saying that 'Moses was but a Juggler, and that one Harriot, being Sir W Ralegh's man, can do more than he', and Richard Cholmeley adds that Marlowe 'read the Atheist lecture to Sir Walter Ralegh and others'.[10] Harriot had studied the culture of the Algonkians, and one of his most Machiavellian conclusions, as Stephen Greenblatt observes, was that their priests advanced religious myths because they made the common people 'have great respect to their Governors'.[11] To encourage belief in Christianity, in order to subdue the Algonkians, Harriot played on this same gullibility, becoming, in Marlowe's purported jest, a kind of Moses, in representing his own mathematical instruments, sea compasses, magnets, magnifying glasses, perspective glasses, and clocks as modern miracles. That Harriot advocated the medicinal use of tobacco and explained its function in religious offerings might also have prompted Marlowe's comment that the Eucharist could have been instituted 'with more Ceremonial Reverence' in 'a Tobacco pipe' (Steane, p. 364).

It is ironic, then, that the strongest literary trace of Marlowe's relationship with Ralegh appears in an exquisite pair of pastoral lyrics, 'The Passionate Shepherd' and 'The Nymph's Reply'. Ralegh shared poetic exchanges with Queen Elizabeth, Henry Noel, George Whetstone, Sir Thomas Heneage, and Edmund Spenser. The first attribution of 'The Nymph's Reply' to Ralegh, however, is by Izaac Walton in 1653.[12] Both verses (which appear in multiple manuscript versions) became popular songs that were first printed together in *England's Helicon* (1600). 'The Nymph's Reply' is written in the pastoral mode favoured by Ralegh in such poems as *The Ocean's Love to Cynthia*. But it is only one of a series of answers to Marlowe's lyric, such as John Donne's 'The Bait', and we can only wonder how familiar Ralegh was with Marlowe. Is it possible that in a moment of scandalous wit he entertained Ralegh with a recitation of 'the Atheist's lecture' containing some of the comic blasphemies retailed by Baines and Cholmeley? If so, is there any reason why this same volatile writer might not also have penned, in a more pious mood, the theological anxieties of *Doctor Faustus* or the militant Protestantism of *The Massacre at Paris*?

We will never know how probing their intellectual curiosity became. But what makes Bradbrook's characterization of the Ralegh circle as an occult 'school of night' seem exaggerated is the appearance of the first edition of Spenser's national epic *The Faerie Queene* as Durham House's premiere literary work, and not George Chapman's mystic *Shadow of Night*. The publication of the 1590 *Faerie Queene* was an event hosted by Ralegh at the apex of Spenser's career. Its Timias–Belphoebe episode allegorizes Ralegh's service to Queen Elizabeth and features an imitation of Ralegh's Petrarchan poetry to her (3.5.45–7), in an elaborate historical allegory in which she cures him with 'divine Tobacco' (3.5.32). Ralegh's 'A Conceit upon this vision of *The Faerie Queene*' (the first of his two commendatory sonnets) judges Spenser's poem to be among the greatest in the Western canon.[13] In it, Spenser compares his fiction's epic geography to 'fruitfullest *Virginia*' as a site of 'hardy enterprise', of discovery and conquest; his poem, like Ralegh's New World territory, was named in Elizabeth's honour. Having inhaled Durham House's heady philosophical atmosphere, Spenser even alludes to Giordano Bruno's theory of infinite universes when he wonders, 'if in every other star unseen / Of other worlds he happily should hear' (2. Proem. 2–3). That the group's speculative enthusiasm was rumoured to have touched on issues of theology, however, continued to hurt its reputation. Like Ralegh, Marlowe brooded on the symbolic importance of Spenser's main protagonist, Prince Arthur, the patron of magnificence. But whereas Ralegh recreates Arthur's dream (1.9.13–15) in his 'Vision' of Spenser's achievement, Marlowe, who had read part of the poem in manuscript, had a more radical response. For in transforming Arthur's crest, 'Like to an Almond tree ymounted hye / On top of green *Selinis*' (1.7.32) into Tamburlaine's 'triple plume', 'Like to an almond tree y-mounted high / Upon the lofty and celestial mount / Of ever-green *Selinus*' (2 *Tamb.* 4.3.119–21), he proposed an alternative to Spenser's ethical and political commitments.

Three years before *The Faerie Queene*, Sidney's *Arcadia*, and *Tamburlaine* were published in 1590, Marlowe initiated a new literary period in which commercial drama successfully competed with poetry and fiction as being one of the most compelling media for exploring issues of contemporary ethics and politics. This shift, epitomized by Marlowe's displacement of Robert Greene as a figure of cultural pre-eminence, shows the impact of the public theatre in shaping literary reputations. What made this cultural change unusually significant was the fact that tragedy had the good fortune to become the primary mode through which the two greatest dramatists of the period, Marlowe and Shakespeare, influenced each other's interpretations of English history. Yet it is only by tentatively forgetting the importance of print that we can recover a sense of the manner in which Marlowe and Shakespeare conceived of their plays as being primarily staged and then, perhaps, subsequently published. When Marlowe died, only *Tamburlaine* and none of Shakespeare's plays had been printed. Although drama flourished through publication, interconnections between stage and page were complex.

Consider, for instance, the embarrassment Greene experienced due to Marlowe's success, when he either saw or heard that his work had been parodied on the stage. Having completed his twelfth work of prose fiction, Greene complained in *Perimedes the Blacksmith* (1588) about an otherwise unknown theatrical production in which he had been satirized in a play written by two 'Gentlemen Poets'. It was in this drama, he insists, that 'two mad-men of Rome' were made to attack with swords part of his literary motto (*Omne tulit punctum*), which had been emblazoned on their bucklers, and scoff that Greene could not make his verses 'jet upon the stage in tragical buskins, every word filling the mouth ... daring God out of heaven with that Atheist *Tamburlan*'.[14] Greene was fond of using '*omne tulit punctum qui miscuit utile dulci*' (he gains every point who mixes use and delight), a famous phrase from Horace's *Art of Poetry*, on his title pages. And he must have been stunned to discover that his poetic creed had been appropriated as the centrepiece of a spectacle of derision by these now unidentifiable collaborative playwrights who favoured Marlowe's exciting and less temperate new drama. But even though his own work had begun to appear dated by comparison, Greene responds that he would rather be considered Diogenes' ass than emulate 'such mad and scoffing poets' who were 'bred of Merlin's race', punning on a variation (Marlin) of Marlowe's surname. Rejecting Marlowe's drama as a bad precedent, he vows instead to 'keep my old course to palter up something in Prose', claiming that he had only answered 'in print what they have offered on the stage'. There is no record of when Greene became a dramatist.[15] But it is likely that the failure of *Alphonsus, King of Aragon*, his answer to *Tamburlaine*, caused him temporarily to retreat into print, after which he ultimately abandoned romance. Greene's attack on Marlowe consequently reveals a faultline dividing the University Wits on the status of drama that was caused by the sudden cultural shift towards theatre occasioned by his rival's success.

A year later, convinced that his romance *Menaphon* would be overlooked because of the growing fascination with staged tragedy, Greene invited his younger friend Thomas Nashe to demonstrate its relevance to the contemporary scene. Nashe responded by attacking Marlowe's tragedies as pretentious and dismissing Thomas Kyd, the author of *The Spanish Tragedy*, as incompetent. Marlowe, Nashe writes, is one of the 'vain glorious Tragedians' and 'idiot Art-masters, that intrude themselves to our ears as the Alchemists of eloquence, who (mounting on the stage of arrogance) think to out-brave better pens with their swelling bombast of bragging blank verse' (3: 311). He uses poetry to 'vent' his angry 'manhood' in 'the spacious volubility of a drumming decasyllabon'. Marlowe is, Nashe continues, no better than Kyd, whose writing ('Seneca read by candle light') is marred by plagiarism, deficient scholarship, and mistranslation. Sharing Greene's antitheatrical prejudice, Nashe mocks the growing number of theatregoers prepared to 'repose eternity in the mouth of a Player' and urges 'the Gentlemen Students of Both Universities' to prefer the tempered eloquence of Greene's '*Arcadian Menaphon*' (3: 12). But Nashe's celebration of an extemporaneous wit capable of fulfilling the highest expectations of art fits his own style better than Greene's, and at the end of his encomium he coyly directs readers to his new satirical pamphlet *The Anatomy of Absurdity* in which he attacks romance writers who aspire to be 'the Homer of Women' (1: 12). 'See how far they swerve from their purpose', he now jests, 'who with Greene colours seek to garnish such Gorgon-like shapes' (1: 16). This betrayal becomes less surprising, however, once we recognize that Greene discredits his own works as 'vanities' in his repentance tracts and adopted a new motto *sero sed serio* (late but in earnest) to signify his change.

Marlowe's overreaching rhetoric also remained vulnerable to Nashe's sarcasm, but his later recollection in *Lenten Stuff* of how 'poor deceased Kit Marlowe' had treated him 'like a friend' (3: 131) indicates that their relationship had changed. Around 1594, Nashe prepared *Dido, Queen of Carthage* for publication and composed a lost elegy on Marlowe, which prefaced some copies. This did not, however, rule out an element of irreverence, and in *Lenten Stuff* he invokes Marlowe's 'diviner Muse' as prelude to his own comic version of *Hero and Leander* (3: 195–201). In his Preface to *Menaphon*, Nashe praised contemporary writers, including Watson and Peele. But even before publication of *The Faerie Queene* made it a contemporary classic, he selects only 'Master *Spenser*, the miracle of wit, to bandy line by line for my life, in the honour of England, against Spain, France, Italy, and all the world' (3: 323). Nashe's preference for Spenser over Marlowe and Kyd indicates the reverence with which Spenser and Sidney were held. Sidney, who died in 1586, had heightened pastoral romance with epic grandeur, written influential literary criticism, and completed a splendid sonnet sequence, paralleling the genres used by most of the wits. Lodge's defence of poetry preceded Sidney's, Greene cultivated the genres of romance, pastoral, and lyric Sidney favoured, and Nashe wrote an ornate preface for the first edition of *Astrophil and Stella*. Spenser, who had been absent from the London scene for almost a decade, embodied this tradition. The Tamburlaine phenomenon consequently forced writers to reconsider their political and ethical commitments. 'If Spenser sees human identity as conferred by living service to legitimate authority, to the yoked power of God and state', Greenblatt writes, 'Marlowe sees identity established at those moments in which order...is violated.' While 'Spenser's heroes strive for balance and control', Greenblatt continues, 'Marlowe's strive to shatter the restraints upon their desires.'[16] Indeed, Marlowe produces in *Tamburlaine* what Patrick Cheney describes as a 'theatrical improvisation in the Spenserian manner' that proposes a comprehensive challenge to the artistic, political, erotic, and theological premises that define his poetic programme.[17] *Tamburlaine, Part One* was Marlowe's most audacious play, and neither he nor his contemporaries ever exceeded its boldness.

Greene's strategy for dealing with Marlowe in the theatre was to write morally acceptable alternatives to *Tamburlaine* and *Doctor Faustus*. In *Alphonus, King of Aragon*, Alphonsus's career recapitulates Tamburlaine's, beginning with a series of combats for sovereignty with lesser kings, continuing with the investiture of his surrogates, and ending with his marriage to the daughter of his greatest rival. His fate is sanctioned by the gods, summarized by his brag, 'I clap up *Fortune* in a cage of gold, / To make her turn her wheel as I think best' (lines 1481–2) which echoes Tamburlaine's claim, 'I hold the Fates bound fast in iron chains, / And with my hand turn Fortune's wheel about' (*1 Tamb.* 1.2.174–5). 'In all this', writes J. Churton Collins, 'we have Tamburlaine – and Tamburlaine crudely – over again.'[18] *Alphonsus* has heightened language, exotic locations, and ample violence, but lacks Marlowe's moral complexity. Instead, Greene splits his play between Alphonsus, the trustworthy and forgiving legitimate heir of Aragon, who fights to recover his throne, and Amurack, the blaspheming, sadistic, and unscrupulous villain he conquers. In *Friar Bacon and Friar Bungay*, Greene repeats this procedure by offering his audience a reparative variation on *Doctor Faustus*. Indicating that damnation is not inevitable, Friar Bacon, the disillusioned conjurer, rejects Marlovian tragedy in recognizing that 'repentance can do much,.../ To wash the wrath of high Jehovah's ire, / And make thee as a new born babe from sin' (lines 1843–9).

The University Wits unanimously responded to *Tamburlaine* by attempting to negate its disturbing vision of heroism in Greene's *Alphonsus* and *Orlando Furioso*; his collaboration with Lodge, *A Looking-Glass for London and England*; Lodge's *Wounds of Civil War*; and Peele's *Battle of Alcazar*. Yet even when supplemented by the anonymous *Locrine*, *Selimus*, and *The Troublesome Reign of King John*, these plays collectively fail either to meet Marlowe's intellectual challenge or match his literary standard. Peter Berek consequently writes that at a time when Henslowe's diary reveals 'the continuous popularity of *Tamburlaine*,' these plays – which he calls *Tamburlaine*'s weak sons – 'invite their audiences to condemn characters for bursting the restraints of conventional beliefs and codes of conduct'.[19] Despite some shared pieties about power, however, these 'weak' writers register a wide range of reactions to *Tamburlaine*, from Greene's martial triumphalism in *Alphonsus* to Peele's ironic account of 'three bold kings' who 'Fall to the earth contending for a crown' in *The Battle of Alcazar*.[20] *Tamburlaine*'s theatrical sons were not weak in the same way, and if the University Wits were unable to engage Marlowe in a significant dialogue on the question of political power, Shakespeare certainly was. Although his second and third parts of *Henry VI* are indebted to *Tamburlaine* and *The Jew of Malta* for their rhetoric of ambition and subterfuge, this influence is subordinated to a very different conception of historical process, based on the perception of weakness, instead of strength, as the defining characteristic of human experience.

Greene, who was acutely aware of his audience's changing tastes in literary fashion, panicked twice at the thought of being displaced, and in doing so he chronicled two of the most important events in English literature. He first panicked in *Perimedes* in 1588 when he felt threatened by Marlowe's success in creating modern tragedy. Then, in *Greene's Groatsworth of Wit*, purportedly written on his deathbed in 1592, he feared that Shakespeare would surpass even Marlowe by monopolizing the medium Marlowe had used to marginalize Greene's own literary efforts. In his famous open letter to Marlowe, Nashe, and Peele (heavily edited by Henry Chettle, who apparently enhanced the text he transcribed), Greene mocked Shakespeare as an 'upstart Crow, beautified with our feathers, that, with his *Tiger's heart wrapt in a Player's hide*, supposes he is as well able to bombast out a blank verse as the best of you'. He is, Greene concludes, 'in his own conceit the only Shake-scene in a country'.[21] Henslowe's records show that several months earlier *1 Henry VI*, performed by Lord Strange's Men at the Rose, was far more popular than the older dramas by Greene, Marlowe, and Kyd that played with it. What Greene appears to be saying is that Shakespeare is a player turned playwright who has learned to 'shake' the stage with blank verse modelled on Marlowe's that rivals his achievement. Greene's rapacious 'Shake-scene' is imagined through a line that recalls phrasing from the yet unpublished *3 Henry VI*, which is cited to seal the allusion to its author. There, the Duke of York, whose son Rutland has been savagely murdered by Queen Margaret's ally Clifford, rejects her cruel invitation to wipe his tears with a handkerchief dipped in his child's blood, by saying:

> O tiger's heart wrapp'd in a woman's hide!
> How couldst thou drain the life-blood of the child,
> To bid the father wipe his eyes withal,
> And yet be seen to wear a woman's face?[22]

In drawing a double analogy between himself, as the beaten York surrendering his paper crown, and Shakespeare, as the inhumane Queen Margaret, tormenting her doomed victim, Greene casts himself and Shakespeare in a fatal contention for poetic kingship. He and the University Wits were under attack by a merciless and unnatural predator: the monstrous crow with a tiger's heart, evoked by Greene's mixed metaphor for Shakespeare, who both robs and devours his rivals.

Yet in his second panic Greene mistook the deeper cause of Shakespeare's new prominence: his unusual ability to elicit empathy, based on a perception of tragic loss as the defining characteristic of human experience. It was this quality that so impressed Nashe, who noted how unusually moved audience members had been in mourning Talbot's death, when *1 Henry VI* was presented by Lord Strange's Men at the Rose in 1592. 'How would it have joyed brave *Talbot*,' he writes, to 'triumph again on the Stage, and have his bones new embalmed with the tears of ten thousand spectators' (1: 212). What Greene never understood was that Shakespeare's relation to Marlowe can be better construed as an open-ended intellectual collaboration than an act of plagiarism. It was during this period that Shakespeare and Marlowe made a remarkable impact on each other's conceptions of tragedy while working on hybrid plays that are now commonly categorized as histories. Marlowe, unlike Greene, does not seem to have been antagonized by Shakespeare's rise to prominence. On the contrary, he seems to have understood that in *Henry VI* Shakespeare views vulnerability rather than strength and self-assertion as the defining feature of human identity. He seems to have been particularly fascinated by Shakespeare's examination of the weak king dilemma, which caused him to base *Edward II* on *Henry VI*, after having consulted the same chronicle histories Shakespeare had previously used to flesh out the Wars of the Roses. Conforming to Shakespeare's tragic paradigm, King Edward, Tamburlaine's opposite, now sombrely asks: 'But what are kings, when regiment is gone, / But perfect shadows in a sunshine day?' (5.1.26–7). Inspired in turn by *Edward II*, Shakespeare would go on in *Richard II* to develop an even more eloquent language of loss, in a project that would climax in *Hamlet* and *King Lear*. What Greene did not understand was that it was not Queen Margaret's Marlovian triumph that was the hallmark of Shakespeare's new

drama – although it is splendidly represented – but the saddened voice of
Northumberland, who, moved by York's suffering, concedes: 'Had he been
slaughter-man to all my kin, / I should not for my life but weep with him, / To
see how inly sorrow gripes his soul' (1.4.169–71). Marlowe became famous
by creating Tamburlaine, the Scythian shepherd who mastered the world. In
deposing Henry VI, the king who would be shepherd, Shakespeare staged
a spectacle of failure that would resonate through his greatest tragedies. By
August of 1592, overwhelmed by the rise of Shakespearean tragedy within
chronicle history, Nashe broke with Greene's antitheatrical bias and became
an outspoken advocate of commercial theatre, whose tragedies, he writes
in *Pierce Penniless*, are 'more stately furnished than ever it was in the time
of Roscius' (1: 215). His enthusiasm was enhanced by the fact that he currently counted himself in the service of Ferdinando Stanley, Lord Strange,
whose company had first performed *1 Henry VI* earlier that year. Indeed,
Gary Taylor even presses the highly controversial proposition that Nashe
collaborated on it.[23]

Contemporary literary criticism has come to appreciate Marlowe and
Shakespeare's involvement in each other's work. Scholars have especially
illuminated Shakespeare's appropriation and containment of Marlowe's poetics, showing how Tamburlaine's evocation of 'That perfect bliss and sole
felicity, / The sweet fruition of an earthly crown' (2.7.28–9), informs Richard
of Gloucester's rapture: 'How sweet a thing it is to wear a crown, / Within
whose circuit is Elysium / And all that poets feign of bliss and joy' (*3 Henry VI*
1.2.29–31). Charles Forker, however, perceptively documents the 'theatrical
and stylistic interchange between the two dramatists' that took place while
both were writing between 1591 and 1592 in a relationship that approaches
'symbiosis'.[24] Although their writing chronologies are a matter of debate,
Shakespeare seems to have initiated their dialogue with *Henry VI*, which,
Jonathan Bate explains, 'opens where *Tamburlaine* closes: with the question of what to do after a conquering warrior is dead and there is no single
strong inheritor to take over'.[25] In opposition to Marlowe's myths of power,
Shakespeare revitalizes the medieval *de casibus* tradition which records 'the
fall of illustrious men', splits the Marlovian hero into moral opposites, includes a broader class model, and varies his rhetoric, as he replaces ambition
and imperialism with self-division and civil war. Marlowe, in turn, was so
intrigued by Shakespeare's challenging reinterpretation that he used *2* and
3 Henry VI as models for *Edward II*, his own experiment in dramatizing
English chronicle history. The immediate consequence of his abrupt change
in direction was a loss of the mighty line, which he sacrificed to achieve
greater breadth and complexity in the play's characterization. Here, in place
of a single commanding figure, Marlowe presented clashing factions, as both

Henry VI and Edward II fall through their respective weaknesses of spirituality and sensuality at the insistence of more ambitious rivals, York and Mortimer, who pay for their aspirations with their lives. The first published titles of Shakespeare and Marlowe's parallel histories preserve this balance between protagonist and antagonist. A version of Shakespeare's third part of *Henry VI* was initially printed as *The True Tragedie of Richard Duke of Yorke, and the death of good King Henrie the Sixt*...(1595), a year after Marlowe's rejoinder had appeared as *The troublesome raigne and lamentable death of Edward the second, King of England: with the tragicall fall of proud Mortimer*. Their titles' shared billing emphasizes Shakespeare and Marlowe's mutual interest in conceiving of English history as revenge tragedy, forever doubled in the unremitting exchange of victor and victim.

By the time Marlowe wrote *Edward II*, Shakespeare had probably already completed the first tetralogy, which, with the addition of *Richard III*, submits 'the scourge of God' to the new providential order of Henry VII in a celebration of Tudor sovereignty ending the Wars of the Roses. Suddenly aware of how conservatively Shakespeare had concluded the series, Marlowe might have intended *Edward II* to resist this movement towards self-justifying moral closure by recalling Shakespeare's insights into the inherent instability of rule, which is invariably a product of self-interest. Marlowe had good reason to be impressed by *The True Tragedy*: it is a radical critique of kingship. What makes the play especially shocking is that York's claim to the throne is stronger than Henry's, who admits his own illegitimacy even as he asks his followers, motivated principally by private revenge, to defend his status. Marlowe's chronicle drama is unique in its elimination of a providential teleology and its suggestion that moral choices are made primarily on the basis of self-interest affirmed through the exercise of power. *Edward II* does not passively endorse Shakespearean history. Instead, it explores the issue of legitimacy that had been posed by *The True Tragedy* but which had been subsequently shaded over by the imperial and nationalist aspirations of *1 Henry VI* (staged last in the trilogy as a 'prequel' in 1592) and *Richard III*, Shakespeare's most doctrinaire early histories. Yet in what is perhaps his last play, *The Massacre at Paris*, Marlowe unpredictably follows Shakespeare's practice of writing what approaches political propaganda, almost as a form of atonement for his more troubling inquiry into historical origins. After Marlowe's death, Shakespeare in his second tetralogy continued to explore the issues they had raised by re-evaluating *Edward II* in *Richard II*, a work that implicitly acknowledges Marlowe's influence, even as it overwhelms its source with nostalgia for a lost sacred order and a more compelling account of history, from the victim's perspective, as perpetual loss.

Shakespeare was so acute in revising Marlovian tragedy because he already had a strong alternative to it in Kyd's *Spanish Tragedy*, which was first staged at approximately the same time as *Tamburlaine*. Written primarily in blank verse with a few passages in prose and rhyme, Kyd's drama shares with Marlowe's the distinction of having established the most effective poetic medium for Elizabethan tragedy. What was unique about Kyd's tragedy, however, was its emphasis on the psychology of victimization. 'Not only *The Spanish Tragedy*', writes Lukas Erne, 'but all of Kyd's plays turn around a thematic pattern constituted of loss, grief, and revenge', as 'they place at their centre a certain type of character: the victim of adverse fortune trying to cope with his or her loss', in a plot involving complex intrigue in a taut dramatic structure. It is this kind of plotting that Marlowe would first adopt in *The Jew of Malta*, in which his 'dramatic style', according to Erne, 'was so clearly affected by *The Spanish Tragedy*'.[26] The most characteristic elements of Kyd's drama are its intense metatheatricality, its blend of mannered elegy and raving madness, and its account of nihilistic revenge. At his best, Kyd dramatized a prevailing sense of disillusionment. Our knowledge of these connections is seriously hindered by the disappearance of his version of *Hamlet*, but it seems likely that Kyd's hero, like Shakespeare's after him, voiced outrage, took revenge, and suffered annihilation in the general blood-letting. Kyd shared a writing room with Marlowe in 1591, whom he denounced for being 'intemperate and of a cruel heart' and for 'attempting privy injuries to men' (Steane, p. 7). Kyd's critique of Marlowe confirms a major difference in their literary reputations. While Marlowe made his mark in the rhetoric of violent triumph, Kyd was best known for expressive complaints voiced by desperate characters, resolved to affirm their identities in terrifying acts of despair. Tamburlaine's boast, 'Is it not passing brave to be a king, / And ride in triumph through Persepolis?' (2.5.53–4), and Hieronimo's lament, 'O eyes, no eyes, but fountains fraught with tears' (3.2.1), stereotype their difference. Hieronimo's volatile mixture of regret, melancholy, and resolve inspired some of the best writing of the next thirty years to explore with even greater intensity the psychology of social dislocation.

Marlowe and Shakespeare's final literary exchange appears to have occurred in the context of poetic patronage. Outbreaks of plague in London between 1592 and 1594 led to restraints on playing, and it was then that Shakespeare cultivated a patron, Henry Wriothesley, the third Earl of Southampton, to whom he dedicated *Venus and Adonis* (1593) and *The Rape of Lucrece* (1594). In *Venus and Adonis*, Shakespeare turned to the Ovidian mythological narrative that Marlowe had perfected in *Hero and Leander*. It is possible that he saw Marlowe's poem in manuscript and posed Venus's failed enticement of Adonis against Leander's successful seduction of Hero as a kind of literary diptych, creating contrasting variations on the theme of tragic desire. Here satisfaction and denial both lead to death. Shakespeare might even have conceded that *Hero and Leander* was better than his own wildly successful *Venus and Adonis*. Although based on a text by Musaeus, Marlowe's epyllion shows a greater proficiency in mastering Ovid's blend of passion and wit. In a well-known series of complaints in the Sonnets (78–80, 82–6), Shakespeare expresses his fear that a rival poet – a 'worthier pen' with 'a better spirit', known for 'the proud sail of his great verse' – will replace him. Despite a plethora of candidates, Marlowe remains the most *credible* rival to merit Shakespeare's anxiety about being outwritten during the plague years. Shakespeare might even playfully allude to *Doctor Faustus*, when he speaks of his rival's 'spirit, by spirits taught to write, / Above a mortal pitch' (Sonnet 86, lines 5–6) in language that Chapman earnestly repeats in seeking assistance from Marlowe's 'free soul' in 'th' eternal clime' of 'spirits immortal' in continuing *Hero and Leander* (3: 183–98). The modern suspicion that Shakespeare and Marlowe were identical has the consequent disadvantage of silencing the artistic and intellectual dialogue embedded in their works.

Shortly after Robert Greene died on 3 September 1592, Gabriel Harvey in *Four Letters and Certain Sonnets* described, with satisfaction, how his enemy – whose pamphlets had made him 'king of the paper stage' – had passed away, sick, indigent, and lice-infested, owing money for his funeral. Harvey's lack of empathy, however, cannot erase one particularly touching detail in his vignette. Amid the squalor, Greene's corpse, following his last wishes, had been crowned with a garland of bay leaves, commemorating his life as a poet. No matter how much he had played down his accomplishments, Greene staged his own death as a laureate. Marlowe never had that opportunity the following May. But his career symbolically began where Greene's ended: with an affirmation of his art. In his famous Prologue to *Tamburlaine*, Marlowe announced a change in direction for English Renaissance theatre, away from the 'conceits' of 'clownage', to a drama of 'high astounding terms', focused on power in history. His major achievement was permanently to enlarge the English literary canon, by transforming commercial drama into literature. But, as Greene looked on, Marlowe encountered in Shakespeare a brilliant rival who would inevitably diminish his paramount reputation once the London theatres reopened in 1594.

NOTES

1. Preface to *Menaphon: Camilla's Alarum to Slumbering Euphues*, in *The Works of Thomas Nashe*, 5 vols., ed. Ronald B. McKerrow (Oxford: Blackwell, 1958), 3: 315. Further references in the text are to this edition.
2. William Covell, *Polymanteia* (London, 1595), sig. R3ʳ.

3. Francis Meres, *Palladis Tamia, Wit's Treasury, Being the Second Part of Wit's Commonwealth* (London, 1598), p. 283.

4. *The Spanish Tragedy* (2.1.3–10), ed. J. R. Mulryne (London: A. and C. Black, 1989).

5. Charles Nicholl, *The Reckoning: The Murder of Christopher Marlowe* (University of Chicago Press, 1992), p. 92.

6. David Riggs, *Shakespeare's Heroical Histories: 'Henry VI' and Its Literary Tradition* (Cambridge, MA: Harvard University Press, 1971), pp. 49 and 51.

7. C. L. Barber, *Creating Elizabethan Tragedy: The Theater of Marlowe and Kyd* (University of Chicago Press, 1988), p. 15.

8. Qtd by Christopher Hill in *Intellectual Origins of the English Revolution* (Oxford: Clarendon Press, 1965), pp. 32–3.

9. 'John Philopatris', *An Advertisement written to a Secretary of My L. Treasurer* (Antwerp, 1592), p. 18.

10. J. B. Steane, *Marlowe: A Critical Study* (Cambridge University Press, 1965), p. 20.

11. See Stephen Greenblatt, *Shakespearean Negotiations: The Circulation of Social Energy in Renaissance England* (Berkeley: University of California Press, 1988), pp. 21–39; and Thomas Harriot, *A Brief and True Report of the New Found Land of Virginia* (New York: Dover, 1972), p. 26.

12. Michael Rudick, *The Poems of Sir Walter Ralegh: A Historical Edition* (Tempe: Renaissance English Text Society, 1999), p. 174.

13. See James P. Bednarz, 'The Collaborator as Thief: Ralegh's (Re)Vision of *The Faerie Queene*', ELH 63 (1996), 279–307.

14. Robert Greene, *The Life and Works of Robert Greene*, 15 vols., ed. Alexander Grosart (London: Huth Library, 1881–6), 7: 7–8.

15. E. K. Chambers, *The Elizabethan Stage*, 4 vols. (Oxford: Clarendon Press, 1923), 3: 323–5, guesses that Greene began writing plays soon after he arrived in London 'about 1586'.

16. Stephen Greenblatt, *Renaissance Self-Fashioning: From More to Shakespeare* (University of Chicago Press, 1991), p. 222.

17. Patrick Cheney, *Marlowe's Counterfeit Profession: Ovid, Spenser, Counter-Nationhood* (University of Toronto Press, 1997), p. 116.

18. *The Plays and Poems of Robert Greene*, 2 vols., ed. J. Churton Collins (Oxford: Clarendon Press, 1905), 1: 72.

19. Peter Berek, 'Tamburlaine's Weak Sons: Imitation as Interpretation Before 1593', RenD 13 (1982), 55–82.

20. George Peele, *The Battle of Alcazar*, lines 51–2, in *The Life and Works of George Peele*, 3 vols., ed. Charles Tyler Prouty (New Haven: Yale University Press, 1952–70).

21. Henry Chettle and Robert Greene, *Greene's Groatsworth of Wit, Bought with a Million of Repentance* (Binghamton: Center for Medieval and Renaissance Studies, 1994), pp. 84–5.

22. Qtd from *The Riverside Shakespeare*, ed. G. Blakemore Evans, et al., 2nd edn (Boston: Houghton Mifflin, 1997), 1.4.137–40.

23. Gary Taylor, 'Shakespeare and Others: the Authorship of *Henry the Sixth, Part One*', MRDE 7 (1995), 145–205.

24. Charles R. Forker, introduction to *Edward II* (Manchester University Press, 1994), p. 20. See also his introduction to *Richard II* (Walton-on-Thames: Thomas Nelson, 2002), pp. 159–64.
25. Jonathan Bate, *The Genius of Shakespeare* (London: Picador, 1997), p. 108.
26. Lukas Erne, *Beyond 'The Spanish Tragedy': A Study of the Works of Thomas Kyd* (Manchester University Press, 2001), pp. xi and 58.

READING LIST

Barber, C. L. *Creating Elizabethan Tragedy: The Theater of Marlowe and Kyd*. University of Chicago Press, 1988.

Bate, Jonathan. *The Genius of Shakespeare*. London: Picador, 1997.

Brooke, Nicholas. 'Marlowe as Provocative Agent in Shakespeare's Early Plays'. *ShS* 14 (1961), 34–44.

Cheney, Patrick. *Marlowe's Counterfeit Profession: Ovid, Spenser, Counter-Nationhood*. University of Toronto Press, 1997.

Ellis-Fermor, Una. 'Marlowe and Greene: a Note on their Relations as Dramatic Artists'. In Don Cameron Allen (ed.), *Studies in Honor of T. W. Baldwin*. Urbana: University of Illinois Press, 1958, pp. 136–49.

Greenblatt, Stephen. *Shakespearean Negotiations: The Circulation of Social Energy in Renaissance England*. Berkeley: University of California Press, 1988.

Leech, Clifford. '*Edward II*: English History'. *Christopher Marlowe: Poet for the Stage*. Anne Lancashire (ed.). New York: AMS Press, 1986.

Nicholl, Charles. *The Reckoning: The Murder of Christopher Marlowe*. University of Chicago Press, 1992.

Shapiro, James. *Rival Playwrights: Marlowe, Jonson, Shakespeare*. New York: Columbia University Press, 1991.

Shirley, James. *Thomas Harriot: A Biography*. Oxford: Clarendon Press, 1983.

Strathmann, Ernest A. 'The Textual Evidence for "The School of Night"'. *MLN* 56 (1941), 176–86.

7

GEORGIA E. BROWN

Marlowe's poems and classicism

For modern readers perhaps nothing is more off-putting than the subject of classicism, with its unfortunate connotations of privilege and cultural exclusivity. In this chapter I want to show how classical culture spawns meanings, overturns ideas, amuses, shocks, and makes new in Marlowe's hands. It is far from dead, and neither does it necessarily work to confirm white, male privilege. The Renaissance had a more inclusive view of the classics than we do.[1] Virgil, for example, was accepted as the author of the pseudo-Virgilian text known as *Virgil's Gnat*, so the arch poet of panegyric, the high priest of epic and imperial expansion, was also the author of a mock-heroic trifle about an insect. The classical authors that Marlowe chose to translate and/or imitate in his poems, including Ovid, Lucan, Musaeus, and, in 'The Passionate Shepherd', Callimachus, were all recognized as dissident writers both by their contemporaries and by the Renaissance.[2] Marlowe chose to identify himself with writers who, in various ways, resisted the political, moral, gender, and aesthetic ideals epitomized by Virgil's *Aeneid*, the text that has come to embody classicism for us. Our appreciation of Marlowe's poems is not only hampered by our narrow understanding of the classical ideal, we also prefer texts that confirm our values of individualism, distinction, and authenticity of voice. We denigrate texts, like Marlowe's poems, which are translations or imitations because they supposedly lack originality, and conform to collaborative models of production which we are only just beginning to appreciate. We tend to agree with James VI, who once advised writers to avoid translation because it impairs one's sovereignty: 'ze are bound, as to a staik, to follow that buikis phrasis, quhilk ze translate'.[3]

We remember Marlowe as a dramatist, but what impressed his contemporaries and immediate successors most was his poetry, especially *Hero and Leander* and 'The Passionate Shepherd'. Marlowe's poems are central to his achievement, not only because he is one of the greatest poetic innovators of the Renaissance, a young man with huge, even arrogant, ambitions to do things in his verse that had never been done before, but also because the poems deal with some of Marlowe's fundamental preoccupations. As imitations and translations, they engage formally, as well as thematically, with ambiguous identities, and explore the margins where the distinctions between self and other, the original and its representation, become confused. Not only do poems such as *Lucan's First Book* and 'The Passionate Shepherd' explore the heroic and lyric modes which constitute the twin poles of Marlowe's dramatic imagination, they are also spaces of continuing confrontations and mediations between the present and the past, and between English and alien elements. Translation and imitation are ways of negotiating spatial and temporal distances, and Marlowe's poems address the very issues that are also raised by his history plays and his dramas of colonial ambition.

The acquisition of Latin by Renaissance schoolboys was a male 'puberty rite', and Marlowe's display of classical erudition advertises his membership of a homosocial elite, but the Elizabethan grammar school system instilled its subjects with many kinds of literacy, including emotional literacy. Imitation of the classics not only taught boys the elements of rhetoric, it also ensured that the articulation of feeling would follow certain conventions.[4] One of the most common models for grief was the classical figure of Hecuba, and Hamlet gauges the truth of his own feeling by its conformity to and divergences from the description of Hecuba's grief as recited by the players (2.2.416–601).[5] In this sense, classical texts helped people to express emotions and desires, and this is equally true of non-dramatic texts like Ovid's *Heroides* or Lucan's *Pharsalia*. If Marlowe and other Elizabethans were taught to feel by the classics, as well as taught how to think and speak, then they inhabit, and are inhabited by, a bilingual culture in the most fundamental ways.

Living between two cultural codes and two linguistic codes, as Marlowe clearly does in his poems, has the most profound consequences for Marlowe's understanding of language and its relation to meaning, especially because one of those codes is Latin. In the preface to his own translation of Ovid's *Heroides*, John Dryden notes that Latin has a predilection for puns:

> 'Tis almost impossible to translate verbally, and well, at the same time; for the Latin (a most severe and compendious language) often expresses that in one word, which either the barbarity or the narrowness of modern tongues cannot supply in more.[6]

Latin is a compressed language and simultaneously evokes a variety of meanings in a highly efficient manner. It is also a language of mutated forms. It is made out of the rearrangement of elements in declensions and conjugations, where a root or syllable is yoked to prefixes and suffixes. English words are more fixed in form, and uninflected English is also much more tied to sequence than Latin is, with the result that Latin can juxtapose sounds and set them against conceptual relationships with more freedom. Translation also raises the question of meaning and where it resides. Should a translation privilege matter over the original's style, or vice versa? As a Renaissance Protestant or Catholic, familiar with a medieval tradition of allegorizing classical texts, does one produce a Christianized translation because the meaning of the text is actually defined by its relationship to eternal truth? To what extent does the meaning of a text lie in its aural and visual codes? How, for example, would you translate a pun, and what would you do with an anagram or an acrostic?

'On the Death of Sir Roger Manwood'

'On the Death of Sir Roger Manwood' (probably written in 1592) is Marlowe's least read poem, which is unfortunate because it is an excellent example of the way Marlowe uses classical culture to undermine the social and political authority classicism is supposed to uphold. Critics have tried to explain Marlowe's authorship of the Latin elegy 'On the Death of Sir Roger Manwood' by arguing that Marlowe harboured a soft spot for a fellow Kentish man, who was one of the judges on the bench during the hearing in December 1589 that cleared Marlowe of any wrongdoing in the death of William Bradley. However, while Manwood was a successful judge, who rose to be Lord Chief Baron of the Exchequer, his final years were characterized by serious and repeated charges of misfeasance. In 1591, for example, he was exposed as trying to sell one of the offices in his gift and rebuked by the queen. The lieutenant of Dover Castle charged him with perverting the course of justice, and the suffragan Bishop of Dover accused him of selling the queen's pardon in a murder case for £240. Manwood may not have been more greedy than other Elizabethan judges, but in 1592, the year of his death, he was confined to his own house, by order of the Privy Council, as the result of a complaint against him brought by a goldsmith. Manwood was only released three weeks later on making humble submission. The Privy Council was investigating his extended possession of a gold chain, which the goldsmith had handed over as security for a loan, and Manwood had insulted them with the high-handed observation that those with hollow causes always run to the powerful, and where truth counts for nothing, might prevails – a protestation of victimization that may strike us as a bit rich coming from the Lord Chief Baron of the Exchequer in dispute with a goldsmith.

Given Latin's penchant for punning and wordplay, and the circumstances of Manwood's later career, there is a hitherto unacknowledged wit in Marlowe's elegy, which derives from the spatial and acoustic nature of words and from the particular nature of Latin as described by Dryden. At one point the *guiltless man*, 'insons', is called upon to weep because his protector, Manwood, is dead.[7] The word 'in-sons' also suggests the idea of being without sound, and the guiltless person is soundless until he weeps. When the poem cries, *Jealousy spare the man*, 'Livor, parce viro', it may well be acknowledging the bad press that surrounded Manwood just before he died. Like 'insons', the phrase 'Livor, parce viro' is a particularly Latin form of wit. The word 'viro' is actually contained within the word 'livor', albeit with a rearrangement of letters. 'Livor', *jealousy*, can indeed spare the man, as it can spell out 'viro' and still have the letter 'l' to spare. The play of word within word is a common feature of Latin tomb inscriptions, as the idea of mortal remains, encased in a tomb, encased in words, plays its own games with secrecy and revelation, emptiness, and reference. At other times, Marlowe's puns introduce a sub-text of money and riches that alludes, uncomfortably, to the facts of Manwood's greedy old age. Manwood is described as 'rigido vulturque latroni', *a vulture to the hardened criminal*, a phrase which praises Manwood, at the same time as it suggests that he is the kind of scavenger that will pervert justice for money. He is also the 'fori lumen', *the light of government*, but the Roman forum was not only the centre of Roman politics, it was also a marketplace, and the term implies the commercialization of the political and juridical which was the cause of Manwood's disgrace.

The elegy is self-conscious about its own elegiac conventions and their limitations, the shores of Acheron are, after all, 'effoetas', *worn out*, as well as *dim*, and Marlowe's elegy is ambivalent, in the literal sense of having two (ambi) valences. It implies criticism and praise, and it looks to both Latin and English. The final line exemplifies its ambivalence: 'Famaque, marmorei superet monumenta sepulchri', *and your fame outlast the monuments of your marble sepulchre*. 'Fama' is a pun which invokes the divergent meanings of fame, rumour, and even ill repute, so the thing that might live for ever is Manwood's bad name. 'Marmorei' generates its own associations with Latin terms such as 'memorare', *to keep in memory*, 'mora' *delay*, perhaps with the idea that the elegy postpones forgetfulness, and 'mors' meaning *death*. At the same time, it invokes English words such as 'memory' and 'marmoreal' in a game of interlingual transposition. Elegies are conventionally aware of their material form, and Marlowe conceives of words, such as 'marmorei' and 'livor', as movable configurations of letters and syllables, rather than as fixed word-forms. The word-games both within and between languages extend the meaning of Marlowe's elegy and reshape thought by generating associations and differences through the formal patterns of words, through what words look like and sound like. If all this seems strange and far-fetched, this is because we have lost the sense of language as an aural and visual object, as something that is spatially conceived and materially determined. There are images, hidden agendas, and riddles embedded in the very textures of writing, which is not only conceived, in the Renaissance, as a transparent medium for communicating truths, but also as an opaque object that generates its own unpredictable meanings.

The visual and verbal games in the epitaph 'On the Death of Sir Roger Manwood' point to a material conception of language that is also articulated in Marlowe's other poems. This conception of language is one of the fundamental consequences of classicism and of living between two codes. The meanings thereby generated are oblique and esoteric, but this is part of their appeal. Paradoxically, as Quintilian notes in the *Institutio Oratoria* (9.2.64), emphasis is a form of occlusion, or hiding. In other words emphasis is achieved by leaving something latent, or hidden, for the audience to discover, and just because we have to work to find something, it does not mean that it is not there, or that it is coincidental.[8] Our idea of the classics is that they are restrained, unified, and uphold the principle of integrity, both on a structural and moral level. But Latin is prone to ambiguity, and through verbal patterning it raises the possibility of depths of meaning which undermine the drive to a clear-cut, simple conclusion. In Stoic and Renaissance Christian philosophical traditions, the puns, word games, and patterns, with their ridiculous yoking together of ideas, would not only have been construed as demonstrations of the plenitude of creation, but also as proof of the deep structural and conceptual coherence of a cosmos that is carefully designed.

Ovid's Elegies

Ovid's Elegies is the title of Marlowe's translation of Ovid's *Amores*, a sequence of three books of love poems addressed by a male poet–lover to his mistress. Each poem is a letter in which the poet describes his feelings in the developing relationship, but this is no ordinary romantic hero, but a man who is bitter, disloyal, violent, sarcastic, and over-sexed, as well as adoring, witty, and passionate. It is unclear when Marlowe undertook the translation of the *Amores* but most critics agree it dates from his time in Cambridge. The first edition included ten of Ovid's elegies (the Elizabethan term for epistolary poems of love or complaint), although later editions extended to translations of all three books. The first edition, which also included Sir John Davies's *Epigrams*, satirical poems which were always published with Marlowe's *Elegies*, was published without a date on the title page, but is thought to date from 1594–5. Such circumspection on the part of printers is usually a sign that there is something dangerous about the publication. Marlowe's decision to translate the *Amores* was certainly a scandalous one,

given that Ovid's text was widely held to be pornographic, and Marlowe's
Elegies were eventually banned by the censors in 1599.

Marlowe's meditation on the materiality of language, which is encouraged
by his familiarity with Latin, is also developed in *Ovid's Elegies*, which explore the different connotations of letters, whether as alphabetical symbols,
or material objects, or epistles, or in the sense of 'Letters' as a sublimated,
quasi-spiritual, artistic activity. For example, Book 1, Elegy 11 describes an
exchange of letters between the lovers and imagines the mistress reading and
writing. In 1.12 the poet curses the very tablets on which he writes, which
were made from wood covered with wax. Alluding to the fact that the writing tablets are folded double, and are hence physically duplicitous, the poet
curses his materials:

> Your name approves you made for such like things,
> The number two no good divining brings.
> Angry, I pray that rotten age you wracks,
> And sluttish white-mould overgrow the wax.
>
> (*OE* 1.12.27–30)

The idea that writing lies because of its physical nature, because of the substance on which it is written, is reinforced by the potential of wax to melt and
mutate. In writing and rewriting the *Amores*, Ovid and Marlowe both participate in a cult of good letters, and the very first elegy carefully establishes
their literary credentials and their awareness of literary conventions, defining their amatory style through a comparison of heroic and elegiac prosody,
where the elegiac metre is shorter than the heroic: 'Love slacked my muse,
and made my numbers soft' (1.1.22). Literature is defined by its mode of
consumption and the introductory elegy makes sure the reader knows that
the poems should be consumed as literary artefacts. However, the cult of
good letters is also, quite literally, a cult of the letter in *Ovid's Elegies*. In
1.3, the poet asks his mistress to love him so that she can become the subject
of his books:

> Be thou the happy subject of my books,
> That I may write things worthy thy fair looks.
> By verses horned Io got her name,
> And she to whom in shape of swan Jove came
> And she that on a feigned bull swam to land,
> Griping [sic] his false horns with her virgin hand.
>
> (*OE* 1.3.19–24)

Io was a mortal woman who was turned into a bull, and the reference to her
myth is yet another witty play with the materiality of writing, as Renaissance

children learned to write on hornbooks, a piece of wood covered with transparent horn, which allowed marks to be erased. Io is 'horned', in the sense that she has horns, because she has been turned into a heifer, and in the sense that she is made in writing: 'By verses horned Io got her name.' The story of Io is also a myth about how writing came into being. In Book 1 of the *Metamorphoses*, Ovid tells us that, after she had been turned into a heifer, and had lost the power of speech, Io identifies herself to her father by letters which she inscribes on the ground with her hoof (*Metamorphoses* 1.647–50). Io gets her name both in the primary scene of writing, as it is described in one of the mythological accounts of the birth of letters, and in the Elizabethan petty school, the practical birthplace of letters, where children scribbled away on their hornbooks, and were inducted in the processes of writing well, in all senses of the phrase.

However, there is something else at play in Marlowe's poem, an association between writing and turning which is suggested by the Latin terms 'versus' meaning *verse*, and the verb 'versare,' which means *to turn*. Line 22 refers to another famous story of metamorphosis, or turning, in the myth of Leda, who was turned into a swan, and line 23 refers to the myth of Europa, who was raped by Jove in the form of a bull. These lines are typical of *Ovid's Elegies* in that they introduce the threat of sexual violence at the moment they attempt seduction. The pun on 'horned' also suggests the cuckold's horns, and, like *Hero and Leander*, *Ovid's Elegies* establishes a link between metamorphosis, or turning, rhetorical power, and transgressive sexuality, which is central to Renaissance interpretations of Ovid. Turning is integral to verse. It is fundamental to metaphor and simile, and both poems exemplify the process whereby the *Metamorphoses*, with its tales of transformation and translation, becomes the quintessential *poetic* text in late Elizabethan England. What Marlowe picks up from Ovid is that literary texts display extreme technical and verbal agility, and furthermore that this rhetorical skill is sexualized. It is used to seduce, whether the object of seduction is the beloved or the reader, and in the case of *Ovid's Elegies* the beloved and the reader of the letters are one and the same. Rhetoric is used to mediate the desires of writers and readers with the result that reading and writing are configured as erotic transactions. Rhetoric even has its own erotic momentum and lets slip all kinds of innuendo which escape the control of the author.

The translation of the *Amores* was a big task. It was also a breathtaking instance of innovation and self-confidence, because it was not only the first translation of Ovid's text into English, it was also the first English text to use the rhymed heroic couplet for an extended piece of writing. Marlowe has yet to receive the credit due to him as one of the Renaissance's greatest poetic innovators. Marlowe is famous for his mighty line, and for his developments in blank verse, but he also put the heroic couplet on the map, after Nicholas Grimald's pioneering experiments with the form, in English, in *Tottel's Miscellany* (1557). Spatial effects are crucial to the couplet, which constructs meanings from the interplay of parts held in space by its strong form.[9] The patterning and arrangement of words carries a lot of the argument in the couplet, which exploits balance and contrast, and lends itself to the processes of comparison, juxtaposition, and apposition. The verse form of the couplet functions in much the same way as metaphor to suggest differences and similarities. Marlowe has not yet perfected his use of the couplet in *Ovid's Elegies*, which tends to think in lines, rather than in couplets, but Marlowe does succeed in arguing spatially. For example, by exploiting the placement of the words in the rhyme scheme, he suggests analogies between 'charms' and 'harms' (3.6.27–8); and he suggests a mutually constitutive relationship between the speaker and bad repute, by rhyming 'am I' and 'infamy' (3.6.71–2). In *Hero and Leander*, Marlowe perfects the heroic couplet, not only exploiting it to create a tone of refined, conversational fluency, but perfecting its comic and erotic potential. The rise and fall of the couplet movement lends itself to comic bathos, but its teasing rhythms also play games of invitation and delay, which collude with Marlowe's overlayering of the erotic and the poetic.

Read together, 'On the Death of Sir Roger Manwood', *Ovid's Elegies*, and 'The Passionate Shepherd' explore the different functions of elegy in Renaissance culture. An elegy was a poem of commemoration, but it was also a love lyric, and as such it had a potential to spill over into satire. *Ovid's Elegies* are a sustained meditation on the pathology of love, its pleasures, psychological perversions, and ideological functions. They are Marlowe's sonnet sequence, and the poet–lover finds himself drawn to a masochistic and sadistic relationship in which he equates virility with poetic success.[10] Nevertheless, while *Ovid's Elegies* are sexy and urbane, in contradistinction to the Spenserian idealization of chastity, they also question the values of urbanity by exposing the aggression and self-delusion of the male sexual sophisticate, and Marlowe's translation makes the speaker more aggressive and scandalous than Ovid. The sequence is full of programmatic statements about the nature of poetry, but those statements are frequently reductive: 'Toys and light elegies, my darts, I took, / Quickly soft words hard doors wide open strook' (2.1.21–2). Writing this kind of verse has the highly practical aim of getting sex, of getting the woman to open her doors, and the elegy is a sour exposé of the role played by the idealization of love in sexual and poetic ambition.

'The Passionate Shepherd'

'The Passionate Shepherd' (1599), like *Ovid's Elegies*, must be read in relation to the Elizabethan political context because it interrogates pastoral and
love lyric, favoured modes of political address to a monarch who Spenser
famously cast as 'fayre Elisa, Queene of Shepheardes all' (*The Shepheardes
Calender, Aprill* 34). Any courtship situation figures the political backdrop
of Elizabethan England because of the implicit pun on court as a verb and
court as a noun, and private love is imagined through its convergences and
divergences from the public world of sentimentalized political transaction.
In 'The Passionate Shepherd', the speaker is a compound of dominance and
suppliance, and the petition for favour can be interpreted as a petition for
patronage. Furthermore, in the context of the model of collaborative authorship which this pastoral lyric exploits, and then occasions, in its implicit
demand for a reply, the petition for favour is also a petition for friendship,
with all the sexual ambiguity latent in the term. It is a request for intellectual companionship that is open to erotic reconstruction.[11] 'The Passionate
Shepherd' was, and still is, one of the most famous Elizabethan lyrics, and
was endlessly copied, imitated, and answered through the seventeenth century. Marlowe's lyric presents itself as an ideal product of courtly society in
which he outdoes the courtiers at their own game. The poem is an idealization of rural life, an attenuation of the harsher historical realities of country
life, in which rusticity is appropriated for urbanity. Ralegh makes this point
when he replies to Marlowe in a poem that introduces time and process into
the prelapsarian ideal of Marlowe's pastoral. Ralegh's phrase, 'sorrow's fall'
(st. 3), invokes the Augustinian idea that sex after the Fall is never satisfying,
and Ralegh's time-drenched parody is critical of the utopianism of 'The Passionate Shepherd' and of Elizabeth's personal mythology of unaging, erotic
attraction.

When the first version of Marlowe's pastoral was published in *The Passionate Pilgrim* (1599), it did not have a title, and its conventional title, 'The
Passionate Shepherd to His Love', fixes the gender of the speaker, when there
is nothing in the poem that ties it to a male speaker or a female addressee,
except its general relation to the tradition of *carpe diem*. The lyric's favoured
figure of paronomasia, the alteration of a single letter, as in live/love, is a game
of sameness and difference, of aural, visual, and referential consonance and
dissonance, which redirects our attention to ambiguity as the principle that
governs the poem. As is also the case with *Hero and Leander*, equivoca-
tion makes 'The Passionate Shepherd' what it is: a masterpiece. In *Hero and
Leander*, the description of Leander (1.51–90) applies the conventions of the
female blazon to a man, as it invokes metamorphic myths, including those of

Circe, Narcissus, and Hippolytus, and demonstrates extreme poetic skill. It plays off what is materially visible against what is imagined, and the description of Leander comes to define the ambiguity of representation, as it comes to stand for the fact that any work of art, however accomplished, both is and is not what it claims to be. The description of Leander, like the text of 'The Passionate Shepherd', is a play of sameness and difference, of male and female, of past and present, of foreign, classical, and English. Ambiguous gender representation emerges as the supreme instance of artistic skill in the Renaissance, but this raises the issue of whether art is a civilizing force, or a force that perverts and is deceitful. The ambiguous speaker of 'The Passionate Shepherd', the girl–boys Hero and Leander, and the cross-dressed boys of the Elizabethan stage all share the same erotic charge, and exploit the hybridity whose representation is the ultimate test of artistic prowess in Elizabethan culture.

As we might expect from Marlowe, the gender politics of 'The Passionate Shepherd' are difficult to pin down because identities are difficult to pin down in the poem. If the invitation is directed by a man to a woman, then the fantasy of a compliant mistress may well figure more aggressive Elizabethan male fantasies of deflowering the great virgin queen. The beloved's silence could certainly express submission, but it could also express resistance. Masculine rapaciousness is checked by the open-endedness of Marlowe's poem, which requires a reply. Indeed Ralegh wrote a reply in which the answer was a clear no. Identity is also difficult to pin down in this poem because of its dense literary quality and its embeddedness in a classical tradition which turns Marlowe's lyric into a collaboration between Marlowe and his predecessors. Marlowe's pastoral draws on another story of a passionate shepherd who tried (unsuccessfully) to woo his love, in the myth of Polyphemus and Galatea (*Metamorphoses* 13.789–897). This myth then became the subject of a singing competition in Theocritus' *Idylls*, an extremely famous text in the Renaissance and a model for pastoral which was as important as Virgil's *Eclogues*. Marlowe's pastoral continues this pattern of transferring voices and stories. It has no single originary source, and is already inscribed within a cycle of collaboration and polyvocality before it explores the pleasures and vices of seduction. In *The Passionate Pilgrim*, the Marlowe–Ralegh interchange is followed by a poem that alludes to the myth of Philomel and Tereus, and is certainly contextualized by this notorious myth of rape, but in Marlowe's pastoral, once the lyric is separated from its traditional title, the rape is potentially male rape, as well as female rape.[12]

The links between the rhetorical and the erotic in this poem are also revealed in the way Marlowe's utopian pastoral vision makes its appeal to the body, as well as the mind. The sensuous appeal of art is articulated thematically, and also in the smooth refinement of the verse, which caresses the ear, and conditions it to expect certain rhythms and sounds. Marlowe's speaker offers to make the beloved 'beds of roses, / And a thousand fragrant posies' (st. 3), playing the game of physical, figurative, and linguistic transposition that is central to this poem, where the addressee is invited to come over here, where nature is transformed into the armoury of seduction, and where one word slips into another. The terms posies and poesies are visually and acoustically very similar and are further linked through the etymology of the word 'anthology', which is literally a collection of flowers. In fact, Elizabethan books were linked to flowers in another way as they were sometimes perfumed, and lavender and other fragrant herbs were sometimes stuffed under their covers, especially embroidered covers. The phrase 'fragrant posies' is not just a pretty poetic image, but a reference to the real synaesthetic appeal of Renaissance texts, and to poetry's ability to move both body and senses.

Hero and Leander

Marlowe's classicism enabled the production of radically new ideas about the nature and value of literature which became the catalyst for the formation of a literary canon, and of a literary community, in late Elizabethan England.[13] Hero and Leander constructs a self-consciously modern, specifically literary persona, which is associated with wantonness, ornament, and excess. It is a poem that avoids conclusions, it questions its own processes, and reveals the world to be a radically unpredictable place where individuals are at the mercy of unpredictable desires.[14] Like all Marlowe's poems, it alludes to texts that are stylistically unwholesome, digressive, and excessively ornamental. Ovid and Musaeus, the principal sources for Hero and Leander, do not embody the chaste, virile style advocated by the influential Roman critic, Quintilian, in his canon of good Roman writing, and Marlowe's engagement with contemporary poetics, in Hero and Leander, also involves an exploration of the racial ideologies that are latent in literary ideals that the Renaissance derived from Roman critics like Quintilian and Cicero.

Hero and Leander (1598) is the only poem by Marlowe that has received anything like the critical attention it deserves. As with all Marlowe's poems, there is no conclusive evidence as to dating, and the shape of the Marlovian cursus remains elusive, but the vast majority of readers place Marlowe's little epic, or epyllion, at the end of his career, and for Cheney, it marks the turn to epic in Marlowe's Ovidian cursus, along with the translation of Lucan. Hero and Leander is about the nature and status of literature, and sets up a mutually constitutive relationship between artistic mastery and erotic success. The more accomplished their rhetoric, the more successful the characters are in getting what they want, and this includes the narrator. Marlowe's epyllion is consummately urbane, witty, and accomplished, a masterpiece of the poetic art that includes all the desirable poetic elements such as allusions to mythology, rich imagery, and a couplet form brought under complete control. At the same time, however, the kind of authorship Marlowe explores in the poem is a transvestite form of authorship which self-consciously effeminizes itself. The gender politics behind the idea of a *master*-piece are undermined in two ways: firstly, by the inability of all characters, including the narrator, to avoid chance and to control sexual desire, and secondly, by suggesting parallels between the narrator's strategies and those employed by the female characters in the game of seduction. Marlowe redefines the author as a transvestite who self-consciously adopts feminized behaviour. In its narrative digressions, for example, the poem succeeds in seducing the reader by imitating the coy behaviour which is usually ascribed to women, as it manipulates the reader's narrative desire by flirting with onward thrust and delay (1.425–30). The story of Mercury and the country maid links the rhetorical and the erotic, as the narrator's narrative accomplishment is recast as erotic arousal. The country maid puts Mercury off to bring him on, just as the narrator puts the reader off, by frustrating their desire to follow the main story of Hero and Leander, to bring them on.

Some of the most famous digressions in *Hero and Leander*, including 1.9–50, 1.55–90, and 1.135–57, are ekphrases, what we might call purple passages, highly accomplished descriptions that could stand on their own as examples of poetic excellence. These descriptions of visual objects also reflect the process whereby the visual becomes verbal, and life endures an unpredictable passage into art, but the ekphrases also contribute to the digressive structure of the poem as they get in the way of the narrative. The beauty of the descriptions arouses wonder, 'But far above the loveliest Hero shined, / And stole away th'enchanted gazer's mind' (1.103–4), but the ekphrases are also transgressive in that they cross over the boundaries of narrative, and enter the realm of dilation, of leisurely expansion and time-wasting, which is a specifically aesthetic space. The result of the text's inability to get on with it is that the text becomes a fetish, an object that is irrationally reverenced, and substitutes itself for erotic satisfaction. The long, but highly accomplished, descriptions stand in for action, stimulate the desire for action, even sexual action given that this is a love story, and convert themselves into the objects the literary consumer admires and desires. In *Hero and Leander*, all literary process is eroticized, including writing, which follows sexual rhythms; reading, which is recast as voyeurism; speaking, which is either a form of seduction or is riddled with unexpected double entendres; and even publishing, as Leander seduces Hero with an argument that establishes parallels between promiscuity and the advantages of an exchange economy (1.224–94).

The poem questions the viability of boundaries and systems of containment, and in doing so it alludes to the racial discourse latent in emerging aesthetic discourse. As an original poem that combines elements of translation and imitation, with invention, it adds foreign elements to the nationalistic, vernacular brew. But hybridity is a threat posed by the famous location of the action. The hometowns of Hero and Leander, Sestos and Abydos, are opposed to each other across the Hellespont, the narrow channel of water that separates Europe from Asia, so their story is one of political and rhetorical miscegenation, as it figures the threat that Asiatic style posed to Roman brevitas, or brevity. Roman critics, like Cicero, were hostile to the florid, luxurious style which they dismissed as Asiatic, soft and even effeminate, and set the Asian against good Roman style which was tough, spare, and manly. Marlowe's poem reflects on colouring as a rhetorical, cosmetic, and racial issue. Hero and Leander are certainly praised for fairness and whiteness, which would seem to confirm the racial ideal. When Leander implores Hero, 'Be not unkind and fair; misshapen [sic] stuff / Are of behaviour boisterous and rough' (1.203–4), he means that, by nature, fair Hero should not be unkind, but his paradox acknowledges that she *is* unkind, and the racial discourse implicit in the idolization of fairness is both asserted and inverted. 'Spotless chastity' (1.368), whiteness (1.65), and purity (1.7–8) are celebrated, but are then challenged by the miscegenating processes of the eroticized marketplace, and the poem's celebration of sexuality. Marlowe's epyllion is a deliberately self-marginalizing text which pursues all kinds of contamination. Like *Ovid's Elegies*, with their own obsessions with gender and racial hybridity, and *The First Book of Lucan*, with its mixture of humour and tragedy, *Hero and Leander* is devalued by a critical paradigm which attempts to keep things clean. Marlowe deliberately pursues mixture and instability in his poems. His texts are hybrids which mix genders, genres, languages, cultures, and tones. In doing so, the products of Marlowe's classical imagination probe his own culture's aesthetic ideals and the way they are founded on ideals of moral, racial, and gender purity. Marlowe's highly influential epyllion articulates a new sense of literary value in a trope of self-promotion through deficiency and scandal. His text is structurally and thematically scandalous, but at least it does not lie, nor advance claims to disinterestedness and moral purity that cannot be maintained.

Hero and Leander opens with a striking description of Hero's appearance in which feminine beauty, constructed as erotic, spectacular, and mesmerizing, as well as threatening and deceptive, is figured through her clothes. Her garments are made of lawn and lined with purple silk decorated with 'gilt stars'. Her green sleeves are 'bordered with a grove' where naked Venus desperately tries to attract the attention of Adonis, and her blue kirtle, or skirt, is stained 'with the blood of wretched lovers slain' (1.9–16). Hero is immediately inscribed in the realm of the artefact and is made into an object of quantifiable and abstract values whose circulation becomes the vehicle for all kinds of capital investments, from the exchange of money involved in buying books, to the symbolic capital Marlowe accrues through his poetic accomplishment. But Hero does not only have visual appeal, she is also a compound of olfactory and auditory delights. Her veil is decorated with flowers and leaves that are so life-like that people, and bees, mistake her breath for the fragrance of what they think are real flowers, and her ingeniously engineered buskins make pleasing chirruping noises when water passes through them, in parody of the sieve imagery that was exploited by Elizabeth to figure her chastity (1.17–36). Hero's appearance is familiar from the sumptuous embroidered clothes that adorned and presented sixteenth- and seventeenth-century bodies, and the compound of delights she offers is typical of a culture alert to the appeal of simultaneous sensations where heavily decorated caps, purses, gloves, and even books were frequently perfumed.

One of the things this chapter has tried to do is to put the senses back into our understanding of Marlowe's poetry. Marlowe's description of Hero's clothes (1.9–50) focuses attention on the somatic consequences of texts and the function of ornament in late Elizabethan culture. The object with all its vibrancy and physical force is apprehended by the senses and becomes part of the process of thought through, not in spite of, its physical nature and physical effects. The imagery and colours of Hero's clothes seem to hide some deeper meaning and demand deciphering. For example, does the picture of Venus and Adonis serve as an admonition against lust, or a celebration of beauty and desire? Colours could themselves be read, and blue usually indicates amity, while green usually indicates love. In this sense, the description functions like an emblem, combining visual and verbal representations, and traces out Horace's dictum, *'ut pictura poesis'*, in the fabric of Marlowe's text. In the Horatian commonplace, poetry is a speaking picture, and painting is a dumb poem, and the description of Hero's clothes focuses attention on the implications of this unfamiliar way of viewing image and text. But colours and patterns can also be chosen for purely decorative purposes and, in a manner typical of the poem, Hero's clothes both invoke and retract their own symbolic significance, fluctuating between their role as sign and their role as product. To the extent that ekphrasis reflects Hero, but also defines her, Hero's description operates on the interface between subject and object, art and nature, and reflects on the processes of canon formation which require the material aspects of writing to be absent. *Hero and Leander* is a poem about the nature of the aesthetic which points to the etymological root of the word aesthetic in the Greek word for the *senses*. Through interweaving of the textual and the corporal, it interrogates the thematics of surface and depth, the hierarchy of text over materiality, and the process that sets rationality over aesthesis, or the processes of the mind over simple sense perception.

Lucan's First Book

Hero and Leander is related to *Lucan's First Book* (1600) through their interest in wandering and truth. *Hero and Leander* pursues the pun Socrates identified in the Greek word for *truth*, 'aletheia', which he defined as 'ale-theia,' or *divine wandering*. *Lucan's First Book* explores *truth* as 'A-lethe-ia', or the condition of being *without forgetfulness* (lethe), which is the truth of the historian. But *Lucan's First Book* is also a digressive text which explores the compatibility of romance structures and narrative history, and the compatibility of poetic and historical modes of truth. Lucan's text immediately became the focus for debates about partisanship and the abuses of history in Roman culture. While Statius praised him, Tacitus argued that Lucan was driven by personal animosity, and so Lucan came down to the Renaissance as a string of questions and ideas about the nature of history, which were precisely the questions Marlowe was exploring in plays such as *The Massacre at Paris*. Not many people now read Lucan, but in the Renaissance Lucan's single surviving text *De Bello Civili*, also known as *The Pharsalia*, was widely read, admired, and quoted, both for its rhetorical power and for its moral and historical content. However, Lucan's biography is as important as his text in explaining his charismatic appeal for the Elizabethans. Lucan embodied the humanist ideal of eloquence married to service to the state, and he was the nephew of no less a figure than Seneca. He successfully held public office under Nero, but quarrelled with the emperor and eventually joined the Pisonian conspiracy. The conspiracy was uncovered and Lucan was forced to commit suicide, aged twenty-six, reputedly quoting lines from *The Pharsalia* as he died.

The Pharsalia is the great epic of classical republicanism, and the manner of Lucan's death inscribed him in the Renaissance imagination as a martyr to tyranny.[15] It tells the terrible story of the civil war between Caesar and Pompey, a shocking tale of depravity and rampant lust for power whose major target is Caesar:

> Destroying what withstood his proud desires,
> And glad when blood and ruin made him way:
> So thunder which the wind tears from the clouds,
> With crack of riven air and hideous sound
> Filling the world, leaps out and throws forth fire,
> Affrights poor fearful men, and blasts their eyes
> With overthwarting flames, and raging shoots
> Alongst the air, and, nought resisting it,
> Falls, and returns, and shivers where it lights.
>
> (*LFB* 150–8)

But Lucan's moral fury encompasses both the depravity of Rome and the weaknesses of the men who were later to become republican heroes. Rome's status as a role model is compromised by its decadence, which provokes a loss of masculinity leading to the collapse of virtue: '[Men] scorned old sparing diet, and ware robes / Too light for women' (165–6), and Lucan combines political radicalism with gender and class conservatism. In his translation, Marlowe plays history against myth, both the myths of classical mythology and the classical and Renaissance myths about Rome as the ideal model for all subsequent political institutions. Marlowe was the first person to translate Lucan into English, and his restless blank verse conveys the savagery and thirst for extremity of Lucan's original, but for all its bloodiness and black humour, Lucan's *Pharsalia* is an invigorating text, one written by a man with furious political commitments, in a culture where literature was a form of public intervention. For readers who find themselves in a culture of political apathy, Lucan's text comes as a shock.

France served as a formative intertext between Marlowe and Lucan. The Duke of Guise, from *The Massacre at Paris*, is modelled on Lucan's Caesar, and Marlowe read widely in the French and English propaganda produced at the time of the French wars of religion, from the late 1580s onwards.[16] Marlowe's translation of Lucan needs to be read in terms of his on-going sceptical engagement with epic, with the nature of heroism, with masculinity, militarism, and the potential for good and for evil in masculine *virtus*, and with his meditations on the relation of the writer to authority. There are two rival traditions of epic: the first is associated with Virgil and the epics of the imperial victors, and the second is associated with Lucan and the epics of the defeated.[17] The victors experience history as a coherent, end-directed story, and the losers experience history as contingency and open-endedness: 'The

world's swift course is lawless / And casual; all the stars at random range'
(641–2), in the words of Marlowe's *Lucan*, so Lucanic epics are episodic and
invoke romance structures. *The Pharsalia* deliberately echoes *The Aeneid* to
underline its own alternative form of epic, one which dissipates the focus on
a single hero. Caesar has the dynamism of the classic hero, but without the
hero's sense of communal responsibility. Republican values and epic masculinity are incompatible, given republicanism's privileging of community
over the exceptional individual or dynasty.[18]

In choosing to translate Lucan, Marlowe was making a public statement about the political and ideological investments of Elizabethan England,
about the idolization of epic, and its concomitant idolization of Tudor cen-
tralizing power, and about the epic conception of laureateship. Nero has
survived as one of the greatest tyrants of history, but what is less frequently
remembered is that he fancied himself as a writer and patron of the arts.
Marlowe uses Lucan to engage with Virgil and Spenser, and their writing of
power, but he also addresses another configuration of writing and power.
In late sixteenth-century England, the image of Elizabeth as an author and
linguist was familiar, although her texts were rarely circulated. Not only did
she exploit ways of investing sovereignty in the voice of the monarch, she
also explored ways of investing sovereignty in writing. Puttenham's *Arte of
English Poesie* (1589) constructs Elizabeth as the ideal of courtly writing,
and as the ideal courtly writer.[19] Lucan supplied examples of the perverse
relationship between authority and authorship – in Nero, and in Caesar, the
author of *De Bello Gallici* – and *Lucan's First Book* engages with Elizabeth's
own paradigmatic textuality. The satiric rage, sourness, vertiginous hyperbole, and hybridity of Marlowe's translation, with its indecorous mixture of
jokes and blood, is an affront to the norms of courtly writing.

Lucan could have been read in Renaissance England as a republican writer,
but he could also have been read as a repository of historical facts and political wisdom on matters such as the role of counsel, which did not necessarily
acquire a republican inflection. At the same time, it is misleading to attenu-
ate the political, as opposed to the specifically republican, impact of Lucan
in sixteenth-century England, bearing in mind that Cuffe was supposed to
have inspired Essex to rebellion by discussing Lucan with him. Marlowe's
translation of Lucan offers him a way of taking up a position within the
most pressing contemporary political debates, when discussion of such issues by a general public, beyond the controlled environments of court and
council, would have been censored. The late 1580s and 1590s were marked
by a revival of interest in Lucan prompted by the civil war in France, fears
over the English succession, and the Babington Plot of 1586, which was tied
to the problems posed by Mary, Queen of Scots.

Mary was a rival to Elizabeth's throne, and her presence on English soil threatened the country with the kind of factional strife described in *The Pharsalia*:

> While Titan strives against the world's swift course,
> Or Cynthia, night's queen, waits upon the day,
> Shall never faith be found in fellow kings.
> Dominion cannot suffer partnership;
> This need no foreign proof nor far-fet story.
>
> (*LFB* 90–4)

The invocation, quotation, and imitation of Lucan in late Elizabethan England was an act of political agency which had contemporary valence. In his *Defence of the Honorable Sentence and Execution of the Queene of Scots* (1587), M. Kyffin cites Lucan to justify Elizabeth's actions:

> If the King of Spaine should come into Fraunce, although perhaps the French King mought take him for his brother, in the sence of the Poet (fratrum concordia rara) yet I doubt he would not take him there for his fellow, omnisque potestas impatiens consortis erit: there is no Kingdome that will abide a Copartner.[20]

Lucan came down to the Renaissance as the focus for debates about the definition of poetry and history. Quintilian canonized this interpretation of Lucan in the *Institutio Oratoria* (10.1.90), when he suggested that Lucan was more suitable as a model for orators than poets. *Lucan's First Book* thematizes the problems of reading in context, most notably in the invocation to Nero, with its joking reference to Nero's large size, 'The burdened axis with thy force will bend' (57). The invocation to Nero is deliberately problematic, and its availability to both panegyrical and satirical interpretations relates the invocation to the problems of interpreting historical narrative, both in relation to the past and in relation to the present, as does the poem's witty avowal that we need no 'far-fet story' (94) to prove that power-sharing is always doomed. *Lucan's First Book* is about the rage for explanation. The terrified Romans run to the augurs and seers in a desperate bid to make sense of a welter of events. The augurs and seers are versions of the historian, and are distinguished by different levels of competence, and by their alignment with different schools of thought (633–41), and each tries to make a truthful, or at least plausible, narrative out of the events.

History tends to be associated with the particular, and poetry with the universal, in Renaissance thought, and *Lucan's First Book* is sceptical about the universalizing thrust of poetry, and its dangerous mythologizing powers. Time and again, rhetoric is used by wicked characters to justify opportunism, apathy, and aggression, by claiming that events and decisions are propelled by some grand design. So, for example, Caesar thinks that the Fates have 'bent' to him (394), when the reader knows that the things that have prompted the army to side with Caesar against Rome are actually the blood-lust of the soldiers, the charisma of Caesar, and the eloquence of the chief centurion Laelius (353–96). At the same time, it is the poetic perspective, with its awareness of the lies and tales that words can tell, that becomes the vehicle for exposing the truth.

Rome does not always serve as a positive model in Marlowe's poems, most notably in his translation of Lucan, where Rome is condemned, as well as being cast as the object of nostalgic longing. Marlowe's classicism defines a discursive space in which he can address the problems of time and distance, the relationship of the past to the present, and of alien and English elements. The classical texts he chooses to address are not invoked as ways of fixing meaning; rather Marlowe generates diverse meanings out of the confrontation between classicism and the present. In Marlowe's hands, classicism renovates understanding and mints new forms.

NOTES

1. Gordon Braden, *The Classics and English Renaissance Poetry: Three Case Studies* (New Haven: Yale University Press, 1978), p. xiv.
2. W. R. Johnson, 'The Problem of the Counter-Classical Sensibility and Its Critics', *California Studies in Classical Antiquity* 3 (1970), 123–51; Patrick Cheney, *Marlowe's Counterfeit Profession: Ovid, Spenser, Counter-Nationhood* (University of Toronto Press, 1997). Cheney notes that Marlowe exploits a counter-Virgilian, Ovidian cursus based on the triad of amatory poetry, tragedy, and epic to contest the political, poetic, and gender ideologies of the Virgilian/Spenserian model. For Virgil and Ovid as contrasting 'literary–political authorities' (p. 6), see Heather James, *Shakespeare's Troy: Drama, Politics, and the Translation of Empire* (Cambridge University Press, 1997).
3. James VI, *The Essayes of a Prentise in the Divine Art of Poesie* (Edinburgh, 1584), M2^v.
4. Walter J. Ong, SJ, 'Latin Language Study as a Renaissance Puberty Rite', in *Rhetoric, Romance, and Technology* (Ithaca: Cornell University Press, 1971), pp. 113–41. Richard Halpern, *The Poetics of Primitive Accumulation: English Renaissance Culture and the Genealogy of Capital* (Ithaca: Cornell University Press, 1991), pp. 19–60; and Lynn Enterline, *The Rhetoric of the Body from Ovid to Shakespeare* (Cambridge University Press, 2000), pp. 23–7. See also Jonathan Bate, *Shakespeare and Ovid* (Oxford: Clarendon Press, 1994), p. 28.
5. Several texts are overlaid in this speech, including Lucan's *Pharsalia*, Ovid's description of Hecuba in *The Metamorphoses*, 13.399–575, and Aeneas's description of Hecuba in Marlowe's *Dido, Queen of Carthage* 2.1.244–6. Overlayering is typical of Renaissance interpretation of the classics.
6. *Essays of John Dryden*, W. P. Ker (ed.), 2 vols. (Oxford: Clarendon Press, 1900), 1: 238.

7. In this chapter all quotations from Marlowe's poems are taken from *Christopher Marlowe: The Complete Poems and Translations*, Stephen Orgel (ed.) (Harmondsworth: Penguin, 1971).

8. See Jonathan Culler, 'The Call of the Phoneme: Introduction', in Culler (ed.), *On Puns: The Foundation of Letters* (Oxford: Blackwell, 1988), pp. 1–16; and Frederick Ahl, *Metaformations: Soundplay and Wordplay in Ovid and Other Classical Poets* (Ithaca: Cornell University Press, 1985).

9. If Lee T. Pearcy's numerological reading of the first edition of *Ovid's Elegies* is correct, in *The Mediated Muse: English Translations of Ovid 1560–1700* (Hamden, CT: Shoe String Press, 1984), pp. 1–36, the sequence signifies through yet another kind of patterning.

10. See Orgel's comments in *Complete Poems*, ed. Orgel, p. 233. M. L. Stapleton, *Ovid's 'Amores' from Antiquity to Shakespeare* (Ann Arbor: University of Michigan Press, 1996), pp. 133–53, argues that *Ovid's Elegies* influences Shakespeare's dark lady sonnets. On the offensiveness of *Ovid's Elegies*, see Ian Frederick Moulton, 'Printed Abroad and Uncastrated: "Marlowe's Elegies with Davies' Epigrams"', in Paul Whitfield White (ed.), *Marlowe, History, and Sexuality* (New York: AMS Press, 1998), pp. 77–90.

11. For excellent discussion of this lyric, see Douglas Bruster, 'Come to the Tent Again: "The Passionate Shepherd", Dramatic Rape and Lyric Time', *Criticism* 33 (1991): 49–72; and Cheney, *Marlowe's Counterfeit Profession*, pp. 68–87.

12. For an extremely suggestive discussion of Elizabeth as Tereus, and Ralegh as Philomel, see Cheney, *Marlowe's Counterfeit Profession*, pp. 76–8.

13. Georgia E. Brown, 'Breaking the Canon: Marlowe's Challenge to the Literary Status Quo in *Hero and Leander*', in White (ed.), *Marlowe, History, and Sexuality*, pp. 59–75; 'Gender and Voice in *Hero and Leander*', in J. A. Downie and J. T. Parnell (eds.), *Constructing Christopher Marlowe* (Cambridge University Press, 2000), pp. 148–63; and *Redefining Elizabethan Literature* (Cambridge University Press, 2004).

14. Robert Logan, 'Perspective in Marlowe's *Hero and Leander*: Engaging our Detachment', in Kenneth Friedenreich, Roma Gill, and Constance B. Kuriyama (eds.), *'A Poet and a Filthy Play-maker': New Essays on Christopher Marlowe* (New York: AMS Press, 1988), pp. 279–91.

15. James Shapiro, '"Metre Meete to Furnish Lucans Style": Reconsidering Marlowe's Lucan', in Friedenreich (ed.), *'A Poet and a Filthy Play-maker'*, pp. 315–25, is excellent but overlooks the importance of Lucan's life.

16. William Blissett, 'Lucan's Caesar and the Elizabethan Villain', *SP* 53 (1956), 553–75. On the French connection in Marlowe's drama, see Richard Hillman, *Shakespeare, Marlowe and the Politics of France* (Houndmills: Palgrave, 2002), pp. 72–111.

17. David Quint, *Epic and Empire: Politics and Generic Form from Virgil to Milton* (Princeton University Press, 1993), pp. 7–9 and 131–209.

18. David Norbrook, *Writing the English Republic: Poetry, Rhetoric and Politics 1627–1660* (Cambridge University Press, 1999), pp. 23–62, esp. p. 36.

19. See Jennifer Summit, '"The Arte of a Ladies Penne": Elizabeth I and the Poetics of Queenship', *ELR* 26 (1996), 385–422.

20. Qtd from Emrys Jones, *The Origins of Shakespeare* (Oxford: Clarendon Press, 1977), p. 120.

READING LIST

Barkan, Leonard. *The Gods Made Flesh: Metamorphosis and the Pursuit of Paganism*. New Haven: Yale University Press, 1986.

Braden, Gordon. *The Classics and English Renaissance Poetry: Three Case Studies*. New Haven, Yale University Press, 1978.

Brown, Georgia E. *Redefining Elizabethan Literature*. Cambridge University Press, 2004.

Cheney, Patrick. *Marlowe's Counterfeit Profession: Ovid, Spenser, Counter-Nationhood*. University of Toronto Press, 1997.

Enterline, Lynn. *The Rhetoric of the Body from Ovid to Shakespeare*. Cambridge University Press, 2000.

Quint, David. *Epic and Empire: Politics and Generic Form from Virgil to Milton*. Princeton University Press, 1993.

8

MARK THORNTON BURNETT

Tamburlaine the Great,
Parts One and Two

At the beginning of *Tamburlaine the Great, Part One*, the Prologue announces a dramatic trajectory that leads from 'jigging veins of rhyming
mother-wits' to 'the stately tent of war'.[1] Within this tent, a metaphor for
the theatrical playing-space, we will be granted the privilege of listening
to the hero's 'high astounding terms' (5); indeed, the extraordinary linguistic impact of Tamburlaine is singled out here as the most self-evident
feature of an innovative dramaturgy and provides, as Patrick Cheney states,
'an advertisement for Marlowe as England's new poet'.[2] But an 'astounding' dimension inheres, too, in the implication that the Prologue will 'lead'
(3) the audience from one kind of theatre to another: members of a flock,
spectators are herded to new horizons in such a way as to make them
the sheep-like followers of the shepherd–bandit. In such a process, the
visual impression of Tamburlaine plays a prominent part, since 'his picture' (7) is seen to belong with his 'astounding' verbal ability. Building
upon the Prologue's suggestions, this chapter argues that *Tamburlaine the
Great* is 'astounding' in multiple respects. Not only do the plays destabi-
lize Elizabethan orthodoxies at the levels of language, class, and ethnicity,
they simultaneously query contemporary constructions of identity and authority, to the extent that existing systems of interpretation and classification are thrown into disarray. So insistent are the plays' unmoorings
of the ideologies of their time that even sexual demarcations, and divine
norms, enjoy a slim purchase. Particularly distinctive about *Tamburlaine
the Great* is the relationship between the two parts: what is formulated
in *Tamburlaine, Part One* is ironized or pushed to a thematic extreme in
Tamburlaine, Part Two, making the plays more complex in their utterances
than might, at first, be assumed. In this sense, it is perhaps more appropriate
to think of *Tamburlaine the Great* as two distinct plays rather than one,
each with its own dynamic and individual reading of the 'astounding' titular
protagonist.

Language and power

Tamburlaine the Great opens by directing attention to the capabilities of, and the drawbacks attached to, language. This is facilitated, at first, via a series of contextual contrasts. Whereas the Persian potentate Mycetes lacks a 'great and thund'ring speech' (*1 Tamb.* 1.1.3) and elects others to ventriloquize his own feeble protests, Tamburlaine speaks confidently and indisputably as his own man. In addition, the speech of Mycetes is marked by impoverished witticisms and limp line endings, which throw into stark relief Tamburlaine's sonorous and resounding pronouncements. More strikingly, Tamburlaine is drawn as a master of linguistic power; that is, his 'vaunts' (*1 Tamb.* 1.2.212) invariably precipitate a material result. Indeed, such is the 'working' (*1 Tamb.* 2.3.25) effect of Tamburlaine's 'words' (*1 Tamb.* 2.3.25) that a disarmed Theridamas is moved to exclaim: 'Not Hermes, prolocutor to the gods, / Could use persuasions more pathetical' (*1 Tamb.* 1.2.209–10). The implication is that Tamburlaine is beyond even the most rhetorically skilled of the deities and thus functions as a type of god himself. By extension, Theridamas, who is privy to the divine communication, joins the ranks of a heavenly elite.

Already in *Tamburlaine, Part One*, however, there are hints that the linguistic facility of Tamburlaine will be short-lived. The 'lavish tongues' (*1 Tamb.* 4.2.67) of Bajazeth and Zabina provide one instance of a louder chorus that will, eventually, rock the hero's verbal pre-eminence. By *Tamburlaine, Part Two*, therefore, it is obvious that the world is inhabited by a number of rival speakers whose skills and expertise are more broadly distributed. *Part Two*, in fact, commemorates the rise of several mini-Tamburlaines, chief among whom is Callapine, the Turkish braggart's son. Interestingly, Callapine in *Part Two* is discovered as an ironic recasting of Tamburlaine in *Part One*. Like Tamburlaine, Callapine rhetorically charms his opposition and ensures that his 'words' (*2 Tamb.* 1.2.10) become 'deeds' (*2 Tamb.* 1.2.10). As a result, at least in part, Tamburlaine experiences the first occasion on which his command of the universe through language begins to falter. 'If words might serve, our voice hath rent the air' (*2 Tamb.* 2.4.121), cries Theridamas, reprimanding a grieving Tamburlaine for deploying hollowed-out articulations and concluding that '[A]ll this raging cannot make [Zenocrate] live' (*2 Tamb.* 2.4.120). The point is clear: Tamburlaine's waning control is linked to his failing prowess with parlance. The remainder of *Part Two* extends the development, with Theridamas standing in for Tamburlaine as an ultimately ineffective speaking exponent. Once again, *Part Two* rephrases *Part One*, revealing a Theridamas who, in his addresses to Olympia, replicates Tamburlaine's own earlier seductions. The difference is that Theridamas's perorations make little impression; Olympia remains unmoved, and an audience leaves the play with the unmistakable conviction that it is not so much the language that has changed but the social climate in which it operates. There is no longer an enabling context for the successful application of Tamburlaine's 'working words'.

One of the reasons for Tamburlaine's success with words is that he reanimates the verbal conventions of the ruling echelons. In this regard, Tamburlaine is 'astounding' in a double sense, for he is represented as generating amazement in class as well as linguistic terms. For instance, the ability to wield aristocratic expressions is arguably more appealing to Tamburlaine than executing the actions described, as when he steals, magpie-like, from Menaphon's royal refrain: ' "And ride in triumph through Persepolis"? / Is it not brave to be a king?' (*1 Tamb.* 2.5.50–1). It is arguably such an appropriation of property not his own that precipitates the class condemnation of Tamburlaine in *Part One*. As Thomas Cartelli notes, Tamburlaine, an 'aspiring commoner', constitutes a 'socially volatile . . . construction', not least because, according to prevailing opinion, he appears as a 'vagrant' (*1 Tamb.* 1.1.45) and a 'thievish villain' (*1 Tamb.* 2.2.3) of 'baseness and obscurity' (*1 Tamb.* 4.3.65).[3] At least in the eyes of the establishment, for Tamburlaine to dare structures ordained as fixed in Elizabethan ideology was a transgression of unthinkable proportions. Precisely what class Tamburlaine is affiliated to is a contentious issue. In the scene where Zenocrate, cowed into submission by her captor's eloquence, graduates from addressing him as a 'shepherd' (*1 Tamb.* 1.2.7) to calling him a 'lord' (*1 Tamb.* 1.2.33), Tamburlaine immediately leaps to a touchy self-defence: 'I am a lord, for so my deeds shall prove' (*1 Tamb.* 1.2.34). It is a moment dense with social import: traditional concepts of class superiority are held up for scrutiny, and the notion of an aristocracy dedicated to achievement rather than blood is privileged. Typically, in *Part Two*, the preoccupation with class is given a subtle twist. By *Part Two*, Tamburlaine, it is suggested, is free of social stigma, having triumphantly defined himself against and within the class codes of his world. This is clarified when Tamburlaine describes his sons' pursuits (dancing and musicianship) and when Zenocrate refers to Celebinus 'Trotting the ring, and tilting at a glove' (*2 Tamb.* 1.3.39) on the back of a 'Scythian steed' (*2 Tamb.* 1.3.38). Such exercises bespeak gentrification, suggesting that Tamburlaine has moved beyond the demotic register of his origins. (Part of that gentrification process was hinted at in the 1992 Royal Shakespeare Company production of the play: in the second half, Anthony Sher (Tamburlaine) entered as a heavier warlord, smug with bourgeois contentment.) Class orthodoxies, then, while being respected, have also been upturned, since Tamburlaine assumes for himself the position and lifestyle of the contemporary gentleman. Even here, however, residual instabilities remain, for Tamburlaine's rise to greatness exposes cracks in an order that prides itself on ideals of an invulnerable social hierarchy.

The paucity of class condemnation in *Part Two* might also be traced to the fact that the environment Tamburlaine presides over has assumed a greater plurality. *Part Two* dramatizes a universe that is more socially diverse and possessed of an increased ethnic orientation. As Orcanes states, in a typical demographic litany, 'We have revolted Grecians, Albanese, / Sicilians, Jews, Arabians, Turks, and Moors, / Natolians, Sorians, black Egyptians' (2 *Tamb.* 1.1.61–3). Emily Bartels has drawn attention to *Tamburlaine the Great's* figures of 'demonized' and ethnically charged 'barbarity', and, certainly, at least in *Part One*, the ethnic status of the protagonist is a vexed consideration.[4] For a crucial component of Tamburlaine's 'astounding' effect is his combination of social mobility and ethnic marginality. Continually, Tamburlaine is arraigned for leading a 'Tartarian rout' (*1 Tamb.* 1.1.71), for being 'Scythian' (*1 Tamb.* 1.2.152) and for manifesting all the stereotypical features of 'Scythians rude and barbarous' (*1 Tamb.* 3.3.271), to the extent that both descriptors – 'Scythian' and 'Tartarian' – appear synonymous with racially adverse slurs. Critics have tended to see in these designations metaphors for nations colonized by or traded with by the Elizabethans. Roger Sales finds in Tamburlaine's Scythian identity an echo of the native Irish, while Richard Wilson draws a parallel between Marlowe's *übermensch* and the Russian emperors courted by the English Muscovy Company.[5] These are helpful points of comparison, but the ultimate meanings of the plays' racial investments are more unsettling and unspecific. For instance, judged alongside the norms of Elizabethan national discourses, the 'Persian' constituency that lambasts Tamburlaine is equated with 'English' orthodoxy, while the 'Scythian' and 'Tartarian' community is linked to various non-'English' forms of racial otherness. A complicating factor is that traditional representatives are crushed or swept aside in the wake of Tamburlaine's onslaughts. As a result, as well as being socially upset, the world delineated has visited upon it a new ethnic dispensation, one that elevates the subaltern and places in jeopardy the entrenched and familiar.

Identification and classification

'Astounding', therefore, is an apt summation of the implications enshrined in Tamburlaine's territorial acquisitiveness and march to cultural visibility. Yet, such are the reverberations initiated by Tamburlaine's ascent to omnipotence that his actions continue to generate ideological irresolution and confusion. Crucially, the plays tease out the consequences attendant upon the upset of instituted values, not least in the area of identity. In both plays, but particularly so in *Part One*, a culture of labelling is granted a keen emphasis. Itself a relative of the impulse to vilify Tamburlaine for leapfrogging his class location, this concern with names and naming lends additional dramatic testimony to the unprecedented impact of Marlowe's Asiatic juggernaut. The importance of the 'name' is first signalled in Cosroe's lament that 'our neighbours that were wont to quake / And tremble at the Persian monarch's name / Now sits and laughs our regiment to scorn' (*1 Tamb.* 1.1.115–17). Even at this early point, an equation between the name, and what the name connotes, is underscored, suggesting that, in *Tamburlaine the Great*, it is not so much facts and actualities that provoke an emotional response as their representational mechanisms.

Given such a preoccupation with nomenclature, it is not surprising that, over the course of the rest of the action, modes of identification are placed in full view. 'He calls me "Bajazeth", who you call "lord"!' (*1 Tamb.* 3.3.67), protests Bajazeth, lashing out at Tamburlaine for an assumed failure to honour his titular authority. Because names connote kudos and influence, they become desirable possessions that rank, alongside gold and crowns, as vital elements in a tyrant's inventory. For Tamburlaine, territorial expansion functions simultaneously as a campaign to remove mighty monarchs and as a project to acquire their more impressive honours and decorations. As he states of his Turkish enemy, 'Thy names and titles and thy dignitaries / Are fled from Bajazeth and remain with me' (*1 Tamb.* 4.2.79–80). Deploying a suitably militaristic metaphor of a transfer of allegiance, Tamburlaine here lays claim to Bajazeth's power, appropriating, through the Turk's humiliation, not only kingdoms but charisma. The effect is to allow Tamburlaine to continue the construction of a social order that bears his own unique signature. Scenes of fraternization with his generals and colleagues are a case in point. 'Deserve these titles I endow you with, / By valour and by magnanimity' (*1 Tamb.* 4.4.134–5), he states to Theridamas, Techelles, and Usumcasane, concluding, 'Your births shall be no blemish to your fame, / For virtue is the fount whence honour springs' (*1 Tamb.* 4.2.136–7). Once again, Tamburlaine unveils a vision of primacy based on living acts rather than inherited privileges, only here he extends the theory, maintaining that an ennobled behaviour is also a guarantor of alternative identifications: with aristocratic conduct successfully imitated, another set of names, which expunge the memory of a plebeian class attachment, can be openly assumed.

But the *Tamburlaine the Great* plays go further than a mere intellectual rehearsal of a name change; as befits dramas that mark themselves out as radical departures, they simultaneously offer an audience visual realizations of the modulation from one identity to another. During the first meeting between Tamburlaine and Zenocrate, Marlowe's aspirant tears off his shepherd's garb in a moment of extravagant divestiture: 'Lie here, ye weeds that I disdain to wear! / This complete armour and this curtle-axe / Are adjuncts more beseeming Tamburlaine' (*1 Tamb*. 1.2.41–3). As the language of his exposure makes clear, Tamburlaine stages a superhuman recreation of himself, moving in the space of three lines from a rustic nobody to a fully fledged knight. The editor working on the scene must, therefore, indicate the nature of the transformation and point up the fact that Tamburlaine, throughout, has been in disguise. That disguise, however (the role of the knight), is itself something of a falsity, since Tamburlaine as yet has not completely demonstrated his fitness for the part. In other words, identity, from the vantage-point of the plays, exists in a negotiable zone and can depend on impersonation and appearance as much as bearing and conduct. There is no straightforward fit between the name and the individual, and a process of personhood takes precedence over a sense of fixed and immutable selves.

In fact, how to name and identify in the *Tamburlaine the Great* plays escalates, at several points, into a crisis of classification. The challenges and difficulties embodied in Tamburlaine are such that he seems to insert himself into no readily comprehensible structure. Time and time again the dramas' chorus of disapproval reaches out beyond social and racial modalities of understanding to embrace more mythological and nebulous schema, an index of Tamburlaine's inassimilable characteristics and implications. In itself this reliance on alternative interpretive methods should not be wondered at, since, as one critic notes, Tamburlaine represents 'a figure who will become the most extended exemplar of a movable "strangeness" that lies outside existing taxonomic arrangements'.[6] On occasions, the endeavour to pin down Tamburlaine is marked by a revealing indecision, with several points of comparison being entertained at one and the same time. The Governor of Damascus, for instance, speculates that Tamburlaine may be a 'man or rather god of war' (*1 Tamb*. 5.1.1), his alternation between human and divine polarities indicating a vexed uncertainty about his opponent's ultimate locations. For Meander, no human connection at all can be involved, although he, too, is driven to contemplate a number of different readings to account for Tamburlaine as a preternatural phenomenon: 'Some powers divine, or else infernal, mixed / Their angry seeds at his conception: / For he was never sprung of human race' (*1 Tamb*. 2.6.9–11), he exclaims. More frequently resorted to than vacillating explanations, however, is the exegetical utility of monstrosity. An incarnation of alterity, and a rebuff to traditional descriptive groupings, Tamburlaine is consistently perceived through a monstrous lens, as numerous approximations demonstrate. Hence, Tamburlaine is 'As monstrous as Gorgon' (*1 Tamb.* 4.1.18), argues the soldan of Egypt, while, to judge from a later depiction, he resembles 'A monster of five hundred thousand heads, / Compact of rapine, piracy, and spoil ... [a] presumptuous beast' (*1 Tamb.* 4.3.7–8, 15). The resilience of monstrosity as an interpretive instrument points, first, to the rapidity with which customary mechanisms of classification are exhausted. At a deeper level, the plays' subscription to understanding through monsters suggests the ways in which the monstrous category can accommodate all manner of deviations from the norm. Even ethnic identifications are pertinent here, as monsters were invariably situated in the margins of known cartographic configurations. No doubt related to this peripheral status is the way in which monsters work in the plays as confirmations of a speaker's sense of belonging to the correct community. By implication, if the monster is mixed and hybridized, the speaker is interpellated within a pure and unadulterated lineage. And, with Tamburlaine's exoticism and difference firmly monsterized, the project to affect his cultural genocide can be freely and legitimately pursued.

Because of the plays' fraught indecision over identification and classification, and because of their inability to approximate Tamburlaine adequately to contemporary networks of understanding, the status of authority itself is compromised. With Tamburlaine successfully encapsulating a number of unorthodoxies and ideological conundrums, there is little space remaining for the purposeful application of establishment policies. Despite the positive transformation undergone by Tamburlaine's enemies over the course of *Part One*, this is not enough to permit either conservative tendencies, or official persuasions, to assume centre-stage. Inside such a scenario, it might appear as if recognized forms of authority have been expunged; however, what the *Tamburlaine the Great* plays in fact discover is a reclamation and reanimation of authority in the guise of the overreacher. *Part One* shows us, first, a swing back to urban forms of institutional power, in that Tamburlaine, earlier branded as one of a band of 'silly country swains' (*1 Tamb.* 1.2.47), gravitates towards the end to Damascus, one of the largest of sixteenth-century eastern cities. The move offers one image of Tamburlaine's accommodation within a culture of civic centrality as opposed to rustic marginality. Another is furnished by the spectacle of Tamburlaine as he presents himself to the assembled throng:

> Then sit thou down, divine Zenocrate,
> And here we crown thee Queen of Persia ...
> To gratify thee, sweet Zenocrate,
> Egyptians, Moors, and men of Asia,
> From Barbary unto the Western Indie,

Shall pay a yearly tribute to thy sire;
And from the bounds of Afric to the banks
Of Ganges shall his mighty arm extend.
And now, my lords and loving followers...
Cast off your armour, put on scarlet robes,
Mount up your royal places of estate...
And there make laws to rule your provinces...
We will our rights of marriage solemnise.

(*1 Tamb.* 5.1.507–8, 517–23, 525–6, 528, 535)

Now rooted, Tamburlaine is constructed as a governor or administrator, one who runs his dominions from a single site and not a plethora of geographical emplacements. Even the expression 'sit down' communicates a sense of movement terminated. Nor are other requirements neglected in Tamburlaine's final assumption of sovereignty: by co-coordinating multiple coronations and his own marriage, he executes the role of archbishop, suggesting that, contestatory actions notwithstanding, a need for formal sanction is still in evidence. Hand-in-hand with the priestly tenor of the conclusion goes a filial subordination to patriarchal authority. Bestowing kingdoms with an aristocratic largesse, Tamburlaine installs the soldan of Egypt, his prospective father-in-law, as a minor dictator whose influence will extend from 'Barbary to the Western Indie'. Such details of topographical extremity are significant, for they help to situate Tamburlaine at a neutral mid-way point while also ridding him of the charge of ethnic exoticism. No longer, then, will Tamburlaine be impugned as a manifestation of barbarity (here, by contrast, civility is honoured) or a representative of racial otherness (both 'Barbary' and 'Indie' are his to dispense with and reject). The whole encapsulates the truth of Tamburlaine's lordship and an incontrovertible celebration of an authority which is challenged only in order to be reinstated.

But that reinstatement itself bristles with unanswered questions. If the perspective of the Elizabethan class system is recalled, Tamburlaine remains a commoner imitating a magistrate, and if the proposed colours of the royal retinue are lingered over, an echo of atrocity is heard. 'Scarlet' robes are uncomfortably close to the 'red . . . furniture' (*1 Tamb.* 4.1.55) donned by Tamburlaine when the 'wrath' he suffers from must 'be quenched with blood, / Not sparing any that can manage arms' (*1 Tamb.* 4.1.56–7). Thus, even as Tamburlaine's oration deploys 'scarlet' as a confirmation of peace, an audience is simultaneously reminded of the fragility of a cultural enterprise dependent upon the preservation of a military regime and upon an attenuated network of faithful associates. Part of Tamburlaine's success, indeed, can be traced to ways in which he inspires loyalty. Throughout the plays, the fellowship shared between the conqueror and his generals is lent a lively attention. Typically, the representation of Tamburlaine's modality of allegiance runs counter to contemporary notions of homage and fealty. For, rather than controlling through obedience to a symbolic figurehead, Tamburlaine ensures the devotion of his followers via the promotion of a shared, self-interested agenda. His 'lawless train' (*1 Tamb.* 1.1.39) unites around a communality of material endeavour and ambition, and his 'sweet friends and followers' (*1 Tamb.* 1.2.60) are bound not so much by abstract political principles as by a personal affinity with Tamburlaine himself. Moreover, the appeal of Tamburlaine is such that, in the same moment, he can assert a masterful superiority and dazzle the uninitiated with narratives of egalitarian glory. To Theridamas he states, 'Both we will reign as consuls of the earth' (*1 Tamb.* 1.2.196), his declaration holding out the promise of a joint rule that is distinguished by its classical antecedents. On occasions, the fellowship Tamburlaine manages takes on an openly political cast, as when his troop crowns him, exclaiming 'Long live Tamburlaine, and reign in Asia!' (*1 Tamb.* 2.7.64). In Tamburlaine's response – 'So, now it is more surer on my head / Than if the gods had held a parliament' (*1 Tamb.* 2.7.65–6) – is encoded a characteristic critique, since the practices of a historically grounded and lawful institution are seen to take second place to the opinions of a recent and illegal fraternity. As is so often the case, *Tamburlaine, Part One* inaugurates a movement that finds an ironic counterpart in *Tamburlaine, Part Two*, with fellowship being subjected to a notably grotesque development. While Tamburlaine continues to benefit from the collegiality of a select group of masculine supporters, he is also delineated as closely allied to the captive kings, even if ironically. For Tamburlaine's chariot is pulled across the stage by his royal prisoners in a spectacular demonstration of physical dependency and proximity. The scene makes available a deflated portrait of camaraderie, of a male alliance that fails properly to function: 'Holla, ye pampered jades of Asia! / What, can ye draw but twenty miles a day?' (*2 Tamb.* 4.3.1–2), Tamburlaine exclaims. The conqueror is here let down by his charges, with the scene as a whole offering striking corroboration of a collapse in reciprocal relations.

Sexuality and spectacle

By rebuking systems of classification and undergirding his own version of social cohesion, and by defying tried-and-trusted identifying mechanisms and repackaging authority, Tamburlaine continues to present an 'astounding' ideological construction. Lending an additionally dissident edge to this impression is the fact that, throughout the plays, Tamburlaine pursues his enterprises on the basis of a non-normative sexuality. Joanna Gibbs writes that 'Tamburlaine appropriates women...as signs of his magnanimity and of his projected invincibility' and, in many respects, this is a well-judged assessment.[7] However, a more leisurely look suggests that, while Tamburlaine collects women as so many possessions, he does so in a seemingly asexual fashion, as his apostrophe to Zenocrate reveals:

> Zenocrate, lovelier than the love of Jove...
> A hundred Tartars shall attend on thee,
> Mounted on steeds swifter than Pegasus;
> Thy garments shall be made of Median silk,
> Enchased with precious jewels of mine own...
> With milk-white harts upon an ivory sled
> Thou shalt be drawn amidst the frozen pools
> And scale the icy mountains' lofty tops,
> Which with thy beauty will be soon resolved...
>   (1 Tamb. 1.2.87, 93–6, 98–101)

At once the address points to a colonial act, with Tamburlaine weighing Zenocrate down with the fruits of his brigandage and marking out the extent of his empire. Confined within things of his own control and creation (the pun on 'enchased' and 'encased' is purposeful), Zenocrate is figured, despite aspiring hyperboles, as Tamburlaine's prisoner-of-war. Yet this owning of Zenocrate is dependent on her being situated in an environment of frosty inaccessibility. As the frigid language suggests, Tamburlaine aestheticizes Zenocrate in such a way as to rob her of a meaningful sexuality. In fact, sexual contact in the speech is conspicuous by its absence, not least because Zenocrate is transmogrified into an iconic abstraction, the cold and remote property of her captor's rhetorical devising.

No doubt with such representations of male–female interactions in mind, several critics have guided Marlowe, via Tamburlaine, into an early modern 'sodomitical' niche. For some, Marlowe's imputed homosexuality can be understood psychologically, as Constance Brown Kuriyama, commenting on *Tamburlaine the Great*, explains: 'the authorial mental state...was probably one of intense conflict of a marked homosexual character'.[8] For others, it is culture rather than psychology that is important. A discussion by Jonathan Goldberg of competing sexualities in the dramatist's work argues that 'Marlowe's identity in his culture comes from his rehearsal of these counter-positions.'[9] Certainly, it is not difficult to pinpoint in *Tamburlaine the Great*, as elsewhere in the Marlovian *œuvre*, a persistent homoeroticism. Hence, compared to the seduction of Zenocrate, the oral delivery aimed at Theridamas invests a greater energy in romantic invitation ('stay with me...Join with me' (1 Tamb. 1.2.187, 201)), to the extent that the Persian addressee finds himself contemplating physical attraction. He is, in his own words, 'conquered with [Tamburlaine's] looks' (*1 Tamb.* 1.2.227). On the one hand, this exchange serves to distance Tamburlaine from the effete same-sex character of the Mycetes scenes; on the other, it reinforces the fact that Tamburlaine's ascendancy vitally hinges upon the charged cultivation of male-on-male relations.

Later parts of the plays elaborate the theme. In Bajazeth, for instance, Tamburlaine finds a convenient 'footstool' with which to 'rise into my royal throne' (*1 Tamb.* 4.2.14–15): the anal puns ('stool') and hints of phallic tumescence ('rise') illuminate an intensely humiliating but also homoerotic encounter. In *Part Two*, similarly, quasi-sexual bonds between men are pursued, although, in this case, they assume incestuous dimensions. Leaving off his grief for Zenocrate, Tamburlaine abruptly instructs his sons in the arts of war. His speech points simultaneously to physical abstinence and penetrative consummation ('Sustain' (*2 Tamb.* 3.2.57), 'fortify' (*2 Tamb.* 3.2.62), 'assailed' (*2 Tamb.* 3.2.66), and 'mount' (*2 Tamb.* 3.2.85)), culminating in the climactic and incorporating pronouncement: 'When this is done, then are ye soldiers, / And worthy sons of Tamburlaine the Great' (*2 Tamb.* 3.2.91–2). Clearly, both psychological and cultural approaches would be critically productive; however, it would be a mistake to lose sight of the plays in favour of the author and the historical context. In this sense, Ian McAdam's discussion of the 'sodomitical' Marlowe is more persuasive in that it resists inordinate sexual speculation; instead, intricacies of dramatic character are foregrounded, with Tamburlaine being read as embodying a 'striving toward adequate manhood'.[10] Whether he deploys men in order to repress them, or marshals them so as to enjoy erotic fraternization, Tamburlaine, one might conclude, is impelled to shore up and perpetuate an unstable masculinity.

No less central to the preservation of Tamburlaine's power is a culture of the spectacle. Both plays exploit a variety of spectacular elements as part of their 'astounding' effect and, in a symbolic economy of awe-inspiring signs and tableaux, it is Tamburlaine himself who makes the most striking impression. Already in the Prologue to *Part One* we have been enjoined to 'View' (7) the Scythian, the suggestion being that the actor playing the part is visually imposing. (In this connection, it is worth noting that Edward Alleyn, the actor most commonly associated with the Tamburlaine role, was famed as a tall, imposing figure.) Further confirmation of the stunning intensity of Tamburlaine's looks arrives when Agydas, in the wake of regarding the silently wrathful conqueror, is moved to take his own life. Merely 'To see [Tamburlaine's] choler' (*1 Tamb.* 3.2.70) is sufficient to precipitate Agydas's suicide in a dramatic moment that is distinctive for allowing the hero a non-speaking authority. But, even as Tamburlaine is looked at as remarkable, so does he participate in a process of self-display. Crucially, Tamburlaine anticipates being put on 'view' as an 'emperor' (*1 Tamb.* 1.2.67). To be an emperor, then, is not simply to act as one but to be seen as one. In addition, Tamburlaine is delineated as displaying other properties apart from himself, such as gold, an 'emblem', as David Hard Zucker states, 'of his military conquests to date'; in this scene, as in others, the protagonist is akin to the contemporary stage-manager or impresario who profits from a heightened theatricality.[11] (In keeping with the plays' preoccupations, the 1992 Royal Shakespeare Company production elected to materialize the shower of gold at this point.) It is perhaps in his enemies that Tamburlaine finds the fittest objects for spectatorial involvement. Not only does Tamburlaine cause his enemies to be gazed at as belittled versions of their once lofty selves; he simultaneously scripts a series of vulgarized pageants in which former opponents are forced to perform. Thus, the caged Bajazeth and Zabina form part of a 'goodly show' (*1 Tamb.* 4.4.63) and, by virtue of their association with vernacular entertainment, are made to experience social diminution. 'Each of these dramatic emblems', states Ruth Lunney, 'can be interpreted . . . as an index to the reality beyond.'[12] And, taking on board the plays in their entirety, that 'reality' extends not so much to the protagonist's unshakable hold on global dominions as to his unravelling composure and declining powers. Notably, the Tamburlaine of *Part Two* is a less able creature than the spectacular showman of *Part One*. 'Behold me here, divine Zenocrate', he thunders, 'Raving, impatient, desperate, and mad' (*2 Tamb.* 2.3.112–13): although Tamburlaine engineers another self-demonstration at this point, it is one that, as his words suggest, communicates only impotence and fallibility. Likewise, even if Tamburlaine elaborates spectacles that echo Christian ceremonies, none is successful. Cutting his arm in a bizarre remodelling of the transfigured Christ, Tamburlaine strives visually to suborn his recalcitrant son but is forced to admit defeat, as Calyphas's comment indicates: 'Methinks 'tis a pitiful sight' (*2 Tamb.* 3.2.131). Calyphas, indeed, is dangerous because he resists being press-ganged into his father's visual system. Whereas Tamburlaine can constitute a sublime 'picture' (*1 Tamb.* Prologue 7), Calyphas appears no more than the 'picture of a slave' and 'of sloth' (*2 Tamb.* 4.1.93). As a result, Calyphas is dispatched, his death an eloquent indicator both of Tamburlaine's spectacular requirements and of a theatre of images at the mercy of increasingly tyrannical imperatives.

In the same way that Tamburlaine is constructed as visually arresting so are his actions imagined as textually undermining. 'Patterns of intertextual reference, texts "deconstructing" or undoing other texts, and authors asserting competing authority recur throughout Marlowe's plays', writes Marjorie Garber.[13] The *Tamburlaine the Great* plays are particularly resonant in this connection in that the protagonist flouts existing textual configurations of power, replacing them with his own models. Initially, at least, Tamburlaine articulates a dismissive attitude towards textual technologies. 'But now you see these letters and commands / Are countermanded by a greater man', he states to Zenocrate, continuing, 'And through my provinces you must expect / Letter of conduct from my mightiness' (*1 Tamb.* 1.2.21–4). Interestingly, such a 'letter' never appears, suggesting that Tamburlaine, in keeping with his early plebeian attachments, is envisaged as operating at a pre-technological stage of development. Later sections of the plays, however, discover Tamburlaine not so much rejecting textuality as taking it over to suit his own purposes. 'I [will] . . . write myself great Lord of Africa' (*1 Tamb.* 3.3.244–5), Tamburlaine announces, his declaration positing martial triumph as a kind of permanent literary testimony of his extraordinary capabilities. In fact, militarism *is* writing for Tamburlaine, as when he describes his sword as a 'pen' with which he will 'reduce' the 'regions' of the 'world . . . to a map' (*1 Tamb.* 4.4.83–4). In this formulation, as David H. Thurn argues, Tamburlaine conceives 'of the world as a space which can be rendered in graphic terms by translating unknown regions into nameable, legible units which participate in a textual system representing total conquest'.[14] But Tamburlaine's appropriation of scribal authority can simultaneously be manipulated in the opposite direction and slip back into a parodic version of its initial incarnation. When Tamburlaine burns the Koran, for instance, he is returned to his original stance in order to suggest that the distance that has been travelled from the scenes of early brigandage may only be illusory. Because Tamburlaine represents, in his view, an omnipotent essence (the seat of language and knowledge), there can be no rival to his version of textual sovereignty.

Burning the Koran also, of course, constitutes the plays' most direct confrontation with an institutional form of religion. By consigning Mahomet's book to an impious conflagration, Tamburlaine openly dares godly power, even if the divinity that is challenged belongs with the Islamic rather than the Christian faith. Compounding the meanings at work in the scene is the fact that, immediately afterwards, Tamburlaine is represented as experiencing physical pain, as if suffering from the effects of Mahomet's retribution. Yet this suggestion is counter-balanced by the diagnosis of the physician, who holds that Tamburlaine's new weakness is specifically tied to humoural imbalances rather than holy interventions. As Fred B. Tromly states, 'Marlowe toys with the ambiguities of causation to create a moment which both invites and frustrates religious interpretation.'[15] To put the point more concentratedly, as does Troni Y. Grande, 'Marlowe . . . complicates . . . the concept of God.'[16] Certainly, in both *Tamburlaine, Parts One* and *Two*, which God, if any, lies behind the unfolding of events is a point of contentious debate. In the same way that Tamburlaine's enemies prevaricate over his ultimate classification, so do they also hedge their heavenly bets in the area of divine allegiance. Irrespective of divisions and dominations, for instance, Orcanes is figured as happily pledging himself to any constituted religious figure-head that appears to support his cause, as when he announces: 'Christ or Mahomet hath been my friend' (2 *Tamb.* 2.3.11). It is one of a number of incongruously comic moments, the second thought of 'or Mahomet' illumi-nating a diverting political expediency. In the *Tamburlaine the Great* plays, then, religious uncertainty and theological confusion co-exist, with no clear sense either of a deity or of a divinely governed scheme. In part the dramas have Tamburlaine to thank for precipitating this state of affairs. For, in the same moment that he empties out godly authority, Tamburlaine fills the spaces established religion has vacated. He is able to move confidently and freely across a number of godly identifications, from chosen leader of 'Jove' (2 *Tamb.* 4.1.116–17) to 'chiefest lamp of all the earth' (1 *Tamb.* 4.2.36), so that he appears to operate in a quasi-divine capacity. There is no god in Marlowe's epic narrative as its protagonist has robbed and reinvented the role.

Nowhere is this assumption of heavenly powers more self-evident than in Tamburlaine's mantra-like assertion, in *Part Two*, that he is the 'scourge of God' (2 *Tamb.* 4.1.156). Yet, despite the escalation of Tamburlaine's bloody megalomania, an audience is pressed to acknowledge that the 'scourge' is increasingly limited in terms of the sphere of his influence and that a mor-tal rather than a divine agency is in charge. The Tamburlaine of *Part Two* is smaller in stature and less assured of independence: his sons squabble among themselves, and he rides a chariot that, on the constricted boards of the Elizabethan stage, must have been able to move only in a series of frustrated and ever-dwindling circles. More importantly, Tamburlaine is im-aged less as the manifestation than as the inexorable victim of approaching extinction, since death and physical decay, not Jove, Mahomet, or Christ, are the plays' new administrators. Given the bodily emphases of the plays, it is appropriate that Tamburlaine should fall prey to a mortality that is registered in starkly anatomical terms. 'See where...Death, / Shaking and quivering, pale and wan.../ Stands aiming at me with his murdering dart' (2 *Tamb.* 5.3.67–9), states Tamburlaine, his formulation suggesting a rein-verted hierarchy that places the Scythian at the base and his former servant at the apex. A momentary respite is granted when Callapine, with other 'vil-lains' and 'cowards', are 'fled for fear' (2 *Tamb.* 5.3.116); however, death is represented in precisely the same manner earlier in the scene, the implication being that the opposition embodied in the Turkish braggart's son can never be adequately defeated.

Notwithstanding the imminence of death, Tamburlaine agitates to bypass it with a final flourish of extravagance. Once the hearse of Zenocrate has been brought on stage, Tamburlaine instructs his eyes to 'enjoy their latest benefit' (2 *Tamb*. 5.3.225), to 'Pierce through the coffin and the sheet of gold' (227) and to 'glut [their] longings with a heaven of joy' (228). Lisa S. Starks writes, quite rightly, that 'Tamburlaine meditates and fetishizes Zenocrate as a neo-platonic object of beauty', and part of that fetishization, one might add, plays itself out in the mummification of the queenly corpse.[17] A number of impulses are inscribed in the summoning of Tamburlaine's 'embalmed... love' (2 *Tamb*. 2.4.130, 138). Ever the showman, Tamburlaine places on display one of his most prized possessions, only here the demonstration serves to emphasize not what has been gained but what is in the process of being lost. Still the irreverent aspirant, Marlowe's hero endeavours to cheat death through the preservation of a living appearance: the spectacle bespeaks an attempt to transcend mortality via an immaculate sublimation with one of its chosen victims. One might even suggest that the combined stress upon ocular satisfaction and joyful penetration conveys a merging of homoerotic and heteroerotic imperatives, since a sexualized objectification and an ecstatic intimacy are both allowed an equal footing. Whatever reading is privileged in these closing stages, Tamburlaine is incapable of subverting his own destiny. A tragically ironic charge is attached to his concluding pronouncement, which bears all the hallmarks of his wilful personality. Bonding, naming, peremptory resolution, and emboldened self-identification are energetically active in his closing realization: 'deprived [of] company... Tamburlaine, the scourge of God, must die' (2 *Tamb*. 5.3.248–9).

Conclusion

The *Tamburlaine the Great* plays assault the eye and the ear, vexing sensibility in the process. They ask uncomfortable questions about how to interpret, and do so from a range of sometimes untenable perspectives. In the same way that the protagonist makes his vaunts substantial, so do the dramas illustrate their preoccupations in action and in image, thereby revealing an intimate connection between ideological implication and theatrical experience. *Tamburlaine, Parts One* and *Two* are indeed 'astounding', both in terms of their dramaturgy and their social and cultural reverberations. Tamburlaine is the figure around which there gathers a constellation of differences and dissidences, which embrace racial alterity, sexual transgression, and governmental illegitimacy. 'Should we applaud such theatre?' Malcolm Kelsall asks.[18] There can be no easy answer to the question, since an audience, like Tamburlaine's captives, often finds itself in a stunned, perplexed, or ambiguous state. In particular, this is because *Tamburlaine the Great*, as Sara Munson Deats notes, 'composes an anamorphic portrait...a masterpiece of indeterminacy'.[19] Variously fractured and seamless, impassioned and implacable, contestatory and conservative, the Tamburlaine narratives represent an irreducible dramatic phenomenon that is both shaped by, and in tension with, the pressures and possibilities of its time.

NOTES

1. *Tamburlaine the Great*, in *The Complete Plays of Christopher Marlowe*, ed. Mark Thornton Burnett (London: Everyman, 1999), *1 Tamb.* Prologue 1, 3. All further references appear in the text.
2. Patrick Cheney, *Marlowe's Counterfeit Profession: Ovid, Spenser, Counter-Nationhood* (University of Toronto Press, 1997), p. 122.
3. Thomas Cartelli, *Marlowe, Shakespeare, and the Economy of Theatrical Experience* (Philadelphia: University of Pennsylvania Press, 1991), p. 67.
4. Emily C. Bartels, *Spectacles of Strangeness: Imperialism, Alienation, and Marlowe* (Philadelphia: University of Pennsylvania Press, 1993), p. 70.
5. Roger Sales, *Christopher Marlowe* (Basingstoke: Macmillan, 1991), pp. 54–9; Richard Wilson, 'Visible Bullets: Tamburlaine the Great and Ivan the Terrible', *ELH* 62 (1995), 51.
6. Mark Thornton Burnett, *Constructing 'Monsters' in Shakespearean Drama and Early Modern Culture* (Basingstoke: Palgrave, 2002), p. 36.
7. Joanna Gibbs, 'Marlowe's Politic Women', in J. A. Downie and J. T. Parnell (eds.), *Constructing Christopher Marlowe* (Cambridge University Press, 2000), p. 171.
8. Constance Brown Kuriyama, *Hammer or Anvil: Psychological Patterns in Christopher Marlowe's Plays* (New Brunswick: Rutgers University Press, 1980), p. 19.
9. Jonathan Goldberg, 'Sodomy and Society: the Case of Christopher Marlowe', in David Scott Kastan and Peter Stallybrass (eds.), *Staging the Renaissance: Reinterpretations of Elizabethan and Jacobean Drama* (New York: Routledge, 1991), p. 80.
10. Ian McAdam, *The Irony of Identity: Self and Imagination in the Drama of Christopher Marlowe* (Newark: University of Delaware Press, 1999), p. 76.
11. David Hard Zucker, *Stage and Image in the Plays of Christopher Marlowe* (Salzburg: Universität Salzburg, 1972), p. 33.
12. Ruth Lunney, *Marlowe and the Popular Tradition: Innovation in the English Drama before 1595* (Manchester University Press, 2002), p. 48.
13. Marjorie Garber, ' "Here's Nothing Writ": Scribe, Script, and Circumscription in Marlowe's Plays', *TJ* 36 (1984), 301.
14. David H. Thurn, 'Sights of Power in *Tamburlaine*', *ELR* 19 (1989), 11.

15. Fred B. Tromly, *Playing with Desire: Christopher Marlowe and the Art of Tantalization* (University of Toronto Press, 1998), p. 89.
16. Troni Y. Grande, *Marlovian Tragedy: The Play of Dilation* (Lewisburg: Bucknell University Press, 1999), p. 65.
17. Lisa S. Starks, ' "Won with Thy Words and Conquered with Thy Looks": Sadism, Masochism, and the Masochistic Gaze in *1 Tamburlaine*', in Paul Whitfield White (ed.) *Marlowe, History and Sexuality: New Essays on Christopher Marlowe* (New York: AMS Press, 1998), p. 183.
18. Malcolm Kelsall, *Christopher Marlowe* (Leiden: Brill, 1981), p. 71.
19. Sara Munson Deats, *Sex, Gender, and Desire in the Plays of Christopher Marlowe* (Newark: University of Delaware Press, 1997), pp. 160–1.

READING LIST

Battenhouse, Roy W. *Marlowe's Tamburlaine: A Study in Renaissance Moral Philosophy*. Nashville: Vanderbilt University Press, 1964.
Burnett, Mark Thornton. 'Tamburlaine: an Elizabethan Vagabond'. *SP* 84 (1987), 308–23.
'*Tamburlaine* and the Renaissance Concept of Honour'. *SN* 59 (1987), 201–6.
'*Tamburlaine* and the Body'. *Criticism* 33 (1991), 31–48.
Hill, Eugene D. 'Marlowe's "More Excellent and Admirable Methode" of Parody in *Tamburlaine I*'. *RenP* (1995), 33–46.
Howe, James Robinson. *Marlowe, Tamburlaine and Magic*. Athens: Ohio University Press, 1976.
Levenson, Jill L. ' "Working Words": the Verbal Dynamic of *Tamburlaine*'. In Kenneth Friedenreich, Roma Gill, and Constance B. Kuriyama (eds.), *'A Poet and a Filthy Play-Maker': New Essays on Christopher Marlowe*. New York: AMS Press, 1988, pp. 99–116.
Levin, Richard. 'The Contemporary Perception of Marlowe's Tamburlaine'. *MRDE* 1 (1984), 51–70.
Martin, Richard A. 'Marlowe's *Tamburlaine* and the Language of Romance'. *PMLA* 93 (1978), 248–64.
Sullivan, Garrett. 'Space, Measurement, and Stalking Tamburlaine'. *RenD* 28 (1997), 3–27.

9

JULIA REINHARD LUPTON

The Jew of Malta

It is the fate of Marlowe's Jew of Malta to find himself forever lurking a few steps behind Shakespeare's Shylock. Barabas is Shylock's evil twin and nasty precursor – a rougher, meaner, and more starkly stereotypical stage Jew whose exorbitant antics bring into relief that glimmer of humanity that partly illuminates Shakespeare's achievement. Yet it is the task of criticism to try to encounter the play on its own terms, though ever attuned to the sequence of literary events that the play will set into motion. Readings of *The Jew* have approached the work from three basic angles: in relation to the formal de-velopment of English theatre and poetry (Eliot, Bevington, Cheney); as a key contribution to European representations of the Jews (Hunter, Greenblatt, Shapiro); and as an exploration of the larger Mediterranean cultural and political landscape in the English imagination (Bartels, Cartelli). This chapter takes the Jewish question as its central focus, but with an eye to the theatrical medium that displays that world for us. The play, I argue, stages different forms of fellowship – of social, religious, and economic association – that configure and reconfigure the different characters of the play in tendentious and fragile alliances.

The word 'fellowship', prominent, for example, in the New Testament but borrowed from the language of Greek social life, is a term that evokes forms of social affiliation that occur outside of or in dialogue with more official modes of civic participation such as citizenship. In a play so dominated by the survivalist egoism of its central character, the focus on fellowship may seem counter-intuitive – unless, that is, we think about social relations in terms of the liquid play of self-interests in tandem with the strange attractors of religious identity. By looking at intersecting circles of fellowship in the play, we may avoid simple oppositions between Self and Other in favour of a template of multiple memberships and shifting allegiances in a public sphere characterized by ethnic, religious, and economic fragmentation and by a complex layering of legal, political, and social institutions. These circles expand to include not only the different groups represented in the play, but also those involved in the production and enjoyment of the drama itself, since the public theatre of Marlowe's day was a space in which new forms of fellowship, of social, sexual, and economic fraternization were emerging with striking vitality and punch, and on ground cleared both physically and symbolically by the reformed Church.

The Jews of Malta

Malta is a small island located off the coast of Sicily, which had some jurisdiction over it; Sicily in turn answered to Spain during the sixteenth century. The Turks had attempted to conquer Malta in 1565, heightening England's interests in helping to maintain Christian control of the strategically sensitive island. Although Malta was part of the dominions of Spain, it was under direct rule by the Knights of St John (also called the Knights Hospitaller and the Knights of Malta), a militant Catholic order with its roots in the Crusades.[1] In Marlowe's play, the rule of the Knights appears to co-exist with a secular system of magistracies, represented by the Governor Ferneze (presumably not himself a Knight of St John) and a 'senate-house', indicating some form of constitutional government inherited from Roman law. Marlowe adds to this scenario fealty to the Turks, whom he represents as having succeeded in their Maltese offensive.

Lodged within these overlapping and often conflicting Spanish, Turkish, Papal, and Maltese political orders sits still another institution with its own limited jurisdiction, namely the Jewish community that had existed in Malta since Roman times. Like other such communities in Christian Europe and the Mediterranean, the Jews of Malta functioned as a semi-autonomous, self-regulating body within the larger political order of Malta. Excluded from the official life of the city and subject to special taxation, the Jews of Malta nonetheless pursued their own forms of social and religious congregation. In Malta, the Jewish community bore the formal title *universitas judeorum* (university of the Jews) with *universitas* naming 'the whole', the corporate unity formed by a group of people living in a host state. When the Jews were expelled from Spain and its dominions in 1492, the Maltese community was also officially dissolved, although its inhabitants were offered the choice of conversion, which some took, often leading to intermarriage.[2] (We see echoes of this path in the romance and conversion of Barabas's daughter Abigail.) In Marlowe's Malta, the Jews have not yet been exiled (though they had been expelled from England much earlier, in 1289). Instead, they engage in trade and money-lending, and we also see them consulting among themselves concerning matters financial and political. A community apart, bound by their own peculiar laws and customs, they are also capable of interchange with Christians on matters exegetical and sexual as well as economic, as seen in Barabas's offer of commentaries on Maccabees to young Mathias, Christian suitor to his daughter.

As Greenblatt has argued, Barabas, like Shylock after him, flourishes in the realm of pre-political association and exchange that make up what political theorists and social scientists call 'civil society' – the modes of informal affiliation and negotiation that shape the give and take of the stock market and the coffee house, the university and the brothel, the trade union and the country club.[3] Excluded from *civic* life, Barabas, like Shylock after him, flourishes in the realm of *civil* society. Although both words pertain to the life of the city, and often function interchangeably, the *civic* refers more precisely to the political participation of citizens in the official rule of the polis, whereas the *civil* refers to those social, economic, and domestic associations, *civilian* rather than properly *civic*, that exist outside the operation of the political per se. It is within the civil space of economic and social exchange that Barabas engineers, manipulates, and falls out of different forms of private association with Jews, Muslims, and Christians. Grouped in their own communities and furthering their economic interests, the Jews became symbols of both *self-interest* and *special interests*, giving a recognizable face and a social body to the dynamic yet disintegrative effects of capitalism on the traditional fabric of communal life.

The identification of the Jews with the atomizing aspects of civil society, however, is not a purely secular phenomenon, but occurs as the result of a theological quandary. The Jews occupy a troubled place in Christian historiography and political thought. They represent the foundation, the 'Old Testament', of a Christianity seen to flow naturally from the promises and prophesies of the Israelites. The hermeneutic practice of 'typology', in which characters, stories, or images from the Old Testament are read as prefigurations of the great events of Jesus' life (e.g., Isaac = Christ), was an organizing principle not only of sermons and religious commentaries, but also of the visual arts and sacred theatre. Yet, if Judaism was simply a foundation designed to support the soaring edifice of the Church, why did the Jews continue to persist as a distinct religion and people? The problem with Judaism from the Christian perspective was its ongoing resistance to the universal invitation of Christianity, a resistance evidenced by the Jews' continued allegiance to such group-defining rites as circumcision and dietary laws.

Barabas, as Greenblatt first noted, is the consummate figure of civil society's uncivil core. Early in the play, Barabas disengages his ambitions from anything political, declaring of himself and his fellow Jews that 'we come not to be kings' (1.1.128). Proclaiming himself his own neighbour, he firmly separates his destiny from that of Malta: '*Ego mihimet sum semper proximus* [I am always nearest to myself], / Why, let 'em enter, let 'em take the town' (1.1.189–90). When Barabas is finally made Governor of Malta by the Turks at the end of the play, he negotiates the former governor's return to office as quickly as possible, in favour of the clearer and more comfortable good of financial gain. Moreover, even within the limited borders of the Jewish community itself, he refuses to cast in his lot with a common good. As he tells his fellow Jews on their way to the senate-house, 'If anything shall there concern our state, / Assure yourselves I'll look – [*Aside*] unto myself' (1.1.171–2). In Marlowe's Malta, the organized Jewish community is dysfunctional at best; separated from the larger body politic, the purely civil body residing within it is in turn subject to internal dissension and fragmentation.

Barabas's renunciation of political ambition in favour of economic gain reflects the actual position of the Jews in the state. When the Jews are called before the senate-house, an at least nominally representative body, they find no representation in it, no formal political place. When Ferneze first asks the Jews for aid, Barabas responds, 'Alas, my lord, we are no soldiers' (1.2.50). The Jews, he is telling us, are permanently and professionally *civilians*, exempt from military and political obligations by their status as resident aliens. The further interchange alternates among civil, civic, and theological definitions of membership and obligation:

> *Barabas*: Are strangers with your tribute to be taxed?
> 2 *Knight*: Have strangers leave with us to get their wealth?
> Then let them with us còntribute.
> *Barabas*: How! equally?
> *Ferneze*: No, Jew, like infidels.
> For through our sufferance of your hateful lives,
> Who stand accursèd in the sight of heaven,
> These taxes and afflictions are befall'n. (*JM* 1.2.58–67)

Barabas links taxation to political membership – why, he asks, should non-citizens be taxed? The Second Knight counters that although the Jews are denied civic participation, they are nonetheless allowed to pursue their economic interests in the civil realm and thus owe some of their wealth to the state. Barabas protests against equal contributions – 'How? equally?' – a response that presumes equity among citizens and resident aliens with respect to taxation. Yet equality by definition pertains only to those included within a legally defined set (whether that of a specific community or of humanity itself), and Barabas will soon discover that the Jews, residing outside the field of formal citizenship, will be taxed quite a bit more than equally.

The grounds for such exclusion are theological, we are told. Because the Jews are 'accursèd in the sight of heaven', Ferneze argues, they must be taxed above and beyond the Christian citizens by the political body that suffers their existence. The scandal of the Jews' survival into the Christian era requires their political exclusion, while their consequent habitation of the purely economic domain of social life justifies their exorbitant taxation. Conversion, however, remains a solution during this phase of Jewish–Gentile relations (distinguishing it, for example, from the race-based Nuremburg laws of the Nazis). The articles read by Ferneze's Officer state that 'Secondly, he that denies to pay shall straight become a Christian' (1.2.72), implying that converted Jews will become naturalized citizens or subjects, cancelling their ties to Judaism in order to enter into the body politic. Political membership, here and throughout the Western tradition, occurs at a cost, requiring the renunciation of local, familial, tribal, or 'particular' allegiances in exchange for more general or universal ones.

The Jews of Malta, however, prefer to maintain their 'hateful lives' – their continued existence as Jews, as well as their economic livelihoods. In this scene and elsewhere in the play, the 'life' of the Jews is a code word for the particularism that they instantiate. Belying the typological pattern of Christian hermeneutics, the Jews have persisted as a religious group; surviving past their due date, an uncanny, even undead quality colours the weird vitality they embody in the Christian imagination. Survival, moreover, implies compromise and pragmatism, a less than strict adherence to heroic or moral codes. We might recall here, for example, the ethos of survival exemplified by Odysseus, who lives into middle age thanks to the deftness of his intuitions. In a different historical register, think as well of the moral and emotional 'gray zone' inhabited by survivors of the Holocaust, faced with the horror of impossible choices; for this generation, and even for their descendants, to live is not-to-have-died with the others.

Barabas derives his name from Barabbas, the Jewish prisoner who was released by the Roman authorities in place of Jesus at the behest of his Jewish accusers:

> Now at the feast the governor was accustomed to release for the crowd any one prisoner whom they wanted. And they had then a notorious prisoner, called Barabbas. So when they had gathered, Pilate said to them, 'Whom do you want me to release for you, Barabbas or Jesus who is called Christ?'
> (Matt. 27: 15–17; cf. Mark 15, Luke 23, John 18)

In the scene before Pilate, the Jews choose to pardon Barabbas, not Jesus, forever marking the former as the one-who-did-not-die-in-the-place-of-Christ, the one who was not substituted for Jesus. To gain this life, however, is to accrue a historical debt: when Pilate washes his hands, the Jews reply, '"His blood be on us and on our children"' (Matt. 27: 25). Released by Pilate on behalf of the Jews, the survival of Barabbas at the expense of Jesus will be irrevocably linked to the formal exclusion of the Jews from political life, their subsequent identification with fiscal dealings and misdealings, and their pursuit of alternative forms of social organization and self-regulation within the commonwealths that host them.

In the trial scene of *The Jew of Malta*, Ferneze, washing his own hands of responsibility for the Jews, explicitly evokes the debt earned by the Jews in the court of Pilate:

> If your first curse fall heavy on thy head,
> And make thee poor and scorned of all the world,
> 'Tis not our fault, but thy inherent sin.
>
> (*JM* 1.2.110–12)

When the Jews of Malta are asked to give up their wealth for the greater good of the state, Barabas refuses. As he declares to Abigail in the development of the scene, 'No, I will live; nor loathe I this my life' (1.2.267). *This my life*: the phrase names the particularized field of religious survival and economic livelihood that places the Jews both in and out of Malta, as a tolerated, semi-autonomous body of resident aliens carrying out economic functions for the larger civic order.

Marlowe fashioned Barabas out of the allegorical figure of the Vice, an archetype of villainy inherited from the stage devils of sacred drama and developed in the minimally secular morality plays of the sixteenth century.[4] As Greenblatt and others have noted, Barabas loses rather than gains in individuality as the play progresses, falling back into his allegorical origins (Greenblatt, p. 150). His infamous autobiography of crimes ('As for myself, I walk abroad a'nights...' (2.3.177–201)) gathers together a poisonous bouquet of generalized anti-Jewish stereotypes interwoven with Machiavellian motifs of policy and self-interest. During this period, the writings of the Italian political theorist were seen as the embodiment of corrupt political pragmatism and devious atheism; Marlowe famously begins his play with a prologue speech by 'Machiavel', resolutely inserting the theological discourse of anti-Judaism into the frame of modern politics, a fusion continued here in Barabas's allegorical autobiography.[5] The speech ends with Barabas's triumphant self-accounting: 'But mark how I am blessed for plaguing them; / I have as much coin as will buy the town' (2.3.202–3). The infinite riches of the biblical concept of blessing have been contracted to the little room of self-interest, which in turn becomes an echo-chamber that traps, redoubles, and caricatures the history of Jewish survival in and as civil society.

The new Jews: from Israel to Islam

Barabas delivers his mythic autobiography in the profane setting of the slave-market, where he will purchase his side-kick, the Turkish Ithamore. The speech functions as a down-payment in the relationship between the Jew and the Turk, who responds in kind with his own briefer but no less vivid accounting of Muslim crimes. Barabas represents his new association with Ithamore as a *fellowship*, an informal alliance based on mutual interests: 'make account of me / *As of thy fellow*; we are villains both: / Both circumcised, we hate Christians both' (2.3.225–7; emphasis added). Barabas founds their fellowship on the mark of circumcision borne by each partner in the new relationship. Circumcision, a sign of covenantal belonging for the Jewish community, becomes a means of linking the Jew to the Muslim, significantly expanding the kinds of pre-political association possible in Malta to include an alliance between members of two distinct non-Christian groups.

Circumcision is a key symbol in biblical typology. In Judaism, circumcision had functioned as a rite of civic initiation linking the members of the Abrahamic covenant to each other and to God. St Paul, in his efforts to build mixed congregations composed of both Jewish and Gentile Christians, transmuted the covenantal signature of circumcision into an interior symbol, a 'circumcision of the heart', that would no longer require a physical cut as the means of initiation.[6] In the post-Pauline world of official Christianities, circumcision became a mark of Jewish obdurance. Moreover, by the time that Marlowe writes his play, the ranks of the circumcised have grown to include the Muslims, bearers of the world-view most immediately at odds with Christian moral and territorial claims. Represented first by the Arabs and then by the Turks, Islam dangerously combined the circumcised legal separatism of the Jews with the universal mission of the Christians. Islam, like Judaism, was a religion living not far away but close at hand, which, far from worshipping many gods, ascribed to monotheisms at least as strict as Christianity's own. Moreover, Judaism and Islam stem from the same Abrahamic lineage as Christianity; the three groups are, in the Muslim phrase, 'People of the Book', neighbouring religions organized around revealed Scriptures that share many of the same prophets and patriarchs. The knowledge of the Law epitomized by Jewish and Muslim monotheism meant that these groups had both more affinity with and more resistance to genuine Christian conversion than their pagan counterparts.[7]

Islam, the youngest of the three Abrahamic religions, came to represent to Christianity a kind of Judaism after the fact, a redoubling of Jewish intransigence to the Christian revelation. As such, Islam executes a second, even crueller blow to Christianity's historical vision, since modern Judaism (from the Christian perspective) is a stubborn carry-over from an earlier moment, but Islam from its very inception administered its proselytizing mission in full knowledge of Christian teachings. The rapid expansion of Islam throughout the Levant, North Africa, the Far East, and the Balkans, however, presented the inverse of Judaism's dispersed, sequestered, and inward-looking communities. The third Revelation announced by Islam rejected Jewish particularism in favour of Christian universalism; like the rulers of European Christendom, the Arab and then Turkish powers used the theme of spiritual equality among the nations to support their missionary, imperial, and commercial projects.[8] For Renaissance Christendom, Islam represented a double scandal, the catastrophic bastardization of both Christian universalism and Jewish particularism.

In *The Jew of Malta*, Marlowe exploits these linkages between Judaism and Islam. The name 'Ithamore', for example, is a variant of the biblical 'Ithamar', the youngest son of Aaron and hence part of the priestly line of the Levites, professional upholders of Jewish ritual law. Islamicizing '-mar' into '-more' (which sounds like 'Moor'), Marlowe signals the fellowship between Jewish and Islamic legalisms signed by circumcision. Ithamore's legal status as a slave also picks up a theme long associated with the Jews, the motif of enslavement to the law. According to Paul, the Jews under the law were like a child–heir, 'no better than a slave, though he is the owner of all the estate; but he is under guardians and trustees until the date set by the father' (Gal. 4: 1–3). In Paul's thinking, the law is a necessary but transitional stage in both the history of world religion and the spiritual development of each individual. Just as a child comes of age and leaves the slavish jurisdiction of his father, so Judaism (and later Islam) should leave behind its laws and enter into the freedom of Christian grace.

Ithamore is a slave who will be manumitted at the time set by his adoptive father, Barabas – he will be emancipated, however, not into Christian freedom but into further fellowship in villainy with the unconverted Jew. When Barabas disinherits Abigail on the occasion of her conversion to Christianity, he adopts Ithamore as his heir and proceeds to poison not only his daughter, but all the nuns with whom she now resides. Moving from Judaism to Christianity, Abigail is a positive instance of the proper typological progression from Old to New Testaments. The doubling of her conversions, like the doubling of her boyfriends, sours the sentimental seriousness of Abigail's turn to Christianity. Nonetheless, Abigail's civic ventures lay out the key exit strategies from Judaism – marriage and conversion – that demarcate the limited forms of openness that Christian commonwealths entertained in relation to their Jewish populations (Wettinger, p. 128).

For Barabas, in keeping with Jewish law on this matter, a Christian daughter is no longer alive for him. In her place, he adopts Ithamore: 'O trusty Ithamore, no servant, but my friend: / I here adopt thee for mine only heir, / All that I have is thine when I am dead, / And whilst I live use half; spend as myself' (3.5.39–43). They then proceed to poison the nunnery with a pot of rice. The adoption of Ithamore, a legal transfer of affect and property conducted in relation to a pot of soup, parodies the biblical story of Esau and Jacob, a favourite topic of typological interpretation. In Genesis, Esau is older brother to the younger Jacob, who will inherit the blessing of their father Isaac through a trick arranged by their mother Rebecca, who sends the younger twin to their blind father with a pot of lentils and a hairy disguise (Gen. 27). In the Jewish tradition, the story narrates the founding line of the twelve tribes of Israel (the name that Jacob will later receive), while Esau becomes a type of various neighbouring groups hostile to Israel. St Paul, on the other hand, takes this and other stories about younger brothers ascending over older brothers as an allegory of the supersession of Christianity over Judaism (e.g., Rom. 9: 10–13). Whereas for the Jews, Jacob is to Esau as Israel is to her enemies, for Paul, Jacob is to Esau as Christianity is to Judaism – a transvaluation and partial reversal of the story's original meaning.

In Marlowe's replay of the story from Genesis, Ithamore delivers the soup that will kill Abigail. He in effect assumes the role of Jacob, receiving the blessing of Barabas / Isaac in the place of the more legitimate sibling. In this allegory, the Muslims are the new Jews, inheriting in the place of the legitimate child (who has sensibly converted to Christianity). If Abigail has made the proper typological transition from Judaism to Christianity, Ithamore travels in the reverse direction, from the second-order Judaism of Islam to the inveterate Judaism that it mimics. The fellowship of Jew and Muslim represents the double negation of the positive conversion effected by Abigail, who becomes their sorry sacrifice.

As such, it is, like all of Barabas's alliances, a fellowship bound to fall apart. The legal formalism of the adoption indicates that their relationship remains one of merely civil association, and will never attain the pathos of a genuine blood tie, a national identity, or a new faith. If circumcision is the initial signature of fellowship for Ithamore and Barabas, it is soon devalued in Ithamore's dismissive remarks once he has fallen under the spell of the courtesan Bellamira. He mocks the Jew's dietary laws, and then links Barabas's poor hygiene to his circumcision: 'He never put on clean shirt since he was circumcised' (4.4.72). What before had bound the two together in mutual enmity against Christians has now been absorbed into a battery of anti-Jewish images that Ithamore glibly recites in his bid for inclusion in Malta's brothel culture. Ithamore closes the scene (and the door on Jewish fellowship) with the cryptic saying, 'The meaning has a meaning. Come, let's in; / To undo a Jew is charity, not sin' (4.4.91–2). Ithamore has learned to speak the language of the Christians, who cynically use the language of typology to oil the economy while keeping their hands clean.

Rezoning

All of this takes place not in the margins of scriptural commentaries, but in the space of the new public theatre. Marlowe's stage would have consisted of the main platform, an inner stage at the back, and a gallery above, regions easily refigured throughout the drama to represent different locales in Malta (the houses of Barabas, the senate-house, the marketplace, the brothel). These rapid scenic remappings, the staple of Elizabethan theatre, are symbolic as well as pragmatic, since each shift rezones Malta's civil and religious sectors not only within the represented world of the play, but also ultimately in relation to the conditions of English theatre itself.

Act 1, scene 1 opens with Barabas 'in his counting house' – perhaps positioned towards the back of the main stage, more likely discovered in its inner stage. The enclosure effectively frames Barabas as a type of Avarice, identifying the Jew with the mercantile economy and with a long line of allegorical Vice figures (Lunney, pp. 107–8). Yet this narrow space soon opens outwards; Cheney imagines Barabas gesturing expansively to encompass the whole stage, 'thereby identifying the room of the counting-house with the room of the theatre' (p. 145). The sweep of the hand locates both Barabas and Marlowe at the crossroads of sacred and civil orders of representations.

Barabas will, however, soon lose this house. The appropriation of Barabas's property and its conversion to a nunnery recalls another familiar typological theme, the transformation of the Synagogue into the Church. For example, in Renaissance art the Virgin Mary is often depicted in front of a building in ruins, alluding to the decline of the Synagogue and its renovation as the Church, of which Mary herself was a favourite symbol.[9] Like Mary, Abigail passes from the Old to the New Testament, a consummate figure of Judeo-Christian womanhood; and like Mary's ruins, her calling takes place in relation to a building that has undergone radical conversion. Shortly, Abigail will appear on the balcony of the new nunnery, habited as a nun, while her father frets beneath her window like a ghost of Passovers past. With the daughter above and the father below, the scene visually schematizes the positioning of superstructure over foundation, Church over Synagogue – the architecture of typology itself.

Yet Barabas has secreted some of his wealth in this typological edifice. Hidden 'close underneath the plank / That runs along the upper-chamber floor' (1.2.297–8), the stash of jewels is an insurance plan, a pocket of movable property that will protect his household against the whims of the state and the Jews' uncertain claims to real estate, depositing the chance of Jewish survival in the crawl space of Christian history. Barabas will use the wealth, as Garrett Sullivan observes in this volume, to 'buy *another* house' – to cultivate another place where the identification of Jewish survival with civil society can continue to unfold. The *converso*, Abigail, is no Virgin Mary; Barabas remains true to his namesake Barabbas, refusing to die into history, and the theological rezoning of Malta remains incomplete.

The play's architecture of conversion and its discontents takes place on the stage of the public theatre. Mobilizing the iconography of the Judeo-Christian turn, the expropriation of Barabas's property has a more contemporary reference as well, namely to Henry VIII's dissolution of the monasteries, including the urban and suburban monastic liberties on which many of London's public theatres now stood. The monastic holdings had always carried the special legal status of 'liberties', not subject to royal and municipal jurisdictions and governed by their own ecclesiastical courts that answered to Rome. When the Church's lands passed to the Crown, the tie with Rome was of course broken, but the lands remained legal 'liberties', free from municipal control. The liberties could thus be leased for various forms of unregulated economic and social activity, including brothels, taverns, and theatres. Blackfriars and Whitefriars, theatres built on liberties within the city of London, retained in their names a reference to their monastic origins.[10]

Like the Jewish community of Malta, the liberties of London isolate civil society as a set of phenomena separate from official civic life – a jurisdiction unto themselves, defined at least initially by religious law, and animated by the free flow of capital, where various forms of fellowship take root in a volatile microclimate potentially at odds with that of the commonwealth that houses it. Moreover, the evacuation of this space for use by the theatre is linked to a complex juridical, political, and theological operation, that of the dissolution of the monasteries. The public theatre is given a Protestant frame – the same frame that allows Marlowe to couch his corrosive representation of Christian hypocrisy under the neutralizing rubric of anti-Catholic satire. These Christians may be nasty, but after all, they are Spanish Catholics, not English Protestants; indeed, the theatrical space we are currently occupying exists thanks to the break with Rome. But – the public theatre is not a church; in fact, it may even be an anti-church, an underworld of carnal, criminal, and economic rather than genuinely spiritual congregation. In this, it shares something with the community of the Jews.

In *The Jew of Malta*, the architecture of the stage discovers within itself a series of real and symbolic transformations – of synagogue into nunnery, of

Catholic monastery holdings into Protestant royal property, and of the old monastic liberties into new theatrical ones. If the Jew is a figure of uncivil society, so too is the actor: each 'congregates', engaging in forms of affiliation and transaction, of dangerous fellowship, that exist with some degree of liberty in relation to the political jurisdictions of city and state. Cheney has noted the mounting equation between Barabas and theatre in the course of the play, culminating in his appearance as an actor–poet–musician in the house of Bellamira in Act 4 and his building of the final stage set in Act 5 (pp. 154–6). Designing and installing a trap for Calymath, Barabas meanwhile plans a bloody end for the Turkish troops in a 'monastery / Which standeth as an outhouse to the town' (5.4.36). Barabas's urban theatre of cruelty finds its suburban counterpart in the liberties just outside the city, the same region 'o'er the walls' of Malta where his body is thrown for a few moments of feigned death and mock resurrection (5.2.58; Mullaney, pp. 58–9).

While the Turkish soldiers are being cooked alive at their own banquet, Barabas hosts their leader Calymath along with Ferneze, Del Bosco, and the Knights of St John in his 'homely citadel'. This final feast is Barabas's literalization of the universal dream of the New Testament, where the sharing of food among Jewish and Gentile Christians is a key feature of the new fellowship in Christ (e.g., Gal. 2: 11–13). Barabas sets a table where Jews, Christians, and Muslims will eat together, abrogating the dietary laws that have kept both Jews and Muslims from the common table of the nations – but his plan, of course, is to drown the Turkish Selim in the soup pot in order to serve him to the Christian governor in exchange for a hefty tip. Moreover, his reward will be collected *from the citizens of Malta* (5.2.29) – from the very legal group that has excluded Barabas from its ranks based on his non-conversion.

The opposite will in fact occur: the bustling stage-engineer, *'very busy'* on his 'dainty gallery', will be cooked in his own pot of soup, cursed by his own blessing, as he falls from the balcony into the inner stage below. This is the play's final rezoning. In a classic set of reversals, the bearer of bad soup is now stewed in his own cauldron, materializing the Hell's Mouth of sacred drama. The inner stage, once cast as the Jew's counting house, is now his coffin. This interior frame discloses our first and last visions of the Jew: from this box he issues, and to this box he shall return. Between these two tableaux, a series of typological remappings has occurred that reflect on the congregational space of the new public theatre. Insofar as Marlowe connects the libertine grounds of the theatre to the civil society of the Jews, the playwright begins to imagine a universe, or at least a *universitas*, a restricted sphere of limited autonomy engaged by a collectivity, in which social, artistic, and religious experiment might take place in some degree of separation from state control and supervision. Marlowe's point is not that the artist, like the Jew, is the Other to the Self projected by a normative and exclusive political order, but rather, more generously and more broadly, that artists, like Jews, can recreate, reinhabit, and remap the civil spaces left over by the incomplete transformations and uncanny survivals of religious forms in modernity. As such, the play constitutes an invitation to think outside the box – the very box of traditional dramatic closure into which Barabas falls with such ferocious style – precisely by making its infinite space echo so deeply from within.

NOTES

1. Emily C. Bartels, *Spectacles of Strangeness: Imperialism, Alienation, and Marlowe* (Philadelphia: University of Pennsylvania Press, 1993), pp. 88–9.

2. Margaret Williams, *The Jews Among the Greeks and Romans: A Diasporan Sourcebook* (Baltimore: Johns Hopkins University Press, 1998), pp. 27, 31; Godfrey Wettinger, *The Jews of Malta in the Late Middle Age* (Malta: Midsea Books, 1985), pp. 116–39.

3. Stephen Greenblatt, 'Marlowe, Marx, and Anti-Semitism' (1978), in Richard Wilson (ed.), *Christopher Marlowe* (Harlow: Longman, 1999), pp. 140–58.

4. On Marlowe and the morality tradition, see David Bevington, *From 'Mankinde' to Marlowe: Growth of Structure in the Popular Drama of Tudor England* (Cambridge, MA: Harvard University Press, 1962); Ruth Lunney, *Marlowe and the Popular Tradition: Innovation in the English Drama before 1595* (Manchester University Press, 2002).

5. On Marlowe and Machiavelli, see Cheney, *Marlowe's Counterfeit Profession: Ovid, Spenser, Counter-Nationhood* (University of Toronto Press, 1997), pp. 136–56. On Machiavelli and the Renaissance political and literary imagination, see Wayne Rebhorn, *Foxes and Lions: Machiavelli's Confidence Men* (Ithaca: Cornell University Press, 1988); and Victoria Kahn, *Machiavellian Rhetoric: From the Counter-Reformation to Milton* (Princeton University Press, 1994).

6. E. P. Sanders, *Paul and Palestinian Judaism: A Comparison of Patterns of Religion* (London: SCM, 1977); Daniel Boyarin, *A Radical Jew: Paul and the Politics of Identity* (Berkeley: University of California Press, 1994); and Mikael Tellbe, *Paul between Synagogue and State: Christians, Jews, and Civic Authorities in 1 Thessalonians, Romans, and Philippians* (Stockholm: Almquist and Wiksell International, 2001).

7. Julia Reinhard Lupton, '*Othello* Circumcised: Shakespeare and the Pauline Discourse of Nations', *Representations* 57 (1997), 73–89.

8. Bernard Lewis, *Race and Color in Islam* (New York: Harper and Row, 1971), pp. 1–28.

9. Erwin Panofsky, *Early Netherlandish Painting*, 2 vols. (New York: Harper and Row, 1971), 1: 133–40.

10. Steven Mullaney, *The Place of the Stage: License, Play, and Power in Renaissance England* (University of Chicago Press, 1988).

READING LIST

Bartels, Emily C. *Spectacles of Strangeness: Imperialism, Alienation, and Marlowe.* Philadelphia: University of Pennsylvania Press, 1993.

Bevington, David. *From 'Mankinde' to Marlowe: Growth of Structure in the Popular Drama of Tudor England.* Cambridge, MA: Harvard University Press, 1962.

Cartelli, Thomas. *Marlowe, Shakespeare, and the Economy of Theatrical Experience.* Philadelphia: University of Pennsylvania Press, 1991.

Cheney, Patrick. *Marlowe's Counterfeit Profession: Ovid, Spenser, Counter-Nationhood.* University of Toronto Press, 1997.

Chew, Samuel C. *The Crescent and the Rose: Islam and England during the Renaissance.* New York: Oxford University Press, 1937.

Greenblatt, Stephen. 'Marlowe, Marx, and Anti-Semitism' (1978). In Richard Wilson (ed.), *Christopher Marlowe.* Harlow: Longman, 1999, pp. 140–58.

Hunter, G. K. *Dramatic Identities and Cultural Tradition: Studies in Shakespeare and His Contemporaries.* Liverpool University Press, 1978.

Kahn, Victoria Ann. *Machiavellian Rhetoric: From the Counter-Reformation to Milton.* Princeton University Press, 1994.

Lunney, Ruth. *Marlowe and the Popular Tradition: Innovation in the English Drama before 1595.* Manchester University Press, 2002.

Wettinger, Godfrey. *The Jews of Malta in the Late Middle Age.* Malta: Midsea Books, 1985.

10

THOMAS CARTELLI

Edward II

As Marlowe has emerged in recent years as early modern England's most modern playwright, *Edward II* has emerged as his most modern play, not merely because it treats the life and loves, and stages the brutal debasement, of a recognizably (if not exclusively) homosexual monarch, but also because it presents a decidedly direct and demystified portrayal of power politics at work, showing political positions to be little more than transparent extensions of the personal desires and ambitions that motivate them. The passions on display in *Edward II*, whether they be Edward's all-consuming love for his favourite, Gaveston, or Mortimer Junior's unrestrained hostility to Edward and Gaveston alike, shape and dominate both the private and political behaviour of the play's two primary antagonists, and contribute mightily to the disordered relations in family and state that obtain throughout the play. As such, they paradoxically present themselves as fit objects of audience censure and disapprobation, and as the primary expressive channels of character formation and audience engagement alike.

Much recent scholarship on the early modern period has been devoted to a reconsideration of the viability of applying traditional theories of the relationship between the four vital bodily elements (blood, yellow bile, phlegm, and black bile) and the four "humours" (sanguine or cheerful, choleric, phlegmatic or stolid, and melancholy) to an understanding of what we late moderns tend to construe as psychological states. An excess of one or other of these elements in an individual's body (say, of yellow or black bile) was thought to produce a humoural imbalance that would make one's temperament chronically aggressive, on the one hand, chronically melancholy on the other. This renewed attention to the physiological sources of externally manifested moods, character-traits, and emotions has brought with it a collateral focus on efforts to moderate such imbalances in the interest of achieving 'the humoural ideal of physiological self-control'.[1] As Michael Schoenfeldt writes with respect to this ideal, 'The Renaissance seems to have imagined selves who differentiate not by their desires, which all more or less share, but by their capacity to control these desires' (p. 17). This 'early modern fetish of control . . . does not demand the unequivocal banishment of emotion'; rather, 'it is unfettered emotion that is most to be feared', the category of passions that is put on display in virtually every scene of *Edward II* (Schoenfeldt, pp. 18, 17). Yet, as Jonathan Gil Harris notes, even the best recent studies tend to 'shy away from sustained analysis of the far more alien and ornery physiology of the passions, whose murky materiality arguably presents a greater stumbling block to moderns' (p. 257). According to Harris, 'The book on the early modern passions is yet to be written', and 'once it is', he imagines, 'the drama of Shakespeare and his contemporaries will figure prominently in its purview' (p. 258). While this is hardly the place to proclaim such a study (which has already been initiated by abler minds), I would, at least, like to situate the present chapter in the context of ongoing efforts to analyse the early modern passions, and to start by claiming that in *Edward II* the passions embodied in the acts and lines of specific characters operate within a very narrow, yet volatile, field of reference, one whose 'murky materiality' manifests fewer ties to humoural theory or physiology than to 'affective economies' of anger and desire that refuse to accommodate themselves to a moral economy of restraint or control.[2] These 'economies' draw their force from a competing ethic that 'brooks' (a much favoured word in this play) no check or curb on expressions of individualist self-assertion or self-esteem.

In *Edward II*, the drama takes place 'inside' in more ways than one and presents its audience with something in the way of a closed set. Although the play derives its plot from Marlowe's dramatic compression of his source-materials in the chronicles of Holinshed and Stow, it often seems to derive its shape and momentum from within, from the abrupt and seemingly un-patterned conflicts of rival passions and personalities. Marlowe cultivates this illusion of plot-autonomy by allowing the intensity of personal interests and unbridled emotion to determine the structure and momentum of his play. We can illustrate this tendency by tracking the movement of an early sequence that proceeds from a moment of calm and apparent reconciliation, but culminates in the most emphatic moment of crisis witnessed in the first movement of the drama. The sequence begins with an uncharacteristic exchange of amicable sentiments between the king and his peers that directly follows (and is the product of) their decision to have the recently banished Gaveston recalled from Ireland:

Edward: Courageous Lancaster, embrace thy king,
　And as gross vapours perish by the sun,
　Even so let hatred with thy sovereign's smile:
　Live thou with me as my companion.

Lancaster: This salutation overjoys my heart.
Edward: Warwick shall be my chiefest counsellor:
   These silver hairs will more adorn my court
   Than gaudy silks or rich embroidery.
   Chide me, sweet Warwick, if I go astray.
Warwick: Slay me, my Lord, when I offend your grace.

                 (*EII* 1.4.339–48)[3]

Edward's analogy between 'gross vapours' and Lancaster's hatred gestures directly at the model of physiological self-control outlined by Schoenfeldt, and Edward's smile suggests his own effort to restore in Lancaster the humoural balance that freedom from hatred should bring. We know, however, from the preceding sequence that Edward is so 'frantic' for his Gaveston (1.4.314) that he will promise anything to have his favourite returned and that the peers' apparently gracious decision to recall Gaveston is informed by the treacherous designs Mortimer Junior has already concocted with the queen: 'But were he here, detested as he is, / How easily might some base slave be suborned / To greet his lordship with a poniard' (1.4.264–6). We see, therefore, thinly disguised behind the decorous exchange of compliment and platitude, the continuing development of a tension that may be suspended for the moment, but must express itself sooner or later. While Edward and Lancaster alike gesture at a restored humoural ideal, the fact that their aims could not be more different reduces that ideal to the residual status of a mannerly figure of speech.

This carefully cultivated reconcilement is soon sundered by the peers' inability to suppress for longer than the interval of a single scene their hatred of Gaveston and by Edward's inability to repress in the sight of the peers his 'passionate' regard for 'his minion':

Edward: The wind is good; I wonder why he stays.
   I fear me he is wracked upon the sea.
Isabella: Look, Lancaster, how passionate he is,
   And still his mind runs on his minion.
Lancaster: My lord –
Edward: How now, what news? Is Gaveston arrived?
Mortimer Junior: Nothing but Gaveston! What means your grace?
   You have matters of more weight to think upon;
   The King of France sets foot in Normandy.
Edward: A trifle! We'll expel him when we please.
   But tell me, Mortimer, what's thy device
   Against the stately triumph we decreed?

                 (*EII* 2.2.1–12)

Mortimer describes a device in which Gaveston is figured as a canker climbing its way to the 'top branches' of 'a lofty cedar tree fair flourishing' where 'kingly eagles perch', thereby expressing his undisguised contempt for Gaveston. Lancaster immediately follows suit and the exhibition of devices is, in turn, succeeded by the series of mocking salutations with which the peers greet Gaveston in person. When Edward 'warrants' the now indignant Gaveston to 'return' these insults 'to their throats', Gaveston does so in a manner that graphically delineates the social and behavioural divide that separates them:

> Base leaden earls that glory in your birth,
> Go sit at home and eat your tenants' beef,
> And come not here to scoff at Gaveston,
> Whose mounting thoughts did never creep so low
> As to bestow a look on such as you.
>
> (*EII* 2.2.74–8)

Apparently outraged by Gaveston's taunt, the peers draw their swords and Mortimer (oblivious to his resolve to delegate such actions to a suitably 'base slave') stabs Gaveston, leading the queen to exclaim, 'Ah, furious Mortimer, what hast thou done?' and leading Edward to say to Mortimer and Lancaster alike, 'Dear shall you both aby [pay for] this riotous deed' (2.2.85, 88), thereby framing their actions in the same discourse of misrule the peers deploy against his relations with Gaveston. As the unchecked fury of Mortimer meets the unchecked passion of Edward head on, the underlying tensions of the play's first movement break out in force with a seemingly autonomous energy of their own.

There is, of course, nothing autonomous about the plot of a play that Marlowe has constructed to elicit just such effects. What his construction of this movement of the play tells us is that he is interested in staging at least two competing forms of disorder in *Edward II*, one focused on Edward's passionate obsession with Gaveston and the other on the arrogance, impatience, and downright fury of Edward's aristocratic opponents, chiefly, though not exclusively, Mortimer. Although Marlowe initially works in concert with his chronicle sources in casting Gaveston in the role of lord of misrule and having him and Edward preside over a carnivalized court in which established hierarchies are literally turned upside-down, within the first hundred lines of the play the peers have already begun to make large contributions of their own to the disordered relations that obtain in Edward's court. Before Edward even has the opportunity to greet Gaveston and endow him with a series of outsized offices and distinctions, the peers make unconditional demands on him whose tenor seldom departs from Mortimer Senior's peremptory 'If you love us, my lord, hate Gaveston' (1.1.79). When, some forty lines later, Mortimer Junior is bid, 'Bridle thy anger', by his fellow peer, Warwick, his response, 'I cannot nor I will not', designation of the king as 'brainsick', and threat to 'henceforth parley with our naked swords', all seem radically incommensurate with his own subject position. The king – who is himself incapable of bridling his own desires – will, of course, soon give Mortimer and the other peers ample cause for such concern. But it seems sufficiently plain that in the first scene of his play, Marlowe is intent on demonstrating that both sides to the controversy are equally unyielding, equally unmindful of anything that one would call the good of the kingdom, much less a humoural ideal founded on temperance.

In this, Marlowe conspicuously departs from the disposition of blame assigned in Holinshed, his primary source, which finds Edward sorely culpable for the wrongs committed through his indulgence by Gaveston and the Despensers alike, and among the peers generally only holds Mortimer Junior accountable for crimes committed in concert with the queen in the last years of Edward's reign.[4] Indeed, by failing to dramatize to any great extent the social and economic crimes committed by Edward's favourites and by making them appear entirely loyal and loving to Edward, Marlowe often makes the peers' objections to them seem excessive, and directed more at their 'base' status as social upstarts than at any crimes more specific than raiding the treasury that they may have committed. Marlowe also – as my preceding commentary on 2.2 should indicate – allows Gaveston in particular to become the channel or mouthpiece for the expression of sentiments that appear specifically designed to make the play's audience sceptical of the peers' avowedly high-minded intentions and high-handed behaviour.

Dramatically positioned as the play's Presenter, Gaveston lays first claim to audience attention as he enters the stage reading a letter from the king and immediately establishes both the amorously negligent nature of his relationship with the king and the embattled terms of his relationship with the peers:

> The sight of London to my exiled eyes
> Is as Elysium to a new-come soul;
> Not that I love the city or the men,
> But that it harbours him I hold so dear—
> The king, upon whose bosom let me die,
> And with the world be still at enmity.
> . . .
> Farewell base stooping to the lordly peers;
> My knee shall bow to none but to the king.
> (EII 1.1.10–15, 18–19)

After negotiating his ironically dismissive interview with the three poor men who petition him for service, Gaveston paints a powerfully seductive picture of what the court will look like when he becomes master of the king's revels:

> Sometime a lovely boy in Dian's shape,
> With hair that gilds the water as it glides,
> Crownets of pearl about his naked arms,
> And in his sportful hands an olive tree
> To hide those parts that men delight to see,
> Shall bathe him in a spring; and there, hard by,
> One like Actaeon, peeping through the grove,
> Shall by the angry goddess be transformed,
> And, running in the likeness of an hart,
> By yelping hounds pulled down, and seem to die.
> Such things as these best please his majesty,
> My Lord.   (*EII* 1.1.60–71)

As the play-proper begins and Gaveston withdraws to the margins of the stage, it is at least conceivable that his cultivated fantasy of an eroticized court life could maintain more of an appeal than that commanded by the fierce but decidedly stiff aggression of the peers, who now seek to assert their claim to the kingdom and the stage alike.[5] In rendering the lords their due in a series of pointed asides, Gaveston deflates their moral self-righteousness and makes the patriotic positions they assume seem what Marlowe shows them to be in the course of the play, namely, defences of their own prerogatives. Wryly commenting '*Mort Dieu*!' in response to Mortimer Junior's thunderous claim that he would sooner put his sword to sleep and 'hang his armour up' than break the oath he made to Edward's father to prevent Gaveston's return, Gaveston plays on the privileged access to the audience he has arguably already achieved in order to demonstrate the claim's dramatic status as self-regarding bluster and bravado. Of course, as the peers leave the stage and Gaveston enters into the embrace of the king who summarily 'creates' him 'Lord High Chamberlain, / Chief Secretary to the state and me, / Earl of Cornwall, King and Lord of Man' (1.1.153–5), it may well be objected that Marlowe also cultivates here the possibility of an opposing point of view. That he does so is clearly signalled both by Kent's comment, 'Brother, the least of these may well suffice / For one of greater birth than Gaveston' (1.1.157–8), and by Gaveston's and Edward's subsequent manhandling, arrest, and dispossession of the Bishop of Coventry: acts that are surely as 'furious' and 'riotous' as those soon to be committed against Gaveston by Mortimer and his fellow peers. And when Gaveston soon thereafter appears seated beside Edward on the throne in the effectual position of England's queen, it may well seem that a form of sodomitical misrule has pre-empted right rule in the court.

Although 'The Elizabethan chroniclers are eloquent, even vehement, about the evil influence Gaveston had over the king, leading him into extravagance and dissolute pleasures, even persuading him to commit adultery... none of this produces a charge of sodomy – the charge is Marlowe's': a 'charge' which, according to Stephen Orgel, Marlowe presents in the very 'terms in which the culture formally conceived it – as antisocial, seditious, [and] ultimately disastrous'.[6] Jonathan Goldberg approaches this 'charge' somewhat differently, claiming that '[among] the categorical confusions of the confused category "sodomy" is categorical confusion itself'. This confusion involves 'a denial of those socially constructed hierarchies' (like the primacy of heterosexual love, the sanctity of marriage, or the established structure of parental authority) that are taken to be normal, normative, or '"natural"'. Within such hierarchies, kings exist 'to maintain social order, yet Edward, from the first line of Marlowe's play, inviting Gaveston to share the kingdom, instigates a sodomitical order', which both opposes and destabilizes established social and political arrangements. Goldberg concludes that '[in] the extended sense of the term, as not only the ruination of the maintenance of male/male hierarchies through friendship, but also as the explosion of the marital tie, *sodomy* is the name for all behavior in the play'.[7]

Goldberg, however, also goes on to claim that 'Marlowe envisions the possibility of sexuality and sexual difference as a separate category', that William Empson 'was closer to the point, when he argued that Marlowe believed that "the unmentionable sin for which the punishment was death was *the proper thing to do*"', and concludes that 'Marlowe is defending sodomy, not an idealized friendship or some spiritual relationship or some self-integrative principle of identity' (p. 124). In this, Goldberg would appear to be hedging somewhat on his claim that 'sodomy is the name for all behavior in the play', including the adulterous relationship of Mortimer and Isabella, by making it appear more as the self-defining ground of homosexual practice and subjectivity. Noting, for instance, that when Edward 'loses Gaveston (indeed, even before he loses him) he replaces him with another man, not with his queen' and that for Edward 'The substitution of man for woman is irreversible', he concludes that 'Marlowe's play negotiates difference – in gender and sexuality – differently' and that 'Modern heterosexist assumptions are not in place' (p. 125). Indeed, when Edward famously answers Mortimer's question, 'Why should you love him whom the world hates so?' by stating 'Because he loves me more than all the world'

(1.4.76–7), Marlowe evocatively frames their relationship in terms of a mutually held affection that is at one and the same time unmistakably sexual and passionately sustained. Although some scholars consider it 'anachronistic and ruinously misleading' to identify 'an individual in [the early modern] period as being or not being "a homosexual"', others maintain that in his construction of both Edward and Gavestion 'Marlowe introduces us to the possibility of a homosexual subjectivity'.[8] While this relationship can also be framed by a humoural calculus of physiological self-control that accounts Edward little more than 'passion's slave' and love itself 'merely a lust of the blood and a permission of the will' (these words, of course, belong to Shakespeare's villainous Iago), for Marlowe same-sex desire may be said to operate outside the prescribed economy where the mind keeps the body in check, in an affective economy marked by excess where the proscribed passions preside.

By the same token, Marlowe stages Edward's passionate devotion to Gaveston as so all-consuming that it repeatedly draws attention to itself as a behavioural phenomenon of pathological proportions and (in Orgel's terms) as a social phenomenon of potentially disastrous consequences. Marlowe, in fact, frequently has a range of other characters on stage call attention to the 'frantic' nature of Edward's passions, which Edward himself puts on display in an entirely self-absorbed and obsessive fashion, as if he were soliloquizing in public:

> *Edward*: He's gone, and for his absence thus I mourn.
>   Did never sorrow go so near my heart
>   As doth the want of my sweet Gaveston;
>   And could my crown's revenue bring him back,
>   I would freely give it to his enemies
>   And think I gained, having bought so dear a friend.
> *Isabella*: Hark how he harps upon his minion.
> *Edward*: My heart is as an anvil unto sorrow,
>   Which beats upon it like the Cyclops' hammers,
>   And with the noise turns up my giddy brain
>   And makes me frantic for my Gaveston.
>   Ah, had some bloodless Fury rose from hell,
>   And with my kingly sceptre struck me dead
>   When I was forced to leave my Gaveston!
> *Lancaster*: *Diablo*! What passions call you these?
>   (*EII* 1.4.304–18)

Lancaster's exclamation and question seem, in this context, entirely understandable. What he witnesses here exceeds both precedent and definition, although they are given both in a closely contemporaneous text, *The Passions of the Mind in General* (1604), where Thomas Wright contends that

> experience teacheth us that men for the most part are not very good judges in their own causes, especially for the Passion of Love, which blindeth their judgement... And indeed the Passions not unfitly may be compared to green spectacles, which make all things resemble the colour of green; even so he that loveth, hateth, or by any other passion is vehemently possessed judgeth all things that occur in favour of that passion to be good and agreeable with reason.[9]

The specific 'passions' that Edward is enacting here could no doubt be called any number of other names, but they arguably represent what Wright would term 'disquietness of the Mind' whose source, 'inordinate affections', are said to 'trouble the peaceable state of this petty commonweal of our soul' (p. 141).

While Marlowe is less interested than Wright might be in answering Lancaster's question, the fact that it is even asked indicates his effort to stage something decidedly extreme or excessive in Edward's display of the 'inordinate affections' he has focused on Gaveston: something that variously equals and exceeds in intensity the passions felt or expressed by the figures named in the inventory of legendary homoerotic relationships Mortimer Senior provides in the speech that moves this scene towards conclusion (see 1.4.385–400). Mortimer Senior notably begins this speech to his son, Mortimer Junior, by indicating how this 'fourth effect of Passions' (Wright, p. 141) might be avoided:

> Leave now to oppose thyself against the king;
> Thou seest by nature he is mild and calm,
> And seeing his mind so dotes on Gaveston,
> Let him without controlment have his will.
> (*EII* 1.4.386–9)

Of particular interest here is the speaker's observation that when left un-opposed, or, in Wright's terms, 'uncontradicted', Edward's 'nature' is 'mild and calm', a reading of Edward's character that suggests that his passions might well be more subdued were he permitted 'without controlment' to 'have his will'. While Wright concentrates his understanding of the passions on states of internal rebellion or sedition, Mortimer Senior contextualizes Edward's passions as the product of the frustration of his will by the peers, effectively dislocating rebellion and sedition from the 'petty commonweal' of Edward's soul and resituating it in the physical confines of the court. In so doing, the elder Mortimer inadvertently indicates that although 'passionate' is a term of disparagement employed by the peers to characterize Edward's arguably 'disastrous' lack of self-control, it is also a condition that the peers themselves help to produce (by inhibiting the free expression of Edward's sexuality) as well as a term that can be employed to describe the impatience, fury, and violence of the peers themselves.

In this respect, it may be said that Edward's 'wanton humour' not only grieves Mortimer Junior more than he admits but more than may be dramatically warranted. Indeed, Marlowe often has Mortimer make the kinds of comments about Edward and Gaveston that are this play's adjuncts to the negative representations of masculine love found in the roughly contemporaneous retellings of Edward's and Gaveston's story by 'E. F.' (presumably Elizabeth Cary), Michael Drayton, and Francis Hubert, representing them as mockeries and deformations of an idealized court that is clothed in the garb of his own stereotypically heterosexist assumptions.[10] Later in the play, when the captive Gaveston is about to be murdered, Mortimer notably refuses even to raise his sword against this 'Corrupter of thy king', considering it 'Shame and dishonour to a soldier's name' to allow Gaveston to fall 'upon my weapon's point' and 'welter in thy gore', as if the act were too suggestive of sodomitic contamination to venture (2.5.9–14). Mortimer sustains this strain of sexual innuendo to the very end of his second-act dialogue with Gaveston as he contemptuously responds to Gaveston's objection to being called a 'thief': 'Away, base groom, robber of kings' renown. / Question with thy companions and thy mates' (2.5.70–1), a phrase that consigns Gaveston to a base sub-culture of homosexual fellow travellers. Such comments when viewed in the context of Mortimer's micro-management of Edward's own torture and murder may even be said to underwrite the provocative contention that 'the notorious legend of Edward's death from an act of anal penetration implicates neither Edward nor Gaveston in "sodomy", but those responsible for that regicidal act', in short, that 'the sodomite is not Gaveston but Mortimer'.[11] It is, in any event, to Marlowe's construction of aristocratic disorder as focused on the rising and falling fortunes of Mortimer, and to the variations he works on his construction of passionate expression, that it is now time to turn.

In the fourth act of *Edward II*, as the party of Mortimer and Queen Isabella gather on stage to consolidate their imminent triumph, the queen attempts to make a sustained public pronouncement that will assign primary responsibility to Edward for the 'civil broils' that have made 'kin and countrymen / Slaughter themselves in others'. In answer to her own rhetorical question 'But what's the help?', she avers that

> Misgoverned kings are cause of all this wrack;
> And Edward, thou art one among them all,

> Whose looseness hath betrayed thy land to spoil
> And made the channels overflow with blood.
> Of thine own people patron shouldst thou be,
> But thou –   (EII 4.4.7–13)

Before she can conclude her anatomy of Edward's abuse of royal authority, she is interrupted by Mortimer, who begins his more pragmatic 'publication' of his party's mission with the statement, 'Nay, madam, if you be a warrior, / Ye must not grow so passionate in speeches' (4.4.14–15). This moment marks both a break and a divergence in the way in which passions are expressed and represented in the play. Whereas the 'furious' Mortimer has heretofore been as much the embodiment as the anatomizer of the compulsive hold that passions can have on character, at this point he attempts to represent himself as both their master and mediator, suppressing their direct expression in the interest of the new public roles he and Isabella have assumed as political actors and agents alike. While the passion of desire or ambition may continue to inform his single-minded drive to power, it will no longer colour his public pronouncements and deeds, being channelled instead into the format of asides, 'unpointed' letters, and close-knit conspiracies as he begins to assume the player's part. Passion is not, in any event, something he wishes to associate with their cause, but prefers to constitute it in terms of what they are waging war against.

In his own ensuing address, Mortimer substitutes for Isabella's 'passionate' rehearsal of Edward's abuses a more concise defence of their enterprise that is premised less on Edward's misgovernance than on the young 'prince's right' to whom Mortimer swears 'All homage, fealty, and forwardness'. While 'the open wrongs and injuries / Edward hath done to us, his queen, and land' are assuredly scored, and a promise made to avenge them 'with the sword' as well as to 'remove these flatterers from the king, / That havocs England's wealth and treasury', Mortimer cleverly publishes their invasion as a restorative act that will allow 'England's queen' to 'repossess / Her dignities and honours' and England's prince his 'right' (4.4.16–26). What gets elided (at least temporarily) in the process is the queen's effort to make Edward's 'looseness' the basis for his overthrow as well as an answering 'looseness' in the queen's relationship to Mortimer which, as Goldberg has taught us, itself falls under the broader definition of sodomy.

This relationship is scored during another brief, but revealing, bout of passionate expression on the part of Leicester, who has been sent to take possession of Edward and to arrest Spencer and Baldock. Bid by Mortimer's henchman, Rice ap Howell, to 'be short' since 'A fair commission warrants what we do', Leicester dwells on that charge in what our text's editor construes as an aside inflected 'with irony':

> The queen's commission, urged by Mortimer!
> What cannot gallant Mortimer with the queen?
> Alas, see where [Edward] sits and hopes unseen
> T'escape their hands that seek to reave his life.
> Too true it is: *quem dies vidit veniens superbum,*
> *Hunc dies vidit fugiens iacentem.*
> But Leicester, leave to grow so passionate.
>   (*EII* 4.7.49–5)[12]

Apparent here is a second discernible change in the way passion is discursively constructed and deployed. Whereas it has heretofore charged and informed both the erotic interactions of Edward and Gaveston and the answering fury and violence of the peers, passion now seems to be understood as a version of *com*passion, as a fullness of feeling that seeks to probe the moral basis of behaviour and, as such, is judged to be out of bounds or keeping with present arrangements. Leicester's passion will, in fact, soon become cause for his replacement by Berkeley who, in turn, will be judged to be 'so pitiful / As Leicester that had charge of him before' (5.2.54–5) and summarily 'discharged' (5.2.40) in favour of Matrevis and Gurney, characters whose primary passion is cruelty and whom Marlowe pointedly downgrades to the status of 'hired thugs' from the gentlemanly status they enjoyed in Holinshed (Forker, p. 285n38). By contrast, the fury with which Mortimer formerly hounded Gaveston to ground has now become subdued to the cooler, controlling vein we see in the next passage where Isabel and Mortimer are considerably more candid about expressing their aims and motivations:

> Fair Isabel, now have we our desire.
> The proud corrupters of the light-brained king
> Have done their homage to the lofty gallows,
> And he himself lies in captivity.
> Be ruled by me, and we will rule the realm.
>   (*EII* 5.2.1–5)

However, as if anticipating Goldberg's contention that 'sodomy is the name for all behavior in the play', Marlowe brings the scene to conclusion with a sudden resurfacing of the fury that has heretofore possessed Mortimer as he responds to the Prince's resistance to his guardianship by stifling the boy and forcibly carrying him away: 'Why youngling, 'sdainst thou so of Mortimer? / Then I will carry thee by force away' (5.2.110–11), behaving for all rights and purposes more like a thug and a bully than as the temporary master of Fortune's wheel.

As the scene switches to the space of Edward's confinement at Killingworth castle, Marlowe works yet another revealing variation on how the passions are constructed in his play. Waxing pathetic at the relentless mistreatment he is receiving at the hands of Mortimer's henchmen, Edward asks to be relieved of his life and is told by Gurney: 'Your passions make your dolours to increase', to which he responds, 'This usage makes my misery increase' (5.3.15–16), effectively becoming the temporary master of a discourse that confines him. With this one astute remark, Edward directly registers the extent to which his passions – which Gurney represents as a form of 'acting out' that exacerbates the feeling or emotion that is acted on – have been materially produced by the brutal practices that have been deployed against him and can no longer be considered the self-generated cause of his abjection. As if to mark this site as the staging-ground of a reversal of authority that has decided implications for his representation of the consequences of aristocratic disorder, Marlowe presents the following exchange between Edward's would-be liberator, Kent, and Matrevis and Gurney:

> *Gurney*: Bind him, and so convey him to the court.
> *Kent*: Where is the court but here? Here is the king,
>   And I will visit him. Why stay you me?
> *Matrevis*: The court is where Lord Mortimer remains.
>   Thither shall your honour go; and so farewell.
> *Kent*: O, miserable is that commonweal, where lords
>   Keep courts and kings are locked in prison!
>   (*EII* 5.3.58–64)

As the play's shifting centre of moral gravity, Kent may well lack the authority to make such pronouncements. More crucial, however, than Kent's passionately expressed platitude is Matrevis's bald assertion, 'The court is where Lord Mortimer remains', which incisively departs from the preferred rhetorical constructions of Mortimer and Isabella that it is the queen's commission that warrants Edward's imprisonment and the prince's right that their protectorship advances.

While it may be said that a passion for dominance does for Mortimer what Thomas Wright's 'green spectacles' do with respect to the passions in general, Marlowe also explores here the socially and morally corrosive effects of *dis*passion, the standing on guard against, or at a distance from, the kind of emotional engagement that so propulsively drives Gaveston and Edward into each other's arms and, more constructively, evokes Leicester's and Berkeley's compassion for the king's plight. By the fifth act of the play, Marlowe has begun to demonstrate what becomes of character when it empties itself out of affect and becomes nothing more than a fixed attitude dominated (as most authorities on the passions prescribe) by reason. Parrying Isabella's report that 'the king my son hath news / His father's dead, and we have murdered him' with the cold assurance of 'What if he have? The king is yet a child' (5.6.15–17), Mortimer discounts his own precedent of what the passions can do when power is wedded to resolve. As Isabella responds to Mortimer's dismissive remark, she paints a picture of a young man as 'frantic' as his father was over the loss of Gaveston but more capable than his father was of redressing his sorrows and fears:

> Ay, ay, but he tears his hair and wrings his hands,
> And vows to be revenged upon us both.
> Into the council chamber he is gone
> To crave the aid and succour of his peers.
> Ay me, see where he comes, and they with him.
> Now, Mortimer, begins our tragedy.
>
> (*EII* 5.6.18–23)

As Isabella anticipates, the new king does more than wax performatively passionate over his father's death. Empowered by 'the aid and succour of his peers', he finds a way to make his passions speak to productive effect. Bid, 'Weep not, sweet son', by his mother, the king privileges the propriety of the open expression of grief, 'Forbid not me to weep; he was my father', and interprets her own 'patience' or coolness in the face of Edward's death as the impropriety it is: 'And had you loved him half so well as I, / You could not bear his death thus patiently. / But you, I fear, conspired with Mortimer' (5.6.31–6). The young king reads in the queen's lack of affect the unmistakable sign of her disaffection, and finds it so inconsistent with the part she should be playing that he consigns her to another role entirely, that of Mortimer's helpmate and co-conspirator.

In a suggestive variation on this theme, after Mortimer is led off stage to his execution, the young king witnesses a resurgence of the queen's passions as she pleads 'As thou received'st thy life from me, / Spill not the blood of gentle Mortimer', into which he reads even more damning evidence of her collaboration with Mortimer: 'This argues that you spilt my father's blood, / Else would you not entreat for Mortimer' (5.6.67–70). While he claims he does not yet 'think her so unnatural' (a word that would effectively couple the act of regicide to adultery and confirm their association with sodomy), he also orders her immediate arrest on suspicion of the charge, in part because 'Her words enforce tears, / And I shall pity her if she speak again' (5.6.84–5). With these words, Marlowe brings an effectual closure to his collateral construction of passion and disorder. Recognizing, as his father and mother could not, that the passions must be accommodated to the moral and legal structures of civil society, the king does not so much renounce pity or compassion as direct it away from the demands of social and legal accountability. A king who can both think and feel, but subdue his feelings to the lordship of his reason, as opposed to his will, Edward III may well supply the missing link both to right rule and the humoural ideal in this play. That he may also supply something less is, however, evinced by the last image with which the play leaves us, as the 'tears, distilling from [his] eyes' are said to be 'witness' of a 'grief and innocency' that is somewhat qualified by the 'wicked traitor's head' he holds in his hands (5.6.99–101).

NOTES

1. Jonathan Gil Harris, Review of Michael Schoenfeldt, *Bodies and Selves in Early Modern England: Physiology and Inwardness in Spenser, Shakespeare, Herbert, and Milton* (Cambridge University Press, 1999), in *ShakS* 19 (2001), 253.
2. I draw the phrase 'affective economies' from the Introduction to Theodore B. Leinwand's estimable recent book, *Theatre, Finance and Society in Early Modern England* (Cambridge University Press, 1999). For a more philosophical approach to the subject of the passions, see Susan James, *Passion and Action: The Emotions in Seventeenth-Century Philosophy* (Oxford University Press, 1997).
3. In this chapter all quotations from the play are taken from the Revels edition of *Edward II*, Charles Forker (ed.) (Manchester and New York: Manchester University Press, 1994).
4. In the Introduction to his edition of *Edward II*, Forker makes a good case for Marlowe's general reliance on the second edition of Holinshed's *Chronicles* (London, 1587) as amended by Abraham Fleming. See Forker, pp. 41–4.
5. See Thomas Cartelli, *Marlowe, Shakespeare, and the Economy of Theatrical Experience* (Philadelphia: University of Pennsylvania Press, 1991), pp. 123–31. The attractiveness of Gaveston to contemporary audiences and readers alike is plausibly evinced by the addition of the following lines to the title pages of editions of the play published in 1598, 1612, and 1622: 'And also the life and death of *Piers Gaveston, / the great Earle of* Cornwall, and *mighty* / fauorite of king *Edward* the second'. The first quarto edition of *Edward II* was published in 1594.
6. Stephen Orgel, *Impersonations* (Cambridge University Press, 1996), pp. 47, 46.
7. Jonathan Goldberg, *Sodometries: Renaissance Texts, Modern Sexualities* (Stanford University Press), pp. 122–3.
8. The former position is taken by Alan Bray in *Homosexuality in Renaissance England* (London: Gay Men's Press, 1982), pp. 16–17, the latter by Bruce Smith in *Homosexual Desire in Shakespeare's England* (University of Chicago Press, 1991), p. 223. Cf. Lawrence Normand, in ' "What Passions Call You These?": *Edward II* and James VI', in Darryll Grantley and Peter Roberts (eds.), *Christopher Marlowe and English Renaissance Culture* (Aldershot: Ashgate Press, 1996), pp. 172–197.
9. Thomas Wright, *The Passions of the Mind in General*, 2nd edn. (London, 1604), in William Webster Newbold (ed.) (New York: Garland Press, 1986), pp. 126–7.

10. See *The History of the Life, Reign and Death of Edward II, King of England, and Lord of Ireland. With the Rise & Fall of his great favourites, Gaveston & the Spencers*. Written by E. F. in the year 1627. And Printed verbatim from the Original (London, 1680); Michael Drayton, 'Piers Gaveston' (orig. 1593–4) in *The Works of Michael Drayton*, J. William Hebel (ed.) (Oxford: Blackwell, 1931), vol. 1; and Francis Hubert, *The History of Edward II* (London, 1629). I discuss these three texts in '*Queer* Edward II: Postmodern Sexualities and the Early Modern Subject', in Paul Whitfield White (ed.), *Marlowe, History, and Sexuality: New Critical Essays on Christopher Marlowe* (New York: AMS Press, 1998), pp. 216–18. Also see Gregory Bredbeck, *Sodomy and Interpretation: Marlowe to Milton* (Cambridge University Press, 1991), pp. 48–77.
11. Mario Di Gangi, 'Marlowe, Queer Studies, and Renaissance Homoeroticism', in White (ed.), *Marlowe, History, and Sexuality*, p. 208.
12. Forker's translation of these lines from Seneca's *Thyestes* reads: 'Whom the rising sun has seen high in pride, him the setting sun has seen laid low' (p. 264).

READING LIST

Bray, Alan. 'Homosexuality and the Signs of Male Friendship in Elizabethan England'. *History Workshop Journal* 29 (1990), 1–19. Rpt in Jonathan Goldberg (ed.), *Queering the Renaissance*. Durham and London: Duke University Press, 1994, pp. 40–61.

Di Gangi, Mario. *The Homoerotics of Early Modern Drama*. Cambridge University Press, 1997.

Goldberg, Jonathan. 'Sodomy and Society: the Case of Christopher Marlowe'. *SWR* 69 (1984), 371–8.

Huebert, Ronald. 'Tobacco and Boys and Marlowe'. *SR* 92 (1984), 206–24.

Robertson, Toby. 'Directing *Edward II*'. *TDR* 8 (1964), 174–183.

Sanders, Wilbur. *The Dramatist and the Received Idea: Studies in the Plays of Marlowe and Shakespeare*. Cambridge University Press, 1968.

Steane, J. B. *Marlowe: A Critical Study*. Cambridge University Press, 1964.

Summers, Claude J. 'Sex, Politics, and Self-Realization in *Edward II*'. In Kenneth Friedenreich, Roma Gill, and Constance B. Kuriyama (eds.), '*A Poet and a Filthy Play-maker*': *New Essays on Christopher Marlowe*. New York: AMS Press, 1988, pp. 221–40.

Thurn, David H. 'Sovereignty, Disorder, and Fetishism in Marlowe's *Edward II*'. *RenD*, n.s. 21 (1990), 115–41.

Waith, Eugene. '*Edward II*: the Shadow of Action'. *TDR* 8 (1964), 59–76.

11

THOMAS HEALY

Doctor Faustus

Enter with Devils, giving crowns and rich apparel to Faustus, and
  dance and then depart.
Faustus: Speak, Mephistopheles. What means this show?
Mephistopheles: Nothing, Faustus, but to delight thy mind withal
  And to show thee what magic can perform.

(*DF* 2.1.83–5)[1]

From the mid-eighteenth century when interest in *Doctor Faustus* revived, critical attention on the play has largely focused on what may be termed its metaphysical concerns. Is Marlowe challenging conventional Christian perspectives on hell and heaven, or does his play ultimately conform with them? Is Faustus a tragic hero or a misguided sinner? Though scholarship on *Doctor Faustus* has increasingly complicated issues surrounding the origin and status of the play's two main versions, ideas of what may be termed high seriousness have dominated debate about its content. For both readers of a text and spectators at performances, attention is commonly concentrated on those scenes that engage most thoroughly with a tragic dimension. The scenes of farce attract much less attention. But what type of play engaged early spectators? How might *Doctor Faustus* have been performed in the theatres of Elizabethan England? This chapter seeks to re-examine the modern preoccupation with *Faustus* as metaphysical tragedy by thinking about it in the cultural milieu from which it first arose. Interestingly, many of the issues raised by the place of the stage in early modern London still seem to resonate strangely within current critical debates about *Doctor Faustus*.

At the start of the Reformation in England, the new Protestants celebrated players along with printers and preachers as crucial conduits through which the reform movement could spread its ideas.[2] By the 1580s, though, some of the more strident elements within the now dominant Protestant Church of England orchestrated a series of pamphlet attacks on the London theatres as sinful places that directly conflicted with the efforts of the godly to win souls to religion. For the city's civic and religious authorities, the theatres were now 'a great offence from the church of God and hindrance to his gospel'.[3] But the court would have none of it; the theatres remained open. Nor did such attacks appear to affect the conduct of thousands of Londoners who regularly flocked to Southwark on the south bank of the Thames to witness performances in the new commercially run theatres being built there. Indeed, by helping to make theatrical distractions seem a questionable activity, such attacks may have helped to heighten the playhouses' attractions.[4]

For the godly, the new commercial theatres of the 1580s had chosen entertainment over edification; they had become places disorderly and unstable. Ideologically, they now exemplified Calvin's fears about 'theatres of the world' where humanity might be stunned, dazzled, and blinded by the world's allurements that falsely promised grace and sweetness.[5] Practically, the playhouse appeared to be in direct competition with the pulpit, with many Londoners choosing the pleasures of the players over the instruction of the preachers. But, for some at least, the stakes were higher than what might simply appear to be a 'ratings war' between Church and playhouse vying for audience share. The Corporation of London argued: 'to play in plague time is to increase the plague by infection; to play out of plague time is to draw the plague by offendings of God, upon occasion of such plays'.[6] The city's ostensible moral health might be directly equated with its physical and commercial health.

Significantly, a number of these contemporary attacks on plays distinguish the drama in textual form from it in performance. While allowing a didactic appropriateness in reading certain plays, when drama was performed it became part of a satanic opposition to the Word of God. Even when a performance might seem to be edifying for its spectators, it was merely the devil's attempt, 'perceiving his comedies begin to stink', to sweeten its moral corruption.[7] Countering this, others defended the drama by arguing that theatrical spectacle was effective in helping to restore moral order, claiming instances when those witnessing performances of murders found themselves drawn to confess similar crimes.[8] Dramatic spectacle, therefore, could also be perceived as an effective vehicle to root out sin and help preserve the godly English. Despite vocal Puritan criticism, English Protestantism never abandons its interest in the drama as an instrument for reform.[9]

Was *Doctor Faustus* originally designed to challenge or subvert such criticisms directed against the stage by deliberately performing the opposite of a traditional morality play, one in which the norms that govern moral certainties about good and evil are displaced and ridiculed?[10] Conversely, was it attempting to marry a dramatic morality tradition inherited from the early reformed Church with the new demands for spectacle and variety in the popular commercial theatres: seeking to prove that entertainment and edification could be successfully conjoined? The difficulties inherent in approaching such questions may be exemplified by considering *Doctor Faustus*'s opening and closing choruses (effectively the same in both the play's main existing versions). The play opens:

> Not marching now in fields of Trasimene
> Where Mars did mate the Carthaginians,
> Nor sporting in the dalliance of love
> In courts of kings where state is overturned,
> Nor in the pomp of proud audacious deeds,
> Intends our muse to daunt his heavenly verse.
> Only this, gentlemen: we must perform
> The form of Faustus' fortunes good or bad.
>
> (*DF* Prologue 1–7)

This seems to propose that the play will meet the expectations of the popular theatre. While indicating that it will not be about famous wars or sex and revenge scandals, it is raising expectations about performing something that will conform to these types of plays (Marlowe still intends to 'daunt his heavenly verse'). There is ambiguity of course; Marlowe may be being ironically literal, indicating that *Doctor Faustus* is genuinely *not* going to be similar to these other types of plays. However, though this chorus proceeds to introduce a standard morality *exemplum*, comparing Faustus with Icarus who flew too close to the sun and consequently drowned, Marlowe employs a language of abundance that promises audience gratification in the excess of what we are about to see performed rather than suggesting controlled moral exposition:

> For, falling to a devilish exercise,
> And glutted more with learning's golden gifts,
> He surfeits upon cursed necromancy;
> Nothing so sweet as magic is to him,
> Which he prefers before his chiefest bliss.
>
> (*DF* Prologue 24–8)

In apparent contrast, at the play's conclusion the final chorus seems to be attempting to extract a more conventional morality summary of its events. What we have beheld is for the audience's edification:

> Faustus is gone. Regard his hellish fall,
> Whose fiendful fortune may exhort the wise
> Only to wonder at unlawful things,
> Whose deepness doth entice such forward wits
> To practise more than heavenly power permits.
>
> (*DF* Epilogue 4–8)

The difficulty is that what an audience has witnessed does not generally correspond with conventional morality instruction. Faustus's rhetorically charged final speech, for instance, is a wonderful piece of theatre that builds to a crescendo of fear and dramatic expectation; it does not provide a sober assessment of his mistaken actions and a reasoned recantation of a misspent life. Richard Proudfoot recently describes how, having initially read this speech in a book of verse, he was keen to see its potential released in performance.[11] But several excellent productions later he is still waiting: what lingers for him is the visual images at the end.

In fact, this speech's dramatic function seems precisely to promote the final spectacle. With increasing energy and pace it helps develop audience suspense around what is going to happen at its conclusion. It collects a series of fragmentary utterances, some or all of which may have religious and philosophical intelligibility for the spectators, but expressed through a rhetoric that is designed to hurry momentum in delivery. In performance, audiences principally respond to the dramatic atmosphere the words enhance, not the speech's intellectual propositions. Intensifying the theatrical thrill over what we are going to see, Faustus's language promotes immediate sensation rather than reflective judgement. This helps explain why following this scene with a chorus that supposedly provides a moral summary of what we have witnessed is frequently experienced as somehow inappropriate – particularly in the earlier 1604 version of the play, which advances immediately from this scene to the Epilogue.

This last chorus, too, might easily be argued as further provoking its listeners to illicit desires rather than cautioning them through moral orthodoxy. A proper godly summary would try to emphasize that Faustus's necromancy was illusionary, a false prop through which Satan catches souls. Here, though, the chorus alluringly proposes that it possesses real force: it does enable a 'practise' of more than is permitted by heaven. We are invited to 'wonder at unlawful things' that have a deepness that 'doth entice', not to exercise reason to dismiss Faustus's choices. Magic continues to be a source of awe; its depths may be sinister but they continue to tantalize. Claiming to warn the curious, the chorus can easily be imagined as tempting a further pursuit of the very things it counsels against.

Thus, merely examining the choric channels that are ostensibly helping to direct audience understanding, we find that Marlowe employs a language that apparently allows him both moral edification and unconstrained spectacle. We might revel in entertainment with at least a vague sense that the play is fundamentally propounding a conventional morality. Conversely, we may sense that *Doctor Faustus* remains dramatically confused because it is neither instruction nor amusing diversion. Rather than successfully marrying the apparent polarities of education and entertainment, Marlowe's language compromises the demands of both, providing no secure understanding of what the play is attempting to achieve.

The performance of the material these choruses frame will, of course, determine our understanding of their accuracy in interpreting the action. But with *Doctor Faustus* what should be played between them remains a vexed question for students of Marlowe and directs us to the difficult issue of text and performance during the Renaissance. What we debate *Doctor Faustus* is about is largely predicated on an inscribed textual document, the play we read. Marlowe, though, almost certainly conceived *Faustus* for theatrical performance. It is highly unlikely that he – and/or others who worked on the play – would have imagined readers studying a text of it. Among current readers carefully analysing its language, pursuing its allusions and contextualizing its philosophical and theological reflections, Faustus's final speech, for instance, can appear to be employing its potent poetic images in the interests of emphasizing their content, a process which helps promote critical debate about the ideas expressed. But in performance it is the emotive effects these images confer that take precedence, helping to build dramatic suspense. Textual stability allows moral pedagogy or other critical models about content to dominate considerations of what a play is intellectually trying to express; performance complicates such issues.

It was about midpoint during the first phase of commercial theatre in London (the period *c.* 1580 to *c.* 1640) that Ben Jonson published his 1616 *Workes*. Presenting some of his plays alongside his poems and masques in the expensive format of a folio volume with a title that conveyed high cultural esteem, Jonson unambiguously signalled his desire that his drama should be examined with the seriousness accorded other elite forms of writing. It was probably the success of Jonson's enterprise that prompted Heminge and Condell to edit a folio of Shakespeare's plays in 1623: *Mr William Shakespeares Comedies, Histories & Tragedies. Published according to the true Originall Copies.*

From these powerful instances, a subsequent editorial practice developed that envisages that the period's dramatists wrote their plays with a sense of them as literary texts, even though the initial printed production of their drama was haphazard in cheap octavo or quarto editions over which they had no control and often seemingly no interest. As the Shakespeare First Folio title proposes, the original copy of the author's play-text might be salvaged and reconstructed, indicating that (more or less) contemporaries of Shakespeare, who died in 1616, wanted to read his drama as he wrote it. Subsequent editorial practice with all Renaissance drama has largely operated to support a view of authorial recovery: emending corruption and returning us as far as possible towards a text that reflects what emerged from the dramatist's hand. It is true that current editors realize that plays of the period often exist in different versions and, thus, that a quest for such an authentic text is never going to be wholly possible; yet the understandable editorial imperative to establish the 'best possible' text is still firmly founded on a premise about an 'authorial' text. While it is the case that numerous seventeenth-century playwrights appear to have taken care to preserve an authorial copy of their plays with a view to their dramas having some life on the page as well as the stage, this does not appear the case in the 1580s and early 1590s when *Doctor Faustus* was first performed.

Doctor Faustus was probably originally produced in 1589 by the Lord Admiral's Company. It was revived by the same company under the owner of the Rose theatre, Philip Henslowe, between 1594 and early 1597 when at least twenty-four performances were given. It was again revived late in 1597 and there are indications of other performances during this period. In early 1601, Thomas Bushell entered an edition called 'the plaie of Doctor ffaustus' for publication, but, if printed, no copy has survived. In late 1602, Henslowe paid William Birde and Samuel Rowley four pounds for 'ther adicyones in doctor fostes'. In 1604 a quarto called *The Tragicall History of D. Faustus* was issued for Bushell, indicating the play was 'Written by Ch.Marl.'. In 1616, John Wright, who had purchased the copyright, published a new edition adding 676 lines to the earlier text, dropping 36, and making numerous minor changes. Yet another version appeared in 1663. It has been notably influenced by *The Jew of Malta* and is generally agreed to have no early authority. A further version again was published in 1697 (acted about a decade earlier) called *The Life and Death of Doctor Faustus, made into a farce, by Mr Mountford etc.* Thus, *Doctor Faustus* continued to attract 'adicyones' for about a century after its first publication. But if Marlowe's *Doctor Faustus* is to be recognized in all these editions as a single play, it is only in the sense of it being a compendium of theatrical possibilities: these seventeenth-century texts illustrate how traditions of performance from the inception of the commercial theatres show no reverence for an author's original vision.

One of the best recent scholarly editions of *Doctor Faustus*, by Bevington and Rasmussen, prints two different versions of it (the 1604 'A' text and the 1616 'B' text) and proposes the author as 'Christopher Marlowe and his collaborator and revisers'.[12] Modern editorial debate about *Doctor Faustus* has centred around which of the two early versions of the play more successfully represents Marlowe's design. The dominant view of the mid-twentieth century was that it was the 1616 edition: most editors of this period follow W. W. Greg's position that the earlier 1604 quarto was defective.[13] But the prevailing recent view has been to prefer 1604.[14] Bevington and Rasmussen believe their editorial work has now established that the 'A' text was set 'from an authorial manuscript composed of interleaved scenes written by two dramatists': Marlowe and a collaborating playwright (Revels edition, p. 64). The 'B' text represents a revised edition.

While elaborate and cogent arguments are advanced by these editors to claim that it is possible to see a somewhat 'rearranged' 1604 text as emerging simultaneously from the pens of Marlowe and an independent collaborator, the rationale behind these claims seems overly dependent on what the editors assume *Doctor Faustus* is dramatically trying to achieve. Under the influence of two centuries of critical tradition, the dominant supposition is that it was originally designed to accomplish the promises implicit in its earliest (surviving) printed title: *The Tragicall History of D. Faustus*. Working on the premise that Marlowe was seeking to emphasize the tragic, most editors and critics assume that the comic scenes were envisaged as diversions or interludes between the more serious actions. There is, though, an overall burlesque-like element to *Doctor Faustus*, and the play does not seek to separate rigidly its moments of comic farce from its moments of high seriousness. There is no evidence that the title *Tragicall History* was used before 1604. In fact, investigating editorial principles for selecting a supposed authorial text with virtually all the plays ascribed to Christopher Marlowe – *Edward II* is the exception – we usually find that they are substantially based on conjecture, often determined by later critical perspectives about what is typically 'Marlowe'. Attribution to an author – one of the central organizational and critical categories we operate by – is actually not a particularly useful method for examining most plays from the Elizabethan period. Unlike Shakespeare and Jonson, the first collected edition of Marlowe's work dates from 1826. It does not claim to be prepared from 'originall copies'.

One of the most difficult questions surrounding *Doctor Faustus* is whether the 'A' version of the play offers a demonstrably different understanding of Faustus's 'history' from the expanded 'B' version. Why did Henslowe pay a substantial fee to enlarge the play? There is some evidence to suggest that the revival of late 1597 was not financially successful. Did he want a different type of play or merely a longer one? Was the play performed in the 1590s the short 'A' text (1,485 lines) we possess, or did it exist in a now lost longer version?[15] Crude farce, tragic seriousness, and scenes that might be one or the other (or possibly both together) are developed in the 'B' text. It is not the case, as is sometimes assumed, that expanding comic high-jinks is the only impetus to the longer 1616 text. The problem of interpretation, though, ultimately comes back to performance. It may be that Rowley and Birde (if it is their 'adicyones' in the 'B' text) believed that they were expanding material that sat sympathetically with their understanding of the play in the light of its theatre history. That is to say, the longer text compared to the shorter might help to give us some idea of how *Doctor Faustus* was played on the stage.

What little hearsay evidence we possess about early audiences' responses to *Doctor Faustus* suggests that theatrical *frisson* was enjoyed. Thomas Middleton proposed that 'the old Theatre cracked' during a performance and 'frighted the audience': that is the wooden construction of the Theatre (an early playhouse in London; it burnt down in 1598) must have shifted a little and given off a cracking sound.[16] At a performance in Exeter, an additional devil (i.e., supposedly a real one) was reported discovered on the stage, causing cast and audience to scatter; while William Prynne writing in 1635 claims there was a visible apparition of the devil on the stage of the Belsavage playhouse during a performance.[17] Henslowe's Diary for 1598 lists among its stage properties a 'dragon in fostes' which no doubt helped 'the scary business that spectators paid for' (Revels edition, p. 50). Seeing *Doctor Faustus* on the early modern stage was probably closer to the experience of a current audience going to a comic horror film than a sophisticated encounter with dramatic tragedy, though, as with some horror films, this does not mean features associated with serious drama might not also be present.

These early accounts remind us, however, that the first audiences would have accepted as unquestionably valid the premise that heaven and hell were locked in a contest for gaining souls, that the supernatural readily impinged on the natural, and that traditionally accepted views about Satan and his kingdom – and about God and his – were largely issues of fact rather than opinion.[18] Faustus's debating proposition to Mephistopheles that 'I think hell's a fable' would have seemed either chillingly naïve or comically preposterous (2.1.115–41). Mephistopheles's response 'Ay think so still, till experience change they mind' would have been generally greeted as a prosaic expression of certitude. Faustus's sophistry during the 'hell's a fable' disputation is intellectually and argumentatively clever but would almost certainly have had no persuasiveness with contemporary audiences. Previously, Mephistopheles has haughtily claimed that he is always in hell because he has seen the face of God and is now eternally deprived of it (1.3.70–87). It is this divine absence that constitutes his continuous torment: a vivid illustration of the negative pride that the satanic traditionally manifests. Faustus counters to suggest that, if this is so, then he will never truly be 'damned' because he is content with his present circumstances: he has no memory of such an encounter. He will 'willingly be damned' and thus not damned in any respect but a technical one. This allows Faustus to express his own pride: 'Learn thou of Faustus manly fortitude, / And scorn those joys thou never shall possess' (1.3.86–7). Yet, such argumentative dextrousness is not really the point. Witnesses to these exchanges would have no serious doubts about hell as a dangerous place. Faustus's confident assertion that 'Think'st thou that Faustus is so fond / To imagine that after this life there is any pain?' (2.1.133–4) would not be part of a rationale shared by the spectators. It is not simply that his logic is flawed; he is just not recognizing reality as it was then perceived.

The expanded end-scenes of the 1616 text help emphasize that Faustus is not some clever 'Humanist' or 'Renaissance' hero who is undermining old-fashioned preconceptions about heaven and hell.[19] One addition allows the good and bad angels to present apparently 'objective' views of the heavenly and hellish. The good angel announces that she is leaving Faustus and shows him the heavenly throne he has lost: 'O thou has lost celestial happiness, / Pleasures unspeakable, bliss without end (5.2.105–6). After this the bad angel shows him a very conventional hell where she gloats that Faustus 'shall taste the smart of all':

> Now, Faustus, let thine eyes with horror stare
> Into that vast perpetual torture-house.
> These are the furies tossing damned souls
> On burning forks; their bodies boil in lead.
> (DF 'B' text 5.2.115–18)

Earlier in the scene, Lucifer, Beelzebub, and Mephistopheles appear independent of Faustus to watch his downfall and 'how he doth demean himself'. Mephistopheles retorts:

> How should he, but in desperate lunacy?
> Fond worldling, how his heart-blood dries with grief;
> His conscience kills it, and his labouring brain
> Begets a world of idle fantasies
> To overreach the devil. But in vain.
> His store of pleasures must be sauced with pain.
> (DF 'B' text 5.2.11–16)

This scene leads to Faustus's final speech, his 'desperate lunacy'. There is no doubt that Faustus meets a gruesome end in the 1616 version and this text adds a further scene (5.3) in which the scholars, having heard 'fearful shrieks' in the night, find Faustus's limbs 'all torn asunder'. The expanded text re-inforces conventional orthodoxy: Faustus is punished; the satanic operates in the world specifically to capture humans vain enough or short-sighted enough to lose sight of the fundamental order that governs the universe. There may be critical argument over whether the 1616 play questions or supports the justice of this order, but there is no doubt that it acknowledges it.

In contrast, there is a great deal more potential ambiguity in the 1604 version. Faustus's final speech stays the same, but what frames it is less directive, making his final cry of 'Ah, Mephistopheles' (5.2.115) and what follows less obvious: fulfilment of terror, relief at seeing a recognized face; a conventional or unconventional damnation? Prior to this scene in both the play's versions we have Faustus's encounter with the old man who urges repentance and Helen who kisses him – 'Her lips sucks forth my soul' (5.1.94). The Christian morality of the scene is straightforward: Faustus is a victim of the sweet allurements that religion warns against. Yet, in all the productions I have seen Helen has been performed as strikingly attractive (the most beautiful was in an all-male production). Even if you agreed with the old man's endeavours, visually, when placed beside Helen, the emotional and aesthetic sympathy was with her. Was it the same in early modern productions, or was Helen presented as an obvious devil in disguise? Regardless, employing the shorter 'A' text it is possible to imagine a spectacle that might leave some feeling that Faustus 'confounds hell in Elysium' (1.3.60) because the absolutes of what hell and heaven consist of are less clearly delineated.

In part, the less directive 'A' text has gained critical favour because it can be read against the grain of orthodox Christian beliefs about heaven and hell. Challenging convention, the play's vision can be more easily related to a popular biographical view of Marlowe that celebrates his heterodoxy – was it not claimed the author had said 'that the beginning of Religioun was only to keep men in awe'?[20] Indeed, for some, Faustus becomes a version of a fatally overreaching Marlowe. But even without the pseudo-biographical link, the 'A' text seems potentially to be questioning what is now largely accepted as superstition, and for many this makes its feel like a more proto-modern play-text, not one linked to the Middle Ages.[21]

Yet, the more likely scenario of the 'B' text's additions is that they were principally conceived to expand and clarify what the companies already felt they possessed in the 'A' text, not to recast or censor the play (this is assuming the printed texts are close to what was performed before and after 1602 when the additions were commissioned by Henslowe – a big assumption!).[22] There is nothing in the 'A' text that dramatically indicates that it needs to be performed differently from the 'B' version. The potential ambiguities about Faustus's end in the 'A' text's last scenes that has caught recent critical and theatrical imaginations, for instance, were probably not seen as ambiguities at all by the companies first acting it. Devils probably rushed on stage at the end, indicating that Faustus was going to be torn asunder in the 'A' text as in the 'B' version. Helping to intensify expectations about the final fiendish spectacle it was understood the 'A' text, too, was leading towards, the 'B' text additions in the last scenes were probably felt to be dramatically sympathetic with the earlier version. On balance, it appears that the 'B' text helps clarify how the 'A' text was previously performed. It is doubtful the additions were an attempt to restrain a more dangerous 'Marlowe' play by redirecting it into more conventional frameworks.

One of the significant expansions in the 'B' version of *Doctor Faustus* is Faustus's encounter with the Pope (3.1). Although this longer scene in the 'B' text ultimately concludes as in the 'A' version, in other respects it well illustrates the dilemma about establishing what either version of *Doctor Faustus* may be trying to accomplish overall. It suggests, too, that for the early revisers this scene's implications were not clear. In the 'A' version, it opens with Faustus recounting the European cities and antiquities that he and Mephistopheles have just visited. They have arrived in Rome and are in the Pope's chamber. Faustus proposes 'that I do long to see the monuments / And situation of bright splendent Rome', rhetorically employing a type of conjuring appeal designed to testify to the strength of his wish (3.1.44–9).

Despite the apparent urgency of this request, though, Mephistopheles proposes that they play some games on the Pope and attending clergy. Faustus readily agrees. What follows is a mocking of the papal court with low comic pranks (upsetting food and wine, roughing up the Pope). The clergy attempt to exorcize Faustus and Mephistopheles with the traditional bell, book, and candle but, the stage direction tells us, they: 'beat the Friars, and fling fireworks among them, and so exeunt'. This is the sum of Faustus's Roman holiday in the 'A' version. In the 'B' text, the scene begins the same up to Faustus's expression of his desire to see Rome. Mephistopheles's proposal to stay to see the Pope, though, stresses the pomp and glory of the papal pageant, making it one of the 'splendent' sights of Rome:

> I know'd you see the pope
> And take some part of holy Peter's feast,
> The which this day with high solemnity
> This day is held through Rome and Italy
> In honour of the pope's triumphant victory.
> (*DF* 'B' text 3.1.52–6)

What they witness is the exhibition of the captured Saxon 'Bruno', a rival Pope who the Holy Roman Emperor attempted to set up. Faustus and Mephistopheles contrive to free Bruno and convey him to Germany. The additions present a more emphatic Protestant context to Faustus's actions: the papal courts declare Bruno and the Emperor 'Lollards' (i.e., of Protestant inclination). The Pope is presented as a largely temporal tyrant interested in his own power. The 'B' text, therefore, contrives to offer a different style to this scene from the 'A' version. Faustus's initial desire to see the great sights of Rome is not immediately abandoned for farce; instead the main preoccupation is with a serious Faustus being anti-papal, pro-German, and favouring Protestantism.

In either version the scene is unique in a post-Reformation English play as the sole instance where the devil acts to chastise the Pope.[23] During the 1580s and 1590s anti-Roman sentiment reached its greatest pitch in England (a combination of the Pope's excommunication of Elizabeth and offer of pardon to any assassin of her – an issue raised in *The Massacre at Paris* – and the circumstances around the Spanish Armada, proclaimed by Philip of Spain as a holy crusade). The English Church promoted the view that Roman Catholicism had become the province of the Antichrist: Satan and the Pope were understood as virtually identical. *Doctor Faustus* is clearly not promoting Catholicism as a desirable or potent religion (the attempt at exorcism shows it has no power, for instance, and the Pope is thoroughly ridiculed), but it is also clearly not associating this religion with the devil. The 'B' version attempts to restore some of Roman Catholicism's sinister temporal power by presenting the Church as anti-Protestant, a negative and corrupted force. It tries to deflect some of the burlesque farce that dominates the scene in the 'A' version by introducing more weighty issues.

In the 'A' version, however, this scene's exaggerated comedy illustrates a quality present throughout the whole of *Doctor Faustus* – one we might term Faustus's and Mephistopheles's adolescent tendency. A feature that occurs regularly in *Doctor Faustus* is that serious issues are suspended or interrupted so that comic spectacle can occur. Some of these instances seem to parallel the more sober actions, such as the antics of Robin and Rafe; others, such as the horse-courser scenes, might be claimed as acting to confer a dramatic sympathy on a mischievous but not evil Faustus – i.e., he doesn't turn into the depraved potentate that he initially announces he wishes to be (e.g., 1.3.105–212). But with the 'A' text's Roman visit, game playing completely displaces any attempt at serious drama. The Faustus of high learning who introduces the scene is readily abandoned for the Faustus of irreverent antic and cheap spectacle. Similarly, at one of the few moments in the play when Faustus genuinely seems on the verge of repentance, Lucifer appears (2.3.70–82). Faustus assumes he is being threatened and is about to die, but Lucifer assures him he has appeared to remind Faustus of his promises and to show him some 'pastimes'. He presents the seven deadly sins, and in response to his question about how he likes the show, Faustus replies 'O this feeds my soul' (2.3.157). The sins are a wonderful piece of circus-like frivolity that it is difficult to imagine any production playing as sinister let alone as weighty. Faustus's response seems in an inappropriate register. As with his happy abandonment of either the past or present glories of Rome for tomfoolery and firework throwing, this scene, too, shows Faustus ready to forsake introspection for pranks and farcical spectacle.

Are these examples principally supposed to illustrate humanity's sinful culpability, prepared to abandon godly salvation for cheap diversions, thus confirming the play's conformity with a morality tradition? Or is *Doctor Faustus* a good illustration of what Mikhail Bakhtin identified as the carnivalesque quality of Renaissance culture, where powerful abstract issues – such as heaven and hell – can be reduced to some form of grotesque material representations, as in the seven deadly sins, allowing them to be laughed at?[24] As Bakhtin argues, the use of carnival de-centres fixed orders, allowing other possibilities and revealing the relativity of established authorities' claims to know how the world is structured. There are certainly scenes in Faustus that sustain a Bakhtinian analysis, such as those with the clownish ostlers, Rafe and Robin, conjuring (2.2 and 3.2, but originally printed as one scene placed after the popish escapade). These two see the benefits of magic as free drink and sex with the maid Nan Spit. They summon Mephistopheles, an act that comically deflates the high magic of Faustus. Indeed, their nonsense incantation – they are of course illiterate – is the only conjuring within the play that appears to possess actual power. Mephistopheles claims to Faustus that he responded to his conjuring only because he could obtain Faustus's soul, not through the magic's inherent power (1.3.45–54). While it is likely that this claim would be mistrusted as the devil traditionally lies, the play also shows that the exorcisms of the Roman Church, too, have no effect on Faustus and Mephistopheles.[25] Mephistopheles is incensed 'by these villains' charms' that have brought him from Constantinople, and he transforms them into a dog and an ape. The ostlers, though, are delighted for they will now be able to get hold of food more easily. Mephistopheles's punishments are experienced as rewards. The satanic quest to reduce higher beings to lower ones, here turning them to literal beasts, is ridiculed by the condition of the ostlers who imagine themselves below the level of the beasts they serve. The traditional hierarchies of heaven and hell are confronted in the debasement and consequent ridiculing of supernatural powers by these clowns who propose different conditions of life from the ones supposedly present in the more serious playing for souls.

Yet, a Bakhtinian perspective applied to the whole play loses sight of the fact that all the characters, socially elite and socially marginal, seem obsessed with showmanship, both in mounting 'plays' and with playing roles within them. Even Lucifer's dismissal of Faustus's terror before he launches his 'production' of the seven deadly sins seems to indicate the devil's own abandonment of satanic gravity because it would interfere with his comic show. The play within a play is a standard device of Renaissance drama, but there can be few instances of dramas so obsessed with constructing plays within plays as *Doctor Faustus*. And, importantly, such play-making is focused around entertainment, with characters wanting to occupy roles that excite spectacle and provide the opportunity for amusement. As Faustus's 'history' develops, the principal use of his powers is to gain a reputation for his conjuring (e.g., the scenes with the Emperor, the Duke of Vanholt, and the students). In the scene with Charles V, despite Faustus's firm instruction that he is only raising spirits that resemble Alexander and his paramour, the Emperor is completely mesmerized by Faustus's illusion: 'Sure these are no spirits, but the true substantial bodies of those two deceased princes' (4.1.65–6). If Faustus is a victim of illusion, many of the play's characters, including the Emperor, also prefer Faustus's illusions to reality. Such a general preoccupation with artifice and fantasy compromises a specific moral warning around Faustus. The Duke of Vanholt's pregnant wife consuming the grapes of India, or the scholars witnessing the first appearance of Helen, are not played as being at mortal risk for benefiting from Faustus's organized performances. They celebrate his courtesy, praise and bless his 'glorious deed' (5.1.32–3). Faustus comes increasingly to perform what the commercial drama generally was seeking to offer its spectators – that which produces contentment and wonder.

Faustus's desire for role-playing reaches one of its most accelerated moments in the Helen scene. Responding to her he decides, appropriately, that he will be Paris and play out his version of the Trojan War:

> I will be Paris, and for love of thee
> Instead of Troy shall Wittenberg be sacked
> And I will combat with weak Menelaus,
> And wear thy colours on my plumed crest
> Yea, I will wound Achilles in the heel
> And then return to Helen for a kiss.
> (DF 5.1.197–202)

But this is insufficient and Faustus changes tack. Helen now is

> Brighter . . . than flaming Jupiter
> When he appeared to hapless Semele
> More lovely than the monarch of the sky
> In wanton Arethusa's azured arms.
> (DF 5.1.105–8)

Faustus is ready to change both Helen's and his own sex (she is the over-whelming Jupiter, he the feminine Semele) and to invite his complete extinction at her hands – Semele insisted on seeing Jupiter in his omnipotence as he appeared to his wife Juno, a guise no mortal can withstand. Faustus seems equally ready to abandon scholarly exactness for inventiveness: Arethusa was transformed to a fountain to protect her chastity from the pursuing Alpheus; she is neither wanton nor a lover of Jupiter in classical mythology. What is revealed in these and the Trojan War images is that Faustus does not want to possess Helen for simple sexual gratification. She stimulates his excitement about role-playing; she feeds his imagination for theatre.

Plays within plays bring attention to a performance as contrived theatre. Aware of 'an audience' on stage watching the play within the play, spectators also become aware of themselves watching 'both' plays. In Renaissance drama, various devices are employed to remind the audience of its 'role' as spectators and, consequently, of their participation in the drama rather than only passively witnessing it. Prologues and epilogues, for example, frame the action within them, but they are also part of the play. As a painting is influenced by what frames it, so the effect of the 'picture' overall includes the frame. In the drama such mechanisms contribute to a difficulty in saying where a play begins and where it ends.

These questions of beginning and ending loom over *Doctor Faustus* because they profoundly affect an understanding of what occurs. Does *Doctor Faustus* end in the 'A' text with him being dragged off to hell, or in the 'B' version with the scholars discovering his dismembered body? Is the final chorus a post-play commentary? What are the implications of the 'scene' where the actors reappear on stage – including presumably a 'restored' Faustus – to take the applause? The appearance of the cast at *Doctor Faustus*'s conclusion helps register that the whole play has been about role-playing, a performance that has as its main endeavour the staging of theatrical opportunities. Faustus is reborn to play another day: twenty-four years on stage, a day in the life of the theatre.

Doctor Faustus is a play designed to facilitate theatrical opportunity: but to what end? As noted above, the commercial theatre of the 1580s and 1590s was seen by some as morally dangerous, by others as morally sound, with seemingly little critical middle ground between defenders and detractors. Yet, it was likely that it was such mixed positions that drew crowds to plays: the simultaneous experience of the comic and the horrific, the blending of pathos and farce, the presence of the exaggerated with the familiar, the edifying and the entertaining – the very features we associate with Marlowe's drama. The play's success on the stage manifestly demonstrates that the companies profitably negotiated the various cultural implications of its shows of delight and magic in their productions.

Ruth Lunney argues that Marlowe's plays break the link between visual signs and traditional perspectives and values.[26] Their signs and characters embrace a 'rhetoric of contradiction' that enables audiences to debate the nature of figures and events. The audience is no longer compelled to approve an intrinsically didactic understanding within well-established frameworks. The result is a new relation between spectator and play where, as the Prologue to *Tamburlaine, Part One* makes clear, we are invited to applaud 'as we please', not as we should.

Should we reconsider how *Doctor Faustus* was contrived? Rather than imagining some authorial ur-manuscript that articulated a precise intellectual vision, might we instead posit that Marlowe and/or his collaborator conceived of *Doctor Faustus* as a play that would be manipulated in performance? Their design was to create a series of scenes that might be linked in different ways in different performances, ones that reflected on ideas of illusion, role-playing, and theatricality around humanity's imagined identities in relation with the supernatural and natural worlds. Performing 'the form of Faustus's fortunes good and bad', this drama was envisaged neither as distinct tragedy nor comedy. A presentation of 'all the world's a circus' rather than 'all the world's a stage', the play proposes that the characters and the spectators share a desire for spectacle that does readily exceed edification. This is a drama that seems constantly to defer clarifying its philosophical or metaphysical speculations while it pursues its various self-generated performances.

For early Protestant reformers, the drama was in the service of religion. For the 'Puritan'-inspired antitheatrical writers from the 1580s, the theatre was 'the chapel of Satan', plays 'the very butchery of Christian souls'.[27] *Doctor Faustus* refuses to acknowledge the determining agency of either of these perspectives because it celebrates the ascendancy of the theatre's own prerogative as a place for playing. The play in either version resists offering a coherent intellectual vision on magic and its relation to religion, or on salvation and damnation. While there is no doubt that it is contrived around a more or less traditional morality vision – Faustus *is* damned – the play's moral structure is constantly being displaced by comic incident. Faustus's faking dismemberment in the horse-courser scenes, for instance, confuses and deflects the horror of his possible dismemberment by the devils. The latter becomes potentially as much a parodic burlesque of the former as vice versa. The play's preoccupations with creating theatre, with organizing performances, may come to seem its ultimate rationale.

NOTES

1. *The Tragical History of Doctor Faustus ('A' Text)* in David Bevington and Eric Rasmussen (eds.), Christopher Marlowe, *Doctor Faustus and Other Plays*, World's Classics (Oxford University Press, 1995). In this chapter all citations are to this version of the play and the 'B' text in the same edition.

2. See Paul Whitfield White, *Theatre and Reformation: Protestantism, Patronage and Playing in Tudor England* (Cambridge University Press, 1993), pp. 1–11.

3. 'Lord Mayor to the Privy Council 3 July 1583' in E. K. Chambers and W. W. Greg (eds.), *Dramatic Records of the City of London, The Remembraxia* (London: Malone Society, 1907), p. 69. See also Peter Lake with Michael Questier, *The Antichrist's Lewd Hat: Protestants, Papists and Players in Post-Reformation England* (New Haven: Yale University Press, 2002), pp. 425–520.

4. Stephen Mullaney, *The Place of the Stage: License, Play and Power in Renaissance England* (University of Chicago Press, 1988).

5. See Houston Diehl, 'Dazzling Theatre: Renaissance Drama in the Age of Reform', *JMRS* 22 (1992), 211–36.

6. 'An answer of the Corporation of London to a petition to the Privy Council from the Queen's Men, *c.* November 1584', in E. K. Chambers and W. W. Greg (eds.), *Dramatic Records from the Lansdowne Manuscripts* (London: Malone Society, 1908), p. 173.

7. See Stephen Gosson, *Plays Confuted in Five Actions* (London, 1582), sigs. G3^v, C4^v–5^r, cited in Lake and Questier, *The Antichrist's Lewd Hat*, p. 500.

8. See Thomas Heywood, *An Apology for Actors* (New York: Garland Press, Facsimile rpt of 1612 edition, 1973).

9. See Margot Heinemann, *Puritanism and Theatre: Thomas Middleton and Opposition Drama under the Early Stuarts* (Cambridge University Press, 1980); and Donna Hamilton, *Shakespeare and the Politics of Protestant England* (Lexington: University Press of Kentucky, 1992).

10. See Stephen Greenblatt, *Renaissance Self-Fashioning: From More to Shakespeare* (University of Chicago Press, 1980), pp. 193–221; Jonathan Dollimore, *Radical Tragedy: Religion, Ideology and Power in the Drama of Shakespeare and his Contemporaries* (Brighton: Harvester Press, 1984), pp. 109–19.

11. Richard Proudfoot, 'Marlowe and the Editors', in J. A. Downie and J. T. Parnell (eds.), *Constructing Christopher Marlowe* (Cambridge University Press, 2000), pp. 45–6.

12. David Bevington and Eric Rasmussen (eds.), *Doctor Faustus 'A' and 'B' Texts (1604, 1616)*, Revels Plays (Manchester University Press, 1993). Hereafter Revels edition. See also Eric Rasmussen, *A Textual Companion to Doctor Faustus*, Revels Plays (Manchester University Press, 1993). See also C. F. Tucker Brooke (ed.), *The Complete Works of Christopher Marlowe* (Oxford University Press, 1910); and the facsimile reprint *Doctor Faustus 1604 and 1616: A Scolar Press Facsimile* (Menston: Scolar Press, 1970).

13. W. W. Greg (ed.), *The Tragical History of the Life and Death of Doctor Faustus by Christopher Marlowe: A Conjectural Reconstruction* (Oxford University Press, 1950).

14. See David Ormerod and Christopher Wortham (eds.), *Christopher Marlowe, Dr Faustus: The 'A' Text* (Nedlands: University of Western Australia Press, 1985);

Michael Keefer (ed.), *Doctor Faustus: A 1604 Version Edition* (Peterborough, Ontario: Broadview Press, 1991).

15. Using the line numbers from the Tucker Brooke edition, Bevington and Rasmussen's Revels edition proposes that the shortness of the 'A' text may be the result of lost manuscript material (p. 65).
16. Cited in E. K. Chambers, *The Elizabethan Stage*, 4 vols. (Oxford: Clarendon Press, 1923), 2: 423. See also Julian M. C. Bowsher, 'Marlowe and the Rose', in Downie and Parnell (eds.), *Constructing Christopher Marlowe*, pp. 30–40.
17. See Chambers, *Elizabethan Stage*, 3: 424; and Bevington and Rasmussen, Revels edition, pp. 49–50.
18. See Stuart Clark, *Thinking with Demons: The Idea of Witchcraft in Early Modern England* (Oxford University Press, 1997).
19. See Roma Gill (ed.), *Doctor Faustus*, New Mermaids (London: Ernest Benn, 1965), pp. xviii–xix.
20. The claim was made by Richard Baines after Marlowe's death and is not reliable. See my *Christopher Marlowe, Writers and their Work* (Plymouth: Northcote House, 1994), esp. pp. 10–21.
21. Greenblatt illustrates how critics come to favour the 'A' text on the basis of their own reading of the content (*Renaissance Self-Fashioning*, pp. 289–90n2). See also Gill, New Mermaids edition, p. xviii.
22. William Empson, *Faustus and the Censor: The English Faust Book and Marlowe's Doctor Faustus* (Oxford: Basil Blackwell, 1987). See also Keefer, *Doctor Faustus*, pp. lx–lxix; and Dollimore, *Radical Tragedy*, p. 119.
23. John D. Cox, *The Devil and the Sacred in English Drama, 1350–1642* (Cambridge University Press, 2000), p. 114.
24. Mikhail Bakhtin, *Rabelais and his World*, H. Iswolsky (trans.) (Cambridge, MA: MIT Press, 1968). See also my *Christopher Marlowe*, pp. 28–9 and pp. 58–60.
25. Gareth Roberts, 'Marlowe and Metaphysics of Magicians', in Downie and Parnell (eds.), *Constructing Christopher Marlowe*, pp. 55–73, discusses the inconsistent use of magic throughout the play.
26. Ruth Lunney, *Marlowe and the Popular Tradition: Innovation in the English Drama before 1595* (Manchester University Press, 2002).
27. Antony Munday, *A Second and Third Blast of Retreat from Plays and Theatres* (London: 1580), p. 89; Stephen Gosson, *The Epermerides of Phialo* (London, 1586), p. 88. Cited in Lake and Questier, *The Antichrist's Lewd Hat*, pp. 450–9.

READING LIST

Barber, C. L. 'The Form of Faustus' Fortunes Good and Bad'. *TDR* 8 (1964), 92–119.
Bluestone, Max. '*Libido Speculandi*: Doctrine and Dramaturgy in Contemporary Interpretations of *Doctor Faustus*'. In Norman Rabkin (ed.), *Reinterpretations of Elizabethan Drama*. New York: Columbia University Press, 1969, pp. 78–91.
Brooke, Nicholas. 'The Moral Tragedy of *Dr Faustus*'. *Cambridge Journal* 7 (1952), 662–87.
Danson, Lawrence. 'Christopher Marlowe: the Questioner'. *ELR* 12 (1982), 3–29.

Dollimore, Jonathan. '*Dr Faustus* (*c.* 1589–92): Subversion Through Transgression'. *Radical Tragedy: Religion, Ideology and Power in the Drama of Shakespeare and his Contemporaries*. Brighton: Harvester Press, 1984, pp. 109–19.

Empson, William. *Faustus and the Censor: The English Faust Book and Marlowe's Doctor Faustus*. Oxford: Basil Blackwell, 1987.

Marcus, Leah S. 'Textual Instability and Ideological Difference: the Case of Doctor Faustus'. *Unediting the Renaissance: Shakespeare, Marlowe, Milton*. London: Routledge, 1996, pp. 38–67.

Roberts, Gareth. 'Marlowe and Metaphysics of Magicians'. In J. A. Downie and J. T. Parnell (eds.), *Constructing Christopher Marlowe*. Cambridge University Press, 2000, pp. 55–73.

Snow, Edward. 'Marlowe's *Doctor Faustus* and the Ends of Desire'. In Alvin B. Kernan (ed.), *Two Renaissance Mythmakers: Christopher Marlowe and Ben Jonson*. Baltimore: Johns Hopkins University Press, 1977, pp. 77–110.

Warren, Michael J. '*Doctor Faustus*: the Old Man and the Text'. *ELR* 11 (1981), 111–47.

12

SARA MUNSON DEATS

Dido, Queen of Carthage and The Massacre at Paris

On first consideration, *Dido, Queen of Carthage* and *The Massacre at Paris* may seem an odd couple to discuss in tandem. In many ways the plays represent polarities within the Marlowe canon. Despite the many questions surrounding the dating of *Dido, Queen of Carthage*, most scholars agree that it is Marlowe's first dramatic effort, perhaps scripted while he was still a student at Cambridge, and *The Massacre at Paris* one of his last, probably written sometime in 1592. Moreover, *Dido* finds its provenance in classical epic, dramatizing Books 1, 2, and 4 of Virgil's *Aeneid* with a veneer of Ovidian shading from the *Heroides*, whereas *The Massacre* is Marlowe's only play based on topical events, a rehearsal of recent upheavals in France. Additionally, whereas *Dido* was first performed by boy actors for a private theatre, *The Massacre* was apparently acted by a professional company. Finally, although many aspects of *Dido* have been interrogated – authorship, date, genre – the text of the play has not been questioned; conversely, *The Massacre* is generally accepted as Marlowe's most corrupt text, most likely the truncated product of memorial reconstruction by a troop of actors.

However, despite these many antitheses, similarities between the two plays abound, a number of which will be examined in this chapter. Although both plays share a traditional scholarly neglect, both have recently evoked considerable critical interest. Moreover, each play presents tragic protagonists – Dido and the Guise – who struggle for national leadership within a complex web of political and amatory events that determine their downfalls, even though in *Dido* the web is woven by the gods, in *The Massacre* by combating political forces. In addition, in typical Marlovian fashion, both plays dramatize multiple inversions of accepted rubrics of politics, gender, and sexuality, and in both plays the accepted audience response to these subversive behaviours has been debated by commentators. Some laud *Dido* as an apotheosis of love over honour; others read it as an affirmation of duty over passion. Similarly, some expositors censure *The Massacre* as a blatant piece of Protestant propaganda, while others praise it as a penetrating appraisal of *realpolitik*. This chapter argues that both plays constitute interrogative dramas that deliberately elicit ambivalent audience reactions to the subversive discourses encoded within the plays.

Ultimately, I seek to demonstrate that comparing these two plays that bracket Marlowe's theatrical career provides valuable insights into the nature of the playwright's dramatic art.

Dido, Queen of Carthage

In many ways, *Dido, Queen of Carthage* is an anomaly in the Marlowe canon. In no other Marlowe play does the male hero share his central position with a female protagonist – one who, according to many commentators, brazenly upstages her lover. In no other Marlowe play is heteroerotic passion the centripetal force of the drama's momentum. Although devils haunt Marlowe's most popular tragedy, *Doctor Faustus*, only in *Dido* do gods and goddesses gambol, glide, and stalk across the stage, bickering among themselves as they meddle in the fates of mortals. Yet despite these atypical aspects, in other respects *Dido* epitomizes both Marlowe's characteristic dramatic strategies and the critical problems surrounding his works.

As with so many of Marlowe's dramas, the authorship of *Dido* has been challenged, the date of the play questioned, and the genre of the drama debated. While no one disputes Marlowe as the primary author, Thomas Nashe's name appears on the title page of the earliest edition (1594), and for many years scholars regarded the play as a schoolboy collaboration between the two university wits, although general consensus now accepts Nashe's contribution as minimal, or perhaps even non-existent.[1] The traditional dating of the play has also aroused scholarly controversy. The view of *Dido* as Marlowe's earliest drama, the apprentice work of a university student, has been challenged by scholars who cite internal evidence, particularly the play's sophisticated dramaturgy and language, to contend that *Dido* is a later play or perhaps a mature revision of a juvenile effort. However, despite the maturity of the drama's verse and the play's skilful stagecraft, majority critical opinion still accepts the traditional dating of the play as Marlowe's earliest work, probably composed around 1585–6.[2] Moreover, the genre of the play has been disputed. Although the title page of the first printed version (1594) announces its genre as *The Tragedie of Dido Queene of Carthage*, as early as the nineteenth century, commentators like Anthony Trollope categorized *Dido* as a 'burlesque' (qtd in Oliver, *Dido*, p. ix). Later, in 1932, T. S. Eliot made his now famous observation concerning Marlowe's serious, savage humour, relating this 'mature tone' particularly to *The Jew of Malta* and *Dido*. Following Eliot, a number of fine studies in the past two decades have established Marlowe as a master of sardonic humour, with *Dido* as a prime specimen of his caustic wit.[3] Finally, the central *dramatis personae* have aroused diverse, even antipodal responses, and the value system affirmed in the play has provoked considerable debate. The disputes concerning the ethical principles endorsed in the play and the appropriate audience response to the two protagonists will probably never be resolved, since, as this chapter will attempt to illustrate, the drama invites alternative, even contradictory interpretations. However, the traditional dichotomous approaches to the play as either a celebration of love or a condemnation of passion have begun to be replaced in recent scholarship by analyses that recognize, and praise, the essential ambiguity of the work.

Thus in many ways, despite its anomalies, *Dido* provides a model for the Marlowe canon. The ambiguous treatment of the two protagonists, elevated through heroic rhetoric while deflated through prosaic action, foreshadows the equivocal development of all of Marlowe's protagonists – Tamburlaine, Barabas, Faustus, Edward, and the Guise. Finally, *Dido* enacts the consistent inversions of hierarchical order that have become Marlowe's dramatic signature.

Dido stages a carnival world in which the norms of gender behaviour, sexuality, and political responsibility are turned topsy-turvy. The play opens with the tableau of Jupiter dandling Ganymede on his knee, besotted by his infatuation for the petulant boy. Like the mortals whose destinies he (at least partially) controls, Jupiter is depicted as a victim of passionate love, displaying the foolishness and excess conventionally associated with amorous seizures. Jupiter seems totally willing to abrogate his divine prerogatives to 'the female wanton boy', to relinquish to the peevish Trojan youth the power to 'Control proud fate, and cut the thread of time' (1.1.29),[4] to subject to his minion's caprices all the deities of heaven and earth. Significantly, therefore, the first example of excessive passion ruling reason is not the smitten Queen of Carthage or even her enamoured sister Anna, but that classical patriarchal icon, Jupiter, King of the Gods. Certainly, Jupiter's dotage for Ganymede is adulterous, homoerotic, and politically irresponsible. However, by associating these subversions with the play's archetypal patriarch (and thus supreme establishmentarian), the play questions the conventional equation of passion with the 'feminine' and duty with the 'masculine', as well as offering a familiar Marlovian alternative to the compulsory heteroeroticism publicly sanctioned at this period. Significantly, in this scene it is Venus, the Goddess of Love and Beauty and thus traditionally the most 'feminine' of the gods, who paradoxically exhorts Jupiter to fulfil his 'masculine duty'.

The relationship between Dido and Aeneas provides the second example of inversion, this time with the woman – not the minion – on top. Whereas

Aeneas dominates Virgil's *Aeneid*, by both word and deed, Ovid's *Heroides* is filtered through the consciousness of Dido. Marlowe's play follows Ovid by placing Dido centre stage, signalling this rearrangement of gender priorities first by the change of eponymous hero from the Trojan warrior to the Queen of Carthage and second by transferring the initiative from Aeneas to Dido. Dido's first meeting with Aeneas introduces a pattern of overture and response that is repeated throughout the play. In the series of interactions between the Queen of Carthage and the Trojan refugee, Dido reverses gender expectations to perform the role of the courtly lover rather than the coy mistress: she initiates and directs the action; she praises Aeneas; and she gives him gifts. In all of their scenes together, Dido's passion remains the galvanizing force, with Aeneas's affection only a flickering reaction to her burning desire. Moreover, Dido's infatuation for Aeneas leads not only to gender reversal but also to the abdication of royal responsibility as the queen flaunts the will of her people, arraying her consort in her royal regalia and parading him through the streets.

The play's second gender rebel (and third exemplar of inversion) is another non-traditional woman, this one clearly not manipulated by divine forces, who also woos the man of her choice and dies of unrequited love. The subplot of the play depicts the amorous frustrations of Anna and the queen's rejected suitor Iarbas, whose unreciprocated passions (Anna's for Iarbas, Iarbas's for Dido) offer dual parallels to Dido's unfulfilled desire. Anna's transgressive ardour for Iarbas also accentuates the gender reversal whereby woman becomes the desiring subject and man becomes the object of desire.

A fourth exemplar of gender reversal burlesques the subversive behaviour of both Dido and Anna. In Act 3, scene 1, Cupid wounds Dido; in Act 4, scene 5, the naughty god finds yet another target for his amorous arrows. The senescent Nurse's lust for the juvenile god inverts a whole host of normative relationships – those between age and youth, male and female, god and human. The ancient Nurse, holding Cupid, pierced by his darts, succumbing to inappropriate lust, and resorting to enticement to achieve her desires, travesties the irrational passion similarly evoked in Dido, and these similarities are accentuated by the repeated tableau of a woman cradling a young boy, a typically Marlovian iconic parody of the Madonna and Child. In fact, the tableau of an adult holding a domineering youth occurs three times in the play. The examples of the elderly Nurse controlled by the imperious child–god, the queen ruled by Cupid disguised as her pampered surrogate son, and the God–King commanded by the cosseted Trojan youth provide indelible emblems for the carnival inversion that the play dramatizes.

Virgil's epic and Ovid's poem narrate only one tragic passion – Dido's obsessive love for Aeneas – with Iarbas's unrequited infatuation for Dido mentioned only in passing. Marlowe's play expands these unhappy amours to include five examples of unequal desire – Jupiter lusting for Ganymede, Dido desiring Aeneas, Iarbas pursuing Dido, Anna yearning for Iarbas, and the Nurse panting after Cupid – some comic, some tragic, some constrained, some voluntary. Moreover, in the upside-down world of the play lovers rarely conform to conventional codes of behaviour: men pursue boys; females woo males; and old crones seek to seduce pink-faced lads. Of the five amours in the play, only one – Iarbas's rather drab suit to Dido – adheres to conventional sex/gender etiquette. These multivalent romances invite dual perspectives. Viewed from a moralistic, pro-duty context, these destructive (or comic) loves can be interpreted as prudential warnings against the perils (or puerility) of uncontrolled desire. However, approached from a more subversive, pro-passion perspective, the polymorphically perverse array of sexualities and gender transgressions represented by these five passions can be seen as undermining, even burlesquing, the inflexibility of traditional amorous systems in the early modern patriarchal society. Yet, whichever reading we endorse, the variety of violations of norms of gender, sexuality, and political behaviour dramatized in *Dido* serve to interrogate compulsory heteroeroticism and many of its standard features, while simultaneously calling into question traditional categories of gender and sexuality.[5]

Similarly, with jaunty disrespect, the play violates traditional generic categories, balancing the lovers' ringing lines and high astounding terms with moments of levity: Jupiter dandling Ganymede on his knees, the humorous wounding of Dido, and the ludicrously lewd old Nurse's attempted seduction of Cupid. Most deflative of all is the treatment of Dido's death. In both Virgil and Ovid, Dido dies alone, with nothing to detract from the solemnity of her tragic immolation. Marlowe's play, however, expands Dido's death scene to include two other suicides, as Iarbas and Anna sprint after Dido into the love-kindled flames, thus, at least according to pro-duty advocates, rendering the play's catastrophe risible rather than piteous or terrible.

Two antithetical interpretations have dominated the criticism of *Dido*. On the one hand, romantic, pro-passion advocates have stressed the tragic elements of the play, embracing the victimized queen and censuring Aeneas as a callous deserter. This romantic reading focuses on the alterations that the play makes in its sources, both Virgil's *Aeneid* and Ovid's *Heroides*, to undercut both Aeneas and the gods, and thus, by extension, to undermine Aeneas's choice of divine dictate over human passion. Primary among these changes is Marlowe's manipulation of his sources to stress both Aeneas's sexual passion for Dido and his betrayal of this passion. Twice Marlowe's Aeneas swears his total devotion to Dido in hyperbolic oaths that are twice broken (3.4.40–50; 4.4.55–60), whereas Virgil's Aeneas truthfully reports that he made no such vows (99).[6] Moreover, when commanded by Hermes to leave Carthage and embark for Italy, Marlowe's Aeneas vacillates between allegiance to Dido and obedience to the gods (4.3.1–30), whereas Virgil's pious Aeneas never questions supernatural fiat (96). Secondly, the account by Marlowe's hero of his unheroic performance during the sack of Troy further tarnishes his epic image. Marlowe radically abbreviates one episode in Virgil to render Aeneas almost indifferent to the loss of his wife Creusa, expands another to stress the prince's pusillanimous desertion of the priestess Cassandra, and adds a third to narrate his failure to rescue Polyxena from the cruel Myrmidons. These changes construct a tripartite prefiguration of Aeneas's abandonment of Dido to her fiery pyre, a foreshadowing punctuated by Polyxena's poignant cry, 'Aeneas stay' (2.1.281), a plea reverberating throughout the dialogue of both Dido and Anna. Finally, commentators endorsing a romantic reading note that just as Marlowe establishes Dido as his title hero, he transfers the initiative from the Trojan prince to the Carthaginian queen. Dominating the stage, Marlowe's Dido woos Aeneas with rich gifts and a magnificent rhetoric that anticipates the cosmic yet sensuous diction of Shakespeare's Cleopatra. In *Dido*, therefore, as in so many of Marlowe's plays, the demonized Other – in this case, the unruly woman – speaks the mightiest lines.

Lastly, a romantic, pro-passion reading also concentrates on the metamorphosis that Virgil's dignified deities undergo in Marlowe's play. The vagaries of Marlowe's quarrelling, conniving gods vitiate their authority, invalidating their epic commands. This irreverent treatment of classical divinity, perhaps revealing the impious influence of Ovid, might also be seen as a subversive undermining of the traditional religious authority legitimating patriarchy.

In response to this romantic approach, a moralistic, pro-duty reading emphasizes the comic elements of the play, adducing alterations in the sources that deface the tragic stature of Dido and thus the romantic ethos that she represents. These additions and alterations include many of the elements noted above: the humorous linking of Dido with both Jupiter and the Nurse, Dido's comic wounding, the play's pervasive association of amorous passion with bribery and linguistic seduction, and the introduction of a sub-plot that multiplies the examples of destructive passion. Anti-romantic exponents assert that these elements combine with the triple suicide to decrease the sublimity of the play's tragic mood and deflate Dido as a tragic hero.

Romantic expositors thus assert that Aeneas and his commitment to duty over love are undercut in Marlowe's drama, whereas pro-duty exegetes insist that Dido and the romantic ethos that she represents are undermined. I suggest that both interpretations have validity. Regarded from one perspective, the play appears to affirm Aeneas's choice of heroic destiny over desire, while derogating love as a kind of seizure, both destructive and ludicrous. However, regarded from another perspective, the play can be seen as celebrating the tragic queen who sacrifices all for love, denigrating the heartless Aeneas who betrays amour for glory. Moreover, an audience listening receptively to the soaring rhetoric of the verse, particularly Dido's plangent lines, while regarding with a blind eye the foolish antics of the leading players, might endorse J. B. Steane's evaluation of the play as a tragic apotheosis of love. Conversely, an audience heeding primarily the unheroic escapades of the victims of passion, while listening with a deaf ear to the play's mellifluous phrases and lyrical cadences, might read the play as either an affirmation of duty or a total spoof of the love versus duty topos, a comic send-up of the high seriousness associated with both the tragic and epic genres. I suggest that the reader/spectator receptive to both the play's heroic verse and its comic interludes will achieve the fullest appreciation of this interrogative drama.[7]

In *The Tudor Play of Mind*, Joel B. Altman locates the ambiguous dramas of the period within the rhetorical tradition of arguing on both sides of the question. According to Altman, the interrogative plays so popular during this period pose questions rather than providing answers. He further maintains that these plays are constructed from a series of statements and counterstatements, both of which are equally valid, thereby imitating the form of a sophistical debate in which thesis provokes antithesis yet without resolving synthesis.[8] We might read *Dido* as an exemplar of this interrogative mode in which antitheses – the tragic and the comic, the romantic and the moralistic – balance precariously, yet without generic or ethical synthesis, as the drama follows the traditional rhetorical practice of this period and argues on both sides of the question.

The Massacre at Paris

Unlike *Dido, The Massacre at Paris* poses no problems with authorship and few with date. No one, to my knowledge, questions Marlowe as the sole author of the work, and critical presumption, based primarily on *Henslowe's Diary*, agrees on 1592 as the probable date of the play's composition and 26 January 1593 as the drama's stage debut. Henslowe also identifies *The Massacre* as an early modern blockbuster, the highest grossing play of the season for Lord Strange's Men. However, critical consensus also insists that the octavo that constitutes the sole extant version of the play is not the drama originally penned by Marlowe and performed with such success by Lord Strange's Men, but rather a pirated memorial reconstruction performed by a band of travelling actors. This judgement is based not only on the abridged nature of the text, which comprises approximately 1,250 lines, but also on the elaborate stage directions, which seem to describe what the author had seen performed, as well as the repeated lines, the garbled language, and the undeveloped characterizations of the *dramatis personae*. Finally, unlike the majority of early modern plays, *The Massacre* was never entered in the Stationers' Register.[9] While earlier critics dismissed the extant text as 'garbled', 'mangled', and 'barely intelligible', they also questioned the value of the original version. Whereas Steane believes that the text that we possess is an impoverished remnant of a potentially great play (pp. 236–46), other commentators have been less optimistic about the drama's potential. H. S. Bennett speaks for this traditional view when he asserts, 'Bad as the state of the text undoubtedly is, there is nothing about it that leads us to believe that, had we the perfect text, we should have a great play. *The Massacre at Paris* is one of the weakest plays of its day' (p. 174).

However, in the past two decades, the much-maligned play has found a number of persuasive apologists, most of whom, although accepting the play as a truncated version of the original, nevertheless find this fragment sufficiently intriguing and Marlovian to invite scrutiny. Moreover, some of these commentators, like Judith Weil and Julia Briggs, although agreeing with the general consensus that the play that has come down to us is far from a masterpiece, nevertheless challenge the widespread assumption that the drama is a piece of crude propaganda, arguing instead that the play possesses often overlooked ironic nuances that render it far more ambiguous than is generally assumed.[10] Following Weil and Briggs, I will seek to rebut the view of *The Massacre* as party line by demonstrating how the ironic structural parallels and ambiguous character portraits of the play create an interrogative drama possessing a sufficient number of typically Marlovian traits to make it of interest to students of the playwright.

Dido dramatizes a carnival world of distorted mirrors; *The Massacre* replicates an urban jungle full of prowling predators and seething with religious violence, intrigue, and treachery. As in *Dido*, the play depicts the lethal mixture of sexuality and politics, presenting multiple inversions of sanctioned sexual and political norms. Henry III's homoerotic love for his favourites mirrors Jupiter's similar subservience to his minion Ganymede, whereas Henry III's privileging of personal affection over kingly duty reflects Dido's elevation of amorous passion over political responsibility. Other liaisons with political implications dramatized in *The Massacre* include Queen Catherine's non-historical infatuation with the Guise and the adulterous affair between the Guise's wife and Henry's minion. As in *Dido*, uncontrolled passion often dictates and distorts policy with fatal results.

Furthermore, despite its amputated and mangled form, *The Massacre* not only provides the ubiquitous inversions but also the multiple perspectives so typical of Marlovian drama. Although earlier critics censured the play as a tasteless piece of chauvinistic propaganda pandering to the lowest jingoist instincts of the early modern audience,[11] in the past two decades commentators have questioned this reductive reading, interpreting the drama as a satire on the treachery or weakness of monarchs and the use of religion as a cloak for Machiavellian policy, as well as a critique of religious violence. The play contains elements of all of these readings as, like *Dido*, it argues on both sides of the questions.[12]

Although ostensibly a vitriolic denunciation of Catholic atrocities committed against innocent Protestants, *The Massacre* features a number of structural parallels that undermine a simplistic dichotomy between good guys and bad guys; indeed, ironically, in a play so centred on sectarian conflict, the good and bad guys are often very similar. The most obvious parallel links the two monarchs, Henry III and Charles I. In two of the most vicious killings in the play, those of the Admiral and the Guise, both Charles and Henry visit their potential victims immediately before the assassinations and lull them into a state of false complacency by their deceitful assurances of protection, and the deaths of both victims seem designed to invite audience sympathy. Moreover, both Charles and Henry are depicted as weak kings, dedicated to hedonism rather than duty and ruled by their mother and either their advisers or their favourites. As the play progresses, the parallels expand to connect Henry with the Guise as well as with Charles. Both the Guise and Henry commit gratuitous murders, while exulting over the deaths of their enemies (cf. particularly the Guise's mocking of the dead Admiral (5.35–41) with Henry's gloating over the death of the Guise (21.95–119)) and the slaughter of the Cardinal of Lorraine, the Guise's brother (22), parallels the similar mindless killing of the clergyman Loreine (7). Through these linkages, Marlowe creates a kind of 'la ronde' of violence whereby Charles makes an alliance with Navarre and later betrays him to side with the Guise and participate in the Duke's atrocities; conversely, Henry initially aligns himself with the Guise, only later to deceive him to side with Navarre and indulge in multiple homicides. Thus the bloodshed and betrayal come full circle and the audience experiences a sickening sensation of déjà vu.[13] Ultimately, as Rick Bowers explains, the play manoeuvres its audience simultaneously to identify with the victims – thus deploring ongoing violence – and with the oppressors – especially the Guise as villain/hero – thus forcing the audience to occupy an intolerable moral position (140), as the drama argues on both sides of the question. Even the valedictory speech of the play, declaimed by the Protestant champion Henry of Navarre, is vitiated by a rhetoric of vengeance which suggests that the cycle of bloodshed will continue.

The play's ambiguous character portraits encourage the audience ambivalence evoked by the play's action. Let us first consider the Duke of Guise. If Dido, the female protagonist pursuing love not power, constitutes an atypical Marlovian hero, the Duke of Guise presents a typical Marlovian overreacher and Machiavel. The Guise, like Tamburlaine, seeks the sweet fruition of an earthly crown and will scruple at nothing to gain the diadem, following the advice of Machevill in *The Jew of Malta* and using religion, in this case his faked ardour for Catholicism, to achieve this goal. Moreover, like his prototype Barabas in *The Jew of Malta*, the Guise revels in his atrocities. Nevertheless, despite a few fine passages of Marlovian hyperbole, the Guise emerges as more of a parody of the Marlovian overreacher than a full-bodied avatar, although whether this results from authorial intention or inaccurate reporting remains problematic. At any rate, although certainly a villain, the Guise is also the play's protagonist, a status validated by the title on our only extant text, which reads, *The Massacre at Paris: With the Death of the Duke of Guise*.[14] Moreover, Marlowe expands the role of the Guise by making him the primary architect of the massacre and the central figure in the action, a role historically shared with Queen Catherine, the Duke of Anjou, and King Charles.[15] However, as Briggs points out, Marlowe has not only expanded the Guise's role in the slaughter of the innocents but has also inserted events from Catholic as well as Protestant sources that function to swerve audience allegiance away from Henry (the ally of the Protestants) and towards the Guise. These include the treachery of Henry to the Guise noted above, the vivid dramatization of the Duke's courage, Henry's forcing the Guise's mourning son to view his father's body, and Henry's brutal mocking of the Cardinal of Lorraine before his strangulation (pp. 265–8). Although we might question the heroic death of the Guise and wonder if these events really evoke greater sympathy for him, as Briggs insists – after all, the Duke has participated in more outrageous cruelties – we might agree that they certainly stress the similarity not only between Henry and the Guise, but also between the pro-Catholic and pro-Protestant assassins.

Henry III, the chameleon king who, according to Paul Kocher, incredibly switches his alliance from the ranks of the devils to the side of the angels, has also aroused vastly different responses from commentators.[16] Weil judges him a headstrong, wilful king with Machiavellian tendencies that link him to Navarre and the Guise (pp. 92–3), whereas, conversely, Andrew W. Kirk identifies him, like Charles, as an exemplum of royal passivity and dependency, who 'dissipates his authority in his enthrallment to his minions . . .' (p. 202). Mario Di Gangi limns a more favourable portrait, presenting Henry as originally a weak and irresponsible king surrounded by a group of disorderly minions who develops into a dignified monarch devoted to one loyal and wise favourite and to the true (Protestant) religion.[17] Henry's political and religious vacillations thus raise a number of questions. Is his shift of allegiance from Catholic to Protestant an act of genuine conversion or the opportunistic choice of another Machiavellian politician? And does the drama affirm this 'conversion' or ironically imply that this radical change is no change at all, since the angels and the devils are really so similar? Finally, is this radical character disjunction – if disjunction it is – influenced by history's ambiguous portrait of Henry III, and thus an aspect of the original text, or is it the result of jumbled reporting?

Finally, Henry of Navarre, the saviour of the Protestants and thus the hero, although not necessarily the protagonist, of the play, has aroused little admiration among commentators – either as an artistic creation or as an ethical individual. Kocher censures Navarre, the character, as 'Marlowe's worst failure in the entire play', a 'patchwork of Protestant commonplaces' ('Contemporary Pamphlets', p. 316). Weil derogates Navarre, the individual, as a sanctimonious Machiavellian, who, like the Guise and Henry III, uses religion as a cloak for ambition (pp. 89–92), a view seconded by Briggs, who speculates that the Protestant leader, like the Guise, may be 'yet another political operator, exploiting religious fervour to bring him one step nearer the crown' (p. 272). If for Weil and Briggs Navarre is a self-willed and self-seeking individual, for Kirk he plays yet another variation on the theme of royal passivity. In contrast to Charles, the dependant monarch ruled by his mother, and Henry, the feckless king originally controlled by his minions, Navarre is too reliant upon providence. Later, however, according to Kirk, Navarre, like Henry, transforms into a Machiavellian figure and this instability calls into question his role as either passive Christian or dynamic leader (pp. 205–6).

Ultimately, the nexus between the garbled text and its ambiguous portraits foregrounds the vexing question: does the problematic quality of the play result from the drama's underlying confusion and lack of direction, as some critics have asserted, or does it derive from the maimed text, as many have assumed, or is it possibly the deliberate result of the play's interrogative mode?

Strange bedfellows

In this chapter, I have tried to demonstrate that *Dido, Queen of Carthage* and *The Massacre at Paris*, the most neglected plays in the Marlowe canon, are worthy objects of study for the student of Marlowe. I have argued that

Dido, so often relegated to Marlowe's juvenilia, is a sophisticated and un-derrated play that zestfully and playfully destabilizes conventional categories not only of gender and sexuality, but also of genre and tone. *Dido* counter-poises flashes of tragic sublimity with sparkles of comic levity while simul-taneously elevating and deflating passionate love, affirming and debunking heroic duty, as it balances contrarieties of genre (comedy, tragedy) and value (romantic, moralistic, satirical) into an intriguing dramatic oxymoron. Also, I have had the opportunity of seeing *Dido* performed by the Fletcher Players of Cambridge University at Corpus Christi College, Marlowe's alma mater, and can testify to its effectiveness as both an entertaining and moving theatri-cal experience. In both its subversiveness and its indecidibility, *Dido* seems surprisingly contemporary.

Unfortunately, *The Massacre at Paris*, at least in its extant text, is a far poorer play, and I doubt that in its present corrupt form it could be suc-cessfully performed today. Nevertheless, despite its stripped verse and stark characterizations, *The Massacre* retains a trenchantly ironic tone and an in-triguingly interrogative mode that identify it as Marlowe's handiwork. More-over, in a historical period wracked with religious terrorism *The Massacre*, with its brutal depiction of sectarian violence and *realpolitik* manoeuvring, seems painfully contemporary.

NOTES

1. See H. J. Oliver's introduction to the Revels edition of *'Dido, Queen of Carthage' and 'The Massacre at Paris'* (Cambridge, MA: Harvard University Press, 1968), pp. xx–xxv.
2. Oliver gives an informative discussion of the pros and cons of the dating contro-versy in his introduction to *Dido*, pp. xxv–xxx.
3. T. S. Eliot, *Essays on Elizabethan Drama* (New York: Harcourt, Brace, and World, 1932), pp. 62–3.
4. In this chapter all citations from *Dido, Queen of Carthage* and *The Massacre at Paris* are to *Christopher Marlowe: The Complete Plays*, Mark Thornton Burnett (ed.), (Dent: London, 1999).
5. See Sara Munson Deats, *Sex, Gender, and Desire in the Plays of Christopher Marlowe* (Newark: University of Delaware Press, 1997), pp. 89–124.
6. All references to Virgil are from *The Aeneid of Virgil*, ed. and trans. Rolfe Humphries (New York: Charles Scribner's Sons, 1951).
7. The most eloquent apologist for the pro-passion reading is probably J. B. Steane, *Marlowe: A Critical Study* (Cambridge University Press, 1964), pp. 29–61. See also John Cameron Allen, 'Marlowe's *Dido* and the Tradition', in Richard Hosley (ed.), *Essays on Shakespeare and Elizabethan Drama in Honor of Hardin Craig*, (Columbia: University of Missouri Press, 1962), pp. 66–8. Advocates of the pro-duty reading include William Godshalk, *The Marlovian World Picture* (The Hague: Mouton, 1974), pp. 38–58; and Mary Elizabeth Smith, *'Love Kindling*

Fire': A Study of Christopher Marlowe's 'The Tragedy of Dido, Queen of Carthage' (Salzburg: Institut fur Englische Sprache und Literatur, 1977).

8. Joel Altman, *The Tudor Play of Mind: Rhetorical Inquiry and the Development of Elizabethan Drama* (Berkeley: University of California Press, 1978), p. 71.

9. See H. S. Bennett's introduction to *The Massacre at Paris*, in *'The Jew of Malta' and 'The Massacre at Paris'* (New York: MacVeagh, 1931), pp. 169–78; and Oliver's introduction to *The Massacre*, pp. xlvii–lxi.

10. See Judith Weil, *Christopher Marlowe: Merlin's Prophet* (Cambridge University Press, 1977), pp. 82–103; and Julia Briggs, 'Marlowe's *Massacre at Paris*: a Reconsideration', *RES* 34 (1983), 257–78.

11. See particularly Wilbur Sanders, *The Dramatist and the Received Idea: Studies in the Plays of Marlowe and Shakespeare* (Cambridge University Press, 1968), pp. 20–37.

12. See Briggs, 'A Reconsideration', pp. 257–78; and Andrew W. Kirk, 'Marlowe and the Disordered Face of French History', *SEL* 35 (1995), 193–213.

13. Briggs, 'A Reconsideration', pp. 257–78; and Rick Bowers, 'The Massacre at Paris: Marlowe's Messy Consensus Narrative', in Paul Whitfield White (ed.), *Marlowe, History, and Sexuality: New Critical Essays on Christopher Marlowe*, (New York: AMS Press, 1998), pp. 131–41.

14. Noted by Patrick Cheney, *Marlowe's Counterfeit Profession: Ovid, Spenser, Counter-Nationhood* (University of Toronto Press, 1997), p. 176.

15. Paul Kocher, 'François Hotman and Marlowe's *Massacre at Paris*', *PMLA* 56 (1941), 366–7.

16. Paul Kocher, 'Contemporary Pamphlet Backgrounds for Marlowe's *The Massacre at Paris* (Part II)', *MLQ* 8 (1947), 316.

17. Mario Di Gangi, *The Homoerotics of Early Modern Drama* (Cambridge University Press, 1997), p. 108.

READING LIST

Bartels, Emily C. *Spectacles of Strangeness: Imperialism, Alienation, and Marlowe*. Philadelphia: University of Pennsylvania Press, 1993.

Briggs, Julia. 'Marlowe's *Massacre at Paris*: a Reconsideration'. *RES* 34 (1983), 257–78.

Cheney, Patrick. *Marlowe's Counterfeit Profession: Ovid, Spenser, Counter-Nationhood*. University of Toronto Press, 1997.

Deats, Sara Munson. *Sex, Gender, and Desire in the Plays of Christopher Marlowe*. Newark: University of Delaware Press, 1997.

Deats, Sara Munson and Robert Logan (eds.). *Marlowe's Empery: Expanding His Critical Contexts*. Newark: University of Delaware Press, 2002.

Downie, J. A. and J. T. Parnell (eds.). *Constructing Christopher Marlowe*. Cambridge University Press, 2000.

Grantley, Darryll and Peter Roberts (eds.). *Christopher Marlowe and English Renaissance Culture*. Aldershot: Scolar Press, 1996.

Godshalk, William. *The Marlovian World Picture*. The Hague: Mouton, 1974.

Harraway, Clare. *Re-Citing Marlowe: Approaches to the Drama*. Aldershot: Ashgate Press, 2000.

Hendricks, Margo. 'Managing the Barbarian: *The Tragedy of Dido, Queen of Carthage'. RenD* 23 (1992), 165–88.

Kirk, Andrew W. 'Marlowe and the Disordered Face of French History'. *SEL* 35 (1995), 193–213.

McAdam, Ian. *The Irony of Identity: Self and Imagination in the Drama of Christopher Marlowe.* Newark: University of Delaware Press, 1999.

Smith, Mary Elizabeth. *'Love Kindling Fire': A Study of Christopher Marlowe's 'The Tragedy of Dido, Queen of Carthage'.* Salzburg: Institut fur Englische Sprache und Literatur, 1977.

Steane, J. B. *Marlowe: A Critical Study.* Cambridge University Press, 1964.

Weil, Judith. *Christopher Marlowe: Merlin's Prophet.* Cambridge University Press, 1977.

White, Paul Whitfield (ed.). *Marlowe, History, and Sexuality: New Critical Essays on Christopher Marlowe.* New York: AMS Press, 1998.

13

RICHARD WILSON

Tragedy, patronage, and power

Stabbed by a Catholic assassin at the end of *The Massacre at Paris*, the dying Henry III of France commands his favourite Epernoun to 'Go call the English agent hither straight', and then begs this 'Agent for England' to return to London and tell 'What this detested Jacobin hath done . . . Salute the Queen of England in my name, / And tell her, Henry dies her faithful friend' (5.5.50–107).[1] There is a tradition that the mute 'English Agent' in this scene is, in fact, the author's self-portrait in his guise as 'Mr Merlin', the English envoy to Henry of Navarre, and so what he has to tell can be interpreted as the play itself, which therefore ends where it begins, restaging for Londoners the perfidies of the French Wars of Religion. And since the text, which dates from late in 1592, may be the last he wrote, this scene in which he might have depicted himself has an uncanny relation to Marlowe's final mission, which, as retraced by Charles Nicholl, seems to have been an attempt to infiltrate the Brussels headquarters of England's Catholic exiles, so as to 'turn' one of them against their candidate for Elizabeth's throne: Ferdinando Stanley, Lord Strange, who happened to be patron of the company then performing the dramatist's works – including *The Massacre at Paris* – on Bankside.

Evidently, this is an episode that situates Marlovian tragedy not only within 'the penumbra of conspiracy surrounding Lord Strange',[2] but also within the nascent early modern literary field, and its overdetermined and potentially lethal negotiations between princes and poets. For though Ferdinando let it be known that he could 'never endure his name or sight when he had heard of his conditions' as a double-agent, and that 'the form of divine prayers used daily in his Lordship's house' proved the playwright had no success there in inciting treason, within six months of the premiere of *The Massacre at Paris* Marlowe was dead, his 'mouth stopped', Nicholl deduces, on orders of 'Her Majesty's special service', to smother the story he had to tell about government provocation of Catholic plots. And a year later Strange was himself poisoned, the victim of Lord Burleigh's masterly web of entrapment.[3]

Dido, Queen of Carthage

The 'stopping' of Christopher Marlowe by English counter-intelligence of-fers a lurid illustration of Michel Foucault's analysis, in his posthumous collection of lectures, *Fearless Speech*, of the birth of tragedy in the problem of truth-telling and the relations between power and the messenger it itches to silence.[4] Killing the messenger, according to Foucault's theory, provided the ground of tragedy in ancient Athens as a breach of *parrhesia*: the pact to speak and hear the truth spoken which was struck between the ruler 'who has power but lacks truth, and the one who has the truth but lacks the power'. Thus, what Greek tragedy presents, again and again, the philosopher pro-poses, is the impasse when the powerful revoke the contract to permit the truth to be spoken which is essential in a culture where 'the king's messenger is still vulnerable, and takes a risk in speaking' (pp. 32–3). Classical tragedy, in this Foucauldian reading, was a fight to the death between sovereign and servant over freedom of speech and the threat of silence. So, it may not be chance that in Marlowe's first and most studiously neo-classical play, *The Tragedy of Dido, Queen of Carthage*, the template for all his plots is laid out as just such a patronage crisis, in the predicament of Aeneas as a truth-teller who risks enslavement, when he sings for his supper at the court of the monarch he calls a 'patroness of all our lives' (4.4.55). The identification of Dido as 'Eliza' in this text is insistent enough to make it clear that this is, in fact, the perilous position of the author himself in the corridors of Elizabethan power. And Aeneas's displaced rival, Iarbas, seems to define the fraught field of Renaissance cultural production – 'When airy creatures war amongst themselves' to win preferment from 'The woman that thou will'd us entertain' – by protesting that the struggle for recognition at the queen's court creates only an art of propaganda, 'Whose hideous echoes make the welkin howl, / And all the woods "Eliza" to resound!' (4.2.7–10). Thus, a competi-tive quotation from the author of *The Faerie Queene* announces, at the very start of Marlowe's career, his analysis of his own professional situation as one of 'golden fortunes clogg'd with courtly ease', which 'Cannot ascend to Fame's immortal house, / Or banquet in bright Honour's hall' (4.3.8–10), until the sponsored writer learns to 'Banish that ticing dame from forth your mouth' (31). And significantly, it is Hermes, the messenger of the gods who is himself the god of commerce and therefore of the playhouse, who has constantly to prompt Virgil's vagabond hero to remember the *Aeneid*, with its higher calling of creative agency, autonomy, and choice:

> Why, cousin, stand you building cities here,
> And beautifying the empire of this queen . . .

Too-too forgetful of thine own affairs...
The king of gods sent me from highest heaven,
To sound this angry message in thine ears:
Vain man, what monarchy expect'st thou here?
                                    (*Dido* 5.1.27–34)

'Here Queen Dido wears th'imperial crown, / Who for Troy's sake hath entertain'd us all, / And clad us in these wealthy robes we wear': Aeneas's surprise reunion with his 'sweet companions' in the lobby of the queen's palace, 'where her servitors pass through the hall, / Bearing a banquet' (2.1.60–72), locates Marlovian drama literally in the waiting-room of royal favour, and in the specific context of that demeaning contest for court costume which was to feature later in so many of Shakespeare's plays, when the actors, blowing their trumpet like 'some noble gentleman that means, / Travelling some journey, to repose', are shown instead 'to the buttery' by their host, albeit with promise of new livery, 'friendly welcome', and want of 'nothing that the house affords' (*The Taming of the Shrew*, Ind. 2.70–100).[5] So, the paradox of this theatre is that of an art that has to be sheltered, like these Trojan refugees, in the halls of the great, reliant on some capricious patron for protection from commercial storms, during its passage to creative freedom. No wonder, then, that Shakespeare based the rehearsal of the players at Elsinore on a recital of 'Aeneas' tale to Dido', as he recognized that what Marlowe was framing in this command performance by a wandering minstrel before the Queen of Carthage was a metatheatrical mirror of his own conditions of production, as author of 'an excellent play...set down with cunning', yet doomed to be 'caviare to the general', and so restricted by the taste of the elite 'whose judgements in such matters cried in the top of' a box-office flop.

In *Hamlet* the Prince recalls how he 'loved' *Dido*, though 'the play pleased not the million', and was acted in public 'not above once' (2.2.416–29). According to Pierre Bourdieu, it was with this memory that Shakespeare voiced his calculation that the cloak of patronage would be a temporary necessity in 'the symbolic revolution by which artists freed themselves from any master except their art'.[6] Yet if Marlowe's admirer could perceive in this student play piped by 'the children of Her Majesty's Chapel' its author's tactical need to dress his work up in the 'rich embroidered coats, / And silver whistles' of the court (4.4.9),[7] he also pinpointed the essence of Marlovian tragedy when he had the old spy-master Polonius cut off Aeneas's speech with the complaint (which Hamlet turns into a cue for beheading) that this text 'is too long' (*Hamlet*, 2.2.479). For in *Dido* the warrant which licenses

the Player King to 'build a statelier Troy' in 'our pleasant suburbs' (5.1.1–
15) beside the river, is always about to be countermanded, along with all the
'instruments that launch'd him forth':

> For this will Dido tie ye full of knots,
> And shear ye all asunder with her hands.
> Now serve to chastise shipboys for their faults,
> Ye shall no more offend the Carthage queen.
> Now, let him hang my favours on his masts,
> And see if those will serve instead of sails;
> For tackling, let him take the chains of gold
> Which I bestow'd upon his followers;
> Instead of oars, let him use his hands,
> And swim to Italy: I'll keep these sure.
>
> (*Dido* 4.4.150–64)

Shakespeare remembered from Marlowe's miniaturized Roman tragedy
the struggle to secure from power 'liberty / Withal, as large a charter as the
wind' (*As You Like It* 2.7.47–8). For clad in such 'base robes' (*Dido* 2.1.79),
when he first sets foot in the city 'Poor and unknown' (1.1.227), that his
genius is unrecognized, Aeneas is garbed by his mentor from her wardrobe,
and even coached by her, before performing, to 'Remember who thou art;
speak like thyself: / Humility belongs to common grooms' (2.1.100–01). His
investiture in 'the imperial crown' and 'golden sceptre' thus confirms the
necessity for an upstart medium to be consecrated with the fiction of royal
licence. But the 'base' actor chafes under 'this diadem' (4.4.35–41) and longs
to escape 'these unrenowned realms, / Whereas nobility abhors to stay', for
the open sea and 'nimble winds' of commerce (4.3.16–24).

So, if *Dido* records a phase in Marlowe's life, about 1586–7, when he was
compelled to infantilize his art in the Chapel Royal, his hero's pledge to an-
chor his future with the queen's, 'That tied together by the striving tongues, /
We may, as one, sail onward' (29–30), proves a mere ruse to seduce the
licensing authorities. As Michael Hattaway writes, it would be easy for a
Marxist critic 'to place Marlowe among the alienated intellectuals' of the
Elizabethan *fin-de-siècle*, 'base of stock, deprived of power, and alienated
from the energies of demotic life'.[8] But this would be to over-simplify his
position-taking in the literary field, trimming, like Aeneas, between private
protection and public presentation. It would be to forget how this dual-
ist structure had liberating effects, similar to those discussed by Bourdieu,
when the Paris salons of the 1840s offered 'young men hoping to live off
art', and separated from their origins by 'the lifestyle they were inventing', a
springboard for their 'conquest of autonomy'.[9] For as the sociologist wrote,

factional 'struggles in the political field may best serve the interest of writers concerned about literary independence' (*Rules of Art*, p. 52). Such certainly seems to be the view of Marlowe himself, judging by the Induction to his play, which presents factions at the court of Jupiter as so many potential backers of Aeneas. In the event, however, before Hermes is despatched to aid the Trojan, the king of heaven 'plucks a feather' from the messenger's wings to adorn his favourite, Ganymede (s.d. 1.1.40). With its hint of the Icarus myth, this petty act of symbolic castration is a true premonition of Marlovian tragedy: a sharp reminder that the cover power gives is liable to be taken back, and that the flight of its herald may always have been sabotaged.

The ambivalent situation of Elizabethan drama, in which playhouses were owned by entrepreneurs while actors were licensed under patrons, meant that free enterprise was always conditioned by 'the vital necessity of maintaining aristocratic protection'.[10] So, *Dido Queen of Carthage* identifies the origins of Marlovian tragedy in the very conditions of his theatre as 'a collusion between courtiers and players against hostile authority', and the pretence that actors 'existed only to gratify the Queen': as Dido 'fetters' the winds of trade (1.1.118), captivating Aeneas with bands (222) like those yoking Venus to Mars (3.4.4), or the thongs lashing Achilles (2.1.205).[11] Thus, the queen will truss her slave with 'bracelets' of his golden tresses (3.1.84), braiding rope to restrain him out of his Apollonian locks (1.1.10, 112, 159). In fact, nothing better illustrates the subjection of Elizabethan drama to political power than this claustrophobic imagery of cables, nets, and hawsers, the prelude to an entire *œuvre* fixated, as Marjorie Garber remarks, on fetishes of bondage, in which characters scheming 'to prison or wall each other up' find closure only in enclosure.[12] So, the 'tackling made of rivell'd gold' with which Dido rigs Aeneas's ships (3.1.116) epitomizes the contradiction of the first modern literary field, which is that such 'a powerful process of autonomization' is initiated 'in the context of dependence on power': autonomy, 'without which there would be no literary field, does not establish itself at the expense of power, which, on the contrary, sustains it'.[13] Yet, if *Dido* sets the agenda for Marlovian tragedy, it is precisely in this actor–manager's flight from his confinement, abandoning his patroness to the pyre she stokes for herself out of the 'letters, lines, and perjur'd papers' (5.1.300) with which he had declared his love. All Marlowe's plays consist of a contest, Garber claims, between speech and text, in which his declamatory heroes 'are slain by their own handwriting, signatures, or seals'.[14] But with this one exception to the Marlovian rule that breath is terminated by writing, we see how this war of speech and script is also waged between city and court, or pit and patron. Marlowe would move on to the Lord Admiral's Men. So, as Aeneas sails, like 'a runagate' (265), from the burning library towards Rome and its amphitheatres, the picture of the sailors, who had been 'clapp'd under hatches', capering to 'merry-make for joy' (240, 260), is an unforgettable tableau of the flotation of an actors' company; so much so that Shakespeare recalled it for the finale of *The Tempest*. *Dido* was a play on his mind when he set his farewell in the same location. And what drew him to it, evidently, was its affirmation of the 'gentle breath' of the playhouse, which filled the sails of the Elizabethan dramatist, as he steered between players, prince, and public, in his creative project, 'Which was to please' (*The Tempest*, Epilogue 11–20).

Tamburlaine

'View but his picture in this tragic glass, / And then applaud his fortunes as you please': if the truancy of *Dido* flags Marlowe's escape from the co-terie to the play-yard, his fanfare to *The First Part of Tamburlaine the Great* proclaims his belief in the emancipating acclaim of the metropolitan crowd. 'Sundry times showed upon stages in the City of London', according to its 1590 title page (rpt in Boas, p. 68), this is a drama which literalizes Dido's tribute to the player as a groom raised to be king, in the epic of 'a Scythian shepherd' (1.2.155) who 'plays the orator' (129) on a tour of arenas, like the Theatre and the Curtain where Marlowe's work was now produced. Thus, it is telling that when Tamburlaine launches his empire as a joint-stock ven-ture with Theridamas, he too images his army as a team of actors – since 'Jove sometimes masked in a shepherd's weed' – in a prospectus that his partner says 'Not Hermes, prolocutor to the gods' could make 'more pa-thetical' (1.2.199–211). It may be that this combination records the merger, late in 1587, of stars of the popular Queen's company with the Admiral's Men. What is certain, Robert Weimann writes, is that the advertisement in the Prologue of the superiority of the new university poet to 'jigging, rhyming' clowns signalled a point when the London stage became 'free and profitable enough to outweigh the stigma attached to such an "unliterary" institution'.[15] So, the liberty accorded the hero of this play relates directly to the ideal situation he describes, where the 'friends that help to wean' his career, and maintain his 'life exempt from servitude... / Till men and kingdoms help to strengthen it' (29–30), have the same restricted role as those factional leaders, such as the Lord Admiral, Charles Howard, who lent companies their names in the years before the stage was 'weaned'. As Tamburlaine boasts, when he seizes his bride Zenocrate from her noble es-cort, such 'lords' were effectively 'kept forced followers' by this system, so long as actors could justify their 'estimates... / That in conceit bear empires

on spears' (62–4). The entire plot of *Tamburlaine, Part One* can therefore
be said to consist of a projection of audience-ratings – equivalent to the
box-office diary of the impresario Philip Henslowe – as the 'orator' wins
crowds that swell from a 'thousand' (121), to 'forty thousand' (2.1.61),
and 'two hundred thousand' (3.3.18), to become 'A monster of five hundred thousand heads' in galleries and pit (4.3.7). Nor were these 'high astounding terms' hyperbole (Pro. 5), since by 1601, 'with 3,750 spectators on
230 days of business, total admissions for London's public theatres would
have been 862,500'.[16]

'I am a lord, for so my deeds shall prove, / And yet a shepherd by my
parentage': in *Tamburlaine, Part One* the social riddle posed by the rise of
the players as 'The strangest men that ever nature made' (2.7.40) is how such
'scum of men' (4.3.9), who 'live confounded in disordered troops' (2.2.60)
and 'seem but silly country swains, / May have the leading of so great a host'
(1.2.34–48). For here the trade-off between power and theatre is determined
by the new reality that 'mighty conquerors', who formerly triumphed 'in
their prowess and their policies', are 'insufficient to express the same', when
'it requires a great and thundering speech' (1.1.1–9). So, from the instant
the Median lords plead to him for 'our liberties' (1.2.75), Tamburlaine's
conquests are a total reversal of the patronage game suggested by Queen
Dido, in which even 'the hallow'd person of a prince' (4.4.40) is subjected
by the player–king to the shackles she intended for Aeneas. From Mycetes,
'the witty king of Persia' (2.4.23), whose failure is that he can never produce the 'dainty show' of 'milk-white steads.../ All loaden with the heads
of killed men' (1.1.76–80), which the real king of wit so regularly presents;
to the Governor of Damascus, whose 'masque in silk and cloth of gold'
(4.2.108) is eclipsed by the dance of Death in which the pageant-master
shows the slaughter of the city's Virgins; the rulers of this play are system-
atically trumped by Tamburlaine's superior dramaturgy. This is truly a war
of theatres, in which victory depends not on feudal sword-fights, but an
'almost complete lack of action, thus giving the great tragedian Edward
Alleyn opportunity to declaim longer passages than had ever been heard
on an English stage'.[17] But the logic of this triumph of words over swords
is ultimately revealed in the degradation of the emperor Bajazeth. For as
Tamburlaine exhibits the monarch in a cage, uses him as a footstool, or feeds
him 'scraps' from his table (87), it is impossible not to see in this abjection the
symbolic revenge of the poet on his own courtly overlords. Thus, when the
sovereign 'brains himself against the cage' (s.d. 5.2.241) Marlowe inverts
the slavish conditions which would condemn so many Elizabethan writers
to infested garrets and violent deaths. And at the end, when Tamburlaine is
compared to Aeneas (5.2.319–33), the suicide of Bajazeth's widow, Zabina,

brings back the fantasy of *Dido*, of a queen reduced to mockery by theft of her theatrical props:

> Hell, death, Tamburlaine, hell!
> Make ready my coach, my chair, my jewels.
> I come, I come, I come, I come!
> [*She runs against the cage and brains herself*]
> (*1 Tamb.* 5.2.255–7)

Tamburlaine, according to the King of Persia he deposes, is an upstart beautified with 'plumes' pulled from the great (1.1.33); and the insult (later shot at Shakespeare), shows how his story continues the struggle begun in *Dido* for the aesthetic 'monarchy' which comes with 'beauty's just applause'. This is a project which, he says, inspired 'all the pens that ever poets held': the dream of 'subduing' the powerful, as Jupiter was seduced by 'the lovely warmth of shepherds' flames' into becoming an actor himself (5.2.98–124). But there is one exception to the conquering thespian's box-office persuasion, and this is the Soldan of Egypt, the father of Zenocrate, who is unmoved when a nameless Messenger reports the hundreds of thousands in Tamburlaine's ranks, insisting his force will be greater, 'could their numbers countervail the stars' (4.1.31). The play ends when the Soldan blesses his daughter's marriage in the name of 'God and Mahomet' (5.2.418); but the stand-off between the monarch who holds power and the Messenger who talks numbers remains unresolved, and suggests that this 'marriage-time' (443) represents the truce between players and politicians in the period of the Armada, when Marlowe was allowed, for this once, to shape his plot with state support. So, if Tamburlaine is, indeed, the personification of Elizabethan theatre, his marriage to the daughter of a king marks, in Marlowe's only happy ending, a high-point of autonomy for the dramatist, but also defines its circumstance and terms. That this autonomy is constrained is immediately evident, moreover, in the Prologue to *The Second Part of Tamburlaine the Great*, which bluntly states the problematic of Marlovian tragedy, when it announces that despite the 'general welcomes Tamburlaine receiv'd, / When he arrived last upon our stage', in this sequel 'death cuts off the progress of his pomp / And murderous Fates throw all his triumphs down'. Thus, it is as if the Soldan, who never reappears, continues to decree that popularity cannot secure legitimacy for the literary field, which will always be subordinated to the arbitrary dictates of a 'murderous' power. In a city where players could be 'thrown down' on a pretext of riot or plague, and 'the Privy Council's directives against vagabonds were aimed precisely at them',[18] the 'general welcomes' of the public could at any time be cancelled by the caprices of the 'Fates'. And so, a drama that restores the people's favourite to the boards, ordering everyone to 'banquet and carouse' (1.6.98), stalls on the consequent death of Zenocrate, as the compact between state and stage dissolves, and the master of revels turns his theatrical resources into a gunpowder plot against the royal court:

> What, is she dead? Techelles, draw thy sword,
> And wound the earth, that it may cleave in twain,
> And we descend into th'infernal vaults,
> To hale the Fatal Sisters by the hair
> And throw them in the triple moat of hell,
> For taking thence my fair Zenocrate.
> Casane and Theridamas, to arms!
> Raise cavalieros higher than the clouds,
> And with the cannon break the frame of heaven;
> Batter the shining palace of the sun,
> And shiver all the starry firmament,
> For amorous Jove hath snatch'd my love from hence,
> Meaning to make her stately queen of heaven.
> (2 Tamb. 2.4.96–108)

Tamburlaine's pledge to 'set black streamers in the firmament' against 'the powers of heaven' (5.3.48), for reneging on the contract agreed in *Dido* to liberate actors from the Fates, sets the funereal scene for Marlowe's ensuing work as a tragedy of art subjugated to authority. The context of this darkening of the Marlovian stage was perhaps the crack-down on theatres due to the Martin Marprelate affair of 1588–9, when writers who had been officially incited to attack the Puritan 'Martin' pamphlets had their work suppressed as blasphemous: 'in that the players take it upon themselves to handle matters of Divinity and State unfit to be suffered'.[19] Thus, on 6 November 1589 Lord Burleigh gave orders 'for the stay of all plays in the City', and on the 12th the Privy Council appointed three Commissioners of Censorship: 'to call before them the companies of players and require them to deliver unto them their books, that they may strike out such parts as they shall find unfit, commanding them that they forbear to present any comedy or tragedy other than they have allowed' (p. 307). In his important study of the office of the Master of the Revels, Richard Dutton infers that it was these orders which ended the career of John Lyly. But he also points out that 'to the best of our knowledge, Marlowe never had problems with the Revels Office', and that 'there is no evidence that his career as a dramatist concerned the Council at all' (pp. 87–9). Thus, Dutton rejects the theory of William Empson that *Doctor Faustus* was mangled by censors.[20] Indeed, he contends that 'the most radical and unconventional dramatist of the era' showed such 'scant respect for established orthodoxy', and steered so 'close to the wind' in allowing the blasphemy of Tamburlaine to go 'virtually unpunished', that his writing proves 'that the expression of provocative opinions was never in itself grounds for censorship'. Marlowe's impunity thereby serves Dutton's thesis that the Elizabethan regime was 'more liberal that it is given credit for' (pp. 86–7 and 89). But what this overlooks, of course, is the impact the prohibitions may have had on the internal logic of Marlowe's plays, and the crucial fact that after this crisis, though they may well go 'virtually' unchecked, the ambitions of his heroes are all punished in the end.

If the orders of November 1589 signalled a new repressiveness in relations between authors and authority, Marlowe was in a fine place to register the change, being on bail 'on suspicion of murder'. He had pitched into an affray alongside a (then celebrated) dramatist, Thomas Watson, who had stabbed a publican's son to death. Neither writer was found guilty when the case came up on 3 December; but Marlowe spent two weeks in Newgate gaol, while 'witty Tom Watson' abandoned theatre to concentrate on activities as a secret agent (Nicholl, pp. 209–18). And there is evidence to suggest these warnings may have altered the course of Marlovian drama, as the *Tamburlaine* texts were revised, it seems, between publication of *The Faerie Queene*, which they quote, on 1 December, and their printing in August 1590. According to the printer, Richard Jones, the two plays had been 'fond and frivolous... digressing and far unmeet' for 'matter of worth', though they amused the 'vain conceited fondlings', who 'greatly gaped' when they were 'showed in London upon stages'. With comic scenes, which 'would prove a great disgrace to so honourable and stately a history', omitted, however, Jones hoped these 'tragical discourses' would prove 'acceptable' to 'gentlemen and courteous readers'. So, it seems that *Tamburlaine* was, after all, reshaped to meet the changed environment, and that Marlowe's work was purged of those 'graced deformities' which had 'been lately delightful' in the playhouse, to make 'the worthiness of the matter' appeal to the 'learned censures' of readers of 'excellent degree', who would now need, among 'serious affairs and studies', to extend it their 'favourable protection' (rpt in Steane (ed.), p. 587). It is hard not to see this servile address as directed at the Commissioners of Censorship. If so, this could explain why a drama which 'achieved the revolution of bringing on stage a figure who was not the sport of Fortune, and held the Fates in chains' (Boas, p. 76) ends so precipitately. We may never know how the original *Tamburlaine* was concluded. But in the revised version,

the hero's death, when he is 'distemper'd suddenly' (5.2.216) after he burns
the Koran, gains irony if seen as an internalization of the blasphemy regu-
lations under which his creator operated. Then the tragedy appears that of
the dramatist himself, overruled by powers 'that sway eternal seats' (5.3.17)
for resisting orders to 'beautify the empire' and instituting his own empire
of art:

> For there my palace royal shall be plac'd,
> Whose shining turrets shall dismay the heavens,
> And cast the fame of Ilion's tower to hell.
> Thorough the streets, with troops of conquer'd kings,
> I'll ride in golden armour like the sun;
> And in my helm a triple plume shall spring,
> Spangled with diamonds, dancing in the air,
> To note me emperor of the three-fold world.
>
> (2 *Tamb.* 4.3.111–18)

'Forth, ye vassals! Whatsoe'er it be, / Sickness or death can never conquer me' (5.1.219–20): Tamburlaine goes to his death with captive kings,
the 'pamper'd jades of Asia' (4.3.1), still harnessed to his chariot. This
pageant-waggon, which has the symbolic function of the cage in *Part One*,
is the hero's *pièce-de-resistance*, upstaging all rival attractions, even where
'great Alexander...rode in triumph' (5.2.69). And as an Elizabethan actors' cart, the vehicle is also the self-referential image of Marlowe's own
profession, its haulage by nobles 'harness'd like horses' and 'lash'd with
whips of fire' (3.5.103–5) expressing a fantastic wish-fulfilment of a
Caesarian dream of the domination of discourse. For a brief instant, at the
start of his career, it seems Marlowe could imagine treating patrons like
'dogs', and threatening to 'bridle all [their] tongues, / And bind them close
with bits of burnish'd steel' (4.1.184–5). But Tamburlaine's dying words
are of being 'drawn...piecemeal, like Hippolytus' by his 'proud rebelling
jades', and of 'heaven's coach, the pride of Phaeton', crashed by its steeds
(5.3.239–46). So, Icarian imagery brings the epic to a close with a definitive
curtailment of theatrical freedom by the men of power. And this 'coach-
man' (4.3.4) himself expresses the impasse into which Marlovian drama
was plunging, when he warns his heirs that 'The nature of thy chariot will
not bear / A guide of baser temper than myself' (5.3.243–4). In reality, nothing could be less like the finesse with which later writers such as Shakespeare
managed paying public and patrician patrons than Marlowe's tragic refusal, with his headstrong charioteer, to please both the market and the
court.

The Jew of Malta

If the ending of *Tamburlaine, Part Two* foretells his inability to realize his aim 'to be a king' of his medium, and 'ride in triumph' like Caesar on the London stage regardless of 'the pleasure they enjoy' above (*1 Tamb.* 2.5.50–64), *The Jew of Malta* which follows registers in its focus on a single character the author's persisting commitment to literary sovereignty. For what this text makes yet clearer is that Marlowe's dramaturgy, 'in which the hero becomes the unifying principle...and interest is concentrated exclusively' on an individual,[21] is, in fact, a function of his quest for unfettered speech. The 'will to absolute play' is what Stephen Greenblatt, in a landmark essay on the play, terms 'the unique capacity for aesthetic experience' of its protagonist, Barabas; noting how much his delight in duplicity, which climaxes in his construction of a 'dainty gallery' to propel his patrons 'Into a deep pit' (5.5.35–8), is that of the playwright himself:

> As Barabas, hammer in hand, constructs the machinery for this climactic false-hood, it is difficult not to equate him with the playwright himself, constructing the plot, and Marlowe appears consciously to encourage this perception: 'Leave nothing loose, all levell'd to my mind', Barabas instructs the carpenters, 'Why now I see that you have art indeed' (5.5.5–6). Deception takes on something of the status of literary art.[22]

'Now tell me wordlings underneath the sun / If greater falsehood ever has been done?' (52–3): the contraption Barabas erects, with its gallery and pit, serves the same purpose as the cage and carriage built by Tamburlaine to secure control of his controllers, and seems, as the aside implies, a working model for Marlowe's stage. Greenblatt interprets this 'will to play' as cued by 'hostility to transcendence'. Yet what specifically motivates Barabas is hostility to interference in a 'kingly kind of trade (5.5.50) which encloses 'Infinite riches in a little room' (1.1.37): like the stage itself. In *Tamburlaine* this enterprise had been terminated from above. But in *The Jew of Malta* Marlowe complicates the scenario by introducing a challenge from below, in the slave Ithamore, who stands in the same relation to Barabas's fictions as a player to a plot. The parallel becomes explicit when Ithamore informs on his master to the prostitute Bellamira while travestying Marlowe's most quoted lyric, 'Come live with me, and be my love' (4.2.116), and we see how this is a drama about authors' rights and ownership of texts. Thus, the first three acts comprise a play-within-a-play – a parody of recent 'revenge' hits such as Thomas Kyd's *The Spanish Tragedy* – in which Barabas exacts poetic justice on those who taxed his fortune by contriving a duel so craftily Ithamore exclaims: 'was there ever seen such villainy, / So neatly plotted, and so well performed? . . . / Why, the devil invented a challenge, / My master writ it, I carried it . . . / . . . they met, and, as the story says, / In doleful wise they ended both their days' (3.3.1–24). Puritans excoriated the playhouse as 'the devil's pulpit'; and with Satan as promoter, Barabas the playwright, Ithamore a player, and the duellists Mathias and Lodowick clueless patrons, this does, in fact, describe not only the conspiratorial status of the Elizabethan play-text, but its subversive relation to spectators. Yet if Ithamore, as performer, has everything to gain from a share in such collaboration, it is possible to detect in Barabas the anxious beginning of the idea of the sovereign author as origin and owner of his meaning. For in this play, where, as the slave says, 'The meaning has a meaning' (4.4.106), what counts is literally possession of the story, which Ithamore steals, despite vowing secrecy to Barabas, to set himself up in a blackmailing parody of the professional writer:

> ITHAMORE: Give me a ream of paper: we'll have a kingdom of gold for't.
> PILIA-BORZA: Write for five hundred crowns.
> ITHAMORE (*writing*): *Sirrah Jew, as you love your life, send me five hundred crowns, and give the bearer a hundred.* – Tell him I must have it.
> PILIA-BORZA: I warrant your lordship shall have't.
> ITHAMORE: And, if he ask why I demand so much, tell him I scorn to write a line under a hundred crowns.
> PILIA-BORZA: You'd make a rich poet, sir.
>
> (*JM* 4.2.136–44)

In *The Jew of Malta* the playwright-as-hero wages war on two fronts, against both the patrons who purloin his profit and the performers who sell his plots. None of Marlowe's play-books were, in fact, published under his name in his lifetime, which reflects their status as the intellectual property of acting companies. But for the second half of this one the protagonist is entirely driven by the struggle to copyright his fictions, like the plan to hang the friar to whom his daughter Abigail leaks his secrets, which he claims is entirely his own, and 'such a plot . . . As never Jew nor Christian knew the like' (4.1.120). This mania to patent originality betrays the anxiety of influence of a charlatan who is, he admits, actually indebted for his schemes to 'old women's words . . . winter's tales' (2.1.25), or tricks 'I learned in Florence' (2.3.23). Thus, the Jew's commercial empire, with his agents 'Obed in Bairseth, Nones in Portugal' (1.1.127–9), and debts 'In Florence, Venice, Antwerp . . . and where not' (4.1.74–5), parallels his story-telling, which is strung out on similarly elastic lines of verbal credit. To monopolize meaning like this, Barabas smiles, 'It is not necessary I be seen' (1.2.313–19); and the dream of such god-like ubiquity and invisibility would indeed shape the institution of authorship for which Marlowe would be a model. But *The Jew of Malta*, which dates from about 1590, was staged not by the Admiral's, but Strange's Men, we know from Henslowe's log; and what it reveals is a script-writer's insecurity in the collective mêlée of Elizabethan theatre, with its mercenary entrepreneurs, fractious companies, pirated quartos, and fickle fashions. Nothing of the good companionship of Tamburlaine's troupe survives, in any case, in this play, where Marlowe may be flaunting his animus towards collaborators when he has the Jew murder all those who, he fears, 'know enough to have my life' (4.1.123). That Barabas poisons the convent where Abigail becomes a nun with porridge he donates for its feast-day (the Theatre was built over such a nunnery), and stifles Ithamore and cronies with an arsenic posy he wafts as part of his act as a French musician, shows how Marlowe relished attacks on playing as a contamination. But no sooner has the mountebank regained control of the *commedia dell'arte* by these means than he makes his fatal mistake, by selling his latest stratagem to the authorities in return, he imagines, for 'our safety' (5.2.23). The end, when Barabas is dropped by the knights into his own trap, has obvious anti-semitic connotations. But it is also this dramatist's most graphic demonstration of the treacherous dependency of patronage relations:

> villains, know you cannot help me now.
> Then, Barabas, breathe forth thy latest fate,
> And in the fury of thy torments strive
> To end thy life with resolution.
> Know, Governor, 'twas I that slew your son,
> I fram'd the challenge that did make them meet.
> Know, Calymath, I aim'd thy overthrow:
> And, had I but escap'd this stratagem,
> I would have brought confusion on you all,
> Damn'd Christians, dogs, and Turkish infidels!
> (*JM* 5.5.82–91)

In the most influential social interpretation of tragedy, the Marxist Lucien Goldmann proposed that the 'tragic vision' of the dramatist Racine reflected the frustration of the official class, the 'nobility of the robe', under the seventeenth-century French monarchy; and it might be tempting to apply a similar analysis to Marlowe in the light of what historians describe as a 'crisis of patronage' in the 1590s, when 'a social contract that had worked well was breaking down', and 'few writers were attaining the rewards they thought they deserved... whether in monetary gifts or political protection'.[23] Thus, we could see Barabas's liquidation in his vat of boiling oil as a metaphor for the disaster experienced, when power disrobed them, by authors such as Lyly, who in 1590 petitioned the queen that thirteen years as her servant, 'a thousand hopes, and a hundred promises... amounteth to just nothing' (Fox, p. 239). The Jew's terror is certainly of being similarly reduced to 'a senseless lump of clay, / That will with every water wash to dirt' (1.2.221–2). But he also warns onlookers not to 'Think me so mad as I will hang myself' – like Judas – 'That I may vanish o'er the earth in air, / And leave no memory that e'er I was' (269–71); and to decode Marlovian tragedy as simply a reflection of external pressure on the author would be to ignore precisely this insistence on the *relative autonomy* of the literary field, and thus the ways in which Marlowe's position-taking ensured the literary specificity of the plays themselves. Until he offers his masterpiece to his Maltese patrons, Barabas is exemplary for the skill with which he plays off factions, performers, and the marketplace he rules. Likewise, biographers relate that when Lord Strange dropped Marlowe for treachery, about 1591, he shifted base again, and 'looked out for another theatrical patron in the Earl of Pembroke' (Boas, p. 173). The brief history of Pembroke's Men was as flag-bearers for the artistic salon run at Wilton near Salisbury by Mary Herbert, Countess of Pembroke and sister of Sir Philip Sidney.[24] So, it cannot be chance that the one work Marlowe wrote for Pembroke's Men, during a period of plague, highlights a showman given remit to stage theatricals in equally escapist conditions, by a patron similarly at odds with the ruling group.

Edward II

Edward II is Marlowe's most finished work, the likely product of study in some aristocratic retreat, and it opens with Piers Gaveston pronouncing a manifesto which sounds like the author reviewing the advantages of patronage over the demands of the groundlings in the pit:

> These are not men for me.
> I must have wanton poets, pleasant wits,
> Musicians, that with touching of a string
> May draw the pliant king which way I please:
> Music and poetry is his delight;
> Therefore I'll have Italian masques by night,
> Sweet speeches, comedies, and pleasing shows.
> (*EII* 1.1.50–6)

Historians are fascinated by *Edward II* as the first English play to confront a new European phenomenon: the rise of the royal favourite at the expense of commons and lords.[25] Intriguingly, a series of such texts issued from the

Pembroke circle.[26] But what clearly excited Marlowe was the opportunity that favouritism gave dramatists to short-circuit both public and politicians; as Gaveston jeers, when he arrives in London to direct private amusements for his lover Edward: 'Farewell base stooping to the lordly peers! . . . / As for the multitude . . . / I'll fawn first on the wind' (18–22). So, the favourite spurns three citizens who typify those playgoers who had just cheered *Tamburlaine* – a groom, a tourist, and a soldier – to make way for a closet staging of a pornographic pageant on the lines of *Dido*, with pages cross-dressed and a naked boy 'in Dian's shape' torturing 'One like Actaeon' to death (58–70). This extravaganza is, in fact, so like the boys' plays banned for scandalizing queen and court, that it becomes clear that the homosexual relations between Edward and his favourites stand as a marker of artistic licence, as much as political factionalism. One reason why the City elders abominated players was, in fact, suspicion that in 'secret conclaves they play the Sodomites or worse'.[27] So, Gaveston's theatricals, in which he mimes 'the Greekish strumpet' Helen (2.5.16), or 'Caesar riding in the Roman street / With captive kings at his triumphal car' (1.1.173–4), can be seen to reflect on Marlowe's chance to revel 'With base outlandish cullions at his heels' in the 'proud fantastic liveries' of Pembroke's faction (1.4.410–12). This reading gains credibility from the fact that Edward's hope of retiring to 'some nook or corner . . . / To frolic with my dearest Gaveston' (72–3), depends on the Pembroke of the play, who is in charge of 'solemn triumphs and public shows' (352) when the king celebrates Gaveston's reprieve from exile with 'a general tilt and tournament' (378), and who offers the fugitive refuge at his 'out of the way' house (2.5.107).

It is likely that *Edward II* was, indeed, presented at Wilton (where Shakespeare was put on for James I) during a ruinous tour by Pembroke's company in 1593. But despite flattering nods to Wiltshire (1.1.127; 3.1.50) and its 'pretty' countess (2.5.109), Marlowe's scepticism about the Earl's capacity to keep such a 'Proteus', or 'god of shapes', in the 'Italian cloak' of a 'dapper Jack' (1.4.413), can be guessed from the fact that the plot turns on Gaveston's ambush, after Pembroke rides 'home, thinking his prisoner safe' (3.2.120). No wonder that Bertolt Brecht was inspired by this drama, since what it represents is its own means and limits of production, and the attack, like that of Edward's nemesis, Mortimer, on the 'idle triumphs, masques, and lascivious shows' (2.2.157) of its own protected stage:

> When wert thou in the field with banner spread?
> But once, and then thy soldiers march'd like players,
> With garish robes, not armour; and thyself,

Bedaub'd with gold, rode laughing at the rest,
Nodding and shaking of thy spangled crest,
Where women's favours hung like labels down.

(*EII* 2.2.182–7)

'Libels are cast again' thee in the street; / Ballads and rhymes made of thy overthrow' (177–8): in *Edward II* the hatred of the king over 'His sports, his pleasures, and his company' (3.3.178) shadows that targeted on Marlowe at the time of the play, and is imaged expressly as a revenge of popular culture on the elite of 'our famous nurseries of arts', the universities (4.6.18). Thus, the lords parade 'against the stately triumph' led by Pembroke with 'homely' shields to 'display rancorous minds' (2.2.12–33); justify rebellion as a traditional game of "prisoner's base" (4.3.69); and exhort 'the murmuring commons' (2.2.160) to 'cast up caps, and clap their hands for joy' (4.3.58). Gaveston had thought his painted 'frolics' superior to shepherds' pastorals (2.2.61–2); so there is cultural irony in Edward's capture by 'A gloomy fellow in a mead': a folkloric Mower who arms a posse 'with Welsh hooks' (4.6.29–45). And if the king's 'frolic with his minion' (1.4.67), got up as Phaeton (16), Midas (210), or the Jove and Ganymede of *Dido* (181), foretells later court masques, which similarly staged allegories such as the trail of 'bright Phoebus through the sky, / And dusky Night in rusty iron car', the 'rout' that trumpets its contempt (4.3.45–7) presages the coming revolution as a culture war, fought when 'commons and the nobles join' (1.4.289) to defend 'the realm and parliament' (4.6.45) against such alien shows.[28] Wilton may have been, as described, a magnet 'To draw a prince' (2.5.113); but Marlowe grasped his situation enough to sense that the 'grey area' of the liveried troupe, operating as 'household servants in a great country house', was doomed (Gurr, pp. 56–7). Sure enough, by 1593 Pembroke's Men 'were fain to pawn their apparel' with which they had toured *Edward II*; and historians infer they were crushed between plague orders and the cost of their repertoire (Gurr, pp. 60–1; Boas, p. 173). In the play, Edward's separation from his new favourite, Spenser, and the scholar Baldock is presented, in any case, as the disbandment of just such a 'company', when the king discards his 'feigned weeds' (4.6.65–99) and resigns his 'transitory pomp' (5.1.108). Since he was only ever a player–king, his washing 'with puddle-water' (5.3.30) at Kenilworth, once the scene of a spectacular water-pageant staged by Elizabeth's lover Leicester, is an apt figure for Marlowe's assessment of the prospects for artistic freedom under aristocratic guard. The 'curate-like' yet 'inwardly licentious' Baldock may be the writer's self-image. If so, the advice Spenser gives him seems a cool analysis of his alternatives as artist or assassin, and the perfect synopsis of Marlovian tragedy as the castration of poetry by power:

> Baldock, you must cast the scholar off,
> And learn to court it like a gentleman.
> 'Tis not a black cloak and a little band,
> A velvet-cap'd cloak, fac'd before with serge,
> And smelling to a nosegay all the day,
> Or holding of a napkin in your hand,
> Or saying a long grace at a table's end,
> Or making low legs to a nobleman,
> Or looking downward, with your eyelids close,
> And saying, 'Truly, an't may please your honour,'
> Can get you any favour with great men.
> You must be proud, bold, pleasant, resolute,
> And now and then stab, as occasion serves.
>
> (*EII* 2.1.30–50)

In *Edward II*, Baldock had read to his patroness 'since she was a child' (29), and if this is also a glance at the publisher of *The Countess of Pembroke's Arcadia* the play can be seen as a riposte to the salon set idealized in Sidney's book, as the king's gruesome murder, which literalizes Gaveston's masque, immerses coterie theatre in the 'mire and puddle' of the 'poor men' abused at the start (5.5.61). Marlowe's negation of patronage seems total when Edward bargains for his life with a last jewel; yet there is suicidal symmetry in the characterization of Lightborn, his killer, as another actor, who performs the atrocity with the artistry of Gaveston ensuring Acteon will 'seem to die' (1.1.70), before he is stabbed himself. For what this author apparently found in the legend of the voyeur ripped apart for spying on a virgin queen was a paradigm of the peril of representing power under Elizabeth, and a frame for his own point of view, torn between demands of public and patron, audience and authority, or commerce and the court.

Doctor Faustus

Yet if *Edward II* registers the impossibility of escape from this fix, in his next work, *Doctor Faustus*, the same myth points up the temptation to pitch power against the playhouse, when the hero presents his *coup de théâtre*, Tamburlaine's masque of emperors, for Charles V, and a gate-crasher, Benvolio, is punished by being struck with Acteon's horns (4.2). This Peeping Tom had simply been enjoying the same vicarious thrill as London playgoers who previewed performances meant for the palace; but the moment of *Faustus*, Nicholl finds, was when Marlowe accepted the niche of 'poet as tutor, secretary and entertainment manager of the powerful' (p. 227) and so this is a play about a scholar seduced by magic patronage, who pays the price of devoting his art to the great. Again, then, nothing could be less like the tact with which Shakespeare, in his play about magical dealings with the mighty, balanced the logic of service with pleas to citizens to 'be friends' (*A Midsummer Night's Dream* Epilogue 15) than Marlowe's inability to off-set power with profit from those knights, students, jockeys, vintners, and ostlers who filled the playhouse, but are here the butt of his hero's tricks. So, the context of Faustus may well have been the time when the drama-tist 'surrender(ed) up his soul', as his character does to 'the arch-regent and commander of all spirits' (1.3.54, 90), to as omnipotent a master as Lucifer, Burleigh, through the guile of as persuasive a recruiter as Mephistopheles: the statesman's son, Robert Cecil. We know that in January 1592 Marlowe was charged with counterfeiting, a crime carrying the death-sentence, but that after an interview with Burleigh he was freed (Nicholl, pp. 283–5). Whether this was when he became a double-agent, betraying his mentors, it must be significant that the next thing this reprieved man seems to have written was Faustus's Devil's Pact:

MEPHISTOPHELES: O what I would not do to obtain his soul!
FAUSTUS: *Consummatum est*: this bill is ended,
And Faustus hath bequeathed his soul to Lucifer.
But what is this inscription on mine arm?
Homo fuge! Whither should I fly?
If unto heaven, he'll throw me down to hell.
My senses are deceived: here's nothing writ!
O, yes, I see it plain. Even here is writ
Homo fuge. Yet shall not Faustus fly.
MEPHISTOPHELES: I'll fetch him somewhat to delight his mind.
(*Enter Devils, giving crowns and rich apparel to Faustus*)
(*DF* 1.5.72–81)

The writing inscribed on his body the instant Faustus signs his satanic con-tract seems an uncanny figure for Marlowe's own relation with authority, and his capacity to write against himself, even as he succumbs to the power that consecrates his art with its commissions and its cloak. Strung between heaven and hell, from where Good and Bad angels come to wrestle for his soul, Faustus's plight describes the author's, that is to say, as he switches one patron for the next. Biographers connect *Faustus* to Marlowe's pene-tration, on Burleigh's orders, of the Catholic cabal of the 'Wizard Earl' of Northumberland;[29] which, if true, means that by 1592 he had produced five plays wearing as many different coats. No wonder that this play presents cosmic history as a ruptured patronage relationship, in which even Mephistopheles, 'servant to great Lucifer', grieves for 'joys of heaven' lost by joining the 'Unhappy spirits' who defected from God imagining 'There is no chief but only Beelzebub' (1.3.40–84). That Lucifer was 'an angel once' and 'dearly loved of God' (64–5) underpins Marlowe's idea of the universality of patronage, with 'every sphere a dominion' (2.1.56). But Faustus's aim to attain 'the signory of Emden' (1.5.24); 'serve the German Emperor' (4.2.16); or 'banquet and carouse' the lecturers at Wittenberg (5.1.6), maps a trajectory for Marlowe's plot which explains why this 'wonder of the world for magic art' (4.1.11) is fixated not on the 'voluptuousness' for which he sells his soul (1.3.92–6), but on staging illusions, like 'that enchanted castle in the air' he conjures for the Duke of Vanholt (4.7.3), or upstaging those of rivals, like the Pope's 'solemn festival' he ruins with 'mirth' and fireworks (3.3.32). For when he begs his diabolical patrons to 'let me an actor be' (3.2.76), and is then 'feasted' among 'the noblemen' at 'royal courts of kings' (3.3.110–23), Faustus projects the only miracle available to Marlowe's associates, which took them, moreover, to identical locales. And this was the irresistible prospect tempting London actors, according to Jerzy Limon, at the time of *Faustus*, with the invitation to exchange the plague-stricken playhouse for contracts to entertain continental royalty.[30] Thus, leaders of the Admiral's Men were issued passports to tour Europe on 10 February 1592. For the dramatist, such a journey to 'the states of Germany' (3.2.123) would have been cover for espionage. So, while his hero's performance of 'rare exploits' at the Hapsburg court (4.1.32–3) was not to be realized by the 'English comedians' until 1607, the fact that their programme for the Emperor then featured *Faustus* confirms how Marlowe inscribed in his tragedy of the Devil's Pact the magical solution power offered his profession, and the artistic opportunities – like the masque of Helen 'performed in twinkling of an eye' as Faustus's masterpiece (5.1.96) – of which his players dreamed (Limon, pp. 117–19).

The messenger of death

'Thus from infernal Dis do we ascend / To view the subjects of our monarchy' (5.2.1): as Lucifer rises to claim Faustus, after twenty-four years entertaining the courts of Europe, he does so not as a medieval gargoyle, but the face of the absolutist state, with its art by contracts and commissions.[31] So, when Shakespeare rewrote *Faustus* in *The Tempest* he made his playwright a prince, and with Prospero envisaged art created by royal fiat.[32] But in 1592 Marlowe could imagine only the disaster when the author is ripped apart by patrons, as God 'bends his ireful brows' (5.2.162) on Faustus, and Lucifer drags him to his 'perpetual torture house' (127), before his colleagues assemble his 'mangled' remains (5.3.17). His *Faustus* was probably never acted by the Admiral's Men in Europe, for it is an irony of this story of a poet torn like Orpheus that the text was cut and pasted by actors, who made it their success after its author's death. The shattered trunk of the work thereby testifies to the contradictions between patrons, players, and public which were its subject and conditions. And though Marlowe signed the last leaf with a claim to autonomy – in a postscript that 'The hour ends the day, the author ends his work' – time was with his pursuers when it 'cut the branch' of his life. 'Dead shepherd', Shakespeare saluted, 'now I find thy saw of might: "Who ever loved that loved not at first sight?"' (*As You Like It* 3.5.82); yet the quotation from *Hero and Leander* affirms the debt of a survivor, who made his own patron a lover, and never forgot his first love was his art. In the game of service Shakespeare learned from his predecessor's failure how to please performer, pit, and prince. But Marlowe, who played this game to lose, created tragedy from his disaster, and in his last unfinished text, *The Massacre at Paris*, even made players into the Catholic enemy, when he had his Duke of Guise plot the Bartholomew's Day atrocity as a masque, in which the 'actors in this massacre' wear the livery of a theatre troupe (1.4.29). Thus, Marlovian tragedy posed the problem of artistic freedom by testing it to destruction. To portray the dramatist, in Guise, as a 'messenger of death' (3.1.3), the English spy was truly describing 'the labour he had to do to produce himself', in Bourdieu's terms, 'as the subject of his own creation' (*Rules of Art*, p. 104). For Marlowe may have been one of those lured by this Duke 'to the seminary at Rheims / To hatch treason 'gainst their Queen' (5.2.110). But Shakespeare seems to have acknowledged that his own sovereignty would never have been won without the tragedy Marlowe inscribed in characters like Guise, who goes to his death costumed as an emperor, determined that though the public may protest, players defect, and power end his play, 'Yet Caesar shall go forth' (5.2.71). So, the great survivor was pleased to repeat this line as the acme of fearless speech,[33] awed by the example of a writer who had shown in his career how 'Caesar did go forth, and thus he died' (94).

NOTES

1. In this chapter all quotations of Marlowe are from *Christopher Marlowe: The Complete Plays*, J. B. Steane (ed.) (Harmondsworth: Penguin, 1969).
2. Charles Nicholl, '"At Middleborough": Some Reflections on Marlowe's Visit to the Low Countries in 1592', in Darryll Grantley and Peter Roberts (eds.), *Christopher Marlowe and English Renaissance Culture* (Aldershot: Scolar Press,

1996), pp. 38–50, esp. p. 40. For 'Marlin the English Envoy', see Philip Henderson, 'Marlowe as a Messenger', *TLS* 12 June 1953, p. 381.

3. Thomas Kyd, qtd in Charles Nicholl, *The Reckoning: The Murder of Christopher Marlowe* (rev. edn, London: Vintage, 2002), pp. 268–9.

4. Michel Foucault, *Fearless Speech*, Joseph Pearson (ed.) (Los Angeles: Semiotext(e), 2001).

5. All quotations of Shakespeare are from *The Norton Shakespeare: Based on the Oxford Edition*, Stephen Greenblatt, Walter Cohen, Jean Howard, and Katharine Eisaman Maus (eds.) (New York: Norton, 1997).

6. Pierre Bourdieu, 'Intellectual Field and Creative Project', Sean France (trans.), in Michael Young (ed.), *Knowledge and Control: New Directions in the Sociology of Education* (London: Collier–Macmillan, 1971), p. 163; *The Rules of Art: Genesis and Structure of the Literary Field*, Susan Emmanuel (trans.) (Stanford University Press, 1996), p. 81.

7. Title page of the 1594 quarto rpt in Frederick Boas, *Christopher Marlowe: A Biographical and Critical Study* (Oxford: Clarendon Press, 1940), p. 49.

8. Michael Hattaway, 'Christopher Marlowe: Ideology and Subversion', in Grantley and Roberts (eds.), *Christopher Marlowe and English Renaissance Culture*, p. 210.

9. Pierre Bourdieu, *The Field of Cultural Production: Essays on Art and Literature*, Randal Johnson (ed.) (Cambridge: Polity Press, 1993), p. 195. Bourdieu is here criticizing the reductive miserabilism of Raymond Williams, 'who, in analysing the English Romantics, simply forgot that this process had liberating effects as well'.

10. Richard Dutton, *Mastering the Revels: The Regulation and Censorship of English Renaissance Drama* (Basingstoke: Macmillan, 1991), pp. 31–2.

11. Peter Thomson, *Shakespeare's Professional Career* (Cambridge University Press, 1992), p. 54.

12. Marjorie Garber, '"Infinite Riches in a Little Room": Closure and Enclosure in Marlowe', in Alvin Kernan (ed.), *Two Renaissance Myth-Makers: Christopher Marlowe and Ben Jonson: Selected Papers of the English Institute, 1975–76* (Baltimore: Johns Hopkins University Press, 1977), pp. 11–13.

13. Christian Jouhard, 'Power and Literature: the Terms of the Exchange, 1624–42', in Richard Burt (ed.), *The Administration of Aesthetics* (Minneapolis: University of Minnesota Press, 1994), pp. 35 and 73.

14. Marjorie Garber, '"Here's Nothing Writ": Scribe, Script, and Circumscription in Marlowe's Plays', in Richard Wilson (ed.), *Christopher Marlowe: A Critical Reader* (Harlow: Longman, 1999), p. 51.

15. Robert Weimann, *Shakespeare and the Popular Tradition in the Theater: Studies in the Social Dimension of Dramatic Form and Function* (Baltimore: Johns Hopkins University Press, 1978), p. 182.

16. Alfred Harbarge, *Shakespeare and the Rival Traditions* (Bloomington: Indiana University Press, 1952), p. 45.

17. G. B. Harrison, *Shakespeare's Fellows* (London: Bodley Head, 1923), p. 43.

18. Andrew Gurr, *The Shakespearean Playing Companies* (Cambridge University Press, 1996), p. 57.

19. Qtd in E. K. Chambers, *The Elizabethan Stage*, 4 vols. (Oxford University Press, 1923), 4: 305–6.

20. William Empson, *Faustus and the Censor: The English Faust-book and Marlowe's "Doctor Faustus"*, John Jones (ed.) (Oxford: Basil Blackwell, 1987).

21. Fredson Bowers, *Elizabethan Revenge Tragedy, 1587–1642* (Princeton University Press, 1966), pp. 105–9.

22. Stephen Greenblatt, 'Marlowe, Marx, and Anti-Semitism', in Wilson (ed.), *Christopher Marlowe*, pp. 152–3.

23. Lucien Goldmann, *The Hidden God: A Study of the Tragic Vision in the 'Pensées' of Pascal and the Tragedies of Racine*, Philip Thody (trans.) (London: Routledge and Kegan Paul, 1964); Alistair Fox, 'The Complaint of Poetry for the Death of Liberality: the Decline of Literary Patronage in the 1590s', in John Guy (ed.), *The Reign of Elizabeth I: Court and Culture in the Last Decade* (Cambridge University Press, 1995), pp. 229–57, esp. pp. 229–30 and 241.

24. For a summary of recent debate about Mary Herbert's influence in the formation of the company which took her husband's name, see Gurr, *Shakespearean Playing Companies*, p. 74; and for the patronage of her son, 'the great Maecenas' William Herbert, see Gary Schmidgall, *Shakespeare and the Poet's Life* (Lexington: University Press of Kentucky, 1990), pp. 72–4. While working under Pembroke Marlowe seems also to have edited the work of his friend Thomas Watson for posthumous publication.

25. See Blair Worden, 'Favourites on the English Stage', in J. H. Elliott and L. W. B. Brockliss (eds.), *The World of the Favourite* (New Haven: Yale University Press, 1999), pp. 167–9.

26. These included Samuel Daniel's *The Tragedy of Philotas* and Ben Jonson's *Sejanus His Fall* (both published in 1605). Jonson also began, but did not complete, a play about Edward II's nemesis entitled *Mortimer His Fall*.

27. Philip Stubbes, qtd in Jonathan Goldberg, 'Play the Sodomites or Worse: *Dido, Queen of Carthage*', in Wilson (ed.), *Christopher Marlowe*, pp. 84–94.

28. For an account of the English Civil War as a contest between the competing cultures Marlowe dramatizes, fought over entertainments and games, see David Underdown, *Revel, Riot and Rebellion: Popular Politics and Culture in England, 1603–1660* (Oxford University Press, 1985).

29. Nicholl, *The Reckoning*, pp. 248–56; and William Urry, *Christopher Marlowe and Canterbury* (London: Faber and Faber, 1988), pp. 70–3.

30. Jerzy Limon, *Gentlemen of a Company: English Players in Central and Eastern Europe, 1590–1660* (Cambridge University Press, 1985), pp. 4–6.

31. See Peter Burke, *The Fabrication of Louis XIV* (New Haven: Yale University Press, 1992), p. 58.

32. See Stephen Orgel, *The Illusion of Power: Political Theater in the English Renaissance* (Berkeley: University of California Press, 1975), p. 45.

33. The line is quoted exactly in *Julius Caesar* 2.2.28.

READING LIST

Archer, John. *Sovereignty and Intelligence: Spying and Court Culture in the English Renaissance*. Stanford University Press, 1993.

Bourdieu, Pierre. *The Rules of Art: Genesis and Structure of the Literary Field*. Susan Emmanuel (trans.). Standford University Press, 1996.

Downie, Alan (ed.). *Christopher Marlowe: Critical Readings*. Cambridge University Press, 1999.

Foucault, Michel. *Fearless Speech*. Joseph Pearson (ed.). Los Angeles: Semiotext(e), 2001.

Grantley, Darryll and Peter Roberts (eds.). *Christopher Marlowe and English Renaissance Culture*. Aldershot: Scolar Press, 1996.

Greenblatt, Stephen. *Renaissance Self-Fashioning: From More to Shakespeare*. University of Chicago Press, 1980.

Gurr, Andrew. *The Shakespearean Playing Companies*. Cambridge University Press, 1996.

Nicholl, Charles. *The Reckoning: The Murder of Christopher Marlowe*. Rev. edn London: Vintage, 2002.

Shepherd, Simon. *Marlowe and the Politics of Elizabethan Theatre*. Brighton: Harvester Press, 1986.

Wilson, Richard (ed.). *Christopher Marlowe: A Critical Reader*. Harlow: Longman, 1999.

14

GARRETT A. SULLIVAN, JR

Geography and identity in Marlowe

Foreign settings in early modern English drama are often assumed to be as vague and imprecise as Shakespeare's famously non-existent Bohemian shore in *The Winter's Tale*. Designed to generate a nebulous sense of Otherness, foreign landscapes are sometimes little more than evocatively alien. Standing as an obvious exception to this view are the plays of Christopher Marlowe, in which dramatic location is carefully chosen: Tamburlaine's imperial conquests carry him from East to West, ever closer to an English audience both fascinated and terrified by his legacy;[1] Barabas lives at the centre of Mediterranean trade and a flashpoint of Euro-Ottoman relations; and Faustus exists on the fault line of Protestant and Catholic conflict.

The care with which Marlowe chooses his settings speaks to his sustained interest in the profound cartographic and geographic innovations of the late sixteenth century. This interest has intrigued critics since at least the 1920s, when Ethel Seaton first pointed out that the itineraries of Tamburlaine's many (achieved and projected) conquests are based upon Abraham Ortelius's influential atlas, *Teatrum Orbis Terrarum* (1570).[2] Relatedly, it is a commonplace of Marlovian criticism to read his protagonists in geographic terms, as transgressors of both moral and physical boundaries. And yet, what scholars have not attended to is the extent to which the precise relationship between geography and identity differs across Marlowe's plays. To see this, we must first take up what are commonly termed the 'new' and 'old' geographies, then consider their importance for three of Marlowe's works, *Tamburlaine the Great*, *The Jew of Malta*, and *Doctor Faustus*. Along the way, we will focus not only on *world* geographies but also on local, *affective* ones, as represented by Faustus's household or Barabas's counting house. By considering geographies both old and new, and both global and affective, we will isolate the importance of the relationship between geography and identity to the representation of Marlowe's central characters.

The late sixteenth and early seventeenth centuries are routinely represented as an epochal moment in the histories of geography and cartography – that of the emergence of the 'new geography'. This moment is understood as marking the turning point from an imprecise and religious or mythopoetic geography to an accurate and scientific one – from, for example, the medieval map centred on the sacred site of Jerusalem to the famous cartographic projection associated with the atlas-maker Gerard Mercator, which allows for the representation of space as homogeneous and uniformly divisible. Characterized by the proliferation of increasingly precise representations of the world (with Ortelius's atlas being a prime example), the new geography was made possible by a number of historical phenomena, such as improved mapping technologies; the growing desire and need for accurate geographic information; and the ever-widening distribution of printed geographic materials, including maps and atlases. It is of the new geography that Marlowe's plays appear to be such a conspicuous product. Like *Tamburlaine*, *The Jew of Malta* reveals geographic precision and specificity; as one critic points out, 'If you look at a map of the Mediterranean you will see how accurate this "placing" of Barabas's wealth-generating is.'[3] *Doctor Faustus* also speaks to Marlowe's interest in new geographic matters, as the titular (anti-)hero sets out 'to prove cosmography' ('A' text 3 chorus 7).[4]

And yet, what has been largely neglected is the presence in Marlowe of important elements of the 'old geography'. Indeed, in his tragedies, and especially in *Tamburlaine*, Marlowe stages the collision between geographies new and old.[5] The conceptual underpinnings of the 'old geography', dubbed by one cartographic historian as 'the topography of myth and dogma',[6] have been compellingly analysed by John Gillies. Gillies draws upon Giambattista Vico's conception of an ancient 'poetic geography'. This conception is predicated on the Greek notion of the '*oikumene* – a word which suggestively combines the senses of "world" and "house"'. From the perspective of the *oikumene*, geographical knowledge was framed by a strong sense of the difference between 'us' and 'them', and between 'in here' and 'out there'. As Gillies puts it, 'In the beginning, then, the Greek image of the "world" was literally bound by their geographic "home". Then, as further geographic knowledge became available, the symbolic architecture of the *oikumene* was simply exported or extrapolated to accommodate it.'[7] Indeed, the conceptual flexibility of this 'symbolic architecture' ensured the *oikumene*'s potency (if not complete hegemony) well into the Renaissance.

As Gillies's example suggests, the classical *oikumene* has as its centre the Mediterranean world. The spatial logic of the *oikumene* is such that it produces a relationship of 'utter divorce and difference' between lands inside this frame and those outside it. Thus passage beyond the bounds of the *oikumene* is symbolically and morally fraught. The lands beyond the *oikumene* are understood as both sources of wonder – home to 'the monstrous . . . and the marvelous' – and sites of possible contamination (*Shakespeare and the Geography of Difference*, p. 8). For this reason, voyaging well beyond the bounds of the *oikumene* is linked with the various forms of transgression associated with encounters with the purely Other. 'Sailing the ocean "to the bounds of things, the remotest shores of the world" . . . presents both a physical and an ontological danger, to, respectively, the voyager and the ordered world which he leaves behind' (pp. 21–2).[8] This old or poetic geography, then, is both grounded in and is the ground for a conception of identity predicated upon the distinction between those inside the frame and those beyond it.

One might imagine that the emergence of the new geography would mark the end of this old, poetic geography and the *oikumene* that underpinned it. However, this shift was not immediately or totally achieved, and its radical nature can be overstated; aspects of the old geography remained vital in the new (Gillies, *Shakespeare and the Geography of Difference*, pp. 156–88). Thus, the late sixteenth century is best understood as a moment at which both old and new geographies are operational. The notion of the *oikumene* continued to have a great deal of cultural power, even though it was sometimes wrested from its original Mediterranean context. What is distinctive about Marlowe is the way in which he deploys the logic of the old geography while also developing the implications of the new; the affective geographies discussed below, for example, all adopt or modify aspects of the poetic geography associated with the *oikumene*. Marlowe's plays can productively be understood as experiments in which the meanings and significances of old and new geographies are, largely through their juxtaposition, developed, explored, and exploded.

Tamburlaine the Great

In his seminal chapter on Marlowe in *Renaissance Self-Fashioning*, Stephen Greenblatt discusses aspects of the new geography in ways that have been influential for understanding the Marlovian conception of identity. Greenblatt argues that

> In *Tamburlaine* Marlowe contrives to efface all [regional] differences, as if to insist upon the essential meaninglessness of theatrical space, the vacancy that is the dark side of its power to imitate any place. This vacancy – quite literally, the absence of scenery – is the equivalent in the medium of the theater to the secularization of space, the abolition of qualitative up and down . . . the equivalent then to the reduction of the universe to the coordinates of a map.[9]

Greenblatt asserts that in this play 'Space is transformed into an abstraction, then fed to the appetitive machine [i.e., Tamburlaine]. This is the voice of conquest, but it is also the voice of wants never finished and of transcendental homelessness' (p. 196). What is true for Tamburlaine, Greenblatt argues, is true for all of Marlowe's protagonists; the Marlovian hero in general is an 'appetitive machine', and 'transcendental homelessness' both is his native condition and finds its perfect expression in 'the reduction of the universe' that Greenblatt associates with the new geography.

What is missing from this account, however, is the recognition that Marlowe stages alternatives to this 'reduction' – as in the case of Damascus in *Tamburlaine, Part One*, a space that is represented as densely social and, thanks to both Zenocrate's lament and the pleading of the city's virgins, is not easily reduced to an abstraction.[10] Moreover, the new geographical spatiality associated with Tamburlaine first appears in the play as something that is *yet to be realized*. If at the outset Tamburlaine can refer to 'my provinces' as if his ambitions for dominion had already been achieved, his other utterances make plain that both his identity and his conquests are yet to come: 'I am a lord, for so my deeds *shall* prove, / And yet a shepherd by my parentage'; moreover, he '*means* to be a terror to the world, / Measuring the limits of his empery / By east and west' (*1 Tamb.* 1.2.23; 34–5; 38–40, emphasis mine). These early scenes are filled with references to what Tamburlaine is yet to do; while, as he later states, ' "will" and "shall" best fitteth Tamburlaine' (*1 Tamb.* 3.3.41), it is nevertheless important to recognize that the spatiality that Tamburlaine intends to usher into being – one in which being a terror and 'measuring the limits of his empery' go hand in hand – is not one that he inherits. If the 'reduction of the universe' Greenblatt associates with Marlowe, Tamburlaine, and the new geography is predominant, it is not represented as the only available spatial model in the play.

The play begins with the representation of a geography of (past) empire to which Tamburlaine is peripheral. The ambitious Cosroe desires to usurp his brother Mycetes's crown, largely on the grounds that Mycetes's rule marks a dark chapter in the history of

> Unhappy Persia, that in former age
> Hast been the seat of mighty conquerors,
> That in their prowess and their policies
> Have triumphed over Afric, and the bounds
> Of Europe where the sun dares scarce appear
> For freezing meteors and congealèd cold.
> (*1 Tamb.* 1.1.6–11)

Cosroe's lament over the fall of the Persian empire should also be read as an apparent introduction to the geographic arena of the play. It marks the first of several references in *Tamburlaine the Great* to the 'triple region[s]' of the world: Asia, Africa, and Europe (*1 Tamb.* 4.4.82). Moreover, this passage evokes the poetic geography outlined by Gillies; Europe is a region beyond the bounds of which the imperial Persian encounters not merely inclement weather, but quasi-supernatural meteorological phenomena ('freezing meteors and congealèd cold'). Cosroe presents us with a version of the *oikumene*, centred more on Asia than the Mediterranean, a space outside of which lie perils that are hinted at in this depiction of the European climate. Moreover, the *oikumene* also serves as a ground for Persian imperial identity, which emerges both out of past conquest and the establishment of a relationship between 'us' and 'them'. Indeed, Cosroe's description suggests that Europe is largely *terra incognita*; after all, conquering Persian emperors have managed no more than to triumph over its 'bounds'.[11] It is quintessentially Marlovian that the *oikumene* on display here literally marginalizes the English and requires that his audience identify with characters who, from the perspective of the London stage, are largely alien.[12]

Tamburlaine's endeavours over the course of both parts of this play can be understood in terms of his desire to dismantle the kind of geography articulated by Cosroe. In one of his most famous speeches, Tamburlaine boasts,

> I will confute those blind geographers
> That make a triple region in the world,
> Excluding regions which I mean to trace
> And with this pen [i.e., his sword] reduce them to a map,
> Calling the provinces, cities, and towns
> After my name and thine, Zenocrate.
> Here at Damascus will I make the point
> That shall begin the perpendicular.
> (*1 Tamb.* 4.4.81–8).

With its dismissive reference to the 'triple region in the world', this speech can be seen as a refusal of the kind of 'blind geography' articulated and assumed by Cosroe. Moreover, we move from an *oikumenical* world-view, with its highly charged boundaries, to a model of spatial organization grounded in little more than Tamburlaine's wilful and arbitrary assignation of the meridian-line to Damascus. If Tamburlaine is to bring 'excluded regions' into his new geographical frame, he makes plain that their inclusion will go hand-in-hand with their extinction: they are to be conquered and renamed after Tamburlaine and Zenocrate. In short, in this speech we witness Tamburlaine pledging to produce a new geographical model at the expense of the *oikumenical* one advanced at the outset of the play.

That being said, the triple regions of the blind geographers are not entirely banished. Not only do other characters continue to think in terms of this model (2 *Tamb.* 1.1.55–77), Tamburlaine himself articulates the ambition to 'conquer all the triple world' (2 *Tamb.* 4.3.63; see also 4.3.118). In short, Tamburlaine seems to move between two positions, one that assumes the 'triple world' model and another that understands it to be hopelessly impoverished. That impoverishment is telegraphed by Tamburlaine's several (anachronistically imperial) references to locations that cannot be accommodated by the model.[13] And yet, part of the poignance of Tamburlaine's final great speech, in which he uses a map to recall his triumphs and lament his failures (2 *Tamb.* 5.3.124–59), lies in the fact that he has not moved outside of Africa, Asia, or Europe; the regions excluded by the 'blind geographers' whom he castigates are the very ones that remain unconquered – even unvisited – at Tamburlaine's death. Importantly, even as the spokesperson for a tyrannical version of the new geography, Tamburlaine continues throughout the play to think in terms (and, indeed, travel within the parameters) of the *oikumene* described by Cosroe at the very outset.

In both its representation of its central character and the spatiality it enacts, *Tamburlaine the Great* is frequently taken to be quintessentially Marlovian: 'Nowhere are Marlovian preoccupations more typically illustrated than in the *Tamburlaine the Great* plays, which centre upon the world conquests of the titular protagonist.'[14] Insofar as the play engages with aspects of both the old and new geographies, *Tamburlaine* certainly is echoed by Marlowe's other tragedies. And yet, it is quite striking, in geographic terms, how distinctive each of these plays is. In *Tamburlaine*, we recognize the complete commensurability of both *spatial* and *social* boundary-crossing – of 'transgression' in its geographic and its moral senses. Such commensurability is not evident in all of Marlowe's plays. What we do encounter is a recurring interest in the relationship between geographies and the construction of identity. Moreover, 'geography' is meaningful for these plays in a broader way than has been recognized. As I have argued elsewhere, geography can be understood 'less [as] a description of the physical landscapes and cultures of a particular region [than as] a conceptual structure through which social and spatial relations are simultaneously materialized and represented'.[15] In Marlowe, it is not only *world* geographies that matter; the *affective* geography of the household, for instance, can serve a crucial function in Marlowe's exploration of the interrelatedness of space and identity. (By 'affective geography', I mean a physical site that functions as an important ground for the identity of a character who perceives himself as being in some way connected to that site and/or the social relations that emerge on or around it. The affective geography is usually but not necessarily a local or domestic one, and the nature of the character's connection to it can take on a variety of forms.) Importantly, when read through the lens of both affective and world geographies, the Marlovian hero is a less consistent, more variegated creature than he is often taken to be when characterized as, say, an 'overreacher'.[16] If Tamburlaine is best understood as an 'appetitive machine' whose identity is expressed through the devouring of lands first 'reduced ... to a map', then the characters of Barabas and Faustus emerge out of significantly different, if equally complex, relations to the geographies of their plays.

The Jew of Malta

Marlowe's plays are often organized around a geographical paradox that emerges from his characteristic opposition of rhetorics of expansiveness and enclosure.[17] This opposition is evident in Barabas's opening soliloquy (*JM* 1.1.1–48). Barabas first situates himself at the centre of an international trade that brings the wealth of many countries to his counting-house. He establishes here the geographic co-ordinates for his trade, revealing that his mercantile activity is squarely in the world described within the classical *oikumene*. (At the same time, and as we have seen, Marlowe's geographic precision is indebted to the cartographic achievements of the new geography.) What is striking is the contrast between the vigorous activity essential to the generation of Barabas's wealth (1.1.40–7) – activity that accommodates much of the Mediterranean world – and the relative immobility of the man who finds the counting of his fortune to be labour enough. This immobility is emblematic. Barabas, unlike Tamburlaine, shows no interest in globe-trotting. Moreover, the significant action of the play occurs after and because Barabas has had both his wealth and his house taken from him. Far from suffering from 'transcendental homelessness', Barabas is one who is attached not only to his wealth but also to Malta; rather than depart with the hidden funds that he has recovered from his confiscated house, Barabas buys *another* house. The only time that Barabas leaves the unnamed Maltese city is when he, wrongly believed to be dead, is thrown over the wall – and even then his exile proves to be among the briefest in all of English literature. If a large part of the allure of 'infinite riches in a little room' (1.1.37) lies in the spatial paradox the very line expresses (the infinite within the extremely finite), this image also evokes Barabas's attachment to a fixed, enclosed space that contrasts with the Mediterranean commerce that serves as a precondition for that space's very existence. Barabas's undeniable transgressiveness cannot be read in terms of a geographic exorbitance – a

Tamburlainian crossing of literal borders. Instead, it reflects his response to the disruption of a particular fantasy of locatedness expressed through the trope of the 'little room' (and echoed in the enclosed spaces of house and city wall).

As the 'little room' contains literal traces of Barabas's commercial dealings, it also metaphorically encloses within it the Mediterranean trade of which those traces are the product. In this regard, the little room is like Malta. As critics have noted, Malta is populated by peoples of various nationalities, most notably Spaniards, Turks, and relocated Knights Templar from the island of Rhodes – all drawn to the island by its status as 'a strategic post for both trading and war' (Bartels, p. 88). Marlowe's Malta is populated by characters whose presence on the island is as much a part of the Mediterranean trade (and the political activity it is imbricated in) as are the riches that Barabas catalogues in his opening soliloquy. As Basso puts it, the wind that brings him to Malta is the one 'that bloweth all the world besides, / Desire of gold' (3.5.3–4). Malta represents a kind of transcultural nexus, less 'home' to anyone than it is 'strategic post'. In this regard, the figure of the Jew, famously rootless, would seem to epitomize the Maltese ethos – and therein lies one of the major ironies of the play. Not only does Marlowe turn those who, from a British perspective, are culturally Other (Turks, Jews, Catholics) into the central players of his drama; he also makes the figure of the Jew into a character who is both outsider and insider, rootless and rooted, indifferent to and interested in the fate of Malta. Barabas's paradoxical position is made plain at the end of the play, when he first helps the Turks invade the city (see also 1.1.189), and then hands over control to the Christian governor, asserting that ''Twere slender policy for Barabas / To dispossess himself of such a place' (5.2.65–6).

Troubled in this play, then, are traditional models of the relationship between geography and identity. If the old (world) geography imagined a Mediterranean centre of the world outside of which existed all that was monstrous, or wondrous, Marlowe stages the activities of that 'Mediterranean centre' knowing full well that those inhabiting it are, from an English perspective, the liminal and threatening. At the same time, he is keenly aware of the marginality of Britain within the ancient version of the *oikumenical* model (as well as of the contemporary marginality of Britain to the various bids for global domination made by Mediterranean-based empires). As for affective geography, it is represented as both the ground for (a fantasy of) identity and always vulnerable to the broader socioeconomic processes that constitute it. While the displacement of Barabas occurs as a result of Ferneze's seizure of his property, the possibility that Barabas's ships, and thus much of his wealth, might be lost at sea is repeatedly emphasized at the outset (1.1.41–100). That the ships arrive safely leads Barabas to boast, 'thus are we on ev'ry side enriched' (103); wealth comes in from both land and sea. But the question has been provoked: just how stable is this fortune? More broadly, what of lasting stability can be built upon this Mediterranean trade and the shifting political alliances upon which it depends? (Of course, the seizure of Barabas's property is linked to such changing alliances. That politics and trade profoundly affect one another is made plain early on, when the return of one of Barabas's ships is impacted by Iberian–Turkish conflict [1.1.95–7].) The world geography generates an affective one – the 'infinite riches in a little room'. And yet that affective geography, and the forms of identity that it underwrites, are jeopardized by the world geography that nurtures them – a geography represented not only by trade, but by the political struggles that arise when all are driven by 'desire of gold'.[18]

Doctor Faustus

In *Doctor Faustus*, the opposition between expansiveness and enclosure can again be mapped onto the distinction between world and affective geographies, the latter represented by Faustus's house in Wittenberg. Faustus begins and ends his twenty-four years of diabolic servitude in this very place. While his reason for returning is never given, Faustus seems to feel it is necessary that he die in the same space in which he first rejected traditional academic disciplines and embraced necromancy (see 'A' text 4.1.101–6).

This return also marks the end of Faustus's engagement with the world geography that had been so important to his identity and ambitions. Faustus's extensive travels, focused less on Asia or the Mediterranean than on northern Europe, serve three major functions: they constitute his attempt to gain geographic and cosmographic knowledge (e.g., 2.1.173–5); they speak to his ambitions to alter and/or control the landscapes and cultures he encounters (e.g., 1.1.58–63); and they both trope and are co-extensive with the spread of his fame (e.g., 4 chorus 1–15). By the end of the play, the hollowness of his pursuits and of the ambitions that drove them are plain to Faustus: 'And what wonders I have done, all Germany can witness, yea, all the world, for which Faustus hath lost both Germany and the world, yea of heaven itself – heaven, the seat of God, the throne of the blessed, the kingdom of joy – and must remain in hell forever' (5.2.21–5). The physical geography emphasized through much of the play is situated precisely in relation to a divine cosmology. Faustus's thought moves outwards, from Germany to the world to heaven itself, thereby locating the arena of Faustus's sublunary concerns within a broader cosmological framework. What is shown here, though, is that Faustus, in his sinfulness, has heretofore neglected to look beyond geographic and cosmographic knowledge to the divine. His pursuits have been driven by forms of worldliness that have finally cost him 'heaven itself'.

Just as Tamburlaine's territorial ambitions are associated with his tyrannical implementation of the new geography, Faustus's aspirations to 'prove cosmography' go hand in hand with his desire for knowledge of and dominion over 'All things that move between the quiet poles' (1.1.58). If an alternative to Tamburlaine's spatiality is to be found in Damascus, in *Doctor Faustus* the alternative lies in his house and study. In this case, the new geography is confounded by Christian cosmology. As Jan Kott has put it, 'The *axis mundi* passes through [Faustus's] Wittenberg study; on it lie Heaven and Hell.'[19] Kott is echoing Mephistopheles's famous assertion, uttered in or around Faustus's house, that 'this is hell, nor am I out of it' (1.3.78; see also 2.1.123–8). Mephistopheles suggests not that Faustus's house is literally hell, but that hell is always carried within the damned; it is both no place and every place. From this perspective, the details of physical geography, as well as their relationship to identity, are both irrelevant and confounded, as 'place' is revealed as an internal state and 'new geographical' co-ordinates are shown to be secondary to the true *axis mundi*. And yet, Faustus returns to a specific location, his house, to die. In a kind of cosmological joke, Faustus seems to have taken Mephistopheles literally: if hell is in his house, it is to that house that Faustus must travel at the end of his twenty-four years. This literalism is echoed by the fact that hell is discussed in increasingly material terms over the course of the play; it becomes more of a *physical* place.[20]

What I have suggested so far is that the new geography is associated with Faustus's 'worldliness'. Also, Faustus construes the cosmological in literal terms, thereby extending the materialist logic of the new geography beyond the sphere of its proper application. And yet, Faustus's house should not be so entirely subsumed into a cosmological order; its meanings and significances are also local and personal to Faustus. Importantly, Faustus's house is represented as a social site, accommodating not only servants such as Wagner, but also friends virtuous (the scholars) and vicious (Cornelius and Valdes). Faustus's initial aspirations to necromancy entail the projected sharing of his wealth and achievements with his 'dearest friends' Cornelius and Valdes (1.1.66, 150–1), who shortly thereafter disappear from the play; later, Faustus attributes his impending demise to his not having lived with one god-fearing friend he describes as a 'sweet chamber-fellow' (5.2.3), while another friend understands Faustus's moroseness as evidence of his having been 'over-solitary' (5.2.8). If Faustus's house stands as the entrance to hell, it is also the site of social exchanges that contain within them the twin possibilities of damnation and salvation. In his travels, and in the 'over-solitariness' that his alliance with Mephistopheles engenders, Faustus alienates himself from the relationships, both good and bad, that are foregrounded at the beginning of the play (e.g., 1.1.66–8; 1.2.34–8). To return to Wittenberg, then, is both to prepare for death and to re-enter a social world that, at the outset, was represented as constitutive of Faustus's identity. If hell is to be found in Faustus's house, so are those (soon to be lost) relationships that helped make him what he was before he embraced necromancy. Herein lies the pathos of Faustus's tragedy: whereas a Christian cosmological order deprives a given place of both its identity and its ability to constitute identities, it is to such a place that Faustus feels compelled to return and from which he is finally so poignantly torn, with his friends praying for him only one room away (5.2.55–64). As the transgressor of both physical and moral boundaries, Faustus resembles the voyager of the ancient poetic geography who has passed beyond the borders of the *oikumene* to 'the remotest shores of the world'. His return expresses a desire to restore both himself and the integrity of the social world that he disrupted through his boundary-crossing.

Faustus's downfall occurs between two poles: that of a global geography that betrays his sinful 'worldliness', and that of an affective geography in which Faustus travels simultaneously to home and to hell. One could conceivably argue that *Doctor Faustus* finally endorses one geographic model over the other – just as critics have vigorously advocated either religiously 'orthodox' or 'heterodox' readings of the text – but what seems most to engage Marlowe is the collision that he stages between contradictory models. As we have seen, Marlowe is drawn to spatial paradoxes of various kinds, paradoxes that are not resolved but put on display; the new geography collides with the old, and affective geographies fight for space with Christian cosmologies. One could provide additional examples of conflicting spatialities in Marlowe. For instance, consider the tension in *Edward II* between the imperatives of a geography of national sovereignty and Edward's desire to live with Gaveston in 'some nook or corner' of the kingdom (1.4.72) – a desire both modified and brutally realized through Edward's lone imprisonment in the dungeon '[w]herein the filth of all the castle falls' (5.5.56). Or the way in which a Tamburlainian rhetoric of spatial conquest extends across erotic relations in *Hero and Leander*:

> For though the rising ivory mount he scaled,
> Which is with azure circling lines empaled,
> Much like a globe (a globe may I term this,
> By which love sails to regions full of bliss).
>
> (*HL* 757–60)[21]

In this poem, the action is located at the cusp of Asia and Europe:

> On Hellespont, guilty of true love's blood,
> In view and opposite two cities stood,
> Sea borderers, disjoined by Neptune's might:
> The one Abydos, the other Sestos hight.
>
> (*HL* 1–4)

And yet, a basic premise of this chapter is that the multiplication of such examples should not lead us to assume a Marlovian canon entirely uniform in its approach to geographic matters. Relatedly, if Marlowe's protagonists can all be characterized as 'transgressive', the nature of their transgressions (both social and geographic) are all distinctive, betraying different relationships to the issues of space and identity that Marlowe explores in his plays. It is the fact of this exploration that marks the most significant continuity across these works. Marlowe's plays can be thought of less as *arguments* about the relationship of geography and identity than as dramatic *experiments* in diversely configuring that relationship, while often offering up multiple geographic models. What do we make of a 'rootless' Jew who embodies emplacedness? Or a vagrant Scythian who conquers and names cities after himself?[22] Or a learned magician who travels to 'prove cosmography' only to find at home both hell and the lost prospect of salvation? It is these kinds of problems and paradoxes that are the raw materials of Marlowe's experiments – experiments in which early modern cultural models for quite literally *viewing the world* are collided, exposed, and explored.

NOTES

1. Patrick Cheney, *Marlowe's Counterfeit Profession: Ovid, Spenser, Counter-Nationhood* (University of Toronto Press, 1997), p. 126.
2. Ethel Seaton, 'Marlowe's Map', *Essays and Studies by Members of the English Association* 10 (1924), 13–35.
3. Lisa Jardine, *Reading Shakespeare Historically* (London: Routledge, 1996), p. 100.
4. In this chapter all play citations are from *Christopher Marlowe: The Complete Plays*, Mark Thornton Burnett (ed.), Everyman (London: J. M. Dent, 1999); references to *Doctor Faustus* are from the 'A' text (1604). Whereas *geography* 'accurately represents the whole known world and its parts according to astronomical observations and fixed geometrical principles', *cosmography* 'considers the form and pattern of the whole celestial scheme' while also 'locating the terrestrial sphere accurately within the celestial spheres of fixed and moving stars' (Denis Cosgrove, 'Mapping New Worlds: Culture and Cartography in Sixteenth-Century Venice', *Imago Mundi* 44 (1992), 65–89, esp. p. 66).
5. John Gillies, 'Marlowe, the *Timur* Myth, and the Motives of Geography', in Gillies and Virginia Mason Vaughan (eds.), *Playing the Globe: Genre and Geography*

in English Renaissance Drama (Madison: Fairleigh Dickinson University Press, 1998), pp. 203–29.

6. John Noble Wilford, *The Mapmakers* (London: Junction Books, 1981), p. 34.

7. John Gillies, *Shakespeare and the Geography of Difference* (Cambridge University Press, 1994), p. 5.

8. The interpolated quotation is from Seneca the Elder.

9. Stephen Greenblatt, *Renaissance Self-Fashioning: From More to Shakespeare* (University of Chicago Press, 1980), p. 195.

10. Garrett A. Sullivan, Jr, 'Space, Measurement, and Stalking Tamburlaine', *RenD* n.s. 28 (1997), 3–27.

11. The marginality of Britain is suggested in a subsequent reference to 'the Western Isles' (*1 Tamb.* 1.1.38).

12. Emily C. Bartels, *Spectacles of Strangeness: Imperialism, Alienation, and Marlowe* (Philadelphia: University of Pennsylvania Press, 1993), p. xv.

13. E.g., Mexico (*1 Tamb.* 3.3.255), 'rich America' (*2 Tamb.* 1.2.35).

14. Mark Thornton Burnett (ed.), 'Introduction', *The Complete Plays*, pp. xvii–xxxiv, esp. p. xviii.

15. Garrett A. Sullivan, Jr, 'Shakespeare's Comic Geographies', in Richard Dutton and Jean E. Howard (eds.), *A Companion to Shakespeare's Works, Vol. 3: The Comedies* (Oxford: Blackwell, 2003) 182–99, esp. 182.

16. Harry Levin, *The Overreacher: A Study of Christopher Marlowe* (Cambridge, MA: Harvard University Press, 1952).

17. Marjorie Garber, ' "Infinite Riches in a Little Room": Closure and Enclosure in Marlowe', in Alvin Kernan (ed.), *Two Renaissance Mythmakers: Christopher Marlowe and Ben Jonson* (Baltimore: Johns Hopkins University Press, 1977), pp. 3–21.

18. Barabas situates his own political manoeuvring in the context of trade: 'Why, is not this / A kingly kind of trade, to purchase towns / By treachery, and sell 'em by deceit?' (5.5.46–8).

19. Jan Kott, *The Bottom Translation: Marlowe and Shakespeare and the Carnival Tradition*, Daniela Miedzyrzecka and Lillian Vallee (trans.) (Evanston: Northwestern University Press, 1987), p. 3.

20. Katharine Eisaman Maus, *Inwardness and Theater in the English Renaissance* (University of Chicago Press, 1995), p. 90.

21. Quotations from *Hero and Leander* are taken from Mark Thornton Burnett (ed.), *Christopher Marlowe: The Complete Poems*, Everyman (London: Dent; and Rutland, VT: Tuttle, 2000).

22. Mark Thornton Burnett, 'Tamburlaine: an Elizabethan Vagabond', *SP* 84 (1987), 308–23.

READING LIST

Burton, Jonathan. 'Anglo-Ottoman Relations and the Image of the Turk in *Tamburlaine*'. *JMEMS* 30 (2000), 125–56.

Dollimore, Jonathan. *Radical Tragedy: Religion, Ideology and Power in the Drama of Shakespeare and his Contemporaries*, 2nd edn. Durham: Duke University Press, 1993.

Floyd-Wilson, Mary. *English Ethnicity and Race in Early Modern Drama.* Cambridge University Press, 2003.

Gillies, John, and Virginia Mason Vaughan (eds.). *Playing the Globe: Genre and Geography in English Renaissance Drama.* Madison: Fairleigh Dickinson University Press, 1998.

Helgerson, Richard. *Forms of Nationhood: The Elizabethan Writing of England.* University of Chicago Press, 1992.

Hiscock, Andrew. 'Enclosing "Infinite Riches in a Little Room": the Question of Cultural Marginality in Marlowe's *The Jew of Malta*'. *Forum for Modern Language Studies* 35 (1999), 1–22.

Klein, Bernhard. *Maps and the Writing of Space in Early Modern England and Ireland.* Houndmills: Palgrave, 2001.

Knowles, James. '"Infinite Riches in a Little Room": Marlowe and the Aesthetics of the Closet'. In Gordon McMullan (ed.), *Renaissance Configurations: Voices/Bodies/Spaces, 1580–1690.* Houndmills: Macmillan, 1998, pp. 3–29.

Shepherd, Simon. *Marlowe and the Politics of Elizabethan Theatre.* Brighton: Harvester Press, 1986.

Vitkus, Daniel. *Turning Turk: English Theater and the Multicultural Mediterranean, 1570–1630.* Houndmills: Palgrave Macmillan, 2003.

15

KATE CHEDGZOY

Marlowe's men and women: gender and sexuality

The society in which Marlowe lived and wrote, and the fictional worlds he created in his writings, were highly gender-segregated. Different physical, emotional, and intellectual qualities were ascribed to men and women, and to a significant extent they inhabited distinct social spaces.[1] These gender divisions shaped the ways in which men and women came to know themselves as such, profoundly affecting the possibilities for sexual desire and expression. The theatre Marlowe wrote for did not merely represent this divided world, it also embodied it: as far as the making and performing of plays were concerned, it, too, was an all-male preserve. Yet the playwrights and actors had to speak to and entertain an audience that, although male-dominated, did include women; and poems like *Hero and Leander* appealed to female as well as male readers.[2] The popularity of works like Marlowe's, depicting a wide range of sexual and social encounters between men and women, may constitute evidence of a shared awareness by his contemporaries of the possibility of testing – and perhaps even transgressing – the boundaries their world had established for itself. Marlowe's plays and poems provide diverse testimonials to the ideals to which the culture of Elizabethan England aspired, and against which it chafed; to its imaginings of alternative ways of organizing gender and expressing sexuality; and to the complex, multifaceted realities of lived experience.

Gender and sexuality can be both orderly and disorderly in the fictional worlds of Marlowe's poetry and drama, working with and against the grain of the social structures they are shaped by and shape. Tracing the interrelations of gender and sexuality in Marlowe's plays and poems, this chapter argues that the significance of Marlowe's treatment of the relations between men and women, and men's relations with one another, lies in his acute perception of the entanglement of their encounters with the political structures and everyday practices of his social world.[3] These issues are explored under two headings. The first section, 'Orderly unions', focuses on heterosexual marriages and political, military, and emotional alliances between men that broadly conform to and work to sustain the prevailing social structures and power dynamics of the worlds depicted in the plays. In the second, 'Disorderly desires', I consider passions and liaisons that threaten to disrupt those structures. In works representing men and women as objects of desire, passionate suitors, ambitious politicians, agents and victims of violence, loyal and treacherous towards family and friends, Marlowe navigated the boundaries of acceptable and transgressive behaviour in ways that both reflected and challenged the values of his society.

Orderly unions

The men and women of Marlowe's society fell in love, experienced sexual passion, and sought happiness through intimate relationships, and his poems and plays vividly depict these emotional dramas. Yet in literature and in life, marriage could not be merely a personal, emotional matter. A cornerstone of the social order, it was vitally implicated with matters of power, wealth, and status. In the patriarchal worlds of Marlowe's dramas, men control marriage and use it to further their own interests. Yet it can also offer women opportunities, albeit in constrained and limited circumstances, to negotiate for themselves a place in society that may hold out some hope of circumventing those constraints.

Opening with a politically charged marriage and ending with a quasi-fraternal union between powerful men, *The Massacre at Paris* vividly illustrates the ways in which the relationships of elite men and women are caught up in the dynamics of power and social order. The play begins with the wedding of Navarre and Margaret, designed to heal divisions between Protestant and Catholic citizens. Yet it immediately has the opposite effect of highlighting conflict: King Charles's wish that 'this union and religious league / . . . / May not dissolve till death dissolve our lives' (1.4–5) is Queen Catherine's cue for an aside revealing her hostility to this reconciliatory project, which she threatens to 'dissolve with blood and cruelty' (1.25).[4] Scene 2 also takes marriage as its starting point, promptly reversing the positive ambitions associated with the opening wedding, as Guise creates an inverted liturgy of negative transformations, apocalyptically expressing his determination that 'If ever Hymen loured at marriage-rites . . . this fatal night / Shall fully show the fury of them all' (2.1–8).

The Massacre at Paris closes with the fraternal union of Navarre and Charles's successor King Henry, who echo the marriage that opens the play by exchanging vows to be faithful and loving until death. They are not required to keep these vows long, however, as King Henry is promptly assassinated; as he did at the beginning of the play, Marlowe makes clear the magnitude of the challenge facing institutions like marriage and kingship that seek to produce and preserve social order. Recalling the words notoriously attributed to Marlowe by Richard Baines ('That all they that love not Tobacco & Boies were fools' and that Christ 'used [John the Baptist] as the sinners of Sodoma'),[5] it might be tempting to read the alliance between Navarre and Henry as precisely the kind of perversion of marriage that Guise invoked in scene 2, an eroticized liaison that early modern audiences would have perceived as sodomitical – that is, as connecting sexual perversion with social disorder. Earlier in the play, Henry's intense attachment to his minions (male favourites) associated him with a self-absorbed, homoerotic hedonism that led to the neglect of his royal responsibilities. Here, though, the alliance with Navarre is homosocial rather than homoerotic, founded in their shared interests as warrior princes in a time of social and political crisis.

The concept of the homosocial, and its connections to and differences from heterosexuality, homophobia, and homosexuality, have been influentially elaborated for literary studies by Eve Kosofsky Sedgwick. She argues that heterosexual public culture is structured by male homosocial bonds, formed when heterosexual men enter into alliances with each other to further their individual and collective interests on the world's stage.[6] Such alliances are often achieved through the exchange of women in marriage, but women exist in this system only as objects, not subjects of their own desires and ambitions. Homosocial bonds can overlap with homoerotic ones, but they can also be homophobic, working to exclude men whose sexual desires for each other may threaten male alliances created and maintained in pursuit of power rather than pleasure. Including, in Sedgwick's words, 'male friendship, mentorship, admiring identification, bureaucratic subordination, and heterosexual rivalry' (p. 186), many of the forms taken by male homosocial bonds are vividly dramatized in Marlowe's plays and poems.

The *Tamburlaine* plays, for example, stage complex variations on the connections between the heterosexual and the homosocial. Tamburlaine's announcement that Zenocrate's 'fair face and heavenly hue / Must grace his bed that conquers Asia' (*1 Tamb.* 1.2.36–7) positions the woman he desires as both the motive and reward of the masculine pursuits of war and conquest. Zenocrate makes no verbal response to this proposal, but her silent presence on stage, bearing mute witness to Tamburlaine's strutting, reminds the audience that his perspective on events is not the only possible one. Tamburlaine's revelation of his armour beneath the shepherd's 'weeds', recalling the magical status transformations of European folktales, is clearly designed to clinch his suit and to entice Zenocrate to submit willingly to becoming his consort as 'Empress of the East' – although as the end of the scene makes plain, submission will be exacted if it is not volunteered (*1 Tamb.* 1.2.252–8).

Tamburlaine's proposal to Zenocrate is bizarrely echoed by his invitation to Theridamas, 'do but join with me, / And we will triumph over all the world' (*1 Tamb.* 1.2.171–2). Though Tamburlaine takes Zenocrate as a sign of Jove's favour, foreshadowing that he will be 'Monarch of the East' (*1 Tamb.* 1.2.185), the partnership he chooses to foreground is the military one of leadership and conquest alongside Theridamas, acknowledging the latter's masculine challenge in order to disarm it: 'Then shalt thou be competitor with me / And sit with Tamburlaine in all his majesty' (*1 Tamb.* 1.2.207–8). Theridamas evidently finds Tamburlaine's rhetoric more seductive than Zenocrate did, submitting in terms borrowed from heterosexual courtship, that echo the 'for better or for worse' bargain of marriage: 'Won with thy words and conquered with thy looks / I yield myself... / To be partaker of thy good or ill' (*1 Tamb.* 1.2.227–9).

Theridamas's admiration for Tamburlaine is echoed by Menaphon, whose blazon of Tamburlaine's body (*1 Tamb.* 2.1.7ff.) celebrates a distinctively virile kind of masculine beauty.[7] The masculine body in Marlowe's works is an object of great fascination, and a site of diverse meanings: the blazon of Leander in *Hero and Leander* (Sestiad 1.61–90) is structurally similar to that of Tamburlaine, but contrasts with it in highlighting gender ambiguity as crucial to Leander's desirability: 'Some swore he was a maid in man's attire / For in his looks were all that men desire' (83–4). Though Tamburlaine's gender is not in doubt, this very virility causes his humanity to be brought into question: like Shakespeare's Coriolanus, he is presented as both more and less than human, quasi-divine and simultaneously monstrous, an evaluation echoed in the description of him as a 'god, or fiend, or spirit of the earth, / Or monster turned to manly shape' (*1 Tamb.* 2.6.15–16).

The alliance between Tamburlaine and Theridamas exemplifies Marlowe's fascination with the relationships between homosocial masculinity and the sphere of power and politics, illustrated in his translation of *Lucan's First Book*, a work that although marginal to the modern Marlovian canon addresses some of its central preoccupations. Its concern with civil war obviously resonates with the subject of *The Massacre at Paris*, and chimes with the examination of political disorder and violence in *Edward II* and *The Jew of Malta*. In Marlowe's translation of Lucan, these concerns are placed in a context of ambition, violence, imperial exploitation, and exotic locations, echoing the terms in which masculine aspirations are fantasized and acted out in *Tamburlaine the Great*, *The Jew of Malta*, and *Doctor Faustus* – three plays that share a fascination with the relationship between the 'lawless', 'vagrant' (*1 Tamb.* 1.1.39, 45) masculinity that drives their protagonists' ambitions, and the construction of certain kinds of socially desirable order. As a scholar whose life has been largely secluded from the world, Doctor Faustus represents a very different kind of masculinity from Tamburlaine. He shares the latter's desire for power, but he sees knowledge, not military conquest, as the key to achieving it ('A' text 1.1.55–65). The institutions that supported serious study in the early modern period accommodated men only, so this is a wholly gendered aspiration – indeed, the masculine world of *Doctor Faustus*, featuring just two women (a servant and an aristocrat) who speak a total of fifteen lines,[8] strongly resembles the all-male Canterbury grammar school and Cambridge college where Marlowe spent most of his life, before passing his final years primarily in the very different, but still exclusively masculine, environment of the London commercial theatre. Faustus's ambition is shared by his friend Valdes, who also resembles Tamburlaine in expressing fantasies of omnipotence in terms that line up the eroticized domination of women alongside imperialism (1.1.121–35). The servants Robin and Wagner act out similar fantasies in a coarser, more comic idiom (1.4.68–70), revealing that this imperial, misogynistic construction of masculinity permeates society.

It is becoming clear that in Marlowe's dramatic worlds women are conceptualized as the objects and medium of power rather than its agents: these are plays which both expose and participate in the subjugation and objectification of women by men.[9] Yet a few women do find ways to achieve some agency, although given the moral and political contexts in which they operate, such achievements rarely constitute a cause for feminist celebration. In *Tamburlaine, Part One*, for example, the move from object status to problematic agency is made by Zabina and Zenocrate in a scene that celebrates them both as paragons of femininity and foils to their men, and installs them on the thrones of Turkey and Persia, respectively, to bear witness to the violent contest between Bajazeth and Tamburlaine (*1 Tamb.* 3.3). Zenocrate's job is to fight with Zabina on the feminine terrain of speech just as her husband will combat Bajazeth on the battlefield – 'manage words with her as we will arms' (*1 Tamb.* 3.3.131) – and their conflict, like that of their husbands, is played out on the terrain of exoticism, sexuality, and status. Each, too, draws her female servant into the argument, paradoxically showing, at this moment where two women fight each other out of loyalty to their menfolk, that women like men can form homosocial loyalties. This happens only rarely, however, in Marlowe's plays, where women's opportunities to elude the control of their fathers and husbands are strictly constrained. The agency Zenocrate attains by virtue of Tamburlaine's love for her is deployed to mediate between him and her father, when she pleads for the siege of Damascus to be lifted. In asking her 'wouldst thou have me buy thy father's love / With such a loss' (*1 Tamb.* 4.4.89–90), Tamburlaine inadvertently highlights the inevitable division of women's loyalties in a patriarchal structure, a theme that Shakespeare would later explore at more length in *King Lear*.

The virgins who plead for Damascus to be spared have found a way to sidestep such patriarchal control. The paradoxical nature of their gender identity, allied to yet distinct from 'all our sex' (*1 Tamb.* 5.1.26), gives them quasi-magical powers to set against Tamburlaine's simultaneously monstrous and divine attributes. If 'the humble suits or imprecations' of women are 'uttered with tears of wretchedness and blood' (*1 Tamb.* 5.1.25), it is tempting to associate this with the widespread Galenic understanding in Marlowe's society of women as wet, flowing, and leaky by nature;[10] yet this play has shown us how very freely male blood can also flow, as the result of male violence. Though their mission is unsuccessful, they do carve out a temporary dramatic space for the articulation of an alternative, feminine set of values concerning war and death, echoed by Zenocrate when she laments the annihilation of 'the sun-bright troop / Of the heavenly virgins and unspotted maids' (*1 Tamb.* 5.1.325–6), and also by the unique character of Olympia, Muslim wife to a Captain who heroically defends his besieged city against Theridamas and Techelles (*2 Tamb.* 3.3). On her husband's sudden death, Olympia kills her son and prepares to stab herself, in order to pre-empt the terrible tortures that may await them if they are captured. But she delays long enough to burn the bodies of her menfolk, 'Lest cruel Scythians should dismember [them]' (*2 Tamb.* 3.4.37). In doing so she upholds, in the face of the barbarian onslaught, civilized values that derive ultimately from the European classical heritage; that a Muslim woman is chosen to be the defender of some of the core values of Marlowe's cultural world is remarkable. Fought over as an eroticized trophy of male conflict, Olympia regains some agency when she tricks Theridamas into stabbing her in the throat, a shockingly sexualized end that nevertheless enables her to avoid his sexual advances, which she literally considers to be a fate worse than death (*2 Tamb.* 4.2).

Zenocrate's failure to secure Damascus prompts her to meditate on her position and such scope for action as it affords her in terms that attempt to turn the painful division of her loyalties into an opportunity for reconciliation (*1 Tamb.* 5.1.385–403). Compare Queen Isabella's efforts, in *Edward II*, to make the orderly union of royal marriage work for her, even as she comes to terms with emotional and erotic rejection by Edward. Though Isabella laments her mistreatment at her husband's hands (1.2.163–6), she reluctantly accepts her wifely duty of obedience in the hope that it will lead to reconciliation, accepting Edward's injunction to work for the recall of his beloved Gaveston. Yet this early commitment to marriage mutates into more disorderly desires, including the adulterous and politically ambitious passion for Mortimer epitomized in Kent's remark that they 'do kiss while they conspire' (4.6.13). Isabella's encounters with Mortimer suggest that feminine grief at the destruction of her marriage motivates her to act in ways that challenge the gender ideologies of the play's world. Her first entrance, greeted by Mortimer with 'whither walks your majesty so fast?' (1.2.46), testifies to an unfeminine purposefulness motivated by the fact that 'the King regards [her] not' (1.2.49). Later, adopting the role of warrior queen, she is dehumanized in a manner reminiscent of *Tamburlaine*, with Edward describing her as one 'whose eyes, being turned to steel, / Will sooner sparkle fire than shed a tear' (5.1.104–5). Her transgressive alliance with Mortimer gives her access to a partnership of power: 'The Queen and Mortimer / Shall rule the realm, the King, and none rule us' (5.4.63–4). Isabella's increasing disorderly behaviour is presented as a factor of her political ambition as well as her emotional distress: indeed, as Joanna Gibbs realizes, the two are intertwined: 'Isabella's affections are informed by the operations of politics.'[11]

The play repeatedly indicates that for both Isabella and Edward, an orderly reconciliation of their competing desires might be possible, so long as it also reconciles the political and personal aspirations that shape Isabella's dissatisfaction. In 1.4, for example, the news of Gaveston's repeal brings about a loving reconciliation between Edward and Isabella, as he offers her golden rewards for pleading for Gaveston, but she insists that the only jewels she would wear around her neck are his embraces, and his kisses are all the treasure she could demand (327–31), in an extended image that inverts the normal gendering of the metaphor of precious metals and jewels, frequently used by Marlowe to symbolize and guarantee heterosexual transactions that sustain male power. It is Edward's refusal to maintain an acceptable balance between the homoerotic, heterosexual, and homosocial aspects of his life as king, between his personal desires and his political responsibilities, that drives Isabella to her disorderly union with Mortimer:

> So well hast thou deserved, sweet Mortimer,
> As Isabel could live with thee for ever.
> In vain I look for love at Edward's hand,
> Whose eyes are fixed on none but Gaveston.
>
> (*EII* 2.4.59–62)

The potential compatibility of homosexual love with heterosexual marriage and the upholding of social order and convention in *Edward II* is underwritten by Mortimer Senior's famous statement that 'the mightiest kings have had their minions' (1.4.390), in a speech which suggests that a king's love for a young man need not be dangerously transgressive, but can affirm orderly cultural values and structures. Mortimer Junior's rejoinder specifies that Gaveston's transgressions infringe class and national distinctions (402–18), stressing that only when these kinds of disorder intersect with homoeroticism does the latter fall into the category of disturbing behaviour.

Mario Di Gangi asserts that 'homoerotic relations in Renaissance England could be socially orderly as well as socially disorderly or sodomitical', and *Edward II* challenges us to figure out what makes the difference.[12]

The complexities of the relations between the homoerotic, homosocial, and heterosexual are acted out in 2.2, when Edward is left alone, and Isabella, Margaret, and ladies-in-waiting enter, along with Baldock, Spencer, and Gaveston. This grouping temporarily constructs an alternative site of values and concerns that contrasts but also intersects, via Isabella's transgressive extramarital alliance with Mortimer, with the social world of the male peers. Strikingly, in this scene, we see a group of women together, whereas normally in Marlowe's works, as noted above, women are isolated from each other, and perceived primarily in terms of their relations to men. Even here, however, the women's appearance ultimately serves to consolidate alliances between the men: in closing the scene by declaring 'Gaveston, think that I love thee well / To wed thee to our niece' (2.2.256–7), Edward underlines the interdependence of homosocial bonds and heterosexual contracts, and the deployment of both in the service of larger political interests, confirming that in this play, the most important thing about 'sexuality, whether homoerotic or heteroerotic', is that it 'implements power' (Bartels, p. 168).

Doctor Faustus renegotiates the relations between male heterosexual desire, the institution of marriage, and male homosocial bonds when Faustus asks for a wife, 'the fairest maid in Germany, for I am wanton and lascivious' (2.1.142). This declaration comes as a surprise from a man who had seemed to find the homosocial world of university learning emotionally satisfactory, and is all the more intriguing because the demand is made to Mephistopheles, with whom he has an intimate and complex relationship that in performance has sometimes blurred the distinction between the homosocial and the homoerotic. Mephistopheles is reluctant to oblige, because even while he tries to dismiss marriage as 'but a ceremonial toy' (2.1.154), he clearly fears the possible repercussions of such a Christian commitment on Faustus's part, and therefore encourages Faustus to accept 'fairest courtesans' instead. The terms in which Mephistopheles conjures up the vision of an ideal woman bear out the homoerotic quality often attributed to him in performance, as he promises Faustus a woman 'as beautiful / As was bright Lucifer before his fall' (*Faustus* 2.1.160–1). But this ethereal vision of androgynous desirability actually materializes in the form of a 'devil dressed like a woman, with fireworks', and Faustus rejects her as 'a hot whore' (2.1.153). Though comic in effect, this depiction of women as devilish, and the dramatic literalization of the slang meanings of 'hot' as sexually voracious and diseased, have a misogynistic edge. Here, Mephistopheles turns marriage, both a symbol and a fundamental element of good order in patriarchal society, into a subversive and disorderly act, taking place in a context that disrupts the hierarchies of gender and sexuality. Such inversion of Christian rituals is associated with witchcraft, symbolically linked at this time with both women and sodomites – think of Mortimer Junior hinting at a discourse of feminine erotic enchantment when he muses on Edward II's love for Gaveston, 'Is it not strange that he is thus bewitched?' (1.2.55). This incident thus epitomizes the association of disorder with unruly gender and sexuality that forms the subject of the next section.

Disorderly desires

The Jew of Malta, like *Doctor Faustus*, mingles comedy and tragedy in its dramatization of the working of gender and sexuality. It plays out a conflict between Abigail's desire to participate in orderly unions, and the disorderly, antisocial impulses of her father Barabas, through the circuits of patriarchal homosocial exchange. Barabas's Jewishness inflects his masculinity in ways that make him irredeemably disorderly within the Christian world-view of the play, and cut him off from any sense of a stake in the social or membership of the commonwealth: as he explains, he is concerned only with his own interests, the private space of the family and its property: 'let 'em [Turks] combat, conquer, and kill all, / So they spare me, my daughter and my wealth' (ll.151–2). Thus he is traumatized by the Christians' appropriation of his house with the intention of turning it into a nunnery, cutting him off from home and wealth in a gesture of exclusion marked by religious and cultural difference as well as gender. The recovery of his wealth is symbolized when he has bought a new house, and Abigail is at home in it (2.2). Abigail seeks to gain some agency by manipulating the opportunities open to a woman in Maltese society, but Jewishness disconnects her and Barabas from the island's homosocial networks. In addition, the lack of any space for female agency in such networks renders her unable to adopt a secure position in the terms made available by Maltese society, oscillating vulnerably between dutiful daughterhood, marriage, and the convent. The transmission of Jewish identity through the maternal line gives an edge to Barabas's attempts to control Abigail's sexuality, and to her repeated attempts to enter the convent, the latter played out, against tradition, the first time as farce and the second time as tragedy. In early modern Europe, patterns of property transmission made the control by elite men of their wives' and daughters' sexuality imperative. It is no surprise, then, that Barabas's description to Abigail's other suitor, Mathias, of how she spurns Lodowick's 'bracelets, jewels, rings' (2.2.264) and 'locks herself up fast' (2.2.267) at his approach, articulates his own fantasy of consigning her to the confinement and enclosure prescribed by Renaissance gender ideologies for the virtuous woman.[13]

Barabas's objectification of Abigail and identification of her with his wealth – 'O girl, O gold, O beauty, O my bliss!' (2.1.54) – is an anti-semitic, but nonetheless exact, articulation of the status of women in most of Marlowe's plays, where they are characteristically imaged as jewels to be exchanged between men. It is echoed, for example, in the simultaneously commodified and bawdy extended conceit of Abigail as a diamond that runs all through the scene in which Lodowick, son of the Governor, conducts his courtship of her via her father (2.2). Taking place in the slave market, this exchange shows how normalized the commodification of persons is in this culture, not restricted to women as objects of exchange among men. In the same scene, Barabas's acquisition of Ithamore to be his 'fellow' (2.2.219) in villainy both extends this commodification to a man – though, significantly, only to one who is racially different – and shows that male homosocial bonds are not intrinsically orderly, but can be transgressive when they are secured between men who are marginalized by normative social hierarchies.

If the exchange of women between men is crucial to the maintenance of male homosocial power, it is becoming clear that women do not always serve as the compliant agents of men's plans, but can act as disruptive and disorderly forces. Several times, Marlowe invokes Helen of Troy as such a woman, one whose desirability has the power to undo the bonds and institutions of martial masculinity. In Helen's most famous Marlovian incarnation, in *Doctor Faustus*, the figure of this desirable woman is used to justify deeds of heroic aggression. Referring to the destruction of Troy, one of the most poignant episodes of ancient culture for the Renaissance, the Third Scholar considers that 'the rape of such a queen' is ample justification for 'ten years' war', and for Faustus himself she merits extending this carnage into the future, and destroying both bonds between men and the institutions – like Faustus's own university at Wittenberg – that symbolize the achievements of male homosocial culture: 'for love of thee, / Instead of Troy shall Wittenberg be sacked; /.../ And [I will] then return to Helen for a kiss' (5.1.96–100). Though Helen was the trophy that incited men to heroic military deeds, Marlowe shows that she can also subvert masculinity. Faustus's erotic submission to Helen, with its disastrous implications for the masculine elite culture he previously upheld, is highlighted by the gender crossings and reversals in the erotic fantasy articulated here: Faustus will be female Semele as well as male Paris, while Helen embodies both the paragon of female beauty and rapaciously masculine Jupiter.

Faustus hopes that Helen will also accomplish a different kind of destruction, erasing the anxieties of conscience from his soul, and requests her as his paramour in the hope that her 'sweet embracings may extinguish clean / These thoughts that do dissuade me from my vow' (5.1.84–5). Yet the reverse occurs: Helen and Faustus leave the stage after his celebrated rhapsody of erotically motivated annihilation, and when he re-enters in the next scene he is distraught with guilt and fear. Helen is forgotten, but Faustus's sexual encounter with her has tipped him into a despairing recognition of the mistake he made in contracting himself to the devil. Lamenting that 'the serpent that tempted Eve may be saved, but not Faustus' (5.2.16), Faustus identifies with Eve, brought by sexuality to a full awareness of his own sinfulness, and positioned, by this process, in a symbolically feminine location that undoes the aggressively ambitious masculinity that initially characterized him.

Like Helen of Troy, Dido is also associated with imperial power, femininity, and catastrophe, and when she anticipates Faustus's longing for Helen in saying of Aeneas, 'in his looks I see eternity / and he'll make me immortal with a kiss' (4.4.122–3), her fate is tragically foreshadowed. *Dido, Queen of Carthage* differs from Marlowe's other plays in having been written for a company of boy actors, rather than for the public theatre where male roles were taken by adult men and boys played women. This may have affected the portrayal of gender and sexuality in a play where female roles are unusually prominent; playful cross-generational homoeroticism takes the place of homosocial liaisons between adult men; and the familiar dynamics of heterosexual encounters in a patriarchal context are often transformed. Anna, for example, fosters Dido's desire for Aeneas by encouraging her to think of herself in implicitly masculine terms, as a powerful ruler seeking a fit consort: 'were you Empress of the world / Aeneas well deserves to be your love' (3.1.68). If this recalls Tamburlaine's wooing of Zenocrate, this echo is underlined by Dido's rhapsody on Aeneas's beauty, unconventionally placing the man as the object of the woman's desiring gaze (3.1.84–95). Dizzyingly combining power, love, and submission, Dido's later order to Aeneas 'in mine arms make thy Italy, / Whose crown and kingdom rests at thy command' (3.4.56–7) reworks a familiar image of female sexuality as a territory to be colonized and ruled by a powerful male, unusual here in being employed by a woman of herself, rather than as a male-authored objectification. This reversal is continued when Dido recreates Aeneas as her late husband Sichaeus – and therefore as her consort – giving him the jewels with which her husband wooed her, in another startling example of the multiple instances of identity-crossings and regenderings that recur in this play.

By creating Aeneas as her spouse, offering him her husband's clothes and place by her at the table, Dido does not merely trouble the normal hierarchy of husband–wife relationships: she also initiates a remaking of family, in which Ascanius becomes their shared child (2.1). Boy children, as much as women, are objects of desire and exchange in this play, something which obviously reflects the fact that it was written for a boys' company, but also expresses a distinctive eroticism, focused on relationships that cross differences of age and status. In 4.5, Cupid poses as Ascanius to play out a scene of grotesquely comic transgressive wooing with one of Marlowe's few lower-class characters, the Nurse. But the play's most celebrated instance of such an encounter is its opening, where the discovery space, often used in Renaissance dramas to reveal erotic intimacy, discloses one of the Renaissance's most celebrated instances of male–male eroticism, as Jupiter dandles the gods' messenger-boy Ganymede on his knee. Mimicking heterosexual courtship, this is a flirtatious relationship, in which the power differential between Jupiter and Ganymede significantly shapes their interactions. The gift to Ganymede of the jewels Juno wore on her marriage-day emphasizes the parallel between the lovely boy and the mature wife, and also anticipates Dido's presentation to Aeneas of her husband's jewels. Acknowledging the commercialized nature of his erotic transaction with Jupiter, Ganymede promises that in exchange for the gifts he demands, 'I'll hug with you a hundred times' (1.1.46–8). Unlike Abigail, he knows how to profit from his status as a sexual commodity.

The contest between Ganymede and Juno for possession of Jupiter is re-enacted in *Edward II*. Seen here from the woman's point of view, it is presented in darker and more bitter terms, as Queen Isabella uses this classical analogy to bewail her rejection by her husband Edward, promising,

> Like frantic Juno will I fill the earth
> With ghastly murmur of my sighs and cries
> For never doted Jove on Ganymede
> So much as he on cursed Gaveston.
>   (*EII* 1.4.178–81)

This perception of Gaveston as occupying the role of beautiful, youthful love object of a more powerful man is widely shared in *Edward II*: Mortimer's acknowledgment that 'the mightiest kings have had their minions' (1.4.390) aligns him with the erotic favourites of Alexander and Hercules, among others. But Gaveston does not see himself as occupying only this subordinated, juvenile position. Rather, he imagines his liaison with Edward as empowering him, and raising him above his lowly origins: 'My knee shall bow to none but to the King' (1.1.19). Homoerotic desire in this case enables a subversion of social hierarchy: Gaveston's 'bliss' (1.1.4) at being invited to share the kingdom with his 'dearest friend' (1.1.2) intertwines genuine love with the pleasure of gaining access to power. Gaveston imagines himself occupying a place at the heart of court culture in this opening scene, elaborating a fantasy of courtly erotic entertainments focused on a spectacle strongly reminiscent of the one that opens *Dido*, in which he occupies the role of powerful spectator and 'a lovely boy in Dian's shape' (1.1.60) will be displayed for his pleasure. Yet with its reference to Actaeon (a hunter who spied on Diana bathing and was destroyed by his own hounds for this voyeurism), this fantasy also highlights the perils of his transgressive desires and ambitions, in terms echoed later when Gaveston prematurely celebrates what proves to be a temporary escape from the lords' 'threats . . . larums, and . . . hot pursuits' (2.5.2). As a result of his capture by the lords, he is unceremoniously dislodged from his privileged position, and his degradation is powerfully imaged as the due result of his transgressions in Lancaster's attack on him as 'Monster of men . . . Greekish strumpet' (2.5.14–15).

A fuller understanding of the debatable homoeroticism of the relationship between Gaveston and Edward can be gained by setting it in the context of the homosociality of the peers, which is undermined by this dyad that they do not control and that refuses to abide by their rules for interaction. One of Edward's key errors, fatally turning the peers against him, is his refusal to ransom Mortimer Senior: the nobles fear that this failure of homosocial obligation could prefigure larger rebellion and disorder in the realm (2.2.140–98). In a world where relations between men can be homosocial or homoerotic, orderly or transgressive, Edward and Gaveston elect to set themselves apart from men who are in every sense their peers. Gaveston paradoxically places his love for Edward, this uniquely public man, in opposition to the public realm, rejecting the values of both 'the lordly peers' and the 'multitude' (1.1.18, 21) in favour of his intimate, personal connection with the king. Edward shares this fundamentally disorderly and transgressive understanding of the relationship between his public role and personal desires: his assurance to Gaveston that 'but to honour thee / Is Edward pleased with kingly regiment' (1.1.163–4) voices at best a troubling confusion about the purpose of power, at worst a problematic willingness to appropriate it for personal ends.

Towards the end of the play, Edward is forced to reflect on his misunderstanding of royal power, in terms that elegiacally recast his previous confidence: 'But what are kings when regiment is gone, / But perfect shadows in a sunshine day?' (5.1.26–7). As power and status melt away from him, Edward is able to retrieve traces of an orderly self through a stoic reassertion of masculinity. Marlowe consistently places a high value on heroic endurance as a mark of masculinity: Tamburlaine's self-wounding is an extreme example, an extraordinary enactment of a masculinity that is confirmed by the combination of stoic fortitude with masochism and vulnerable openness that Coppélia Kahn argues typifies the martial heroes of Shakespeare's Roman plays.[14] Edward displays a surprising kinship with these heroes when he undergoes a shaving with puddle water designed to be harsh enough to disfigure him, in conditions bad enough 'to poison any man, / Much more a king brought up so tenderly' (5.5.5–6), revealing a tolerance for suffering that echoes Tamburlaine's masochistic heroics: 'He hath a body able to endure / More than we can inflict' (10).

But death, of course, is more than even Edward's newly stoic masculinity can endure, and the precise form of his death has been a key moment for many interpreters of the play, particularly those who are concerned with its complex dramatization of the interrelations of gender and sexuality. Though modern editions often add stage directions specifying – as Mark Thornton Burnett's Everyman edition does, for example – that '[LIGHTBORN *murders* EDWARD *by penetrating him with the red-hot poker*]', Marlowe's dramatic text is in fact less explicit about the manner of Edward's death. Lightborn demands the preparation of a red-hot spit, a table, and a featherbed at 5.5.30–3, but by the time the execution is carried out some eighty lines later, the spit appears to have been forgotten, and only the table is mentioned. As the action unfolds, it moves away from the spit, so punitively homophobic interpretations of Edward's death that suggest that its manner is a punishment fitting his supposedly sodomitical crime can only do so by subjecting the text to a certain amount of ideological strain. Interpreting this scene for academic criticism or performance, we should attend to the uncertainty of the text, and resist the temptation to make it simpler and more shocking than it is.

Conclusion

In this chapter, I have argued that the representation of gender and sexuality in Marlowe's works is deeply implicated in the structures of his society, and needs to be interpreted with an eye to the social, ethical, and political repercussions for the fictional worlds he creates of orderly and disorderly forms of gendered and erotic behaviour. One work that offers exceptionally rich material for this subject, the Ovidian erotic narrative poem *Hero and Leander*, has proved difficult to accommodate to this argument, even though in Marlowe's time the poem's verbal formulations of sexual desire and gender identity – like those of another Marlovian love poem, 'The Passionate Shepherd' – were immensely influential. The dazzling poetry of *Hero and Leander* expresses a delirious pleasure in physical beauty and in eroticism, grounded by a saucily anti-romantic perspective on love. *Hero and Leander* shares with the plays a sense that erotic desire often emerges in situations where there is a power differential, an attention to the body as both attractive and vulnerable, and an awareness of the immense differences between men and women. Yet, insofar as it 'takes as its theme the utter arbitrariness of desire',[15] and represents its interactions between men, women, and gods in essentially asocial ways, it proves resistant to the kinds of politically grounded interpretations I have offered of the plays.

Ovid, Marlowe's primary inspiration in *Hero and Leander*, provided Renaissance writers with a richly varied repertoire of situations and images for investigating and representing sexual passion and its effects, in highly gendered ways, and his influence is often visible in Marlowe's plays. Marlowe was the first translator of Ovid's Elegies into English, and with their cool eroticism and anti-romantic stance, they provide an important context for his representation of love, gender relations, and sexuality in his more famous works. Indeed, Marlowe's plays could be read as a complex response to the challenge laid down by 'violent Tragedy' in Book 3, Elegy 1 to 'move grave things in lofty style' (23) and 'men's acts resound' (25). In 1599, a volume containing ten of Marlowe's Ovidian Elegies along with a collection of forty-eight political epigrams by Sir John Davies was publicly burned. It has often been assumed that this was primarily a gesture of political censorship, in which Marlowe's frivolous erotic poetry was condemned by its proximity to Davies's satirical epigrams. But Ian Frederick Moulton has recently argued that this event should in fact be interpreted in relation to Marlowe's distinctive handling of gender and sexuality in his translation. Moulton contends that because 'Marlowe's translation of the Elegies celebrates effeminacy and argues for the pleasures of subjection',[16] in the context of a world where, as we have seen, the maintenance of appropriate gendered and sexual behaviours was crucial to social and political stability, the poems could be read as offering a threateningly disorderly vision of the heterosexual coupling that was supposed to form the cornerstone of patriarchal society. This complex and ambiguous mingling of the political and the erotic in a literary production that was written out of, and addressed to, a predominantly masculine imaginative and social universe, but that exposed the ideological precariousness of the gender relations that shaped and sustained it, provides a fitting last word on the volatile and multifaceted presentation of gender and sexuality in Marlowe's writings.

NOTES

1. Sara Mendelson and Patricia Crawford, *Women in Early Modern England 1550–1720* (Oxford University Press, 1997).

2. On women theatregoers, see Jean E. Howard, *The Stage and Social Struggle in Early Modern England* (London: Routledge, 1994). Sasha Roberts, *Reading Shakespeare's Poems in Early Modern England* (Basingstoke: Palgrave, 2002) reveals that women were enthusiastic readers of Ovidian verse like Marlowe's.

3. Except for the rivalrous encounters of Zenocrate and Zabina in *Tamburlaine*, and Dido and Anna in *Dido, Queen of Carthage*, women's relations with each other are significantly absent.

4. In this chapter Marlowe's works are cited from *The Complete Plays*, Mark Thornton Burnett (ed.), Everyman (London: Dent, 1999), and *The Complete Poems*, Mark Thornton Burnett (ed.), Everyman (London: Dent, 2000).

5. Qtd in Jonathan Goldberg, 'Sodomy and Society: the Case of Christopher Marlowe', in Richard Wilson (ed.), *Christopher Marlowe* (London: Longman, 1999), pp. 54–61.

6. Eve Kosofsky Sedgwick, *Epistemology of the Closet* (New York: Harvester Wheatsheaf, 1991), p. 184.

7. The blazon is a poetic form which describes a body by enumerating its constituent parts: see Nancy J. Vickers, 'Diana Described: Scattered Woman and Scattered Rhyme', *CritI* 8 (1981), 265–79.

8. The Hostess appears only in the 1616 text; in the 1604 text, the Duchess is alone. References to *Doctor Faustus* are to the 1604 text.

9. Emily C. Bartels, *Spectacles of Strangeness: Imperialism, Alienation, and Marlowe* (Philadelphia: University of Pennsylvania Press, 1993), p. 25.

10. Gail Kern Paster, *The Body Embarrassed: Drama and the Disciplines of Shame in Early Modern England* (Ithaca: Cornell University Press, 1993).

11. Joanna Gibbs, 'Marlowe's Politic Women', in J. A. Downie and J. T. Parnell (eds.), *Constructing Christopher Marlowe* (Cambridge University Press, 2000), pp. 164–76 (p. 165).

12. Mario Di Gangi, 'Marlowe, Queer Studies, and Renaissance Homoeroticism', in Paul Whitfield White (ed.), *Marlowe, History and Sexuality: New Critical Essays on Christopher Marlowe* (New York: AMS Press, 1998), pp. 195–212 (p. 204).

13. Peter Stallybrass, 'Patriarchal Territories: the Body Enclosed', in Margaret W. Ferguson, Maureen Quilligan, and Nancy J. Vickers (eds.), *Rewriting the Renaissance: The Discourses of Sexual Difference in Early Modern Europe* (University of Chicago Press, 1986), pp. 123–42.

14. Coppélia Kahn, *Roman Shakespeare: Warriors, Wounds, and Women* (London: Routledge, 1997).

15. Claude J. Summers, '*Hero and Leander*: the Arbitrariness of Desire', in Downie and Parnell (eds.), *Constructing Christopher Marlowe*, pp. 133–47 (p. 133).

16. Ian Frederick Moulton, *Before Pornography: Erotic Writing in Early Modern England* (Oxford University Press, 2000), p. 104.

READING LIST

Bredbeck, Gregory W. *Sodomy and Interpretation: Marlowe to Milton*. Ithaca: Cornell University Press, 1991.

Deats, Sara Munson. *Sex, Gender, and Desire in the Plays of Christopher Marlowe*. London: Associated University Presses, 1997.

Di Gangi, Mario. *The Homoerotics of Early Modern Drama*. Cambridge University Press, 1997.

Findlay, Alison. *A Feminist Perspective on Renaissance Drama*. Oxford: Blackwell, 1998.

Goldberg, Jonathan. *Sodometries: Renaissance Texts, Modern Sexualities*. Stanford University Press, 1992.

Henderson, Diana. *Passion Made Public: Elizabethan Lyric, Gender and Performance*. Urbana: University of Illinois Press, 1995.

Orgel, Stephen. *Impersonations: The Performance of Gender in Shakespeare's England*. Cambridge University Press, 1996.

Shepherd, Simon. *Marlowe and the Politics of Elizabethan Theatre*. Brighton: Harvester Press, 1986.

Smith, Bruce. *Homosexual Desire in Shakespeare's England: A Cultural Poetics*. University of Chicago Press, 1991.

16

LOIS POTTER

Marlowe in theatre and film

Since Marlowe's four major plays are so different from each other, it is not surprising that their performance histories have been equally different. Initially, three of them at least were famous as vehicles for Edward Alleyn, the actor who created, and perhaps literally owned, the roles of Tamburlaine, Faustus, and Barabas (*Edward II* was probably written for a different company). *The Jew of Malta*, one of the most successful plays of the 1590s, was so completely associated with him that no one else dared play Barabas until after Alleyn's death in 1626. The play was revived in 1633, and there may also have been a production of *Tamburlaine the Great* as late as 1641, just before the outbreak of the Civil War and the closing of the London theatres.[1] References to *Faustus*, *Tamburlaine*, and *The Jew of Malta* in Civil War pamphlets suggest that performances were still part of collective memory, though the plays were no longer associated with Marlowe's name.[2]

Completely forgotten after the Civil War, *Edward II* and *The Jew of Malta* were the first Marlowe plays to receive serious attention from an eighteenth-century editor, probably because they seemed the most stage-worthy. They appeared in Robert Dodsley's *Old English Plays* in 1744 and 1780, respectively, and *The Jew of Malta* was revived in 1818 in an adaptation by Solomon Penley which incorporated lines from *Edward II*. But the Marlowe who was recreated in the nineteenth century was more like a mad Romantic genius, thanks in particular to the inaccurate belief that he had been killed by a rival 'in his lewd love'.[3] Well into the next century, he was admired chiefly for *Faustus* and *Tamburlaine*, plays about men with 'aspiring minds', which looked all the more impressive because they seemed unstageable. From the 1920s and 1930s onwards, however, the accumulation of new evidence about the circumstances of the poet's death and its possible connections with the Elizabethan secret service gradually began to reveal a more cynical Marlowe, perhaps more interesting to the late twentieth century. As a result, *The Jew of Malta* once again attracted directors, while *Edward II* came almost to dominate the Marlowe canon.

Doctor Faustus

Doctor Faustus has the longest and most complicated acting tradition, not only because it exists in two different texts but also because its subject matter does not belong exclusively to Marlowe. Throughout the seventeenth century, there are records of its performance by English actors (often alongside *The Jew of Malta*) in the countries now known as Germany, the Czech Republic, Austria, and Poland.[4] Since the Faust legend was already known in these countries from other sources, including the German *Faust-Book* that Marlowe had read in translation, it is difficult to distinguish his influence from that of the native tradition. Successive adaptations, in Britain and abroad, which made the play increasingly spectacular and comic, only developed what, judging from contemporary references to bushy-haired devils with fireworks, was already there. As Michael Hattaway puts it, 'it was the spectacle of the devils and not the mind of the hero that was at the centre of the play'.[5] A version published in 1663, probably used in revivals in 1662 and 1675, replaces the scene at the Pope's court with one in Babylon, presumably to avoid giving offence to Roman Catholic sympathizers at the Restoration court.[6] It also borrows lines from *The Jew of Malta* (which must have dropped out of the repertory by then). By now, Faustus was making trees move and calling up an army of devils. The actor William Mountford, who probably played Mephistopheles to Thomas Betterton's Faustus,[7] took the farcical possibilities still further. His *Life and Death of Doctor Faustus, made into a Farce, with the Humours of Harlequin and Scaramouche* (published 1697), was, as its title indicates, a vehicle for two comic actors. Faustus's great speech to Helen of Troy became 'O Mephostopholis! what would I give to gain a Kiss from off those lovely Lips' (p. 6). In later Harlequin plays, the clown and the doctor merged into the 'Harlequin Doctor Faustus' who appears in eighteenth-century pantomimes.

Goethe's *Faust*, a great and almost unactable work (Part One, 1808; Part Two, 1832), was largely based on German folk drama and puppet shows, but Goethe had also read Marlowe's play (Heller, p. 118). So *Faustus*, now seen in the light of the later masterpiece, shook off its farcical associations to become the most widely studied work by a contemporary of Shakespeare. Its earliest revivals set it in the context of medieval/Renaissance thought. William Poel's productions in 1896 and 1904 for the Elizabethan Stage Society were part of a movement to perform Elizabethan drama in the kind of theatre for which it was written. Faustus wore the surplice depicted on the play's 1624 title page and conjured with a formula from Reginald Scot's *True Discovery of Witchcraft*. Though Poel cut heavily, he did not reject all the comic material, and the scene at the Pope's court is said to have been genuinely funny.[8] On the other hand, Nugent Monck directed *Faustus* at the first Canterbury Festival (1929) as part of a double bill with the medieval morality play *Everyman*; not surprisingly, it was 'an austere discourse on the wages of sin'.[9]

The most interesting pre-war production (New York, 1937) starred the twenty-one year old Orson Welles, with an African–American actor, Jack Carter, as Mephistopheles.[10] Welles also co-directed (with John Houseman) and designed the production himself; music was by the writer Paul Bowles. The text, though heavily cut, nevertheless retained the Seven Deadly Sins (as puppets), some of the clown scenes, played as slapstick, and all the Faustus–Mephistopheles scenes, somewhat rearranged. A keen amateur magician, Welles used lighting and actors in black against a background of black velvet to create spectacular effects in the scene at the papal court. A procession of dishes for the Pope's feast came to a halt as a suckling pig and other animals rose twelve feet in the air and danced. Then,

> three Cardinals' hats flew off like giant saucers. When the Pope's own miter rose from his head and a flash box exploded under his skirt amid cries of terror and fiendish laughter, the procession broke up, leaving Faustus alone on a stage that was suddenly and completely bare.[11]

Welles's own performance benefited from his own identification with the role of the doomed genius (p. 235). Like *Macbeth*, the Faust legend has sometimes been credited with a sinister effect on performers. Two other Faustuses who had achieved success in films attracted similar facile comments about selling their souls for success when they returned to play Faustus in the theatre – Richard Burton in 1965 and Jude Law in 2002.[12] Houseman's memoirs even inspired a production that combined Marlowe's play with Welles's version to dramatize a theatre producer's diabolical bargain.[13]

Welles had used twentieth-century technology to make *Faustus* both funny and horrific. The relation between these two aspects of the play has been the main problem for most directors. Michael Benthall's Old Vic production of 1961 combined spectacle with psychological realism, as when the hilarious practical jokes at the Pope's court were followed by Faustus's cursing by the friars and his own wry awareness that their ritual was needless for someone already damned. Paul Daneman's young intellectual was never unaware of his situation: even his simple line, 'I'll go on foot', when Mephistopheles offered him a choice of conveyances, hinted at his disenchantment with magical technology. In keeping with a newer direction in Marlowe criticism, Clifford Williams at the Royal Shakespeare Theatre (1968) achieved irony at Faustus's expense by depicting the magical apparitions as they 'really' were – hideous and grotesque – not as they appeared to their enraptured

2 In Clifford Williams's production of *Doctor Faustus* for the Royal Shakespeare Theatre, Stratford-upon-Avon, in 1968, the Duchess of Vanholt (Diane Fletcher) flirtatiously feeds Faustus (Eric Porter) the grapes that Mephistopheles (Terence Hardiman) has just brought her, while her complaisant husband (Richard Simpson) looks on. Photograph by Thomas Holte.

victim. In the production, the austere Faustus and Mephostopheles mingled easily with such clearly comic figures as the Duke and Duchess of Vanholt (Plate 2). Adrian Noble's production at the Royal Exchange, Manchester (1981), was praised for its skilful integration of the comic scenes with those involving Faustus. 'Mephostophilis moves invisible about the outer stage, turning the pages of the book for Robin as he has just done for Faustus, helping with the pronunciation of Demogorgon and whispering in Dick's ears some of the drinks that await him in the tavern.'[14]

Faustus has also been done on a small scale, with extensive, often symbolically relevant, doubling. As if agreeing with Mephistopheles's 'Why, this is hell', John Barton's Royal Shakespeare Company touring version with Ian McKellen (1974) took place entirely in Faustus's study. The Good and Evil Angels were a hand-puppet and a voodoo doll, operated and voiced by Faustus himself; the Seven Deadly Sins were also puppets. The play seemed to be happening entirely in Faustus's mind, yet, as if to undercut his apparent freedom, devils spoke the Chorus's lines, so that, as Robert Cushman (*Observer* 1 Sept. 1974) pointed out, the entire play seemed diabolically controlled. Doubling has tended to enforce a pessimistic reading. In an Oxford college production of 1984, even the Old Man, masked and enveloped in heavy robes, finally turned out to be Mephistopheles.[15] David Lam's Young Vic production of 2002 used only seven actors, initially depicted as monks studying in a library. In the show of the Seven Deadly Sins, Faustus himself took the role of Pride, and Helen of Troy appeared only as a mirror into which Faustus gazed, rapturously addressing a fantasy of himself. At the end, after the Chorus spoke the moral, the actors resumed their stations at the library table and Mephistopheles once again handed Faustus the magic book.

Although numerous films narrate versions of the Faust story, Marlowe's play has figured in only two. Though a critical disaster, the 1967 film based on Nevill Coghill's highly publicized Oxford production of 1965, with Richard Burton and Elizabeth Taylor, had some interesting ideas: in the pageant of the Deadly Sins, Wrath turns into Tamburlaine and Covetousness into Barabas. The 1994 Faust, written and directed by Jan Švankmajer and set in modern Prague, incorporates some of Marlowe's dialogue along with that of other versions of the legend, both popular and literary.

Tamburlaine

Tamburlaine, simply because it is a two-part play with a large cast, has achieved relatively few revivals, most of them conflations of the two parts. The first conflation was performed at Yale University in 1919; Nevill Coghill's revival in Worcester College gardens (1933) confined itself to Part Two.[16] Whereas at Yale Tamburlaine was sympathetically portrayed as an angry young alternative to the elderly establishment that had just conducted World War I, the earliest successful commercial production, by Tyrone Guthrie (1959), starred Donald Wolfit as a barbaric, frightening, and increasingly insane hero. Basil Ashmore's adaptation, which Guthrie in turn cut and adapted, was written in 1948, with Tamburlaine as a Hitler figure (Geckle, pp. 55 and 65). This anti-war approach has dominated most subsequent productions.

In Keith Hack's 1972 Tamburlaine for the Edinburgh Assembly Hall and the Glasgow Citizens' Theatre, a striking set featured corpses on gallows and wheels, with a central platform, striped in white, red, and black, which was also Tamburlaine's chariot, sometimes seeming dangerously likely to careen into the audience. Torchlight reflected off the gold-adorned costumes; the lights were brought up, non-naturalistically, when Tamburlaine showed Theridamas his heap of treasure. The play was divided into three acts to show a clear progression from triumph to suffering to death, with a different Tamburlaine in each act (Rupert Frazer, Jeremy Kissoon, and Mike Gwilym) so as to work against excessive identification with the hero. The text was altered and transposed (Mycetes became Bajazeth's uncle, a new Chorus acquired many more lines): one reviewer called it 'Brecht's *Tamburlaine*'.[17]

Peter Hall's National Theatre production of 1976, though condensed into a long two-part play, gave the fullest text yet seen. In their excellent and detailed review of this production, J. S. Cunningham and Roger Warren praise Hall for bringing out the play's symbolism and parallels through the different colours referred to in the text, with other colour-coding to indicate the diversity of Tamburlaine's journeys and conquests.[18] Though Hall did not describe the play as 'Brechtian', his diary entries from the rehearsal period record his gradual discovery that the dialogue 'must be shared with the audience – told like a story teller'.[19] The 'engaging air of teasing connivance' with which Tamburlaine (Albert Finney) and other characters addressed the audience brought out the play's humour as well as its bewildering savagery (Cunningham and Warren, p. 162).

While there have been attempts at small-scale productions, *Tamburlaine* has generally worked best on a large scale. It has been played in France (dir. Antonio Diaz-Florian at the Cartoucherie de Vincennes, 1989), in the style familiar from the work of Peter Brook and Ariane Mnouchkine: a multinational cast, lots of music, an experiment in style. Terry Hands's production for the anniversary of Marlowe's death, in the small Swan Theatre in Stratford (1993), was even more effective when it transferred to the larger Barbican stage in London. Starring Antony Sher as an athletic and animalistic hero, who swung on ropes and walked head-first down a pole, it emphasized cruelty and blood not only visibly but sometimes also palpably, particularly for those in the front row, who felt assaulted by 'theatrical terrorism'.[20] Even more than the other productions mentioned, it divided its audience between, on the one hand, admiration of sheer spectacle and energy (Plate 3), and, on the other, horror at the way it was used. There was no summing up after the hero's death, no closure; instead, the last line, which Sher apparently spoke with different emphases in different performances, was 'And shall I die, and this unconquered?' 'This', as Martin Wiggins wrote in a perceptive review, 'might have meant heaven, or the Swan theatre, or the rest of the known world' (p. 84).

The Jew of Malta

Both *The Jew of Malta* and *Edward II* have owed many of their revivals to pairings with the better-known Shakespeare plays, *The Merchant of Venice* and *Richard II*. The only pre-twentieth-century production of *The Jew of Malta* (1818) was prepared for the star actor Edmund Kean, who had already been successful as Richard III, Othello, and Shylock. The play was

3   Antony Sher as Tamburlaine in Terry Hands's conflation of the two parts for the Royal Shakespeare Company, performed at the Swan Theatre, Stratford-upon-Avon, in 1993.

given a spectacular production, with a cast of twenty-one speaking parts. Though Penley developed the love interest involving Mathias and Lodowick (mainly by using the dialogue of Edward II and Gaveston!), he cut Barabas's part where it was bawdy, grotesque, or potentially blasphemous, as in the irreverent comparison of his wealth to Job's. Barabas did not poison the convent (though Abigail died anyway), nor did he frame one friar for the murder of the other. In his first scene with Ithamore he made it clear that he was exaggerating his villainy in order to draw Ithamore out. One of Penley's few additions to the role occurred when Barabas heard of Abigail's death, paused, and then briefly explained his lack of emotion:

> Oppression's burning pow'r hath dried
> The source of frail humanity for ever.
> No, no, I cannot shed a tear.
>
> (*JM* 4.1)

Penley's prologue, which replaced the one spoken by Machiavelli, praised Marlowe as 'the bright star to Shakspeare's glorious sun' but dissociated the theatre from the anti-semitic sentiments in the play, which tactlessly premiered during the Passover season.[21]

A similar desire to dissociate the production from the play has led to considerable ingenuity in later revivals. Some directors have followed Kean's path and created a noble Barabas; others have attempted to disinfect the play by using humour or rather, as James L. Smith argues, by over-emphasizing T. S. Eliot's interpretation of the play, usually paraphrased as 'savage farce'.[22] In the Phoenix Society production of 1922, which audiences found hysterically funny, Barabas (Balliol Holloway) was 'a monster of iniquity' and his death was simply one more joke (Smith, p. 12). Responses to the play were more evenly balanced in two major British productions commemorating the 1964 quatercentenary of Marlowe's birth. Both Clifford Williams (RSC, Aldwych Theatre, London, 1964, then Stratford, 1965) and Peter Cheeseman (Victoria Theatre, Stoke-on-Trent, 1964) were at home in black comedy, perhaps the most popular genre of the decade. When the Williams production was recast and revived at Stratford in 1965, alongside *The Merchant of Venice*, Eric Porter played both Barabas and Shylock; curiously, contemporary photographs show that he looked more dignified as Marlowe's character. When Barabas and Ithamore hovered over the poisoned porridge, Barabas's curse on Abigail was not only frightening but also prophetic of his death, when he again cursed in the boiling cauldron. But much of the production was farcical: goggle-eyed friars, nuns with ridiculous coifs, and a prostitute and pimp too moronic to carry out their own villainous intentions. This combination of involvement and distancing was another 'Brechtian'

4   Ferneze (John Carlisle) confronts Barabas (Alun Armstrong) in Barry Kyle's production of
The Jew of Malta (Royal Shakespeare Company at the Swan Theatre, Stratford-upon-Avon,
1987).

feature. It seems to have prevented reviewers from dwelling on the play's
anti-semitism.

In 1987 the play was again performed at Stratford opposite a production of *The Merchant of Venice*, but the roles of Shylock and Barabas were
played by different actors and there was no attempt to draw out the similarities between the two plays. While Barry Kyle's *The Jew of Malta* brought
out the modern implications of the story, particularly in the treatment of
the sympathetic, victimized Abigail, it also stressed the villainy of Ferneze,
played by John Carlisle (who doubled as Machiavel) as a worthy antagonist for Barabas and a whited sepulchre in his austere robes (Plate 4). As
Barabas, Alun Armstrong, expertly playing off the audience, gave such a
fine comic performance that *The Jewish Chronicle*'s reviewer, though he
agreed that the play was anti-semitic, added, 'It is also anti-Christian and
anti-Moslem. Indeed, it is anti-everything except . . . a good laugh.'²³ Some
directors of the 1990s, feeling that a purely comic approach was an evasion
of responsibility, attempted to deal with the problem, like Penley in 1818,
by historicizing the play. Stevie Simkin, who directed it for King Alfred's
Performing Arts Company, Winchester, in 1997, set it in a factory in Nazi-
occupied Warsaw in 1939.²⁴ A German officer, who also plays Ferneze, forces
the other characters – Polish Jews, non-Jewish Poles, and German Nazis – to

perform the play to show the Jews their inferiority. In the course of the production, the Jews develop strategies for subverting the text and in the final scene all the actors revolt and remove their costumes, revealing their 'real' clothes; only 'Ferneze' is left, ridiculous and imprisoned in his role, to speak the final lines.

In 1999 Ian McDiarmid, who had already played the role in the BBC's radio homage to Marlowe in 1993, recreated it at the Almeida Theatre, directed by Michael Grandage. One reviewer felt that the comic element was taken so far that 'it was difficult to take the Christian persecution seriously',[25] another that the production, after deliberately detaching the play from its historical context by cutting Machiavel's Prologue, had exploited that context by making Barabas a loving father whose adoption of Ithamore after Abigail was an expression of the need for love. Despite the many farcical and metatheatrical moments, the final image evoked by the play was of a father 'heroically resisting a Nazi death-oven',[26] and, as Ferneze uttered his final couplet, 'Barabas's face appeared at the porthole cut into the boiling cauldron' (Smith, p. 128).

The more visually expressive production style of the non-English-speaking theatre perhaps makes it easier to subvert an unacceptable meaning without subverting the play itself. Bernard Sobel (Gennevilliers and the Théâtre de la Renaissance, Paris, 1976) emphasized the distinction often made by critics between the grandly cosmopolitan trader of the first part of the play and the gleeful killer of the second part. At first, Barabas (René Loyon) was elderly, bearded, bespectacled, and fairly dignified. When the Maltese confiscated his wealth, however, the production style suddenly changed. From a trap-door, a hand emerged, holding an enormous cardboard nose; Barabas put it on, removed his beard, adopted a hunchback and limp like Richard III, and curled his hands into claws, becoming a stage caricature of a Jew.[27] When this grotesque character disappeared into the cauldron, a curtain fell in front of him, emphasizing the theatricality of his role (Jacquot and Vigouroux, p. 360). The Prologue was spoken not by Machiavel but the ghost of Marlowe, who, speaking of laws written in blood, touched the still-bleeding wound on his own face (p. 352). Thus, the production was contextualized both in Marlowe's own milieu and in later history.[28] Again, in 2002, when Gert Voss played Barabas in an Austrian production directed by Peter Zadek, the character began by removing 'a grotesque mask of the kind that Nazi propagandists such as Julius Streicher used to characterize Semitic features'.[29] The emphasis on the constructed nature of his stereotype apparently made it possible, even in Hitler's homeland, to be comic as well as satiric; this Barabas ended up 'feeding poisoned seed to the birds' (Billington).

Edward II

The most remarkable development in Marlowe's performance history is the extent to which, by the late twentieth century, *Edward II* became almost equal to *Doctor Faustus* as Marlowe's most performed and adapted play. Two factors contributed: its adaptation by Bertolt Brecht, whose influence on mid-twentieth-century Marlowe productions has already been evident, and a turn-of-the-century fascination with homosexuality and homophobia. The potential autobiography in the play could have been known to its first modern directors but, given the Oscar Wilde trial of 1895, it is not surprising that the earliest revivals – by William Poel in London in 1903 and Frank Benson at the Stratford-upon-Avon festival in 1905 – largely played down the sexual element. The *Manchester Guardian* reviewer, C. E. Montague, commented that it was hard to make Isabella and Gaveston 'both intelligible to a modern audience and at the same time true to Marlowe's intention'.[30] Both Poel and Benson made Gaveston a 'typical' Frenchman, impudent and frivolous; Poel called him a 'quite delightful stage character' (Speaight, p. 180), and in 1905 a reviewer praised the 'light-heartedness' with which he met his fate.[31] Benson's production was seen in the context of the Shakespearean kings he had played, particularly his sympathetic Richard II; reviewers usually called Edward a 'weakling'.[32] Poel conveyed the horror of the king's murder through suggestion: Lightborn entered behind the bench where Edward was sleeping and pressed his hand over Edward's forehead. The curtains closed; a shriek was heard; Lightborn re-entered with Matrevis and Gurney, putting his gloves back on (Speaight, p. 180). In Benson's version, what shocked the audience was not the murder but the later appearance of Mortimer's head in a bucket, which upset 'the fairer portion of the house' so much that the business was cut after the first performance.[33]

Successful productions of *Edward II* by the Phoenix Society in London (1923), and in translation in Prague (1922) and Berlin (1923), may have inspired Brecht's decision to adapt the play (with much verbatim use of the 1912 translation by Walter Heymel) for performance at the Munich Chamber Theatre in 1924; another cause is said to have been the success in Berlin of its more famous twin, *Richard II*, in 1922.[34] *Leben Eduards des Zweiten von England* was the first play Brecht directed, with many devices that later came to be trademarks of his style: a ballad singer; captions with the dates of events (mostly inaccurate); and stylized white faces to indicate the terror of the soldiers in the battle scenes (p. 401). Brecht's own terse writing stresses the play's cruelty as well as the irreverence shown to authority figures. Gaveston sees himself, and is seen, as 'King Eddie's Whore', a portrayal impossible in the English and American theatre of this period. Yet Edward's betrayal has religious overtones, and his refusal to give up either Gaveston or his crown makes him stronger and more sympathetic than Marlowe's character. After successful performances in Germany, the play inspired other adaptations, some of which mingled Brecht with Marlowe, and it reached the English National Theatre in 1968 (directed by Frank Dunlop).

The two most significant English revivals of the Marlowe original, however, were at Cambridge: John Barton directed Toby Robertson in 1951, and when Robertson himself directed Derek Jacobi in 1958 Laurence Kitchen wrote that 'this play is a masterpiece fit for a national repertory'.[35] Robertson also directed Ian McKellen in a double bill with *Richard II* in 1969 (after the original Edward had dropped out). The director later recalled that in 1958 'it seemed extraordinary that you should actually do this on the stage at all', while in 1969, the year after the abolition of pre-production censorship by the Lord Chamberlain, it was possible to show Edward and Gaveston kissing.[36]

Charles R. Forker's exhaustive performance history of the play traces the process by which successive productions became less like history plays and more like polemics against a homophobic society.[37] In the Manchester Royal Exchange production of 1986 (directed by Nicholas Hytner) characters wallowed in the mud, as Edward's humiliation became the metaphor for the entire play. By the 1980s, the control of sexual behaviour had become a major issue in the Anglo-American world. Section 28, an amendment to Britain's Local Government Act in 1988, forbad the sponsoring of events, including 'artistic' ones, which might 'promote homosexuality'.[38] There was much debate at the time as to what 'promoting' might mean, and Marlowe's was one of the names that surfaced as an example of a 'gay' author. Apart from making *Edward II* unexpectedly topical, antagonism to Section 28 also created interest in other Marlowe plays that might be considered 'queer theatre', such as *Dido* (a touring production in 1993, directed by Michael Walling, opened in a gay nightclub).[39] Assumptions about Marlowe's life were also imported into productions of the better-known plays, as in the all-male *Faustus*, with Gerard Murphy in the title role, directed by Barry Kyle for the Royal Shakespeare Theatre in 1989 (a number of similar productions occurred around this time). Murphy's own production of *Edward II* in the same year mixed medieval and contemporary styles, locating Edward and Gaveston in the gay nightclub scene and giving Mortimer a moustache and hair style reminiscent of Hitler's. By contrast, Gaveston wore black leather, then a white outfit that reminded reviewers of Elvis Presley. Simon Russell Beale as Edward was contemptuous and decadent when around Gaveston (Plate 5), later becoming an anguished figure, and finally meeting what appeared to be a horrific death by red-hot poker. Though, as has been pointed

5 Edward II (Simon Russell Beale) with Gaveston (Grant Thatcher) and other followers antagonize the barons. Directed by Gerard Murphy (Royal Shakespeare Company at Swan Theatre, Stratford-upon-Avon, 1990).

out, there is no indication that Marlowe intended the final scene to resemble Holinshed's description,[40] this martyrdom reflected the sense of persecution among the gay community. One group that was brought into being by Section 28, OutReach, appeared in the *Edward II* film by Derek Jarman, released in 1991. Jarman, who had been diagnosed as HIV-positive at the end of 1986 and who died in 1994, published his screenplay under the title *Queer Edward II*, as a polemic 'dedicated to the repeal of all anti-gay laws, particularly Section 28'.[41] If Mortimer was a uniformed fanatic and Isabella a vampire who kills Kent by biting him in the neck, one reason may be the influence of an earlier film, *Sod'Em*, that Jarman planned but never made (the screenplay was published in 1996). In a future dystopia an actor called Edward, who has played Edward II, has to buy Marlowe's play under the counter. At the end, after book-burnings and pursuit, Edward and his boyfriend wake up in bed. Similarly, in the *Edward II* film, there is a surprise ending, as Lightborn kisses and releases Edward; it is Mortimer and Isabella who end up in a cage, with young Prince Edward, wearing his mother's clothes, playing on top. Though this may sound like a revenge fantasy, Jarman claimed a historical basis for it: one writer apparently told Edward III that his father had escaped from Berkeley Castle to North Italy (p. 158).

Also seeking topicality, during the controversy over American President Bill Clinton's attempt to liberalize the attitude of the US armed forces towards homosexuality in its ranks, the Washington Stage Company gave an *Edward II* (directed by Jim Stone, May 1993), set in a gun-carrying gangster-era with considerable gender cross-casting. In Budapest (directed by Jozsef Ruszt) it was set in a slaughterhouse with blood-smeared walls;[42] in Vienna's Burgtheater (1998) Edward was a 'pitiful, worn and gaudy circus clown who is abused, beaten, laughed at and thrown about, yet who manages to capture our sympathy'.[43] Unlike most other Edwards, Joseph Fiennes in 2001 (directed by Michael Grandage, Sheffield Crucible) was praised for showing spiritual growth as 'a tragic hero who acquires majesty only by losing kingship'.[44] Noting that the production emphasized the characters' sexuality far more than the text did, Benedict Nightingale decided that, in the climate of the early twenty-first century, a modern audience might 'find mere words and looks evasive'.[45] When Timothy Walker's production of *Edward II* was paired with *Dido, Queen of Carthage* and *Richard II* in the 2003 season of 'Regime Change' at Shakespeare's Globe, there was nothing evasive about its treatment of the relationship between the king and his favourites. Some members of this theatre's notoriously vocal audience initially expressed both shock and amusement at the sight of Edward and Gaveston kissing in the opening scene, as well as at the tall and powerful (male) Isabella leading her army, sword in hand, a nightmare vision of the dominating female. As

Edward, Liam Brennan gave full value both to the outrageousness of the early scenes and to the purity of his later devotion to the memory of those who had suffered on his account; the escalating conflict between king and barons was sometimes cultural and sometimes political, but always insoluble.

Tim Carroll's production of *Dido* suggested why: power is in the hands of cruel and greedy children. By contrast with the 'gentle heavens', whose role in his sufferings Edward refuses to acknowledge, the classical gods of *Dido* were children playing at dressing up, in clothes and shoes too big for them; when acting as *dei ex machina*, they swooped in from above via a playground slide. Since the roles of Cupid, Ascanius, and Ganymede were spoken by adult actors holding baby dolls, the Ganymede scene was comic rather than homoerotic. On the other hand, the adult passions of the human actors were treated with great sympathy. Aeneas (Will Keen) was extraordinarily moving in his account of the fall of Troy, while Dido (Rakie Ayola), initially charming and comic as she ran through the wildly changing emotions brought on by Cupid's arrows, was even more touching in her final despair than Brennan's Edward in his acting out of the stage direction 'the king rageth'. The juxtaposition of the two plays – one carefully Elizabethan though with touches of historical detail, the other resolutely modern in appearance – was ultimately unsettling. If Mortimer and the other barons sometimes seemed like adults who don't find children amusing, it was clear by the end that they were no more mature than their opponents.

Edward II is also the only Marlowe play to inspire a major ballet. Commissioned by the Stuttgart Ballet from choreographer David Bintley, with music specially composed by John McCabe, it was first performed in Stuttgart on 15 April 1995, then at the Birmingham Hippodrome on 9 October 1997. Its interpretation was similar to Jarman's and Murphy's, with Mortimer and his 'mob', in black leather, leaping 'in militaristic formation, banging their fists against the scenery'.[46] The first night in Stuttgart received a 15-minute ovation and in Britain the choreography was praised for its 'epic range, from delicacy to brutishness'.[47] Edward and Gaveston had 'perhaps the most sheerly beautiful music' while Edward and Isabella danced together 'with exquisite frigidity' and Mortimer seduced her 'in three pas de deux of accelerating passions and evil'.[48]

The Massacre at Paris

An adaptation of *The Massacre at Paris* was performed in France in 1972, the 400th anniversary of the St Bartholomew's Day Massacre.[49] Patrice Chéreau, who later directed *La Reine Margot*, a sensational film treatment of the Dumas novel inspired by the same event, created a famous production dominated by a swimming pool that became increasingly red in colour as the blood flowed. The Glasgow Citizens' Theatre revived the play in 1981 as a piece of high camp, emphasizing its function as a spectacle for Queen Elizabeth I (who, seated at the back of the stage, was its only spectator). An adaptation by the American Shakespeare Repertory Theatre in New York, January, 1987, began by telling its audience that they would be 'treated as Huguenots', filled their space with actors dressed as guards and prisoners, and occasionally turned searchlights over them. The play ended with the Huguenots taking up the murderers' chant of 'Tuez, tuez', proving that, in power, they would be equally intolerant.[50] A surprising number of other productions were given in the 1990s, including a frank send-up, at Pembroke College, Cambridge, which was advertised as 'The Complete Wars of Religion – Reduced'.

Marlowe's anniversary and its aftermath

Unlike the 1964 commemoration of Marlowe's 400th birthday, which led mainly to the yoking of his plays with those of his more famous contemporary, the commemoration of Marlowe's death in 1993 gave the opportunity for his works to stand alone. The BBC produced all six plays on the radio between May and October 1993, including *Dido* (a shortened version of the touring production already mentioned) and *The Massacre at Paris*.[51] The anniversary also inspired a number of plays based on Marlowe's life – or, rather, his death.[52] But the Marlowe best known to audiences at the beginning of the new millennium was the one depicted in the immensely popular film *Shakespeare in Love* (1998). Since its premise is that writers' lives have no reality compared to that of their imagined worlds, it might seem surprising that Rupert Everett's Marlowe is played neither as an overreacher nor as someone likely to have held any of the views in the Baines Note. He is charming, effortlessly authoritative, and, in his advice to the floundering young Shakespeare, always right. Many scholars, especially those interested in Marlowe as a gay writer, were annoyed at what looked like a sanitization of the historical character in the interest of popular success and the Academy Award that the film eventually won. In fact, Marlowe, as he appears in the film, is a character in Shakespeare's mind, not in his own. Even though his name does not appear in the credits, Everett's Marlowe sometimes has almost the same effect as Mercutio, who, according to a legend retailed by Dryden, was supposed to have been killed by Shakespeare halfway through *Romeo and Juliet* to prevent him from taking over the play. This is why Shakespeare's initial sense of guilt over Marlowe's death, though supposedly mistaken, is also quite justified. Ironically, the popularity of the film led to a resurgence of interest in Marlowe himself. At least some of the novels and screenplays written in the 1990s seem likely to result in the making of films about Marlowe in Lust (see Lisa Hopkins in this volume). While this interest probably began as parasitic on the cult of Shakespeare, it is possible that it will nevertheless take on a life of its own.[53]

NOTES

I should like to thank Darlene Farabee, Russell Jackson, Kelly Nutter, Michèle Willems, and Zdeněk Stříbrný for their help with the research toward this essay.

1. Anthony B. Dawson (ed.), *Tamburlaine the Great*, New Mermaids (London: A. and C. Black; New York: Norton, 1997), p. xxx.
2. See Lois Potter, 'Marlowe in the Civil War and Commonwealth: Some Adaptations and Parodies', in Kenneth Friedenreich, Roma Gill, and Constance B. Kuriyama (eds.), *'A Poet and A Filthy Play-Maker': New Essays on Christopher Marlowe* (New York: AMS Press, 1988), pp. 73–82.
3. See Thomas Dabbs, *Reforming Marlowe: The Nineteenth-Century Canonization of a Renaissance Dramatist* (Lewisburg: Bucknell University Press, 1991).
4. Otto Heller, 'Faust and Faustus: A Study of Goethe's Relation to Marlowe'. *LnL* 2 (1931), 109–10.
5. Michael Hattaway, *Elizabethan Popular Theatre: Plays in Performance* (London: Routledge and Kegan Paul, 1982), p. 167.
6. Richard H. Perkinson, 'A Restoration "Improvement" of *Doctor Faustus*', *ELH* 1 (1934), 305–24.
7. Their names are written next to these roles on the British Library copy of the play. See Richard Proudfoot, 'Marlowe and the Editors', in J. A. Downie and J. T. Parnell (eds.), *Constructing Christopher Marlowe* (Cambridge University Press, 2000), p. 44.
8. Robert Speaight, *William Poel and the Elizabethan Revival* (Cambridge, MA: Harvard University Press, 1954), pp. 114–15.
9. William Tydeman, *Text and Performance: Doctor Faustus* (Houndmills: Macmillan, 1984), p. 47.
10. Simon Callow, *Orson Welles: The Road to Xanadu* (London: Jonathan Cape, 1995), pp. 264–7.
11. John Houseman, *Run-Through, 1902–1941* (New York: Simon and Schuster, 1972), p. 234.
12. For the Nevill Coghill production starring Richard Burton, see Humphrey Carpenter, *OUDS: A Centenary History of the Oxford University Dramatic Society 1885–1985* (Oxford University Press, 1985), p. 198.
13. Genesis Repertory (2002). See *http://www.oobr.com/top/volNine/five/faustus.htm*.
14. Russell Jackson, '*Doctor Faustus* in Manchester', *Critical Quarterly* 23 (1981), 3–9 (8).
15. Directed by Simon Pearson, New Company, New College, Oxford, November 1984. Reviewed by Mark Thornton Burnett, *MSAN* 5 (1985), 8.
16. George L. Geckle, *'Tamburlaine' and 'Edward II'*, Text and Performance (Houndmills: Macmillan, 1988), p. 51.

17. T. J. Cribb, 'Brecht's *Tamburlaine*', *Essays in Theatre* 6 (1988), 95.
18. J. S. Cunningham and Roger Warren, '*Tamburlaine the Great* Rediscovered', *ShS* 31 (1978), 155. See also, for a detailed comparison of the Guthrie, Hall, and Hands productions, David Fuller, '*Tamburlaine the Great* in Performance', in Sara Munson Deats and Robert A. Logan (eds.), *Marlowe's Empery: Expanding His Critical Contexts* (Newark: University of Delaware Press, 2002), pp. 61–81.
19. Peter Hall: *Peter Hall's Diaries: The Story of a Dramatic Battle*, John Goodwin (ed.) (London: Hamish Hamilton, 1983), pp. 232, 246, 247.
20. Martin Wiggins, review in *CahiersE* 44 (1993), 81.
21. *Marlowe's Celebrated Tragedy of The Jew of Malta, in five acts, with considerable alterations and additions, by S. Penley, Comedian, as Performing with unanimous Approbation at the Theatre Royal, Drury Lane* (London, 1818), p. i.
22. See James L. Smith, '*The Jew of Malta* in the Theatre', in Brian Morris (ed.), *Christopher Marlowe* (London: Ernest Benn, 1968), pp. 5–9.
23. David Nathan, *Jewish Chronicle* 1 April 1988.
24. Carolyn D. Williams, review in *CahiersE* 55 (1999), 75–7.
25. Peter J. Smith, *CahiersE* 57 (2000), 127.
26. Laurie Maguire, review in *MSAN* 19 (1999), 6.
27. For a detailed account of this production, see Jean Jacquot and Nicole Vigouroux, 'Le Juif de Malte de Marlowe et la mise en scène de Bernard Sobel, Ensemble théâtrale de Gennevilliers', in Jean Jacquot (ed.), *Les Voies de la création théâtrale* (Paris: Editions du Centre National de la Recherche Scientifique, 1978), 6: 341–96.
28. When the production was revived at the same theatre (in 1999), with a new translation, the Prologue was restored to Machiavelli, who spoke it in complete darkness (Guy Boquet, review of *Le Juif de Malte*, *CahiersE* 56 (1999), 114–15).
29. Michael Billington, *Guardian* Saturday Arts 19 January 2002.
30. C. E. Montague, *Manchester Guardian* 29 April 1905.
31. *Stratford-upon-Avon Herald* 5 May 1905.
32. *Birmingham Gazette* 28 April 1905.
33. *The Stage* 4 May 1905.
34. Jürgen Schebera, *Leben Eduards des Zweiten von England. Stücke* 2, 2 vols. (Suhrkamp Verlag: Frankfurt-am-Main, 1988), 2: 395–400.
35. Laurence Kitchen, *Observer* 17 August 1958.
36. Interview with George L. Geckle, in Geckle, '*Tamburlaine*' and '*Edward II*', p. 95.
37. Charles R. Forker (ed.), *Edward the Second*, Revels Plays (Manchester University Press, 1994), pp. 99–116.
38. For a discussion of this Act and the reactions to it, see Kate Chedgzoy, *Shakespeare's Queer Children: Sexual Politics and Contemporary Culture* (Manchester University Press, 1995), p. 187.
39. Anne Khazam directed *Dido* for the Edinburgh and London Fringe Festivals in 1991. She gives a good account of this production, 'Directing Dido', in *MSAN* 12 (1992), 2–4.
40. See Stephen Orgel, *Impersonations: The Performance of Gender in Shakespeare's England* (Cambridge University Press, 1996), p. 48; also, in Downie and Parnell, *Constructing Christopher Marlowe*, the essays by Simon Shepherd (p. 114) and Lawrence Normand (pp. 190–1).

41. Derek Jarman, *Queer Edward II* (London: BFI Publishing, 1991), dedication.
42. Reviewed by Annamaria Kiss in *MSAN* 15 (1995), 4–5.
43. Annamaria Kiss, review of *Edward II*, directed by Claus Peymann, Vienna Burgtheater, opening February 1998, *MSAN* 18 (1998), 9–10.
44. Michael Billington, *Guardian* 15 March 2001.
45. Benedict Nightingale, *Times* 15 March 2001.
46. Judith Mackrell, *Guardian* 11 October 1997.
47. Ismene Brown, *Daily Telegraph* 13 October 1997.
48. Guy Rickards, *http://www.chester-novello.com/work/8534/main.html*.
49. See Francine St-Orge, 'Jean Vauthier and *The Massacre at Paris*', in *MSAN* 11 (1991), 6–7. Vauthier's production was also adapted for radio and performed under the title of *La Mort Facile (Easy Death)*.
50. Directed by Janet Farrow and Douglas Overtoom. Review by Daniel J. Vitkus in *MSAN* 7 (1987), 4–5. This production was part of a series of Marlowe revivals, given on an exceptionally small stage and emphasizing the erotic content of the plays. The others were *Edward II* and *The Jew of Malta* (both 1985, reviewed *MSAN* 5 (1985)), *Dido* (1986, reviewed *MSAN* 6 (1986)), *Tamburlaine* (1986, reviewed *MSAN* 6 (1986)), and *Doctor Faustus* (1994, reviewed *MSAN* 14 (1994)).
51. For a good review of the entire sequence, see Stephen Longstaffe, 'Marlowe on Radio Three', in *CahiersE* 43 (1998), 75–82.
52. See Lois Potter, 'Marlowe Onstage: the Deaths of the Author', in Downie and Parnell (eds.), *Constructing Christopher Marlowe*, pp. 88–101.
53. For a comparison between the Marlowes of *Shakespeare in Love* and the 1978 BBC TV series *Will Shakespeare*, available on video in 1995 and 1998, see Frank Ardolino, 'Marlowe in *Will Shakespeare* and *Shakespeare in Love*', *MSAN* 9 (1999), 2–4.

READING LIST

Cribb, T. J. 'Brecht's *Tamburlaine*'. *Essays in Theatre* 6 (1988), 95–107.

Cunningham, J. S., and Roger Warren. '*Tamburlaine the Great* Rediscovered'. *ShS* 31 (1978).

Downie, J. A., and J. T. Parnell (eds.). *Constructing Christopher Marlowe*. Cambridge University Press, 2000, pp. 88–101.

Friedenreich, Kenneth, Roma Gill, and Constance B. Kuriyama (eds.). '*A Poet and a Filthy Play-maker*': *New Essays on Christopher Marlowe*. New York: AMS Press, 1988.

Geckle, George L. *Text and Performance: 'Tamburlaine' and 'Edward II'*. Houndmills: Macmillan, 1988.

Hattaway, Michael. *Elizabethan Popular Theatre: Plays in Performance*. London: Routledge and Kegan Paul, 1982.

Jarman, Derek. *Queer Edward II*. London: BFI Publishing, 1991.

Morris, Brian (ed.). *Christopher Marlowe*. London: Ernest Benn, 1968.

Tydeman, William. *Text and Performance: 'Doctor Faustus'*. Houndmills: Macmillan, 1984.

Wraight, A. D. *Christopher Marlowe and Edward Alleyn*. Chichester: Adam Hart, 1993.

WEBSITES

http://home.earthlink.net/~jhdemous/Robert/Edward/edward.html
  Photos of Brecht's *Edward II* at the Jean Cocteau Theatre, New York.
http://www.chester-novello.com/work/8534/main.html
  An account of the John McCabe score of the ballet based on *Edward II*.
http://memory.loc.gov/ammem/fedtp/ftfst1.html
  Production notebook, script, programme, costume designs, score, posters,
  etc., for Welles's famous production.
The Prospect production of *Edward II*, starring Ian McKellen, has been released on
  audiotape.

17

LISA HOPKINS

Marlowe's reception and influence

Marlowe was barely cold before people began the process of trying to make meanings of both his death and life. He was stabbed to death on Wednesday 30 May 1593. On Sunday 23 June 1593, less than a month later, George Peele was paid £3 by the Earl of Northumberland, who may well have known Marlowe personally, for his poem *The Honour of the Garter*, which praised both Marlowe and his friend Thomas Watson, who had died in late 1592. Four days later, Thursday 27 June, was the date affixed by Marlowe's friend (and possible collaborator) Thomas Nashe to the end of his *The Unfortunate Traveller* (though it was not published until 1594), which draws a parallel between Marlowe and the notoriously lascivious Italian poet Ludovico Aretino. *The Unfortunate Traveller* also refers to the supposed necromancer Heinrich Cornelius Agrippa and his entertainment for the Emperor Charles V, episodes which seem to be echoed in *Doctor Faustus*. Indeed, Marlowe seems to have been playing on Nashe's mind, because 8 September saw the entry in the Stationers' Register of his *Christ's tears over Jerusalem*, which castigates atheism and may have been an attempt to dissociate himself from his dangerous acquaintance.

Meanwhile, on 6 July of the same year, Marlowe's *Edward II* had been licensed for publication by William Jones (no known quarto was published until 1594, but there may have been an earlier one which is now lost), and on 28 September *Hero and Leander* was entered in the Stationers' Register by John Wolf; it must already have been circulating in manuscript, though, because on 22 October Thomas Edwards's *Narcissus*, praising Watson and Marlowe and showing clear signs of knowledge of *Hero and Leander*, was entered in the Stationers' Register, also by John Wolf. In September as well, Gabriel Harvey composed his 'Newe Letter of Notable Contents' (published in October), which calls Marlowe a 'Lucian' and mentions the death of 'Tamburlaine', but seems to imply that he had died of the plague. This used to be taken as one of the various erroneous accounts of the death of Marlowe, but Charles Nicholl has argued convincingly that it refers in fact to the death of Peter Shakerley.[1]

The next year, 1594, saw the publication of *Dido, Queen of Carthage*, saying on the title page that it was written by Marlowe and Nashe, and of Robert Ashley's *Of the Interchangeable Course, or Variety of Things in the Whole World*, a translation from the French of Loys LeRoy, which seems to take the idea of Tamburlaine's footstool from *Tamburlaine the Great* rather than the original text,[2] and thus shows Marlowe's continuing influence. Borrowings from Marlowe are also apparent in *Taming of a Shrew*, entered in the Stationers' Register on 2 May 1594.[3] More surprisingly, references to the trial of the queen's Jewish physician, Dr Lopez, who was arrested on charges of treason and attempted poisoning on 5 February 1594, occur in the Horse-courser scene of *Doctor Faustus*; obviously Marlowe himself cannot have written these, but the insertions show the continuing relevance and appeal of the play. Also entered in the Stationers' Register, on 17 May 1594, was *The Massacre at Paris*, and though no ensuing edition is known to have been published, the play was performed by the Admiral's Men at the Rose on 19 June, and nine times subsequently between then and 25 September. *Doctor Faustus* was also revived by the Admiral's Men from 2 October, possibly with new material, since it generated large profits.[4] There followed a lull in the interest in Marlowe, but 1598 saw the publication of both *Hero and Leander*, by Edward Blount, with Marlowe's name on the title page and a dedication to Thomas Walsingham, and of *Mucedorus*, which, Paul Kocher argued, imitated the goblet scene of *Doctor Faustus* (p. 37). *Hero and Leander* was followed later in the same year by a new version published by Paul Linley and concluding with Chapman's continuation, as well as by publication of *The Second Part of Hero and Leander. Conteyning their further Fortunes*, by Henry Petowe.

The memory of Marlowe the man was being revisited almost as much as his works were. We have no way of knowing what oral reports circulated about his death, though it would seem likely that there were several. Soon, though, written ones began to appear, and many of these are notable for the way they focus either on the suggestion of sexual or religious deviance or misconduct, or on hints of a parallel between the fates of Marlowe and of his characters. Thomas Beard's *Theatre of God's Judgements*, published in 1597, contained the following account of Marlowe's death:

> It so fell out that in London streets, as he purposed to stab one whom he ought a grudge unto with his dagger, the other party perceiving, so avoided the stroke that withal catching hold of his wrist, he stabbed his own dagger into his own

head, in such sort that notwithstanding all the means of surgery that could be wrought, he shortly after died thereof.[5]

Beard's account is likely to have only a tenuous basis in fact (no other account mentions medical assistance having been offered, and it is unlikely that there would have been time for this to have occurred), but it is nevertheless of interest for the emblematic way in which it conceives of Marlowe's death: accidentally killing oneself while attempting violence against another is exactly what befalls the villain D'Amville in Tourneur's *The Atheist's Tragedy* as a punishment for his unbelief.

Next year, 1598, came the publication of Francis Meres's *Palladis Tamia*, containing two mentions of Marlowe's death:

> As Jodelle, a French tragical poet, being an epicure and an atheist, made a pitiful end, so our tragical poet Marlowe for his epicurism and atheism had a tragical death.

> As the poet Lycophron was shot to death by a certain rival of his, so Christopher Marlowe was stabbed to death by a bawdy serving-man, a rival of his in his lewd love.[6]

Again this is clearly unreliable, and indeed it is not even easy to see how the two accounts might square with each other, but what is obvious is that like Beard, Meres is determined to make meaning(s) out of Marlowe's death. Marlowe, it seems, died in a way which, paradoxically, both provided him with a suitable punishment and confirmed his status as canonical poet and tragedian. Meres's stance is an interesting one, because implicit in it is the idea that God himself is not unlike a poet or tragedian administering poetic justice to mortals. Marlowe, presumably, was blind not to see this (the wound to his eye usefully figures the 'blindness' of atheism); by contrast, Meres's own perception of the pattern confirms both his orthodoxy and his literary credentials.

The earliest reliable account of Marlowe's death is William Vaughan's in *The Golden Grove*, also published in 1598. This contained the following reference to Marlowe:

> Not inferior to these was one Christopher Marlow, by profession a playmaker, who, as it is reported, about 7 years ago wrote a book against the Trinity. But see the effects of God's justice: so it happened, that at Deptford, a little village about three miles distant from London, as he meant to stab with his poignard one named Ingram, that had invited him thither to a feast, and was then playing at tables, he quickly perceiving it, so avoided the thrust, that withall drawing out his own dagger for his defence, he stabbed this Marlowe into the eye, in such sort that his brains coming out at the dagger's point, he shortly after died.

Thus did God, the true executioner of divine justice, work the end of impious atheists.[7]

This is right on so many counts, correctly identifying the scene of the crime and the name of the killer, that we might well feel inclined to trust it even in respects for which there is no other corroborative evidence, such as the tantalizing detail about the book against the Trinity. Charles Nicholl has argued that the unusual accuracy of Vaughan's information is attributable to his connection with the family of the Earl of Essex (although David Riggs has recently attributed it rather to the fact that William Vaughan was the nephew of Blanche Parry, Chief Gentlewoman of Elizabeth I's bedchamber).[8] However that may be, Vaughan also has connections with another odd Marlovian development: on 4 July 1602 he wrote a letter from Pisa mentioning a Catholic English priest called John Matthew who used the alias Christopher Marlowe (Nicholl, p. 359), presumably in some sort of homage to the late poet, though one would have thought this was a rather inflammatory act.

The putative connection of Essex with Vaughan suggested by Nicholl is an intriguing one, because the way in which Marlowe's own fictional characters were used to incriminate him both before and immediately after his death is a tactic deployed by Essex on other occasions. On 7 February of that year the Lord Chamberlain's Men put on Shakespeare's *Richard II* at the Earl of Essex's behest, apparently in a bid to get the audience into a suitable frame of mind for the Essex Rebellion, scheduled for the following day. This tactic of using literary works for political purposes might perhaps be thought reminiscent of the presence of the signature 'Tamburlaine' in what became known as the Dutch Church Libel, the anti-immigrant manifesto found pasted to the wall of the Dutch churchyard which precipitated the arrest of Marlowe and Kyd. Essex certainly took a keen interest in literature in general, not least because it tended to cause him trouble: Rowland White wrote to Sir Robert Sidney on 7 November 1595 that 'The Earl of Essex is infinitely troubled with a printed book the Queen showed him'[9] – the book in question being Robert Persons's *A Conference about the Next Succession to the Crown of England* – and he, like Cleopatra, feared that his story would be acted after he was dead. The literariness of the intrigues surrounding Marlowe's death might well seem to be characteristic of Essex, though unless further evidence miraculously appears, this must remain pure speculation.

Up until the Civil War, Marlowe's own place in literature was, of course, well assured, and is confirmed not only by the continued popularity of his works but by numerous references to him by other writers. In *As You Like It*, for instance, Shakespeare includes some unusually pointed mentions of Marlowe as a 'dead shepherd' who made 'a great reckoning in a little room',[10] alludes to Leander, quotes 'The Passionate Shepherd to his Love', and jokes about 'elegies on brambles' (3.2.347–8) and 'honest Ovid' (3.3.6), both of which appear to refer to the recent public burning of Marlowe's pioneering translation of *All Ovid's Elegies*. These allusions seem to form part of a wider debate about the meanings of Marlowe's work in general, and of *Hero and Leander* in particular: M. Morgan Holmes suggests that 'Hero and Leander's tragedy had become, among the "smart set" of 1590s London, a site of conflict between competing philosophical and social visions of how desire ought to be inscribed in order to shape individual and collective destinies'; Holmes sees Chapman's and Petowe's continuations as attempts to reassert orthodoxy, countered by the fact that '[i]n 1599 ... Thomas Nashe's *Lenten Stuff* and William Shakespeare's *As You Like It* joined the fray and showed that "all men" did not, in fact, expect or even desire the same things'[11] – that, in short, some might prefer their own sex to the opposite one.

Nor was *As You Like It* Shakespeare's only acknowledgement of the influence of Marlowe. Shakespeare quoted Marlowe in *The Merry Wives of Windsor*, may have collaborated with him on the three parts of *Henry VI*, and is clearly influenced by him in a host of plays, including *Richard III*, *Richard II*, *The Merchant of Venice*, and *The Tempest*, together with the narrative poem *Venus and Adonis*, often taken to be a response to *Hero and Leander*. (There is also, of course, a view that Marlowe is the rival poet of the sonnets, though the paucity and ambiguity of the surviving evidence makes it seem likely that, like the causes of Marlowe's death, this theory will never be comprehensively confirmed or disproved.) And as well as Chapman and Petowe, a whole host of other Renaissance writers clearly signalled responses to Marlowe, including John Marston, who in the Induction of *Antonio and Mellida* has Feliche call Matzagente a 'mount tufty Tamburlaine';[12] Thomas Middleton, whose Harebrain in *A Mad World, My Masters* will not let his wife read *Hero and Leander*; Ben Jonson, who includes a parody of *Hero and Leander* in *Bartholomew Fair*; and Barnabe Barnes, whose *The Divils Charter* (1607) is clearly indebted in its devil-raising scenes to *Doctor Faustus*.

Marlowe's reputation endured well into the century after his death. In 1633, Thomas Heywood oversaw the publication of *The Jew of Malta* with a dedication to 'Mr Thomas Hammon, of Greyes Inn', who had been Marlowe's classmate at the King's School, Canterbury, and had later followed him to Corpus Christi College, Cambridge.[13] Heywood's own play *The Captives* shows clear signs of indebtedness to Marlowe: Godfrey quotes 'Who ever loved, that loved not at first sight', and a friar who is in fact already dead is 'killed' by another, as in *The Jew of Malta*.[14] One of those

who seems to have been particularly affected by this 1630s revival of interest in Marlowe was John Ford, who in *Love's Sacrifice* parodies both
Tamburlaine and, it has been suggested, Edward Alleyn's acting style.[15] Indeed Marlowe is a powerful presence throughout Ford's work. Sharing an
interest in the socially displaced, whom they typically term 'mushrumps',
both Marlowe and Ford create characters who, as Lawrence Danson says
of Marlowe's heroes, 'amaze or dismay us by the sheer tenacity of their will
to be always themselves', and Richard McCabe has commented suggestively
that '*Perkin Warbeck* might well be regarded as *Tamburlaine* rewritten by
Ford.'[16] Marlowe's presence is felt in *'Tis Pity She's a Whore* in particular, where the opening lines, with their reference to atheism, seem overtly
to evoke his legend. When Bergetto's belly 'seethes like a porridge-pot' he
reminds one of Barabas's poisoned porridge, and there are marked parallels between Giovanni and both Doctor Faustus and Tamburlaine – indeed
there is a suggestive switch from one mode to another of Marlovian excess
in Giovanni's progression from the doomed but essentially harmless scholar
Faustus to the atrocities of Tamburlaine.[17]

After this period appreciation of the distinctive qualities of Marlowe's
œuvre seems noticeably to have waned. Although there are traces of both
Marlovian verse and Marlovian ambition in Milton, particularly in the conception of Satan, Marlowe was generally forgotten. Arguably his greatest
work, *Doctor Faustus*, was debased into farcical and harlequin versions,
and indeed deafness to his voice was such that on 8 April 1654 'a come-
die called *The Maidens Holiday*' was entered in the Stationers' Register
as 'by Christopher Marlow and John Day', an attribution which no one
now accepts. Conversely some critics, including Milton's nephew Edward
Phillips, even asserted that Marlowe had not written *Tamburlaine*, an as-
cription which no one now doubts; Phillips in his *Theatrum Poetarum*
called Marlowe 'a kind of a second *Shakesphear*' but assigns *Tamburlaine* to
Thomas Newton, author of *A Notable Historie of the Saracens*, and when in
1681 Charles Saunders's *Tamerlane the Great* was censured as 'only an Old
Play transcrib'd' Saunders claimed never to have heard of Marlowe's play,
or to have found anyone else who had either.[18] This, as J. Douglas Canfield
points out, is partly because a different version of the story of Tamburlaine,
Rowe's *Tamerlane* (1701), now dominated the stage, and spoke more clearly
to the prevailing concern with modes of masculinity and heroism.[19] Not until
the publication in 1744 of Dodsley's *Old Plays*, including *Edward II*, did the
tide begin to turn again in favour of Marlowe.

When it did turn, however, it did so rapidly. Both life and works were
comprehensively rediscovered by the Romantics, for whom Marlowe becomes an avatar of poetic rebellion. In 1808 Charles Lamb, in *Specimens*

of English Dramatic Poets, praised the death scene of Edward II, and 1818 saw the publication at London, in separate texts, of W. Oxberry's editions of *The Jew of Malta, Edward II, Doctor Faustus, Lust's Dominion*, sometimes then attributed to Marlowe, and *The Massacre at Paris*, as well as the publication of the first German translation of *Doctor Faustus*. On 24 April that year, moreover, Edmund Kean revived *The Jew of Malta*, in what seems to have been the first time that a Marlowe play had been seen on the stage since the 1633 *Doctor Faustus*. In 1820 W. Oxberry published the two parts of *Tamburlaine* and Hazlitt's Lectures *Chiefly on the Dramatic Literature of the Age of Elizabeth*, praising Marlowe, appeared. The year also saw the publication at London of J. P. Collier's *Poetical Decameron*, discussing Marlowe. In 1825 Hurst and Robinson's *Old English Drama*, including *Dido, Queen of Carthage*, appeared, and John Payne Collier announced the 'discovery' of the *Massacre at Paris* leaf, a much longer version of a speech from the play, which he said was in the hands of the London bookseller Rodd.[20] Collier's known habits of forgery leave a question mark over the authenticity of this, but *The Massacre at Paris* certainly does read like a garbled and truncated text, and there is nothing intrinsically improbable in the 'Collier leaf'. In 1826 came the publication of the first collected edition of Marlowe, probably by George Robinson, and in 1827 Oxberry's editions were all brought out together, along with *Dido, Queen of Carthage*, as *The Dramatic Works of Christopher Marlowe, With prefatory Remarks, Notes, Critical and Explanatory*, by W. Oxberry, Comedian. Interest also began to grow abroad, and Goethe's praise of *Doctor Faustus* in 1829 – 'How greatly is it all planned!' – led in 1831 to the publication of the first German translations of *The Jew of Malta* and *Edward II*.

In 1844 Leigh Hunt praised Marlowe in his *Imagination and Fancy*, and indeed, as Irving Ribner notes, 'Marlowe's reputation was gradually revived by Romantic critics of the nineteenth century.'[21] *Hero and Leander* was an obvious influence on Byron, and after the early death of that other celebrated atheist Shelley, comparisons were often made between the two. Marlowe was also an important influence on Shelley's wife Mary. In her first novel, *Frankenstein*, she must have been acutely aware that the Faustian ambition of her hero leads him into paths which parallel the first, and unsuccessful, request which Marlowe's Doctor Faustus makes of Mephistopheles, which is for a wife, and the fissured, motherless families found in so many of her works parallel the fragmented families which are characteristic of Marlowe's plays.[22] (Later, her father William Godwin was to write a life of Faust, which comes directly after his treatment of Agrippa, avowed source for Mary Shelley's novel;[23] moreover, Faustus too, like Victor Frankenstein, had Ingolstadt connections.)[24] Equally, the idea that the Monster might become 'the scourge of your fellow creatures' irresistibly recalls Marlowe's Tamburlaine, who termed himself the Scourge of God.[25] Marlovian influences are also strongly present in Mary Shelley's fourth novel, *Valperga*, where, after the death of his father, the hero/villain Castruccio journeys to the court of Edward II, where he becomes a favourite first of the king and later of Gaveston, after the latter's return from exile in Ireland. Mary Shelley is relatively reticent about the homosexual relationship of Edward and Gaveston, though its notoriety would mean that she need have no fear of not being understood, and indeed to some extent she is able to use Marlowe as a code to convey her meaning. Later in the century, there were even two operas by Berlioz (*Les Troyens* and *La Damnation de Faust*) which covered Marlovian ground, while a passion for *Hero and Leander* got the young Edmund Gosse into trouble with his puritanical father. Indeed so intense was late nineteenth-century interest that Thomas Dabbs has recently proposed that 'Marlowe was originally invented by Victorian scholars, critics, and educators and then handed on to us.'[26]

Marlowe after the Romantics continues to become a figure of generalized rebellion but also becomes more specifically an icon of homosexuality. Of particular interest in this context are the references to him by Swinburne and echoes of him in the work of Bram Stoker, whose employer Henry Irving was heavily involved in the erection of a statue to Marlowe in Canterbury in 1891, and who had at least an indirect debt to Marlowe, since, as much recent work has pointed out, his creation of Dracula was influenced by Irving's portrayal of Goethe's Faust.[27] Since *Dracula* has also been read as a response to the trial of Stoker's close friend Oscar Wilde, it looks as though Marlovian references may be acting here as something of a shorthand code for homosexuality.

Homosexuality has also been a key element in many twentieth-century homages to Marlowe, particularly in fictionalizations of his life. Many of these are of poor literary quality, but one or two offer some interesting vignettes. They can pretty much be said to begin with C. E. Lawrence's play *The Reckoning*, acted at the Royal Academy of Dramatic Art in 1934, followed three years later by a brief but suggestive reference in the Eric Ambler thriller *Background to Danger*, where, trapped in a vulcanizing tank and expecting to die, the hero Kenton 'began to repeat to himself some odd scraps of verse of which he was fond – a sonnet of Donne's, a piece of Wilfred Owen's, part of "Kubla Khan", a speech from Marlowe's "Tamburlaine" '[28] – a suggestive list of the rebellious and dissident.

Interest in Marlowe hotted up as the twentieth century progressed. The 1953 discovery of the Corpus Christi portrait and the 1955 proposal by Calvin Hoffman that it should be identified as Marlowe led to renewed interest in his life, as did the 1976 discovery by R. B. Wernham of the Flushing coining episode, and the two quatercentenaries of his birth and death, in 1964 and 1993 respectively. Indeed, Marlowe narrowly avoided experiencing one of the oddest of reincarnations in the twentieth century: the stage name originally proposed by Columbia Pictures for the actress eventually known as Kim Novak was 'Kit Marlowe'. He did become the recipient of the rather dubious honour, for a reputed atheist, of having a window dedicated to him in Westminster Abbey on 11 July 2002, which controversially included a question mark after giving his date of death as 1593, with the clear implication that he survived and wrote the plays of Shakespeare. The window was the result of an initiative by the Marlowe Society (of England, rather than the American branch, which has no truck with such theories), who were also responsible for the perhaps even more unlikely decision to commemorate Marlowe in the form of a Christopher Marlowe Rose, bred by David Austin Roses and unveiled at the 2002 Chelsea Flower Show, whose orange-red colour was intended to recall the slashes in the doublet in the putative Corpus Christi portrait. (For reasons I am unclear about, the scent is said to be tea with a hint of lemon.) There was also a growing flurry of novelizations of his life, including Anthony Burgess's *A Dead Man in Deptford* and Judith Cook's *The Slicing Edge of Death* (both published in 1993), Stephanie Cowell's *Nicholas Cooke: Actor, Soldier, Physician, Priest*, Liam Maguire's *Icarus Flying*, Robin Chapman's *Christoferus or Tom Kyd's Revenge*, Iain Sinclair's *Slow Chocolate Autopsy*, and, most recently, Stephanie Merritt's *Gaveston*.

In general, these modern retellings portray very much the Marlowe of legend, often with particular emphasis on fidelity to the picture of him offered by the Baines Note. Stephanie Cowell's *Nicholas Cooke: Actor, Soldier, Physician, Priest* is centred on the London theatrical scene of the 1590s and has its adolescent hero meet Marlowe, here called Morley, who gets him apprenticed to John Heminges. Cowell's Marlowe endorses the speculations of Giordano Bruno, hobnobs with Thomas Hariot, and flirts with atheism and homosexuality. Liam Maguire's *Icarus Flying* has Marlowe dying not in a brawl at Deptford – it is a Christopher Morley who is killed there instead – but from a combination of pox and exhaustion. He is both atheist and homosexual, though guilty and confused about the latter, being made to say 'He's a boy or a fool who does not like tobacco' rather than the received version of 'All they that love not tobacco and boys be fools'. He joins the School of Night – an organization which is here considerably larger than it is generally envisaged as being, and of more conservative ends – to prove that he is not a Catholic. But despite all these attempts to conform, his plays get him into trouble: the School of Night, as the Masons are said to have done with Mozart, believe their rituals have been parodied in *Doctor Faustus*, Essex is offended by the portrait of Gaveston, and Marlowe appears to crack under the pressure. Chris Hunt's *Mignon*, which is very sexually explicit, positively revels in its hero's sexuality, and has its Marlowe dedicating 'Come live with me and be my love' to a young French boy before disappearing from the novel.[29] Finally, Anthony Burgess's *A Dead Man in Deptford*, stylishly post-modern, has a Marlowe much happier with his own homosexuality, though he is eventually killed for motives which are obscure but which seem to centre on his relationship with Ralegh, while *Slow Chocolate Autopsy: Incidents from the Notorious Career of Norton, Prisoner of London*, Iain Sinclair's collection of stories about the seamy past of London, goes one step further in its postmodernity by musing of Marlowe's imminent murder, 'The trick would be how to put a spin on such an obvious narrative device, how to keep the yarn out of the hands of the conspiracy freaks. How to muzzle Anthony Burgess. God forbid that Ackroyd should pastiche this one. Death, what a banality!'[30]

Perhaps the most interesting of the novelizations is Robin Chapman's *Christoferus or Tom Kyd's Revenge*, because it moves beyond imaginative reconstruction of Marlowe himself to offer, in addition, critical comment and interpretation of his works. After the nice touch of observing that Chapman's 'adjectives came in cow-like droves mooing at the subject noun', and suggesting that Baines and Frizer committed the murder in the service of Rome, the novel first offers close reading – in *Hero and Leander* '[o]nce again Christofer wins a doubtful argument with a feline rhythm and the pounce of rhyme' – and then a full-blown and not uninteresting analysis of *Doctor Faustus*:

> first we have Faustus as an unseen presence in the Vatican, a spy in other words. Next comes Mephostophilis, a fellow agent from Hell, who can grant Faustus anything – at a price. Call Faustus Christofer and Mephostophilis Baines, who then serves whom and who, come to that, i[s] the Archbishop? Answer: an important papal authority from the very seminary Christofer attended. The Archbishop refers to a ghost – the Cockney name for a spy or informer is *ghost* – and says Christofer comes from Purgatory. On the face of it an unexceptionable provenance entirely suited to such a relentless spirit except Christofer once told me there were three courtyards at the seminary of Rheims which were commonly known as Heaven, Purgatory and Hell. And the English students took their air and exercised themselves at football in Purgatory.

Doctor Faustus, in this account, is thus Marlowe writing his own literary life, slyly offering a coded representation of the twilight world of espionage in which he moved.[31]

Marlowe appeared in drama too, most notably in Peter Whelan's *The School of Night*, set at Scadbury, where Marlowe is preparing to stage *Dido*,

Queen of Carthage for a visit from Ralegh. Whelan sees Marlowe as fore-shadowing the literary dissident, and also as fundamentally dependent on the fortunes of Ralegh. Whelan's Marlowe plays the part of Venus in *Dido, Queen of Carthage*, is homosexual, prays to 'Dog' rather than 'God', and wants to continue the School of Night's inquiries into truth, which both Ralegh and Thomas Walsingham now wish to abandon as too politically risky. Walsingham proposes instead to have Marlowe escape to Venice with the aid of 'Tom Stone', the pseudonym of Shakespeare, who wittily compares with Marlowe ideas for a possible *dénouement* for *Othello*. Walsingham's wife, however, has other ideas, and arranges for Frizer to murder Marlowe.[32] This echoes Eugénie de Kalb's theory that Audrey Walsingham was the person most likely to have procured the death of Marlowe,[33] but there is in fact no evidence that Thomas and Audrey Walsingham had married or even met by 1593.

In one way, the modern world which produces these adaptations can be seen as Marlowe's natural home. *Edward II*, in particular, has spoken very powerfully to the more open homosexual identities of our own time; as well as Derek Jarman's film version of it, there is also a recent ballet, with music by John McCabe, choreography by David Bintley, and costumes by Jasper Conran, and accompanied, when performed by the Birmingham Royal Ballet in 1997, by a mock 'Daily Herald' for 19 October 1330 which compared Isabella with Princess Diana. Stephanie Merritt's novel *Gaveston* also plays on this idea. Merritt's novel is narrated by Gabriele Harvey, whose name offers a neat play on the snippets about Marlowe's career afforded by Gabriel Harvey. Gabriele is a graduate student specializing in the Arthur myth and the niece of media mogul Sir Edward Hamilton-Harvey, a man in possession of a secretary called Roger Mortimer who nearly did a PhD on Thomas Mann, and a beautiful French–Canadian wife called Isabelle. Gabriele finds herself caught up in the takeover of her department and the subsequent appointment of a new professor, the devastatingly handsome film theorist and cultural commentator Piers Gaveston, who woos her in an offhand way to which Gabriele, entranced by his looks, eagerly responds, even agreeing to become engaged to him before her world is turned upside down when the Sunday papers reveal that Piers is in fact having an affair with her uncle. After the ensuing media scrimmage, Piers dies in a motorbike accident which Gabriele is certain is suicide, leaving her alone but tentatively newly bonded to her uncle by the fact that both have loved him.

Merritt is a regular reviewer of new novels for *The Observer*, and her own book, which has more pretensions to literary status than many of the novelizations of Marlowe's life, is certainly readable, and at times interesting.

The language and habits of the media don are very well observed, and so too is much of the manoeuvring around the demise of the department of literature and its rebirth as a Faculty of Cultural Studies, and the accompanying academic bitching: '"There are three words that express my vision for this new faculty," he began ("Me, me, me," whispered Jake Lennox, rather too loudly . . .).'[34] There are some other nice touches, too: the history play's role as condition-of-England text is replicated in the fact that Piers Gaveston is preparing a television series on what Englishness means, as well as in the way that Gaveston echoes not just the Marlowe character but also, subtly but unmistakably, Princess Diana, whose death prompted a national reconsideration of contemporary modes of Englishness. This resemblance is established by the media scrum which causes Piers's death – which takes place, like the princess's, in August – and then continues at his funeral, the allusion to a divorce, Sir Edward's likening of himself to a candle in the wind (p. 41), which was the title of the song sung by Elton John at Diana's funeral, and Sir Edward's ultimate decision to do 'an interview. On telly – one of those special one-hour jobs . . . all trembly lips and apology' (p. 376), which is an obvious allusion to the princess's infamous *Panorama* interview. The history play's meditation on historiography is duplicated in the novel's formal experimentation, since it opens with the Diana-like funeral of Piers, brings the events up to date, and then moves beyond to muse on the inevitability or otherwise of the outcome.

What is unclear, though, is who all this is aimed at. The title will obviously appeal to those with an interest in Marlowe, but apart from one brief reference to *Doctor Faustus* (p. 169 – made, suitably enough, by Gaveston) and the facts that the heroine is at St Dunstan's College and that her father is buried in Marlow, the novel is entirely unselfconscious about its own indebtedness, to a degree which at times borders on the ludicrous – it is a bit rich that no one in a department of literature should ever for a moment suspect that a character called Piers Gaveston might be homosexual, and I also cannot credit that the revelation of a public figure's homosexuality would cause such a devastating public reaction in London in the twenty-first century. Nevertheless, the novel drops it like a bombshell which no one could possibly have suspected, depressingly suggesting that four hundred years have made remarkably little difference in what is and isn't acceptable in English public life. However much it may strain at its readers' belief at this point, though, Merritt's novel does undoubtedly serve as evidence that Marlowe was not only dangerous in his own time, but can also still be used as a very sharp tool for probing and examining what might be dangerous in other times too.

NOTES

1. Charles Nicholl, *The Reckoning* (London: Jonathan Cape, 1992), p. 64.

2. See William J. Brown, 'Marlowe's Debasement of Bajazet: Foxe's *Actes and Monuments* and *Tamburlaine, Part I*', *RQ* 24 (1971), 38–48 (45).

3. See Fredson Bowers, 'Marlowe's *Doctor Faustus*: the 1602 Additions', *SB* 26 (1973), 1–18 (3).

4. See Paul H. Kocher, 'Nashe's Authorship of the Prose Scenes in *Faustus*', *MLQ* 2 (1942), 17–40 (38–9).

5. Thomas Beard, *The Theatre of God's Judgements* (London, 1597), pp. 147–8.

6. Francis Meres, *Palladis Tamia* (London, 1598), sig. OO6.

7. William Vaughan, *The Golden Grove Moralized in Three Books* (London, 1598), sigs. C4^v–C5.

8. David Riggs, 'The Killing of Christopher Marlowe', *StHR* 8 (1999), 239–51 (245).

9. Sylvia Freedman, *Poor Penelope: Lady Penelope Rich, An Elizabethan Woman* (Bourne End: Kensal Press, 1983), p. 111.

10. William Shakespeare, *As You Like It*, Agnes Latham (ed.) (London: Routledge, 1987), 3.5.81 and 3.3.11–12.

11. M. Morgan Holmes, 'Identity and the Dissidence it Makes: Homoerotic Nonsense in Kit Marlowe's *Hero and Leander*', *ESC* 21 (1995), 151–69 (155).

12. John Marston, *Antonio and Mellida*, G. K. Hunter (ed.) (Lincoln: University of Nebraska Press, 1965), Induction, p. 86.

13. See John Baker, in 'Readers' Queries', *N&Q* 241 (1996), 306.

14. Thomas Heywood, *The Captives, or The Lost Recovered*, in *Thomas Heywood: Three Marriage Plays*, Paul Merchant (ed.) (Manchester University Press, 1996), 2.3.132–3 and 4.2.

15. See Antony Telford Moore, 'Ford's Parody of Edward Alleyn', *N&Q* 241 (1996), 190–1.

16. Lawrence Danson, 'Continuity and Character in Shakespeare and Marlowe', *SEL* 26 (1986), 217–34 (217); Richard A. McCabe, *Incest, Drama and Nature's Law 1550–1700* (Cambridge University Press, 1993), p. 241.

17. John Ford, *'Tis Pity She's a Whore*, Brian Morris (ed.) (London: Ernest Benn 1968), 3.8.18 and 1.1.4–8; Cyrus Hoy, '"Ignorance in Knowledge": Marlowe's Faustus and Ford's Giovanni', *Modern Philology* 57 (1960), 145–54.

18. F. S. Boas, *Christopher Marlowe: A Biographical and Critical Study* (Oxford: Clarendon Press, 1940), p. 300.

19. J. Douglas Canfield, 'Shifting Tropes of Ideology in English Serious Drama, Late Stuart to Early Georgian', in J. Douglas Canfield and Deborah C. Payne (eds.), *Cultural Readings of Restoration and Eighteenth-Century English Literature* (Athens: University of Georgia Press, 1995), pp. 195–227 (pp. 197–8).

20. For a full account of the circumstances, see Joseph Quincy Adams, 'The *Massacre at Paris* Leaf', *Library* 14 (1934), 447–69.

21. Ribner, 'Marlowe and the Critics', *TDR* 8 (1964), 211–24 (212). On Marlowe's reputation in the Restoration and Romantic periods, see also MacLure, pp. 8–12.

22. Percy Shelley, while at Eton, was said to have been found by a master trying to raise the devil much as Doctor Faustus does (Radu Florescu, *In Search of Frankenstein* (Boston: New York Graphic Society, 1975), p. 42).

23. See Gareth Roberts, 'Necromantic Books: Christopher Marlowe, Doctor Faustus and Agrippa of Nettesheim', in Darryll Grantley and Peter Roberts (eds.), *Christopher Marlowe and English Renaissance Culture* (Aldershot: Scolar Press, 1996), pp. 148–71 (p. 160).
24. See Michael H. Keefer (ed.), *Christopher Marlowe's Doctor Faustus: A 1604-Version Edition* (Peterborough, Ontario: Broadview Press, 1991), p. xxvi.
25. Mary Shelley, *Frankenstein*, Maurice Hindle (ed.) (Harmondsworth: Penguin, 1985), p. 147. All further quotations from the novel will be taken from this edition and reference will be given in the text.
26. Harry Levin, *The Overreacher: A Study of Christopher Marlowe* (Cambridge, MA: Harvard University Press, 1952), p. 63; Edmund Gosse, *Father and Son*, Peter Abbs (ed.) (Harmondsworth: Penguin, 1983), p. 227; Thomas Dabbs, *Reforming Marlowe: The Nineteenth-Century Canonization of a Renaissance Dramatist* (Lewisburg: Bucknell University Press, 1991), p. 14.
27. See for instance David J. Skal, '"His Hour Upon the Stage": Theatrical Adaptations of *Dracula*', in Nina Auerbach and David J. Skal (eds.), *Dracula* (London: Norton, 1997), pp. 371–81 (pp. 372–3).
28. Eric Ambler, *Background to Danger* (1937; London: Vintage, 2001), p. 226.
29. Stephanie Cowell, *Nicholas Cooke: Actor, Soldier, Physician, Priest* (London: Norton, 1993); Liam Maguire, *Icarus Flying: The Tragical Story of Christopher Marlowe* (London: Ormond Books, 1993); Anthony Burgess, *A Dead Man in Deptford* (London: Random House, 1993); Chris Hunt, *Mignon* (London: Gay Men's Press, 1987). I am indebted to Annaliese Connolly for help in researching novelizations of Marlowe's life. A number of these novels are also discussed in Kenneth Tucker, 'Dead Men in Deptford: Recent Lives and Deaths of Christopher Marlowe', *RORD* 34 (1995), 111–24 (though there are oddities in this essay such as Tucker's consistently referring to A. D. Wraight as 'he' and his uncritical acceptance of her controversial insistence that Marlowe wrote an early and now lost play on Scanderbeg (p. 118)).
30. Iain Sinclair, *Slow Chocolate Autopsy: Incidents from the Notorious Career of Norton, Prisoner of London* (1997; London: Phoenix, 1998), p. 8.
31. Robin Chapman, *Christoferus or Tom Kyd's Revenge* (London: Sinclair-Stevenson, 1993), pp. 88, 107, and 161.
32. Peter Whelan, *The School of Night* (London: Warner Chappell, 1992). For an account of a further fictional encounter between Marlowe and Shakespeare, in D.C. Comics' *The Sandman*, see Michael D. Bristol, *Big Time Shakespeare* (London: Routledge, 1996), chapter 5.
33. Eugénie de Kalb, 'The Death of Marlowe', *TLS* 1218 (21 May 1925), 351.
34. Stephanie Merritt, *Gaveston* (London: Faber and Faber, 2002), p. 168.

READING LIST

Boas, F. S. *Christopher Marlowe: A Biographical and Critical Study*. Oxford: Clarendon Press, 1940.
Bristol, Michael. *Big Time Shakespeare*. London: Routledge, 1996.
Dabbs, Thomas. *Reforming Marlowe: The Nineteenth-Century Canonization of a Renaissance Dramatist*. Lewisburg: Bucknell University Press, 1991.

Holmes, M. Morgan. 'Identity and the Dissidence it Makes: Homoerotic Nonsense in Kit Marlowe's *Hero and Leander*'. *ESC* 21 (1995), 151–69.

Hoy, Cyrus. '"Ignorance in Knowledge": Marlowe's Faustus and Ford's Giovanni'. *Modern Philology* 57 (1960), 145–54.

MacLure, Millar, ed. *Marlowe: The Critical Heritage, 1588–1896*. London: Routledge, 1979.

Nicholl, Charles. *The Reckoning*. London: Jonathan Cape, 1992.

Ribner, Irving. 'Marlowe and the Critics'. *TDR* 8 (1964), 211–24.

Riggs, David. 'The Killing of Christopher Marlowe'. *StHR* 8 (1999), 239–51.

Tucker, Kenneth. 'Dead Men in Deptford: Recent Lives and Deaths of Christopher Marlowe'. *RORD* 34 (1995), 111–24.

The 'Reading list' at the end of each chapter may be supplemented by the following reference works.

Biographies

The newest and most complete biography is Constance Brown Kuriyama, *Christopher Marlowe: A Renaissance Life* (Ithaca: Cornell University Press, 2002). See also Lisa Hopkins, *Christopher Marlowe: A Literary Life* (Basingstoke: Palgrave, 2000); Charles Nicholl, *The Reckoning: The Murder of Christopher Marlowe* (1992; revised edn, London: Vintage, 2002); William Urry, *Christopher Marlowe and Canterbury*, Andrew Butcher (ed.) (London: Faber and Faber, 1988); and A. D. Wraight and Virginia F. Stern, *In Search of Christopher Marlowe: A Pictorial Biography* (1965; Chichester: Adam Hart, 1993).

Older biographies include: John Bakeless, *The Tragicall History of Christopher Marlowe*, 2 vols. (1942; Hamden, CT: Archon, 1964); Frederick S. Boas, *Christopher Marlowe: A Biographical and Critical Study* (Oxford: Clarendon Press, 1940); C. F. Tucker Brooke, *The Life of Marlowe*, attached to his edition of *Dido* in the R. H. Case *Works* (seen Editions, below); and Mark Eccles, *Christopher Marlowe in London* (Cambridge, MA: Harvard University Press, 1934).

Just out is Roy Kendall, *Christopher Marlowe and Richard Baines: Journeys through the Elizabethan Underground* (Madison, NJ: Fairleigh Dickinson University Press; Cranbury, NJ: Associated University Presses, 2003).

Forthcoming biographies include those by Park Honan and David Riggs.

Editions

The most recent complete paperback edition is the two-volume set edited by Mark Thornton Burnett: *Christopher Marlowe: The Complete Plays*,

Everyman (London: Dent; Rutland, VT: Tuttle, 1999); and *Christopher Marlowe: The Complete Poems*, Everyman (London: Dent; Rutland, VT: Tuttle, 2000). See also E. D. Pendry and J. C. Maxwell (eds.), *Christopher Marlowe: Complete Plays and Poems*, Everyman (London: Dent, 1976); and Stephen Orgel (ed.), *The Complete Poems and Translations* (Harmondsworth: Penguin, 1971). An older modern-spelling edition in hardback is R. H. Case (ed.), *The Works and Life of Christopher Marlowe*, 6 vols. (London: Methuen, 1930–3).

Through Oxford University Press's World's Classics Series, David Bevington and Eric Rasmussen have edited *Christopher Marlowe: 'Tamburlaine, Parts I and II', 'Doctor Faustus' A- and B-texts, 'The Jew of Malta', 'Edward II'* (Oxford University Press, 1995). See also Patrick Cheney and Brian J. Striar (eds.), *The Collected Poems of Christopher Marlowe* (New York: Oxford University Press, forthcoming).

The most recent old-spelling edition is *The Complete Works of Christopher Marlowe*, Roma Gill (ed.), 5 vols. (Oxford: Clarendon Press, 1987–8), with critical commentary: vol. 1, Gill (ed.), *Poems, Translations, and 'Dido, Queen of Carthage'* (1987); vol. 2, Gill (ed.), *Doctor Faustus* (1990); vol. 3, Richard Rowland (ed.), *Edward II* (1994); vol. 4, Gill (ed.), *The Jew of Malta* (1995); vol. 5, David Fuller and Edward J. Esche (eds.), *'Tamburlaine the Great, Parts 1 and 2', and 'The Massacre at Paris with the Death of the Duke of Guise'* (1998).

Previously, the standard old-spelling editions have been Fredson Bowers (ed.), *The Complete Works of Christopher Marlowe*, 2nd edn, 2 vols. (Cambridge University Press, 1981); and C. F. Tucker Brooke (ed.), *The Complete Works of Christopher Marlowe* (Oxford: Clarendon Press, 1910).

Recently, the Revels Plays series has been publishing revised editions of Marlowe's works, including in paperback: Charles R. Forker (ed.), *Edward II* (Manchester University Press, 1994); and David Bevington and Eric Rasmussen (eds.), *'Doctor Faustus', A- and B-Texts (1604, 1616)* (Manchester University Press, 1993). The Revels Plays is also issuing Revels Student Editions: J. S. Cunningham and Eithne Henson (eds.), *Tamburlaine the Great* (Manchester University Press, 1998); and David Bevington (ed.), *The Jew of Malta* (Manchester University Press, 1996). Older editions in hardback include: J. S. Cunningham (ed.), *Tamburlaine the Great* (Manchester University Press, 1989); N. W. Bawcutt (ed.), *The Jew of Malta* (Manchester University Press, 1978); H. J. Oliver (ed.), *'Dido, Queen of Carthage' and 'The Massacre at Paris'* (Cambridge, MA: Harvard University Press, 1968); and Millar MacLure (ed.), *The Poems: Christopher Marlowe* (London: Methuen, 1968).

Similarly, the New Mermaids series is updating its Marlowe editions, including Martin Wiggins and Robert Lindsey (eds.), *Edward II* (London: A. and C. Black; and New York: Norton, 1997); and two recent editions of *The Jew of Malta*: T. W. Craik (ed.) (London: A. and C. Black; and New York: Norton, 1992), and James R. Siemon (ed.) (London: A. and C. Black; and New York: Norton, 1994).

Bibliographies

Annotated bibliographies include the three-series instalment in *ELR*: Patrick Cheney, 'Recent Studies in Marlowe (1987–1998)', *ELR* 31 (2001), 288–328; Ronald Levao, 'Recent Studies in Marlowe (1977–1987)', *ELR* 18 (1988), 329–41; and Jonathan Post, 'Recent Studies in Marlowe: 1968–1976', *ELR* 6 (1977), 382–99.

See also Bruce E. Brandt (ed.), *Christopher Marlowe in the Eighties: An Annotated Bibliography of Marlowe Criticism from 1978–1989* (West Cornwall: Locust, 1992).

Two older bibliographies cover Marlowe studies through 1977: Lois Mai Chan (ed.), *Marlowe Criticism: A Bibliography* (Boston: Hall, 1978); and Kenneth Friedenreich (ed.), *Christopher Marlowe: An Annotated Bibliography since 1950* (Metuchen: Scarecrow Press, 1979).

Concordances

Recent concordances are Robert J. Fehrenbach, Lee Ann Boone, and Mario A. DiCesare (eds.), *A Concordance to the Plays, Poems, and Translations of Christopher Marlowe* (Ithaca: Cornell University Press, 1982), which is keyed to Bowers's second edition (see Editions, above); and Louis Ule, *A Concordance to the Works of Christopher Marlowe* (Hildesheim: Olms, 1979), which modernizes spelling and reprints parallel texts of modern- and old-spelling versions.

Periodicals/magazines

The Marlowe Society of America publishes *The Marlowe Society of America Newsletter*, long edited by Bruce E. Brandt and now edited by Rick Bowers; and *The Marlowe Society of America Book Reviews*, edited by Duke Pesta.

Other research tools

An invaluable resource is Millar MacLure (ed.), *Marlowe: The Critical Heritage 1588–1896* (London: Routledge, 1979), which collects commentary on Marlowe during the three centuries identified in the title.

Similarly, Vivien Thomas and William Tydeman (eds.), *Christopher Marlowe: The Plays and Their Sources* (London: Routledge, 1994), collects sources for the plays.

Collections of essays

The following collections reprint essays already published elsewhere: Richard Wilson (ed.), *Christopher Marlowe* (Harlow: Longman, 1999); Emily C. Bartels (ed.), *Critical Essays on Christopher Marlowe* (New York: Hall; London: Prentice, 1996); Harold Bloom (ed.), *Christopher Marlowe* (New York: Chelsea, 1986); John Brown Russell (ed.), *Marlowe: 'Tamburlaine the Great', 'Edward the Second' and 'The Jew of Malta': A Casebook* (London: Macmillan, 1982); Judith O'Neill (ed.), *Critics on Marlowe* (Coral Gables: University of Miami Press, 1970); and Clifford Leech (ed.), *Marlowe: A Collection of Critical Essays*, Twentieth Century Views (Englewood Cliffs, NJ: Prentice-Hall, 1964).

The following collections print new essays: Sara Munson Deats and Robert Logan (eds.), *Marlowe's Empery: Expanding His Critical Contexts* (Newark: University of Delaware Press, 2002); J. A. Downie and J. T. Parnell (eds.), *Constructing Christopher Marlowe* (Cambridge University Press, 2000); Paul Whitfield White (ed.), *Marlowe, History, and Sexuality: New Critical Essays on Christopher Marlowe* (New York: AMS Press, 1998); Darryll Grantley and Peter Roberts (eds.), *Christopher Marlowe and English Renaissance Culture* (Aldershot: Scolar Press, 1996); Kenneth Friedenreich, Roma Gill, and Constance B. Kuriyama (eds.), *'A Poet and a filthy Play-maker': New Essays on Christopher Marlowe* (New York: AMS Press, 1988); Alvin B. Kernan (ed.), *Two Renaissance Mythmakers: Christopher Marlowe and Ben Jonson* (Baltimore: Johns Hopkins University Press, 1977); Brian Morris (ed.), *Christopher Marlowe* (New York: Hill, 1968).

Marlowe on the Internet

For the homepage of the Marlowe Society of America, log on at: *http://web.ics.purdue.edu/~pwhite/marlowe/*. Includes MSA Newsletter Archive (currently being added, only one issue from 1985 currently available) and the MSA Book Review Archive.

See also the Marlowe Society (in England) homepage: *http://www.marlowe-society.org/*.

For other sites, see the following:

- The complete works of Marlowe:
  http://www.perseus.tufts.edu/Texts/Marlowe.html. Perseus Project: University of Tufts.
- Christopher Marlowe (1564–1593):
  http://www.luminarium.org/renlit/marlowe.htm. Includes links to some biographical material, essays and articles on Marlowe, and various other links.
- The life of Christopher Marlowe:
  http://swc2.hccs.cc.tx.us/HTMLS/ROWHTML/faust/marlowe.htm. Southwest College. Includes biography and useful links page.
- Christopher Marlowe collection at Bartleby.com.
  http://www.bartleby.com/people/Marlowe.html. Includes some works, one link to an article on Marlowe and Kyd.
- Christopher Marlowe.
  http://www.theatrehistory.com/british/marlowe001.html. TheaterHistory. com. Contains a brief biography taken from the book *Elizabethan and Stuart Plays*.
- T. S. Eliot's 'Notes on the Blank Verse of Christopher Marlowe':
  http://www.bartleby.com/200/sw8.html. Originally from *The Sacred Wood: Essays on Poetry and Criticism* (1922).
- Christopher Marlowe and *Doctor Faustus*: A Unit for High School English Teachers: *http://www.teachersfirst.com/lessons/marl-1.htm*.
- Online literary criticism collection: Christopher Marlowe:
  http://www.ipl.org/div/litcrit/bin/litcrit.out.pl?au=mar-13. Internet Public Library. Includes several critical articles. Links to more articles on five of the plays.

INDEX

CAMBRIDGE COMPANIONS TO LITERATURE

Period and thematic

The Cambridge Companion to Greek Tragedy
edited by P. E. Easterling

The Cambridge Companion to Old English Literature
edited by Malcolm Godden and Michael Lapidge

The Cambridge Companion to Medieval Women's Writing
edited by Carolyn Dinshaw and David Wallace

The Cambridge Companion to Medieval Romance
edited by Roberta L. Krueger

The Cambridge Companion to Medieval English Theatre
edited by Richard Beadle

The Cambridge Companion to English Renaissance Drama, second edition
edited by A. R. Braunmuller and Michael Hattaway

The Cambridge Companion to Renaissance Humanism
edited by Jill Kraye

The Cambridge Companion to English Poetry, Donne to Marvell
edited by Thomas N. Corns

The Cambridge Companion to English Literature, 1500–1600
edited by Arthur F. Kinney

The Cambridge Companion to English Literature, 1650–1740
edited by Steven N. Zwicker

The Cambridge Companion to Writing of the English Revolution
edited by N. H. Keeble

The Cambridge Companion to English Restoration Theatre
edited by Deborah C. Payne Fisk

The Cambridge Companion to British Romanticism
edited by Stuart Curran

The Cambridge Companion to Eighteenth-Century Poetry
edited by John Sitter

The Cambridge Companion to the Eighteenth-Century Novel
edited by John Richetti

The Cambridge Companion to Gothic Fiction
edited by Jerrold E. Hogle

The Cambridge Companion to Victorian Poetry
edited by Joseph Bristow

The Cambridge Companion to the Victorian Novel
edited by Deirdre David

The Cambridge Companion to Crime Fiction
edited by Martin Priestman

The Cambridge Companion to Science Fiction
edited by Edward James and Farah Mendlesohn

The Cambridge Companion to Travel Writing
edited by Peter Hulme and Tim Youngs

The Cambridge Companion to American Realism and Naturalism
edited by Donald Pizer

The Cambridge Companion to Nineteenth-Century American Women's Writing
edited by Dale M. Bauer and Philip Gould

The Cambridge Companion to the Classic Russian Novel
edited by Malcolm V. Jones and Robin Feuer Miller

The Cambridge Companion to the French Novel: from 1800 to the Present
edited by Timothy Unwin

The Cambridge Companion to the Spanish Novel: from 1600 to the Present
edited by Harriet Turner and Adelaida López de Martínez

The Cambridge Companion to the Italian Novel
edited by Peter Bondanella and Andrea Ciccarelli

CAMBRIDGE COMPANIONS TO CULTURE